More Praise for *Food Nations*

"*Food Nations* is a cornucopia of fascinating information about why we eat what we eat. There is much in this wide-ranging book to stimulate anyone with an interest in the past, the present, and even the future of food."
—Harvey Levenstein, author of *Revolution at the Table*

"That food and drink are at the very center of the body politic is dramatically enforced in this revelatory collection of essays, unified by the proposition that food is power and power, food. If anyone can doubt that food is as serious a subject as politics or business, let him read any one of these essays and stay amazed."
—Betty Fussell, author of *My Kitchen Wars*

"*Food Nations* joins a growing body of scholarship that proves emphatically that food matters. Warren Belasco and Philip Scranton have provided a valuable service by bringing these important essays together and deserve the thanks of the scholarly community."
—Hasia R. Diner, author of *Hungering for America*

"Food studies is serious business and *Food Nations* is a major contribution to our understanding of the business of food. This meticulously researched book is a most welcome addition to an exciting new field."
—Barbara Kirshenblatt-Gimblett, author of *Destination Culture*

Selling Taste in Consumer Societies

EDITED BY
**WARREN BELASCO AND
PHILIP SCRANTON**

Routledge
Taylor & Francis Group
New York   London

Published in 2002 by
Routledge
29 West 35th Street
New York, NY 10001

Published in Great Britain by
Routledge
11 New Fetter Lane
London EC4P 4EE

Routledge is an imprint of the Taylor & Francis Group.
Copyright © 2002 by Routledge

Printed in the United States of America on acid-free paper.

10 9 8 7 6 5 4 3

Library of Congress Cataloging-in-Publication Data

Food nations : selling taste in consumer societies / edited by Warren Belasco and Philip Scranton.
    p. cm. — (Hagley perspectives on business and culture)
    Includes bibliographical references and index.
    ISBN 0-415-93076-6 — ISBN 0-415-93077-4 (pbk.)
       1. Food Habits—Congresses. 2. Food industry and trade—Social Aspects—Congresses.
    I. Belasco, Warren James. II. Scranton, Philip. III. Series.

GT2855 .F66 2001
394.1'2—dc21

2001019497

Contents

Preface

PHILIP SCRANTON

*A*s the rapid rise to prominence of food studies suggests, scholars and general readers alike have become fascinated with the cultural and historical dimensions of multiple cuisines. The research collected in this volume both resonates with and steps beyond these themes, engaging the peculiar relationships between food, nationalism, and politics in Parts II and V and those between food, business, and culture in the volume's middle segments. At the outset, two distinguished analysts of foodways and food history, my coeditor Warren Belasco and the redoubtable Sidney Mintz, set the disciplinary context for these empirical studies and identify key issues that have animated and continue to stimulate researchers' efforts. The temporal and spatial boundaries within which our contributors strive to analyze and understand the significance of food and drink, on the first count, run from the latter nineteenth century to the present, and on the second, span societies in North America (Anglo and Latino) and continental Europe. Moreover, this volume draws together perspectives and methods from anthropology, sociology, folklore, and ethnic, business, and cultural history, with a nod here and there toward technology studies, marketing, and gender analysis. This is as it should be, for an "emerging field" (in Warren Belasco's phrasing) frequently exposes the fruitful connections that can be made between collateral areas of scholarship that hitherto had been regarded as separate, if not disparate.

The studies published here were initially presented at a two-day conference in November 1999, "Food and Drink in Consumer Societies," sponsored by the Hagley Museum and Library, Wilmington, Delaware. The editors would like to express their appreciation to Dr. Glenn Porter, Hagley's director, who has long supported the nontraditional conference themes emanating from the Center for the History of Business,

Technology and Society. Adam Albright designed the conference's compelling visuals, and Carol Lockman smoothly handled reams of correspondence, mastered and managed a host of details, and tracked our expenditures and budget commitments. Roger Horowitz, the center's associate director, joined Warren Belasco and me in reviewing scores of paper proposals in order to assemble the program, and is, I believe, responsible for hatching the "Food and Drink" idea in the first place. Hagley's events staff and planners handled the physical and organizational preparations with their usual skill, and fully deserve the thanks that is perhaps not often enough forthcoming.

Colleagues in history, anthropology, and museum scholarship served admirably as commentators on the individual sessions, providing our authors with a set of critical reviews that preceded those offered by the editors. Our gratitude goes to Fath Davis Ruffins of the National Museum of American History, Smithsonian Institution; Arwen Mohun and David Shearer, History Department, the University of Delaware; and Judith Goode, Anthropology, Temple University, for their efforts and insights. As the third volume in Hagley's collaboration with Routledge, *Food and Drink* has benefited from the close guidance of Deirdre Mullane, who proposed this series in the wake of our 1998 "Beauty and Business" conference. At Routledge Derek Krissoff and then Vik Mukhija ably assisted us with editorial advice and the management of successive preparatory steps leading toward publication. Our thanks to them and to Routledge's ever-able copy-editors. Last, the editors must express their debt to Sidney Mintz, who offered the keynote address at the conference despite a crushing schedule of other commitments, and to the dozen authors whose careful revisions yielded the essays that are presented here. It is our hope that readers will find these investigations of food, culture, politics, and history as engaging and rewarding as did the enthusiastic audience that first heard them on two bright November days in Delaware.

Part One

CONTEXTS

Chapter 1

FOOD MATTERS: PERSPECTIVES ON AN EMERGING FIELD

WARREN BELASCO

*F*ood is important. There is in fact nothing more basic. Food is the first of the essentials of life, our biggest industry, our greatest export, and our most frequently indulged pleasure. Food means creativity and diversity. As a species, humans are omnivorous; they have tried to eat virtually everything on the globe, and their ability to turn a remarkable array of raw substances into cooked "dishes," "meals," and "feasts" is evidence of astounding versatility, adaptability, and aesthetic ingenuity. Food is also the object of considerable concern and dread. What we eat and how we eat it may be the single most important cause of disease and death.[1]

As psychologist Paul Rozin puts it, "food is fundamental, fun, frightening, and far-reaching."[2] Its meanings and usages extend far beyond nutritional maintenance. Food, observes anthropologist Arjun Appadurai, is "a highly condensed social fact" and "a marvelously plastic kind of collective representation."[3] Food indicates who we are, where we came from, and what we want to be. In *Kitchens*, his elegant study of the culture of restaurant work, sociologist Gary Alan Fine writes: "Food reveals our souls. Like Marcel Proust reminiscing about a madeleine or Calvin Trillin astonished at a plate of ribs, we are entangled in our meals. The connection between identity and consumption gives food a central role in the creation of community, and we use our diet to convey images of public identity."[4] If we are what we eat, we also are what we don't eat. People moralize constantly about what they will and will not eat. To eat is to distinguish and discriminate, include and exclude. Food choices establish boundaries and borders. In the modern era this process of culinary differentiation may entail major modification of traditional foods; few people today eat exactly what their grandparents ate fifty years ago, and many of us also like to cross group boundaries to "eat the Other." Adding to this disparate mix of shifting identities is the fact that the way food is produced, prepared, and consumed usually reflects a society's gender roles. Given this sexualized component, food is often highly eroticized—a fact well known to psychologists, marketers, blues singers, and poets alike.

Food also has tremendous historical importance. Anthropologist Sidney Mintz argues that the domestication of plants and nonhuman animals for food in the Neolithic era (10,000 years ago) was "probably the single greatest technical achievement in the human record, more important than the internal combustion engine or nuclear energy. It was, from the beginning and long before these other triumphs, a remarkable way to capture and control energy."[5] Indeed, nature writer Evan Eisenberg speculates that the forbidden "fruit" memorialized in Genesis was actually Mesopotamian wheat, and the seducing serpent may have been one of the snakes customarily used to protect granaries from rats. With settled agriculture came more work, more children (and more pain for Eve), and the general "fall" from hunter-gatherer Eden: "With time, with irrigation, mountains of grain became the foundations of cities. To protect the grain from marauding nomads, armies arose and enslaved those whose grain they protected. To dig the great irrigation canals and keep them clear, slaves were called for, and bureaucrats, and despots. Humans were winnowed like grain, separated by function, wealth, power. Civilization arose, and writing, and real estate."[6] Grain also fed animals that harbored the primary infectious diseases of settled societies. In his best-selling survey of global geographical history, biologist Jared Diamond puts it succinctly: agriculture spawned guns, germs, and steel—the principal material drivers of civilization and conquest.[7]

We also know that European exploration and colonization had a lot to do with food. It can even be argued that the Americas' greatest gift to humanity was not the U.S. Constitution, Hollywood, or rock 'n' roll, but mundane potatoes, tomatoes, and maize, while the importation of Old World farm animals, weeds, and grains probably did more to destroy Native American life than any European musket or sword. Henry Hobhouse writes in *Seeds of Change*: "The starting point for the European expansion out of the Mediterranean and the Atlantic continental shelf had nothing to do with, say, religion or the rise of capitalism—but it had a great deal to do with pepper. The Americas were discovered as a byproduct in the search for pepper."[8] And out of that search for pepper came the foods of the Columbian Exchange that revolutionized the diet, economy, social structure, and politics of the entire world. William H. McNeill writes that "potatoes, by feeding rapidly growing populations, permitted a handful of European nations to assert dominion over most of the world between 1750 and 1950."[9] For food writer Betty Fussell, it was corn, another Native American staple, that "made the whole world kin," for corn became the great common denominator underlying much of the globe's meat, mush, and mash.[10] Focusing on a different carbohydrate in *Sweetness and Power*, Sidney Mintz suggests that the slave-based cultivation of sugar in the New World literally fueled the industrial revolution, as well as the destruction of large parts of the tropical world. Not to be outdone by the carbohydrate-determinists, Mark Kurlansky argues that it was trade in North Atlantic cod that "changed the world."[11] Whatever the prime commodity, there is no question that the last five hundred years have witnessed an enormous global redistribution of nutrients, and it is no coincidence that today's billion or so beneficiaries of what might be called the Great Imperial Barbecue suffer from caloric overload, while the ex-colonies that initially supplied those wonder foods now house the poorest fed third of the world's six billion people. The richness of a society's diet is a primary indicator of its "development."[12]

Food means power, power means food. And power means conflict, even violence. Many of the world's wars may be viewed as a series of colossal food fights. Take, for example, the rise of what might be called the American agro-military complex. It took a lot of blood to establish the territorial base on which America's agricultural hegemony and caloric overload now depend. Between 1776 and 1783 the colonists fought the British to allow American farmers to expand west of the Alleghenies and to sell their surpluses freely on the world market. In the 1860s the North fought the South to keep an agricultural system based on slavery from competing with an agricultural system based on "free" labor. Throughout the nineteenth century the U.S. Army waged a series of wars to replace aboriginal and *mestizo* herdsmen and farmers with European herdsmen and farmers. In 1898 we picked a war with Spain that netted us better access to cheap sugar and fruit. Our twentieth-century wars further reinforced American agricultural dominance in world markets.[13] The Cold War, too, was waged and perhaps even "won" through kitchen debates, grain deals, breadlines, and the Green Revolution; the current trade battles over biotechnology, hormones, NAFTA, WTO, and GATT may be evidence of further food fights to come. Wars also have a way of transforming food practices and habits (as Martin Bruegel's article here shows). Many major breakthroughs in modern food processing were initially developed for military purposes. And the Vietnam War was indirectly responsible for the ethnic/natural/ healthy foods revival that sparked the culinary renaissance of the last thirty years.[14]

So food has weight, as most people know. And yet not long ago, at the annual meeting of the American Studies Association, I spoke at a session whose title, "Why American Studies Scholars Should Study Food," implied a certain defensiveness about the subject at hand. Looking at the ASA program, I did not see any panels devoted to justifying the study of gender, race, movies, television, or music. Those battles were won long ago, or at least I hope so. But when it comes to telling others about *our* interests, we food scholars may still evoke a sense of surprise. It is not really a matter of outright disrespect, but rather, mostly bemused wonder—Is this what academics do these days?—with also a hint of feeling threatened. We "food people" may be feared for two very different reasons. Either we're perceived as overly discriminating gastronomes (à la Craig Claiborne) who will slight the booboisie for their unrefined palates, or we're feared as the muckraking "food police" (à la Upton Sinclair) who will tell people what's *really* in those hors d'oeuvres. And there is some basis for both perceptions. Reflecting the culinary nostalgia of many food writers, journalists John and Karen Hess state: "the history of American food is the destruction of its taste."[15] And social radicals have long seen the adulterated industrial diet as a telling metaphor for the sins of capitalism, as when George Orwell quipped: "We may find in the long run that tinned food is a deadlier weapon than the machine gun."[16] In either role, as gourmet or as muckraker, we're going to spoil the meal of those who would rather dine in peaceful obliviousness.

I suspect that many "food people" face similar responses at their respective institutions. To be sure, some scholars have carved out respected, if also small, food-related subdisciplines as ethnographers, folklorists, and rural, medical, or nutritional sociologists. But what about the main research discipline represented in this volume, history? Overall it is safe to say that food has until quite recently been largely invisible in academic history. True, there are many amateur antiquarians and enthusiasts who have written very useful histories of particular foods, dishes, cooks, or cuisines. While such accounts perform invaluable service in preserving information and traditions, few of them pay much attention to the things that interest professional historians—power, social relations, context.[17] But you could look through ten years' worth of programs of the annual meetings of the American Historical Society, Organization of American Historians, or the American Studies Association and not find more than a dozen sessions (out of thousands) devoted to food.

The great French naturalist Jean-Henri Fabre (1823–1915) wrote: "History celebrates the battlefields whereon we meet our death, but scorns to speak of the plowed fields whereby we thrive; it knows the names of the King's bastards, but cannot tell us the origin of wheat. That is the way of human folly." While historians are now a lot more interested in social life at the grass roots, they still largely ignore the grass itself that makes life possible. And young scholars who are interested in food history are routinely advised not to go near the subject until their *second* book, *after* tenure.[18]

Since the 1980s some of us older scholars *have* been writing our second or third books about food, and these works form the base for what this essay's title brands the "emerging" field of food studies. Yet it is an indication of the tenuous nature of this food scholarship that much of the work of the past twenty years has been initiated for reasons related to *other* research agendas. Food is rarely the primary motivation for the inquiry. Rather than being the *end* focus, it tends to be a novel *means* to illuminate already accepted disciplinary concerns. Thus labor historians writing about unionization might get involved with food when they look at migrant farmworkers, slaughterhouses, or canneries.[19] Women's historians might look at housework, home economics, or anorexia to illustrate gendered power relations.[20] Agricultural historians will obviously tell us about farming, but like many farmers, they are often more interested in economics and politics than in nutrition and cuisine.[21] As one agronomist told me, most conventional farmers are concerned with the production of commodities, not the consumption of food. (A similar split may divide ethnographers of peasant farming from those studying peasant meals.) Social historians, like sociologists, may use food to illustrate organizational dynamics, stratification, or social construction.[22] Cultural historians, like folklorists and literary analysts, are often less interested in food itself than in the role of food as a metaphor, symbol, an agent by which people communicate and interact.[23]

I, too, took this indirect path into food studies when I began the project that became *Appetite for Change: How the Counterculture Took on the Food Industry*.[24] I started to look at the counterculture's critique of mainstream American cuisine not because I wanted to study the food system, but because I was interested in the hegemonic process: the way mainstream culture deals with subcultural dissent and deviancy. Originally I intended to treat the organic and natural foods movement as just one chapter in a series of case studies of "retailing revolt"—blue jeans, rock 'n' roll, bikers, and so on. Only after I started the food chapter did I decide that issues of food production and distribution are important in themselves—and not just because they can illuminate some *other* dynamic or theory (in my case, hegemony). But this repositioning of food from useful tool to primary focus is relatively rare. And many of the food scholars whose work I admire have moved on to other, nonfood subjects, as if to say that food alone is not enough to sustain a scholarly career.[25]

Why this puzzling shyness about food? Even though most historians seem to be avoiding food, history does have something to tell us about why people are surprised that food can be studied seriously, and more important, about why people are so oblivious to food, especially to where it comes from and to the wider social, political, and psychological implications of our food behaviors.

For one thing, westerners—and academic westerners in particular—are heirs to a classical dualism that prizes mind over body. As philosophers Deane Curtin and Lisa Heldke write in *Cooking, Eating, Thinking*: "Our tradition has tended to privilege questions about the rational, the unchanging, and the eternal, and the abstract and the mental; and to denigrate questions about embodied, concrete, practical experience."[26] (So deeply ingrained is this preference for the disembodied intellect that much of the *au courant* "cultural studies" work on "the body" is exceptionally rarefied, as if to suggest that material matters can be taken seriously only when etherized into theory.) Reinforcing this dualism are remnants of the "Protestant ethic" that once dominated Anglo-American culture. Both Harvey Levenstein and Peter Stearns suggest that Americans periodically dive off the deep end into orgies of self-flagellating health food faddism and futile dieting because they are too hung up by Protestant prudery to enjoy their food.[27] While it is unclear that we Americans are *that* self-denying—consider the environmental impact of this country's unrelenting consumerist self-indulgence!—there may indeed be some archetypal, dualistic disdain for something as mundane, corporeal, indeed animalistic as eating. "Put a knife to thy throat," urges Proverbs 23:2, "if thou be a man given to appetite." "Govern thy appetite well," advised the arch-Puritan John Milton, "lest Sin Surprise thee, and her black attendant Death."[28] To some extent, we may still live with our Victorian (if not Puritan) heritage. The Victorians constructed many elaborate dining rituals partly because they harbored a deep suspicion of eating, which—like sex—they viewed as basically *uncivilized.*[29] The novelist Joyce Carol Oates puts it nicely: "Civilization is a multiplicity of strategies, dazzling as precious gems inlaid in a golden crown, to obscure from human beings the sound of, the terrible meaning of, their jaws grinding. The meaning of man's place in the food cycle that, by way of our imaginations, we had imagined might not apply to *us.*"[30] In other words, food is gross.

Food studies have also been hindered by another Victorian relic—the idealized bourgeois division between the female sphere of *consumption* and the male sphere of *production*. While the separate spheres did not reflect the daily realities for most women—to this day women are major food producers across the globe—the polarization certainly influenced the development of middle-class academia, for it effectively segregated women professionals in less-valued disciplines closer to the home, particularly dietetics, home economics, and nutrition education. In the history of those professions we can find substantial middle-class/moralistic intolerance for the food practices of ordinary people, and the distrust was often mutual—thus strong popular resistance to prissy admonitions to "eat right."[31] Conversely, the male-dominated realms of industrial agriculture, food technology, mass retailing, and corporate management have generally received more public respect and academic prestige.

This institutionalized bias delayed serious attention to food even after the women's movement subverted the separate spheres. While more women began to enter all fields of academia in the 1960s, it took several decades before scholars could begin to consider the traditional female ghetto of domesticity without Victorian era blinders and prejudices, and even today, feminists who do treasure their cooking heritage and skills may risk the skepticism and scorn of colleagues. For example, when soliciting contributions to *Through the Kitchen Window*, a marvelous collection of women's writings about food and cooking, women's studies scholar Arlene Avakian was condescendingly asked how her "cookbook" was going. Even more dispiriting was the suggestion by Harvard biologist Ruth Hubbard—the first woman to hold a tenured professorship in her department—that a positive book about cooking threatened women's "liberation" from the kitchen: "Haven't we had enough of women being viewed through the kitchen window?" To this Avakian replies: "the work of cooking is more complex than mere victimization. . . . If we delve into the relationship between women and food we will discover the ways in which women have forged spaces within that oppression. Cooking becomes a vehicle for artistic expression, a source for sensual pleasure, an opportunity for resistance and even power. By reclaiming cooking we insure that we are not throwing the spaghetti out with the boiling water."[32] In recent years there have been significant—and sympathetic—reappraisals of women's food work,[33] but the identification of food with patriarchal oppression still slants the scholarship, as evidenced, perhaps, by the fact that there is much more work devoted to women's eating disorders than to women's positive connections to food.

The association of cooking with enslavement leads to another major reason for food's relative invisibility: technological utopianism. For millennia food has meant unrelenting drudgery, not just for cooks, but also for all food workers—farmers, field laborers, butchers, grocers, and so on. Since at least the early nineteenth century there has been a strong drive, in a sense, to "disappear" food, to make it less visible and less central as a burden or concern. Thus at the turn of this century many feminist utopians embraced almost any idea that would get food out of the home and thus free women: the meal in a pill, foods synthesized from coal, centralized kitchens, and "self-service" electric appliances and convenience foods. Similarly, farmer-utopians dreamed of push-button, fully automated factory farms as a way to save their children from backbreaking labor and rural isolation.[34] Today we can recognize that those dreams came true, in a perverse sort of way, but the result was further distancing from the traditional rituals and practices of food production.

Even more important in distancing us from nature and tradition have been the efforts of the food industry to obscure and mystify the links between the farm and the dinner table. While these efforts were stepped up in the mid-nineteenth century (reflected in the above-mentioned gendered separation of production from consumption), they date at least as far back as the first multinational food conglomerate, the East India Company, which was dedicated to bringing exotic foodstuffs to the British dining room and whose annual report in 1701 observed: "We taste the spices of Arabia yet never feel the scorching sun which brings them forth."[35] In other words, this food company was rather proud that, thanks to its noble service in distant lands, the average British consumer did not have to experience the strenuous (and sometimes violent) production processes by which his sausage got peppered or his tea sweetened. Perhaps the most vivid recent example of how we no longer have to feel the "scorching sun" of food production is the meatpacking industry, whose main thrust over 150 years has been to insulate consumers from any contact with the disassembly of warm-blooded mammals into refrigerated, plastic-wrapped chops and patties. In his magnificent environmental history of Chicago, *Nature's Metropolis*, William Cronon writes that the late nineteenth-century meatpacking industry encouraged "forgetfulness": "In the packers' world it was easy not to remember that eating was a moral act inexorably bound to killing."[36] By the 1920s, the relationship between supplier and customer, plough and plate, was largely anonymous, as noted by agricultural geneticist Edward East: "Today one sits down to breakfast, spreads out a napkin of Irish linen, opens the meal with a banana from Central America, follows with a cereal of Minnesota sweetened with the product of Cuban cane, and ends with a Montana lamb chop and cup of Brazilian coffee. Our daily life is a trip around the world, yet the wonder of it gives us not a single thrill. We are oblivious."[37] If consumers in the 1920s were already complacent about what East called the "globe-girdling" food supply system, they are even more "oblivious" now, when the "forgetfulness" applies not just to spices, sugar, or meat, but to virtually everything we consume: tomatoes, bread, pasta, shrimp, apple juice, and so on. Food is so vague in our culture in part because, thanks to processing, packaging, and marketing, it *is* an abstraction. As farmer-poet Wendell Berry writes, the ideal corporate customer today is the "industrial eater . . . who does not know that eating is an agricultural act, who no longer knows or imagines the connections between eating and the land, and who is therefore necessarily passive and uncritical. . . ."[38] And furthering the critical challenges to those attempting to uncover the complex commodity chains connecting field and fork is the fact that modern meals themselves are so ephemeral, for people do not eat as regularly or as socially as they used to. Given the unbearable lightness of eating these days (to borrow from novelist Milan Kundera), it is not surprising that it takes some effort to see food as a subject worthy of serious scrutiny.

Yet, despite these difficulties and delays, there is no question that more people are studying food than ever before. While it may be premature to announce the birth of a new discipline of food studies, signs of increased activity are everywhere. In addition to the food panels now beginning to appear regularly (albeit still sparingly) at mainstream academic conventions, there have been several major international conferences devoted entirely to food, and these have in turn resulted in published collections (including the present volume, which is an outgrowth of a conference on "Food and Drink in Consumer Societies," held at the Hagley Museum and Library in Wilmington, Delaware, in November 1999.)[39] These gatherings are especially noteworthy for their interdisciplinarity, as nutritionists, agronomists, biochemists, and ecologists mingle with historians, sociologists, folklorists, and film critics. New academic journals are appearing, independent food studies associations are growing, and publishers are establishing food series. While book-length monographs are still relatively rare, this appears about to change, as evidenced by a proliferation of readers containing chapter-length harbingers of work-in-progress.[40] Meanwhile, as a possible sign of disciplinary maturity, publishers are issuing quasi-canonical collections of classic essays and food studies textbooks, especially in the social sciences, the area with the longest history of sustained scholarly interest.[41] There is also a lively trade press market for food-related memoirs, essays, and annotated historical recipes.[42] Culinary history societies are mushrooming across the country. There are dozens of excellent Web sites devoted to the serious analysis of foodways, not to mention the thousands of sites dedicated to cooking, gastronomy, nutrition, and restaurant reviews.[43] Several universities have established food studies graduate programs, while other graduate students seek to "do food" within conventional disciplines.

The historian must ask: Why now? In part, scholarship is following the wider urban, middle-class culture, which since the 1970s has become much more interested in food-related matters of taste, craft, authenticity, status, and health. Food scholars belong to the same social professional/managerial class that has fueled an unprecedented expansion, elaboration, and differentiation in food consumption options, and that affluent, well-educated, trend-conscious public is literally hungry for analysis and perspective. Thus food scholars often find that journalists and documentary filmmakers are especially enthusiastic about this new work. So, too, are food professionals—chefs, managers, cookbook writers, and so on. (Indeed, many of the new food studies graduate students are former food workers seeking to intellectualize and expand their practical experiences and interests.) At the same time, as mentioned above, mainstream scholars have found food to be a useful tool for expanding ongoing research inquiries, especially into class, gender, ethnicity, consumer culture, material culture, and environmental studies. Academic administrators are increasingly supportive of the field because it is inherently interdisciplinary and also because it attracts strong course enrollments. And just as the counterculture discovered food reform as a means for political protest in the Vietnam era, the academic left has also found food studies to be a congenial and fertile base for activist analysis of hunger, inequality, neocolonialism, biotechnology, and globalization.[44] Concerns about food security, diversity, corporate accountability, and ecological sustainability underly much of the food scholarship today and animate many new food studies courses, where students often attempt to recover and illuminate the invisible links in the global food chain. Finding out where our food comes from is an important step toward taking responsibility for our food's full cost, which Thoreau defined as "the amount of life exchanged for it, immediately or in the long run."[45]

While the present volume does not purport to tally the "full amount of life exchanged" in the entire food chain, it does offer many important comparative and historical insights into that much-contested market zone where supply meets demand. It is thus fitting that the introductory remarks come from Sidney Mintz, whose *Sweetness and Power* stands as the model of "following production to where and when it became consumption. . . ."[46] Noting that the modern industrial food system is far more complex than the relatively closed, self-contained food systems studies by the classical anthropologists, Mintz offers five "conundrums" or "contradictions" facing those of us attempting to understand contemporary consumer culture: food is so important yet is taken for granted; food patterns are hard to change yet they do change often and rapidly; modern consumers value individualism and choice and yet also expect maximum security and protection; modern men and women are becoming more and more alike and yet view and treat food very differently; and modern eaters—particularly Americans—seem especially inconsistent in their "oscillation between Baskin-Robbins and the jogging track," between outrageous gluttony and equally excessive guilt. In addition, we are invited to contemplate the growing disparity between our own excesses and the acute food insecurity of billions elsewhere in the world. Mintz's meditation on these paradoxes provides a very useful springboard for the book's historical/anthropological studies of modern food consumption.

Part II, "The Construction of National Cuisines," raises more provocative questions, particularly about the old saw, "you are what you eat." When speaking of national cuisines, the axiom often conjugates into "we are what we eat." But who is this collective "we"? Do we define a national cuisine by bioregion? By foodshed? By arbitrary lines on an inaccurate map? What if those lines keep changing? How many people does it take to comprise a "we"? And in what context? As voters? As soldiers? As cooks? Customers? And what about the word "eat"? Which foods? When? Where? There are so many different ways that people eat. Which meals count as signifiers of "national identity" and which ones are simply occasions for "filling up" or "grabbing a bite"? (As Mintz notes, much of the food consumption literature, particularly the journalistic variety, focuses on what people eat on special occasions rather than on a daily basis.) And then there's that troublesome identity word "are," derived from "to be," "is." What is "identity" anyway? And which one? Most of us have quite a few. Perhaps Whitman had it right when he proclaimed that the self is so full of contradictions and "multitudes" as to be ultimately "untranslatable."

Judging from Part II's three essays, it seems that "national cuisines" may be most important to the people who stand to profit the most from their construction, especially politicians, food marketers, and other food professionals. While it is unclear how important national cuisines are to people's daily lives, attempts to identify and institutionalize national cuisines may be very significant from a marketing standpoint—as national branding campaigns (just as large food companies seek to add value to their products through the invention and licensing of marginal differences). It also seems clear that the idea of national cuisine is quite modern, even though the claim may seek to root itself in assertions of tradition, custom, soul, *terroir*. Thus Kolleen Guy's essay, "Rituals of Pleasure in the Land of Treasures: Wine Consumption and the Making of French Identity in the Late Nineteenth Century," offers a close look at the social invention and institutionalization of one particular marker of national identity wine, especially the classified, chateau-bottled variety. Here the self-interested motives of the primary players are quite clear, indeed blatant: national politicians marshaling French militarism; local politicians attempting to boost regional economies; wine growers, manufacturers, and wine merchants promoting their varieties; plus (strangely enough) temperance crusaders attempting to wean alcoholic workers from the harder stuff. The class dynamics of the wine story also illustrate how nationalism can trump socialism. (I would not be at all surprised if Marx and Engels were aware of the ongoing battle of the French vineyards as they wrote about the false consciousness of nationalism.) And as a case study in national branding, the success of French wine interests in establishing a highly regulated classification system has inspired and confounded wine competitors in the rest of the the world. By successfully capitalizing on the mystique of *terroir*, the French wine industry also created a lucrative line extension: the chateau tourist trade, which has served as a model for sip-and-taste tourism throughout the world. While the French may not have been the first to hook international travelers with the bait of culinary authenticity, they were spectacularly good in cornering the high end connoisseur market. And by using *terroir* to resist foreign suppliers, the French also unwittingly established a patriotic model for the current sustainable food movement—particularly the celebration of the "local" and "regional" over the forces of "globalization" and "McDonaldization."

The interaction between globalization and the invention of national cuisine is one of the many intriguing themes of anthropologist Richard Wilk's paper, "Food and Nationalism: The Origins of 'Belizean Food.'" Here the recent (and ongoing) construction of a marketable identity takes on a particularly forced, if not desperate aspect. Compared to France, Belize does not have much *terroir* to market (turtles and river fish do seem a rather fragile concept on which to build a national franchise), so the brand has to be fabricated out of assorted imports and colonial fragments. Indeed, the situation is not all that different from ours in the United States, where, as Donna Gabaccia has shown, the various cuisines of imagined authenticity, whether regional, ethnic, or national, have little organic relationship to indigenous culture or environment and derive mainly from a hodgepodge—or creolization—of alien dishes and myths.[47] (Thus Wilk's characterization of Belizean food practices as "heterogeneous, polyglot, disorderly, and even incoherent" could apply not just to our own practices here in the Americas but also to much of the post-Columbian world.) Yet, strangely, the more people move around, the more they seem to value home cooking, or rather a somewhat generalized, stereotyped version of it, as is clear with the case of Belizeans who have come to the United States. The role of emigration in establishing notions of national cuisine applies to many other immigrant groups: the further away from the mother country, the more crystallized the culinary identity. Conversely, just as the most interesting generalizations about nineteenth-century American cuisine came from visitors to the United States, Belizeans seem to rely on foreign expatriates to tell them what is most truly Belizean. Readers should beware that following all the twists in Professor Wilk's compelling tale of the tortured search for authenticity may make them want to burn their ethnic cookbooks and stick to fast food, which may be the only honest, contextually appropriate cuisine for our tribe. This essay also stands as a bracing antidote to conventional laments about the destruction of "national cuisines" by "globalization," for as Wilk shows, international flows of money and people may actually promote—and indeed require—the construction of local identities.

Further blurring the distinction between the "mass" and the "authentic" is Steve Penfold's essay, "'Eddie Shack Was No Tim Horton': Donuts and the Folklore of Mass Culture in Canada," which suggests that we live in a decidedly postmodernist situation where fluffy confections that have no link at all to *terroir* can take on the role of nationalistic, even jingoistic, icons. As Penfold shows, the donuts in question actually came from south of the border, as did the machinery and marketing model, the company is based in Ohio, and they're popular in only part of Canada. It's hard to argue that the donuts even taste different from the Yankee variety. Yet serious aspirations and concerns do lurk beneath the sugary crusts, especially dreams about the simple life, civic integrity, and the resistance of Canadian Davids to the American Goliath. Actual ingredients have little to do with this. So here is a clear illustration of another food studies axiom: that what we think about food may have little to do with the actual material properties of the food itself. Tim Horton's example may be a *reductio ad absurdum* of that axiom, but it's not all that different from a lot of so-called national foods. So what if these Canadian donuts actually came from the United States? The Irish potato comes from Peru; much of French food and wine came from Italy; the all-American hamburger and barbecue come from Asia. What makes the donut story different, however, is the self-reflexive irony attached to it. While there certainly are many Canadians who take the notion of distinctly Canadian cuisine quite seriously, it does not appear that the donut mavens really do. Rather, there's a tone of defeat or at least weariness in the story, a sense that given the facts of international trade and politics, it may be a bit unrealistic to expect David to fend off Goliath. The Horton story suggests that people may know that modern eating is so compromised, globalized, creolized, and McDonutized that it is really impossible to think in terms of food identities that mean a lot any more. Given the absurdity of the whole proposition anyway, why *not* make a donut the national food? The ironic self-effacement in the folklore of donuts may sound Canadian, but it seems much more universal, for irony rules everywhere, not just in Canada.

Irony rules in part because increasingly sophisticated consumers are well aware that much of what we take to be "tradition" is quite recent and is quite invented.[48] This leads to Part III, "The Business of Taste," which explores the construction of taste for new foods. According to all three papers in this section, there is no simple relationship between supply and demand, production and consumption. It is equally simplistic to argue that marketers just *serve* existing consumer needs or, conversely, that self-interested marketers can easily *manufacture* consumer wants.

Martin Bruegel's essay, "How the French Learned to Eat Canned Food, 1809–1930s," offers a hybrid of the "service" and "manufacturing" models. While canning technology was largely invented in France, initially for military purposes, it took almost a century before French food processors were able to convince civilians to use the product. Citing Joseph Schumpeter's adage that inventions do not always find profitable markets, Bruegel reminds us that culture often trumps technology. Throughout the nineteenth century French consumers were simply not "ready" to eat canned food, mainly because they (rightly) questioned its taste and safety. Class demographics also played a major role, for in addition to being expensive, canned goods contradicted the lower-class popular preferences for local, fresh, "natural" foods. In this sense the economic interests of processed food manufacturers conflicted with the those of Kolleen Guy's wine and cheese makers, who sought to expand markets by promoting the mystique of premodern *terroir*. Modernizing French food habits thus took considerable "education." In particular, Bruegel cites the role of schools and the military as essential institutions of modernization. Home economics classes "trained" women in the preparation of processed foods, while military service taught men to accept them. On the production side, manufacturers also standardized can sizes, improved safety, and lowered prices. Wider civilian use followed in the 1920s, when social and economic changes further enhanced the appeal of convenience foods. So while the French did eventually "learn" to eat canned food, the contradictory appeal of *terroir* may have reduced the pace of French dietary industrialization compared to that of Great Britain and the United States, where the working classes embraced a quick-and-easy diet somewhat sooner.[49]

The role of cultural institutions in "educating" modern consumers is also highlighted in Amy Bentley's piece, "Inventing Baby Food: Gerber and the Discourse of Infancy in the United States." Like cold cereals, candy bars, and fast food "Happy Meals," canned (or, more precisely, jarred) baby foods have socialized several generations to the taste and patterns of industrialized, convenience-based cuisine. Infant-feeding patterns also reveal much about changing parenting philosophies and practices. How did American mothers come, in just a few decades, to discard time-honored, naturally economical, nutritionally superior infant feeding practices, particularly the traditional preference for prolonged breast-feeding and delayed introduction of solid foods? The answer, Bentley suggests, lies partly in the evolution of "expert" opinion. Historians generally hesitate to use professional advice literature as an accurate reflection of what people actually do, since, as historian Harvey Green writes of Victorian drug warnings, "what was prohibited was probably closer to reality than the recommendation."[50] In the case of child-care advice, however, mothers of the early twentieth century may have been particularly ready to listen, in part due to the Progressive-era cult of expertise, and in part because migration, urbanization, and mass culture were rapidly undermining traditional support networks. The "medicalization" of food by chemists, who confidently reduced "eating" to the "dietary intake" of biochemical "nutrients"—protein, calories, minerals, and the newly discovered vitamins—further enhanced the prestige and influence of nutrition professionals. The same dietitians and home economists who were "teaching" young women to use canned foods also favored processed baby foods, particularly after the pioneering Gerber Products Company saturated popular magazines and professional journals with its well-honed promotional "narratives" of safety, service, and convenience. Bentley's suggestion that professional opinion was more than a little compromised by economic self-interest has considerable resonance today, when influential task forces studying dietary guidelines, pesticides, and biotechnology are staffed by experts with close ties to the industries they scrutinize. It often takes some historical hindsight to unmask the interests behind what contemporaries take to be "sound science."

In "Searching for Gold in Guacamole: California Growers Market the Avocado, 1910–1994," Jeffrey Charles addresses the timeless challenge facing sellers of new products: how, in a supposedly "free market" economy, to hook consumers who "freely" choose *not* to embrace their product. The avocado offers a clear case of a commodity that was in large supply long before there was any clear demand. Like much of California's fruit and vegetable industry, the avocado business resulted not from consumer need but from real estate speculation—especially the boosterish advertising of California as a pastoral/romantic paradise where almost anyone could set up a lucrative orchard and profit handsomely in Edenic bliss. As Steven Stoll shows in *The Fruits of Natural Advantage* (1998), late-nineteenth-century settlers may have been drawn to California's valleys by romantic dreams, but from the very start they faced the harsh realities of an erratic climate, opportunistic pests, insufficient labor, and an uncertain, remote market. To meet these challenges the most successful growers (mainly of grapes, citrus, and stone fruit) specialized in one or two varieties; reshaped the landscape to suit their intensive, irrigation-dependent monoculture; devised a labor system dependent on a floating proletariat of migrant workers; sponsored university research and development of a chemical arsenal to protect their crops; and formed cooperative packing and marketing associations to control competition and foster demand in distant cities.[51] Avocado growers faced all of these difficulties plus some additional cultural obstacles, for their product was hard to classify within prevailing culinary concepts. Efforts to market the avocado as a nutrient-dense wonder-fruit failed to win the degree of enthusiasm achieved by growers of oranges, raisins, and plums in the 1920s, while its association as a female-oriented salad vegetable deterred male consumption. (Perception was everything. A "health" pitch worked well in the infant-food market, where parental anxieties ruled—hence Gerber's success—while Calavo's adult-oriented health promotions got nowhere.) Only with the postwar ethnic revival did avocados achieve a solid (but seasonal) niche as a Latin-American staple, especially in guacamole, which serves as an important accompaniment to decidedly *non*healthy salty snacks. Ironically, this modest marketing success came precisely when California growers were facing stiff competition from Mexico, where the fruit actually originated. In short, Charles' article is a compelling lesson in the limitations of "top-down" marketing, as well as another example, along with Wilk's Belizean cuisine, of how the romance of ethnicity can coexist with the globalization of trade.

Part IV elaborates several of the book's main themes by examining the relationship between ethnicity, class, and business. In "As American as Budweiser and Pickles? Nation-Building in American Food Industries," Donna Gabaccia views the construction of "national cuisines" through the lens of immigration history. Which mass-produced foods are particularly "American" and what was the role of immigrant entrepreneurs in creating those national (and "nation-building") brands? Examining the biographies of several particularly successful food industrialists, Gabaccia finds that these immigrants succeeded by importing European technologies and business management practices—so much for American exceptionalism! At the same time, given the dominant culture's strong intolerance, they did best in the mass market by dropping explicit "ethnic" identities, even in selling products stereotypically associated with foreign expertise, particularly beer (Busch) and wine (Gallo). Just as certain foods are gendered in culinary discourse—meat is "male," salads are "female"—Gabaccia detects a pattern of xenophobic discrimination even in industries not easily identified as "ethnic," as native-born businessmen dominated certain staple industries like cereal manufacturing and canning, while immigrants tended to stick to the industries that, perhaps not coincidentally, also received the brunt of moralistic purity campaigns, particularly baking, meatpacking, and brewing. Gabaccia's suggestive reading of business patterns reminds us that while multiculturalism may suit today's market segmentation strategies, in the turn-of-the-century heyday of Fordist mass production, prejudice and Anglo-conformity shaped America's culinary identity.

Bigotry ruled at the local retail level, too, according to Tracey Deutsch. In "Untangling Alliances: Social Tensions surrounding Independent Grocery Stores and the Rise of Mass Retailing," Deutsch takes us back to the same era when nutritional experts were successfully pitching canned goods (Bruegel) and processed baby foods (Bentley), when some entrepreneurs established well-known national brands (Gabaccia) while others failed (Charles). This was also the period when the chain store made significant headway not just in mass retailing but also as the staple symbol of crass modernism. Longing for the lost mom-and-pop grocery reigns today, even as Americans patronize ever-larger conglomerated hypermarkets. Challenging our sentimentality, Deutsch argues that consumers had sound reasons for flocking to the chains, which, in addition to being cheaper, offered greater autonomy, choice, and dignity, especially for women and excluded minorities. "Stores were about power as much as price." Offering a fascinating peek at the complex social relationships involved in buying food, Deutsch shows us why other "self-service" innovations like automobiles, motels, and fast-food restaurants proved so liberating, and why it might be hard to uproot them. The grocery chain story thus poses especially strong questions for those of us who see a return to localized, intimate buyer-seller arrangements (for example, farmers, markets, community-supported agriculture, co-ops, family-run stores) as essential for community revival and environmental sustainability.

While both Gabaccia and Deutsch relate the history of the standardized mass market, Sylvia Ferrero focuses on the more multicultural yet also highly globalized postmodern food scene in "*Comida Sin Par.* Consumption of Mexican Food in Los Angeles: 'Foodscapes' in a Transnational Consumer

Society." Like Deutsch, Sylvia Ferrero offers a bottom-up view of the power relations involved in food consumption and entrepreneurship. Relying on anthropologist Arjun Appadurai's seminal work on the invention of national cuisines in the context of the ultracomplex, international, late-twentieth-century economy, Ferrero shows how modern immigrants and hyphenated Americans construct profitable "foodscapes" that maintain in-group solidarity and communicate distinctiveness even as they attract the outside patronage of affluent culinary tourists. Given the imminent rise of Hispanics to status as America's number one minority group, Ferrero offers a hopeful glimpse of a multicultural future in which immigrants prosper without full assimilation. And in shedding new light on how ethnic entrepreneurs cater to the elusive search for authenticity, Ferrero's ethnographic/semiotic analysis of Mexican-American restaurants, groceries, and cookbooks adds useful research methodologies to the largely historical slant of this collection.

The recent history of Mexican foodways receives further attention in Jeffrey Pilcher's study, "Industrial *Tortillas* and Folkloric Pepsi: The Nutritional Consequences of Hybrid Cuisines in Mexico." Using food to relate the story of Mexican economic and social "development," Pilcher's essay thus serves as a useful transition to the book's final section, which treats food in the context of political policy. In particular, Pilcher shows how state-sponsored modernization and globalization can have mixed meanings and implications for the world's poor. Like Wilk on Belize, Pilcher illustrates Sidney Mintz's now-classic distinction between the "inside" and "outside" meanings of a trend.[52] From the "inside," dietary change does not necessarily mean the loss of cultural identity. Just as Ferrero's "transnationals" maintain group solidarity even as they cross borders, so too have Mexican peasants retained a sense of history and heritage even as they adopt new foods; indeed, imported snacks and soft drinks are often incorporated into traditional rituals and food practices. From the "outside," however, peasant participation in the global food market means grave economic and nutritional perils; it takes money (and a job) to purchase these unhealthy foods. Indeed, one consequence of this greater involvement in the market is the northward flow to the Los Angeles "foodscapes" studied by Ferrero. At the same time as peasants are eating more industrial foods, the more affluent residents of the most industrialized societies are eating like peasants at restaurants run by refugees from impoverished peasant communities. Looking for the "outside" meaning of this strange synergy, I vaguely recall an adage that one of the spoils of war is the opportunity to eat the vanquished—or at least the vanquished's beans. Pilcher also offers a useful amendment to the cliche, "you are what you eat": while eating fast foods may not necessarily make you an American in cultural identity, it *will* give you an American waistline and arteries.

Keith Allen's article, "Berlin in the *Belle Époque:* A Fast-Food History," further confirms that eating fast food is not necessarily the same as eating American. Fifty years before McDonald's revolutionized dining habits, the German restaurant Aschinger's developed many of the primary elements of the fast food formula, particularly speed, predictability, filling portions, economies of scale, reasonable prices, low labor costs, and franchising. Aschinger's ability to win customers away from mom-and-pop neighborhood eateries reinforces Deutsch's argument that grocery chains elevated American consumers. According to Allen, Aschinger's "low prices enabled the cabman, the skilled workman, even the seamstress to enjoy the same fare and clubby, dark-wood atmosphere as the minor clerk, the civil servant, and the student." At the same time, Aschinger's cuisine and identity was distinctively German, much the way Howard Johnson combined modern management and marketing techniques with an appeal to New England culinary and architectural traditions. (Here again we see how the globalizing, massifying dynamics of modern capitalism coexist with—indeed, depend upon—folksy allusions to the premodern.) And being distinctly German also led to the company's eventual demise—and thus its obscurity in fast food history. Siding with the Nazis in the early 1930s, the Aschinger family acquired their primary Jewish competitor, profited handsomely as caterers and suppliers during the war, then suffered appropriately afterwards. Allen's story is thus a reminder that success and failure in the food system are always an intensely political matter.

The connection between food and state politics is clear in another case study in failure, Mauricio Borrero's piece, "Food and the Politics of Scarcity in Urban Soviet Russia, 1917–1941." While virtually all of the other articles in this book deal with the way consumer capitalism allocates resources and power, Borrero addresses early Soviet attempts to redistribute food outside of a commercial market, mainly through direct rationing and through state-subsidized public dining rooms. Both experiments were direct outgrowths of nineteenth-century utopian thought, and both models still loom large in radical critiques of the late-capitalist food system. Borrero's explanation of the Soviet's inability to alleviate hunger through direct redistribution thus has implications not only for our understanding of how the Cold War was "won," but also for current analysis of hunger today, when, just as in the Soviet Union, there is plenty of food on the world's farms but no simple way to get it to everyone who needs it.[53]

In all, this volume raises many questions for the future of the food system. How do we get food to the needy when the prevailing market favors the well-fed? How will science and technology serve more universal human needs? How, in the context of greater globalization of trade and culture, do we protect the local and individual? Who will invent the traditions, tastes, and identities of the future? Will the current struggle over genetically modified foods follow the paths established by canning and baby foods, or will corporate biotechnology be derailed by *terroir* tourism? Will universal "McDonaldization" proceed along the lines originally set out by the national brands and chains of the early twentith century, or will it be subverted by the rising numbers of "transnationals" now crowding the world's cities? How do we feed ten to twelve billion people sustainably, equitably, healthfully, *and* tastefully? History may not tell us how to solve these conundrums, but it can certainly suggest how we got into them.

NOTES

1. Parts of this essay appeared as "Why Food Matters," *Culture & Agriculture* 21 (Spring 1999): 27–34.
2. Paul Rozin, "Food Is Fundamental, Fun, Frightening, and Far-Reaching," *Social Research* 66 (Winter 1998): 9–30.
3. Arjun Appadurai, "GastroPolitics in Hindu South Asia," *American Ethnologist* 8 (1981): 494.
4. Gary Alan Fine, *Kitchens: The Culture of Restaurant Work* (Berkeley: University of California Press, 1996), p. 1.
5. Sidney Mintz quoted in Paula M. Hirschoff and Neil G. Kotlers, eds., *Completing the Food Chain: Strategies for Combating Hunger and Malnutrition* (Washington, DC: Smithsonian Institution Press, 1989), pp. 115–116.
6. Evan Eisenberg, *The Ecology of Eden: An Inquiry into the Dream of Paradise and a New Vision of Our Role in Nature* (New York: Vintage, 1998), pp. 95–97.
7. Jared Diamond, *Guns, Germs, and Steel: The Fates of Human Societies* (New York: Norton, 1997).
8. Henry Hobhouse, *Seeds of Change: Five Plants That Transformed Mankind* (New York: Harper & Row, 1985), p. xi. See also, Herman J. Viola and Carolyn Margolis, eds., *Seeds of Change: A Quincentennial Commemoration* (Washington, DC: Smithsonian Institution Press, 1991).
9. William H. McNeill, "How the Potato Changed the World's History," *Social Research* 66 (Winter 1998): 67. See also, Larry Zuckerman, *The Potato: How the Humble Spud Rescued the Western World* (New York: North Point Press, 1998).
10. Betty Fussell, *The Story of Corn* (New York: North Point Press, 1999), p. 6.
11. Sidney Mintz, *Sweetness and Power: The Place of Sugar in Modern History* (New York: Viking, 1985); Mark Kurlansky, *Cod* (New York: Penguin, 1997).
12. Gary Gardner and Brian Halweil, *Underfed and Overfed: The Global Epidemic of Malnutrition* (Washington, DC: Worldwatch Institute, 2000).
13. Harvey Levenstein, *Revolution at the Table: The Transformation of the American Diet* (New York: Oxford, 1988), and *Paradox of Plenty: A Social History of Eating in Modern America* (New York: Oxford, 1993).
14. Amy Bentley, *Eating for Victory: United States Food Rationing and the Politics of Domesticity* (Champaign: University of Illinois Press, 1998); Elaine Tyler May, *Homeward Bound: American Families in the Cold War Era* (New York: Basic Books, 1988); Karal Ann Marling, *As Seen on TV: The Visual Culture of Everyday Life in the 1950s* (Cambridge: Harvard University Press, 1994), pp. 242–283; John H. Perkins, *Geopolitics and the Green Revolution: Wheat, Genes, and the Cold War* (New York: Oxford University Press, 1997); Warren Belasco, *Appetite for Change: How the Counterculture Took on the Food Industry* (Ithaca: Cornell University Press, 1993).
15. John Hess and Karen Hess, *The Taste of America* (New York: Penguin, 1977), p. 17.
16. George Orwell, *The Road to Wigan Pier* (1937); Warren Belasco, "Food, Morality, and Social Reform," in *Morality and Health*, ed. Allan M. Brandt and Paul Rozin (New York: Routledge, 1997), pp. 185–199.
17. Among the best of such nonacademic "culinary histories": Harold McGee, *On Food and Cooking: The Science and Lore of the Kitchen* (New York: Collier Books, 1984); Reay Tannahill, *Food in History* (New York: Crown, 1988); Margaret Visser, *Much Depends on Dinner* (New York: Grove Press, 1986); Visser, *The Rituals of Dinner* (New York: Grove Weidenfeld, 1991); T. Sarah Peterson, *Acquired Taste: The French Origins of Modern Cooking* (Ithaca: Cornell University Press, 1994); Gerry Schremp, *Kitchen Culture: Fifty Years of*

Food Fads (New York: Pharos Books, 1991); Waverley Root and Richard de Rochemont, *Eating in America: A History* (New York: William Morrow, 1976); Andrew F. Smith, *Popped Culture: A Social History of Popcorn in America* (Columbia: University of South Carolina Press, 1999) and *Souper Tomatoes: The Story of America's Favorite Food* (New Brunswick: Rutgers University Press, 2000); Elisabeth Rozin, *The Primal Cheeseburger* (New York: Penguin, 1994).

18. Jennifer Ruark, "A Place at the Table: More Scholars Focus on the Historical, Social, and Cultural Meanings of Food, but Some Critics Say It's Scholarship Lite," *Chronicle of Higher Education*, July 9, 1999: A17–A19. Fabre quoted in Arthur Butler, *Essays on Wheat* (New York: MacMillan, 1919), p. v.

19. James R. Barrett, *Work and Community in the Jungle: Chicago's Packinghouse Workers, 1894–1922* (Champaign: University of Illinois Press, 1987); Roger Horowitz, *"Negro and White, Unite and Fight!": A Social History of Industrial Unionism in Meatpacking, 1930–90* (Champaign: University of Illinois Press, 1997); Levenstein, *Revolution at the Table*.

20. Susan Strasser, *Never Done: A History of American Housework* (New York: Pantheon, 1982); Joan Jacobs Brumberg, *Fasting Girls: The History of Anorexia Nervosa* (Cambridge: Harvard University Press, 1988); Laura Shapiro, *Perfection Salad: Women and Cooking at the Turn of the Century* (New York: Farrar, Straus, and Giroux, 1986); Bentley, *Eating for Victory*.

21. Gilbert Fite, *American Farmers: The New Minority* (Bloomington: Indiana University Press, 1981); John Fraser Hart, *The Land That Feeds Us* (New York: Norton, 1991); Peter A. Coclanis, "Food Chains: The Burden of the (Re)Past,"*Agricultural History* 72 (1998): 661–674.

22. Stephen Mennell, *All Manners of Food: Eating and Taste in England and France from the Middle Ages to the Present* (Urbana: University of Illinois Press, 1996); Donna R. Gabaccia, *We Are What We Eat: Ethnic Foods and the Making of Americans* (Cambridge: Harvard University Press, 1998).

23. Stephen Nissenbaum, *Sex, Diet, and Debility in Jacksonian America: Sylvester Graham and Health Reform* (Westport, CT: Greenwood, 1980); Harvey Green, *Fit for America: Health, Fitness, Sport, and American Society* (New York: Pantheon Books, 1988); Marling, *As Seen On TV*.

24. Belasco, *Appetite for Change*.

25. It should be noted that several of the authors collected in this volume *have* produced or are currently working on second books in food studies: Mintz, Bentley, Pilcher, Belasco.

26. Deane W. Curtin and Lisa M. Heldke, "Introduction," in *Cooking, Eating, Thinking: Transformative Philosophies of Food*, ed. Curtin and Heldke (Bloomington: Indiana University Press, 1992), p. xiv.

27. Levenstein, *Revolution at the Table*, and *Paradox of Plenty: A Social History of Eating in Modern America* (New York: Oxford University Press, 1993); Peter N. Stearns, *Fat History: Bodies and Beauty in the Modern West* (New York: New York University Press, 1997).

28. John Milton, *Paradise Lost* (1667), quoted in March Egerton, ed., *Since Eve Ate Apples* (Portland, OR: Tsunami Press, 1994), p. 18.

29. Brumberg, *Fasting Girls*; Kenneth L. Ames, *Death in the Dining Room & Other Tales of Victorian Culture* (Philadelphia: Temple University Press, 1992); Kathryn Grover, ed., *Dining in America, 1850–1900* (Amherst: University of Massachusetts Press, 1987).

30. Joyce Carol Oates, "Food Mysteries," in *Not for Bread Alone: Writers on Food, Wine, and the Art of Eating*, ed. Daniel Halpern (Hopewell, NJ: Ecco Press, 1993), pp. 25–37.

31. Strasser, *Never Done*, pp. 206–207; Levenstein, *Revolution at the Table*, pp. 44–59, 98–108; Shapiro, *Perfection Salad*, pp. 127–190.

32. Arlene Avakian, ed., *Through the Kitchen Window: Women Writers Explore the Intimate Meanings of Food and Cooking* (Boston: Beacon Press, 1997), pp. 4, 6.

33. Strasser, *Never Done*; Marjorie L. DeVault, *Feeding the Family: The Social Organization of Caring as Gendered Work* (Chicago: University of Chicago Press, 1991); Carole M. Counihan, *The Anthropology of Food and Body: Gender, Meaning, and Power* (New York: Routledge, 1999).

34. Dolores Hayden, *The Grand Domestic Revolution:A History of Feminist Designs for American Homes, Neighborhoods, and Cities* (Cambridge: M.I.T. Press, 1981); Kenneth Roemer, *The Obsolete Necessity: America in Utopian Writings, 1888–1900* (Kent, OH: Kent State University Press, 1976); Strasser, *Never Done*, pp. 67–84; Warren Belasco, "Future Notes: The Meal-in-a-Pill," *Food and Foodways*, 8 (2000): 253–271.

35. This quotation is one of the dozen or so wise sayings chiseled into the interior dome of the Library of Congress Main Reading Room.

36. William Cronon, *Nature's Metropolis: Chicago and the Great West* (New York: Norton, 1991), p. 256.

37. Edward M. East, *Mankind at the Crossroads* (New York: Charles Scribner's Sons, 1924), p. 64.
38. Wendell Berry, "The Pleasures of Eating," *Journal of Gastronomy* 5(2) (1989): 126.
39. Other notable conference collections include: Arian Mack, ed., *Food: Nature and Culture* (New York: New School University, 1999); Raymond Grew, ed., *Food in Global History* (Boulder, CO: Westview, 1999); Carola Lentz, ed., *Changing Food Habits: Case Studies from Africa, South America, and Europe* (Amsterdam: Harwood, 1999).
40. Again, in addition to the present volume, examples of such edited things-to-come include: Ron Scapp and Brian Seitz, eds., *Eating Culture* (Albany: State University of New York, 1998); John Germov and Lauren Williams, eds., *A Sociology of Food and Nutrition: The Social Appetite* (Victoria, Aus: Oxford University Press, 1999); Sian Griffiths and Jennifer Wallace, eds., *Consuming Passions: Food in the Age of Anxiety* (Manchester, UK: Mandolin, 1998); Anne L. Bower, ed., *Recipes for Reading: Community Cookbooks, Stories, Histories* (Amherst: University of Massachusetts Press, 1997); Donna Maurer and Jeffery Sobal, eds., *Eating Agendas: Food and Nutrition as Social Problems* (New York: Aldine de Gruyter, 1995). That the early 1980s were not so prolific is shown by the fact that, for many years, the only such reader—and a very good one at that—was Linda Keller Bown and Kay Mussell, eds., *Ethnic and Regional Foodways in the United States: The Performance of Group Identity* (Knoxville: University of Tennessee Press, 1984).
41. Carole Counihan and Penny Van Esterik, eds., *Food and Culture: A Reader* (New York: Routledge, 1997); Curtin and Heldke, *Cooking, Eating, Thinking*; Barbara G. Shortridge and James R. Shortridge, eds., *The Taste of American Place: A Reader on Regional and Ethnic Foods* (Lanham, MD: Rowman and Littlefield, 1998); David Bell and Gill Valentine, *Consuming Geographies: We Are Where We Eat* (London: Routledge, 1997); Alan Warde, *Consumption, Food, and Taste* (London: Sage, 1997); John Germov and Lauren Williams, eds., *A Sociology of Food and Nutrition: The Social Appetite* (Victoria, Aus: Oxford University Press, 1999); William A. McIntosh, *Sociologies of Food and Nutrition* (New York: Plenum, 1996); Alan Beardsworth and Teresa Keil, *Sociology on the Menu* (London: Routledge, 1997); Richard Pillsbury, *No Foreign Food: The American Diet in Time and Place* (Boulder, CO: Westview, 1998); Brigid Allen, ed.,. *Food: An Oxford Anthology* (New York: Oxford University Press, 1995); Paul Levy, ed., *The Penguin Book of Food and Drink* (London: Penguin, 1998); Kerry S. Walters and Lisa Portmess, eds., *Ethical Vegetarianism: From Pythagoras to Peter Singer* (Albany: State University of New York Press, 1999).
42. Avakian, *Through the Kitchen Window*; Mark Winegardner, ed., *We Are What We Ate: 24 Memories of Food* (Orlando, FL: Harcourt Brace, 1998); Ruth Reichl, *Tender at the Bone: Growing Up at the Table* (New York: Broadway Books, 1998); Elizabeth Ehrlich, *Miriam's Kitchen* (New York: Penguin, 1998); Richard Sterling, ed., *Travelers' Tales: Food* (San Francisco: Travelers' Tales, 1996); Andrew Dalby and Sally Grainger, *The Classical Cookbook* (Los Angeles: J. Paul Getty Museum, 1996).
43. A very useful guide to such sources is Gary Allen, *The Resource Guide for Food Writers* (New York: Routledge, 1999).
44. See, for example, Philip McMichael, *The Global Restructuring of Agro-Food Systems* (Ithaca: Cornell University Press, 1994); Alessandro Bonanno, et al., eds., *From Columbus to ConAgra: The Globalization of Agriculture and Food* (Lawrence: University of Kansas Press, 1994); Wes Jackson, et al., eds., *Meeting the Expectations of the Land: Essays in Sustainable Agriculture and Stewardship* (San Francisco: North Point Press, 1984); Janet Poppendieck, *Sweet Charity? Emergency Food and the End of Entitlement* (New York: Viking, 1998); Deborah Barndt, ed., *Women Working the NAFTA Food Chain: Women, Food, and Globalization* (Toronto: Second Story Press, 1999).
45. Henry David Thoreau, quoted by David Orr, *Earth in Mind: On Education, Environment, and the Human Prospect* (Washington, DC: Island Press, 1994), p. 172.
46. Mintz, *Sweetness and Power*, p. 1. See also Sidney W. Mintz, *Tasting Food, Tasting Freedom: Excursions into Eating, Culture, and the Past* (Boston: Beacon Press, 1996).
47. Gabaccia, *We Are What We Eat*.
48. For an introduction to the social construction of food issues and concerns, see Maurer and Sobal, *Eating Agendas*; Stephen Mennell, *All Manners of Food: Eating and Taste in England and France from the Middle Ages to the Present* (Champaign: University of Illinois Press, 1995); Anne Murcott, ed., *The Sociology of Food and Eating: Essays on the Sociological Significance of Food* (Aldershot, UK: Gower, 1983); Stephen Mennell, Anne Murcott, and Anneke H. van Otterloo, eds., *The Sociology of Food: Eating, Diet, and Culture* (London: Sage, 1992). Peter Farb and George Armelagos, *Consuming Passions: The Anthropology of Eating* (Boston: Houghton Mifflin, 1980).
49. For the earlier success of convenience-based cuisine, see Mintz, *Sweetness and Power*, especially pp. 74–186; Levenstein, *Revolution at the Table*.

50. Harvey Green, *The Light of the Home: An Intimate View of the Lives of Women in Victorian America* (New York: Pantheon Books, 1983), p. 38.
51. Steven Stoll, *The Fruits of Natural Advantage: Making the Industrial Countryside in California* (Berkeley: University of California Press, 1998).
52. Mintz, *Sweetness and Power*, p. 151.
53. Frances Moore Lappe, Joseph Collins, and Peter Rosset, *World Hunger: Twelve Myths*, 2nd ed. (New York: Grove Press, 1998); Douglas H. Boucher, ed., *The Paradox of Plenty: Hunger in a Bountiful World* (Oakland: Food First Books, 1999).

Chapter 2

FOOD AND EATING: SOME PERSISTING QUESTIONS

Sidney W. Mintz

I want to consider here the distinctive role played by food, in con-
tradistinction to all other commodities, in American everyday life.
Though most seem only recently to have been discovered, anthropological
studies of food and eating are of surprisingly long standing. One thinks, for
example, of William Robertson Smith, whose work on sacrifice and the Old
Testament can be said to have marked the beginnings of the scientific
study of food in relation to religion.[1] But most anthropologists would probably begin with Bronislaw Malinowski's *Argonauts of the Western Pacific*, or
even more, his *Coral Gardens and Their Magic*.[2] In these works food is
shown to play a central part in the economic, social, and political life of
every Trobriand Islander; Malinowski skillfully leads the reader into the
web of relationships that tie people together, and lets us see how food
moves along its threads. Others might think first of Malinowski's student,
Raymond Firth, whose *A Primitive Polynesian Economy* documents the economic life of the people of Tikopia.[3] My own favorite is Audrey Richards's
Land, Labour and Diet in Northern Rhodesia.[4] The people she studied, the
Bemba, had already been thrust upon a path of considerable change, but
they were trying to maintain many features of their familiar way of life.
Richards uses Bemba agricultural and nutritive patterns as a way of show-
ing us how the people produce, distribute, and consume their daily food,
and how it colors all of their relationships.

These authors worked in societies in which, at the time that they were
being studied, the foods coming from outside the society, whether measured by bulk or by symbolic weight, were of trivial significance in local
diets. Richards did describe at length and with clarity the effects of Western
colonialism, especially politically and economically, on the Bemba. But for
the most part their food continued to be truly Bemba food, and only grudg-

ingly did the Bemba give way to the relentless pressure of external forces upon diet and food habits.

It may seem strange that the largely closed character of the food systems of societies such as these made consumption in them an easier subject for anthropologists to study. Though the boundaries between societies are *always* being crossed, it was nonetheless possible in these cases to treat production, distribution, and consumption as a single systemic web and, indeed, to view enlargements of that web, or alterations in its parts and their relations, as mostly political in significance. To state it crudely, as food was distributed, political authority expectably accompanied it. Alterations in productivity might indeed arise from technological change under such conditions, but the links between increased productivity and the nature and scale of consumption were of a characteristically modest kind. What I mean by this is that increased local productivity in societies of this sort did not lead inexorably to greater production, wider markets, longer hours of work, higher pay, larger houses, more visits to the psychoanalyst, bigger shopping malls, or persisting (and sometimes declining) numbers of unemployed or homeless people. Or to say it differently again, these societies did not respond to *internally* widened opportunities in ways that we would find familiar. The studies carried out by anthropologists demonstrated that people typically worked hard, took pride in their work, ate with great pleasure, and used food (and other goods) ceremonially. But their economies could be explained to a noticeable extent in terms of themselves—with production, distribution, and consumption forming an almost seamless whole. I do not want to exaggerate this contrast to the modern; it has been done too much. But I also do not want to mute it or ignore it.

In the modern world, where change is rapid and productive and distributive activities are often widely separated from each other, anthropological fieldwork cannot usually encompass both production and consumption, so that analyses structurally parallel to the ethnographies of the past are awfully difficult to bring off. When it's food that's being produced, distributed, and consumed, the problems multiply. Treatments such as Mary Weismantel's *Food, Gender and Poverty in the Ecuadorian Andes*[5] do much to help us understand how new foods and new schedules, enhanced and enforced by migration and the splitting of the family labor unit, remake local life. But our grasp of the relationships between production and consumption is still constrained, once market forces penetrate social relationships on the level of everyday life. Because of the changes those forces make possible, our understanding of the consumption of food in modern society confronts conundrums, apparent contradictions, contrasts, and polarities of a kind. It never seems to turn out to be quite as simple as we might think. And so it may be useful to try to spell out a few of the questions this subject raises. The ideas I have to offer here will not fall upon you as fresh as driven snow, but perhaps there is benefit in reviewing some things, even those we may know already.

Food is enormously important, first of all, as sustenance. If you cannot eat, soon enough you will not be able to stay alive. But food is also a symbolic marker of membership (or nonmembership) in practically any sort of social grouping. Whether it be ceremonial or everyday, public or private, kin-based or not, at work or at play, religious or secular, social groups characteristically employ food to draw lines, confirm statuses, and separate those who do, and do not, belong. But because we must eat regularly and often, simply to stay alive, the very everydayness of food saturates it with the perfunctory. Thus the first conundrum, I think, is food's enormous importance to survival, on the one hand, and our tendency to take it very much for granted, on the other. The plentifulness of food feeds the symbolic—and yet, were it much less plentiful among us, its symbolic "weight" or power would doubtless increase. Audrey Richards pointed out long ago that hunger is a far more powerful drive than sex;[6] but most of us, most of the time, enjoy more food than we even need. As a consequence, this most vital of substances is made humdrum, prosaic, and hardly a dignified subject to dwell upon.

A second contradiction inheres, I think, in the ways people feel about the particular foods that they eat. I used to argue that it would be easier to make a radical change in a country's politics than to change its fundamental diet. In the years since the collapse of the Soviet Union, I have come to think that, more than ever. Imagine convincing the Russian people to give up black bread in order to eat rice instead! Or the people of China, to give up rice to eat black bread! Such food habits are so close to the core of what culture is that they sometimes function almost like language. As with language, on many occasions people define themselves with food; at the same time, food consistently defines and redefines *them*.

Despite this, we know—and we get additional evidence daily—that people can change their diets radically and quickly: a simultaneous conservatism, even obduracy, wedded to an odd lability or mimicry, this contrast lends mystery to food behavior—and the mystery is unsolved, I think. The rapid acceptance and spread of Japanese food, particularly raw fish, among even working-class Americans in recent decades is, for me, at least, ample evidence of this second point. As a young soldier I remember my barracks-mates telling me that the Japanese were subhuman because they ate raw fish. My counterarguments—that "we" ate raw clams and oysters— were brushed aside as entirely irrelevant. Yet today many blue-collar Americans can tell raw tuna from raw salmon by their texture on the tongue—an accomplishment that probably would have made their grandparents throw up. Here, then, the conservative or usual, and the trendy and new, arise in unexpected conjuncture. I suspect that all of us can point to comparable contrasts worldwide.

A third, important contrast or conundrum in the study of food inheres in the knotty problem of governance in a democratic capitalist society such as this one, obsessed by its culturally specific notions of individual freedom: how to provide protection to the citizenry on one hand, yet maintain freedom of choice on other. It seems to me that this is particularly acute in the U.S. case, where the freedom to consume has acquired much additional strength in the last decade or two, and where concepts of individuality no longer skirt the issue of the sacred right to buy, but often assimilate it, even more than before. That is to say, I think it can be argued that the critique once commonly leveled at consumerism—that individuality was becoming a function of consumption—is now widely assumed to *be* the status quo, a kind of given, not some fearsome future to be deplored or prevented. Because of this, the relationship between choice and individuality is central to any serious reflection about how the state and the economy cohere or disjoin. Standing athwart the channels through which sellers and buyers negotiate, the state confronts ambivalent demands. How it shields its citizens—from dangerous automobiles, say, or smoking, or *Salmonella*—without restraining their custom becomes each day a more pressing concern. Nor are the answers that readily apparent, except in the most egregious cases. The recent changes by government in regard to the advertising and sale of medicinal foods—"nutraceuticals"—nicely captures the state's uncertainties about safety versus the free market.

I think that there are two other conundrums or inconsistencies—I'm not sure what best to label them—I wish to refer to here. The first is to some extent gender-based. Both men and women in this society are brought up with powerful, if somewhat different, concepts of what individuality is and how one achieves it. But food—what it is, one's right to consume it unencumbered, what it symbolizes—has different significance according to gender. Think a moment about the obvious: men and women are equal and becoming more equal every day, we hope, but they do *not* eat alike, and do not even seem likely to want to. Even if we omit the still-important, though declining, issue of who cooks the food, women will probably find much more glaring than do men the gender contrast that food-related behavior reveals and dramatizes.

And finally, there is what I think of not so much as a contradiction or conundrum, but as the issue food raises of where morality begins and ends. This is, I think, a legitimate anthropological question, because cross-cultural reflection provides comparative insight. But it is not exclusively an anthropological issue, and it merits at least a minute's attention later on. Why is food in American life so powerful a vehicle for moral considerations? And to what extent might we go beyond simply asserting that morality enters into the way we relate to food?

I offer you, then, five themes among many, with which to puzzle over food and consumption in modern society:

1. that food is critical to life, nutritively and symbolically, yet usually prosaic and everyday;
2. that people are both intensely conservative in their food habits, yet startlingly open to change, even rapid change;
3. that democratic governments must struggle over food issues because, among other things, they are obliged to protect their citizens from harm, but can interfere only at some political risk with citizens' rights to buy as they wish;
4. that the relationship between food and individuality, in this society at least, works out differently for men and for women; and finally,
5. that the penetration of the sphere of eating by strong moral considerations is a cross-culturally relevant issue, because in many societies the very presence of the moral order in matters of food would be considered somewhat out of place.

Let me now address these matters briefly, in order.

Audrey Richards was right to point out that hunger is more powerful than the sex drive. If she sounds wrong, it is because those who are both young and very well fed have had no opportunity to learn how right she was. Even a short fast—36 or 48 hours— would convince any of us otherwise. At the same time, food overflows with symbolic significance, which is linked to its fundamental nutritive function in subtle ways. And yet, despite its importance both nutritively and symbolically, there is a strong propensity to routinize food, both in the eating and as a prosaic and intrinsically boring subject of discussion, at least for intellectuals. This difference between the importance of food and the way it is treated and regarded is exaggerated in a society such as our own, in part because of our staggering affluence. Were not so many of us so sturdily overnourished, the importance of food would be more readily acknowledged.

Roland Barthes's assertion[7] many years ago that, with the emergence of modern society, food has been transformed from a substance that fits with a certain ritual, atmosphere, or occasion into a substance that epitomizes that which it is supposed to accompany, is apposite. He noted that this transformation of food makes sense especially under conditions of affluence. When people are really hungry, especially when they are hungry nearly all the time, the secondary meanings of food expectably diminish, sometimes to the vanishing point.

Though he was speaking of modern France, what Barthes claimed seems to have become a more general characteristic of modernity. "We are witnessing an extraordinary expansion of the areas associated with food," he wrote:

> [F]ood is becoming incorporated into an ever-lengthening list of situations. . . .
> food is also charged with signifying the situation in which it is used. It has a
> twofold value, being nutrition as well as protocol, and its value as protocol

becomes increasingly more important as soon as the basic needs are satisfied. . . .
In other words, we might say that in contemporary . . . society, food has a constant tendency to transform itself into situation.[8]

My own take is that the more food becomes "situation," the less it matters intrinsically what the food is. In other words, while I think Barthes's assertion was prophetic, turning food into situation probably changes importantly how the *specific* food itself is perceived. But this does not alter the familiar difficulty of taking for granted that upon which we most depend. I think that all of us who want to study food are aware of this inalterable problem.

That people both stay very much the same in what they eat, and yet can change features of their diet swiftly and radically, is hardly news. But what I find striking is how little we really understand about this apparent inconsistency. One important aspect of the contrast for me is that we don't always begin our analysis by looking at what people *usually* eat. I think that the significance of the difference between conservatism and trendiness in food can be made to yield analytically only by considering the backdrop of customary eating against which new foods or food novelties are tried.

As an example, we might think of the Chinese and McDonald's. While McDonald's has enjoyed legendary success in the People's Republic of China and will no doubt continue to do so as long as the astonishing rate of economic growth there holds up, it needs to be remembered, first, that there are nearly 1.4 billion Chinese; and second, that hardly any of them— a couple of hundred thousand is not really very many, you see—have eaten a Whopper *twice*. But even more important than the number of Whoppers they have eaten is what they eat when they are *not* eating Whoppers. A powerful and old daily reliance upon a central complex carbohydrate; its accompaniment by respectable quantities of vegetables, especially leafy vegetables; and the daily consumption of vegetable protein in the form of beans, bean curd, and so on, is the backdrop to Chinese experimentation with novelties.[9] If we try to imagine the American backdrop to the eating of a Whopper, however, it seems certain that we will end up aware of striking differences. Otherwise said, what a Whopper *is* is not forecast by its intrinsic nature but by the cultural matrix within which it is perceived and consumed. This is a research sphere, by the way, into which the historical study of foods and food habits must enter strongly, and no amount of laboratory testing, in my opinion, is likely to tell us very much that is cross-culturally useful.

The broad issue of regulation and commerce has, of course, been transformed in recent decades. In the sphere of food, the cases involving mad cow disease, the spread of *Salmonella* and *Escherichia*, and the place of genetically modified food plants are maddeningly complicated and will not be solved in the immediate future. In the United States, they pose particularly difficult problems because consumers make conflictful demands upon the state: they want both to be left alone when they buy, as in all else, yet they want to be protected. It would be easy to exemplify the issue with, say, gun control. But food furnishes us with subtler and more tantalizing problems.

Spheres of concern such as terminology all confront an apparently antiquated regulatory system. As we all know, the Food and Drug Administration makes no attempt to regulate the term "natural," because there seems to be no way to define it. Other such spheres of concern are the boundary between food and medicine, which seems prone to change and difficult to defend; the health issues raised by concentrated food animal production in confined spaces, particularly of poultry and swine; and the regulation of seafood, especially raw seafood. It is possible that issues of this kind are in practice never wholly resolved, and so it may be with those concerned with food. The banana wars, so called; the European resistance to American beef; the resulting boycott of French *foie gras* and Roquefort; the French reaction, which included the leveling of a future McDonald's site in the south of the country—this complex sequence concerned at every stage the right to buy and the state's obligation to protect its citizens. Food seems to have a rich potential for exciting such displays.

The food and gender issue deserves much more than the passing attention it will get here. But I think I am right when I say that we do not yet possess a thorough analysis of the ways foods are differentially perceived along gender lines and what differences fit in with this one. Several years ago I asked one of my undergraduate students to research how young females prepared for a date that would include dinner out. Though I do not have contrasting information on how young males prepared, I am certain you would not call it preparation in the same sense. Young women often ate shortly before going out, and might consume small quantities of oil to forestall rapid intoxication. The foods they chose were selected at least in part according to what might be consumed gracefully. Under such constraints, it is hardly accurate to claim that they were "choosing" the foods they ate—or, at least, we can claim that males and females do their choosing differently. The contrast has probably changed somewhat as culinary competence declines nationally. But this contrast between males and females seems to me potentially very fruitful analytically. It can of course be made in other societies as well. But because the terms and details vary enormously across cultures, such contrasts could prove freshly illuminating. What in the way of values and preoccupations do young Americans bring to the table with them that influence the way they pick from the menu? This sounds, perhaps, like a "psychological" question. But I think it has to do with cultural differences.

My last point has to do with morality and food. Again, I mean to be brief. The infusion of moral considerations into food habits is not exclusively American, of course; but it surely is important in America. A recent report by Rozin, Fischler, and their colleagues briefly compares food attitudes in the United States, Japan, Flemish Belgium, and France.[10] The authors argue that in the United States, health concerns, particularly among women, may play a decidedly negative role in food habits. But what I have in mind is not so much health concerns as the complex of feelings associated with eating particular foods or with eating what one wants to eat. As with so many other activities, Americans seem especially prone to characterize eating habits as morally good or bad, and to juggle their food intake in an attempt to create a moral equilibrium. I have referred to this elsewhere as the oscillation between Baskin-Robbins and the jogging track, but of course that is mere hyperbole for the ethnographic details it conceals. Gluttony is the least interesting and the most obvious of the seven deadly sins. But few societies seem to spend so much energy being arithmetical about it as do we Americans.

It has often been said that virtue requires sin as its backdrop. That may be so, but societies vary in the extent that they require such frequent invocations of sin in order to stay virtuous. This suggests that there may really be two different questions here. The first is whether the United States, for example, differs from other societies in the ways that we define the morally positive and the morally negative. Our moral judgments appear to turn largely on issues of individual strength—strength of will, lonely courage, restraint, inner discipline—rather than on fear of public disapproval, letting down the side, disappointing others, skipping the rules. This stress upon the solitary source of moral rectitude is certainly not an American monopoly, but it does seem very American. The second question, then, would be whether in the United States issues of food and eating serve more as arenas for the playing out of moral issues than is the case in other societies. I think the answer to this second question is affirmative. I find it difficult to imagine a French equivalent to the lonely nighttime battles waged at the refrigerator door by so many Americans.

As to the first question, my intuition is that our moral concern with highly individualized performance, regardless of context, is extremely high. Of course our acceptance by others matters enormously to us; but it does not soften the private judgments we continuously make of ourselves. Sure, we don't want to let down our side. But what we carry with us inside our heads is a separate yardstick of our performance.

It may not be entirely clear why food and eating should be so prone to moral takeover. But certain aspects of American social and economic life—among them the pervasive affluence, the ubiquity of food-dispensing devices, the intensely peddled attractiveness of diversity in food, the strong underlying stress upon fats and sugars (both epitomes of "the rich life,"[11] both essentials in packaged foods), and the circumambient thrill afforded Americans by the *idea* of sin—may play a part. Our social history, I think, conspired to make our relationship to food morally contested. People who were mostly poor, mostly hopeful, and mostly running away from somewhere else would almost inevitably see the fruits of their labor as rewards, as fulfillment—indeed, as freedom itself. Eating one's full in safety, resting on the laurels of an infinity of successful escapes, sitting back to say: "I have eaten my full, I am content, I am free, I am *American*"—this can become a thanksgiving speech for Everyman.[12]

Of course these remarks culminate in neither conclusions nor dramatic insights. An anthropology of food and eating that moves decisively beyond the brilliant work of a Firth or a Richards still remains to be written. But it may be nonetheless useful to try to pin down some of the polarities with which we can construct the debates to come. It would require the most foolish of optimisms for us to look at the global food picture with calm. As nearly two and a half billion human beings in China and India enter the twenty-first century, the growing desire for more food by more people confronts us. Africa's chronic malnutrition grows ever more serious. In the West, and especially in the United States, the spread of obesity and related disorders provides a mocking contrast to the dietary needs of so many millions elsewhere. These problems are not only—or perhaps not even primarily—economic, but also cultural and social. Accordingly, the social sciences have a serious obligation to make what sense they can of the present situation and to seek practical answers to real questions. But I am sure that this antipasto will have left you adequate room for the *primi, secondi,* and all that will now follow.

NOTES

1. William Robertson Smith, *The Old Testament in the Jewish Church* (Edinburgh: Adam and Chas. Black, 1881), and *Lectures on the Religion of the Semites* (New York: Appleton, 1889).
2. Bronislaw Malinowski, *Coral Gardens and Their Magic.* 2 vols. (London: George Allen & Unwin, 1935), and *Argonauts of the Western Pacific* (New York: E. P. Dutton,1950).
3. Raymond Firth, *A Primitive Polynesian Economy* (New York: Humanities Press, 1950).
4. Audrey Richards, *Land, Labour and Diet in Northern Rhodesia* (London: International Institute of African Languages and Cultures, 1939).
5. Mary Weismantel, *Food, Gender and Poverty in the Ecuadorian Andes* (Prospect Heights, IL: Waveland Press, 1988).
6. Audrey Richards, *Hunger and Work in a Savage Tribe* (London: George Routledge & Sons, 1935).
7. Roland Barthes, "Toward a Psychosociology of Contemporary Food Consumption," *Annales E.S.C.* 16 (Sept.-Oct. 1975): 977–986. Reprinted in Forster, R., and O. Ranum, eds., *Food and Drink in History* (John Hopkins University Press, 1979).
8. Ibid.
9. Sidney Mintz, "Swallowing Modernity," in J. L. Watson, ed., *Golden Arches East* (Stanford: Stanford University Press), pp. 183–200.
10. P. Rozin, C. Fischler, et al., "Attitudes to Food and to the Role of Food in Life," *Appetite* 33 (2) (1999): 163–180.
11. Sidney Cantor and Michael Cantor, "Socioeconomic Factors in Fat and Sugar Consumption," in M. Kare and O. Maller, eds., *The Chemical Senses and Nutrition* (New York: Academic Press, 1967) p. 429–446.
12. Sidney Mintz, *Tasting Food, Tasting Freedom* (Boston: Beacon Press, 1996).

Part Two

THE CONSTRUCTION OF NATIONAL CUISINES

Chapter 3

RITUALS OF PLEASURE IN THE LAND OF TREASURES: WINE CONSUMPTION AND THE MAKING OF FRENCH IDENTITY IN THE LATE NINETEENTH CENTURY

KOLLEEN M. GUY

"*I* have always professed the highest esteem and even a sort of ven-
eration for the noble wine of the Rhine; it sparkles like champagne,
it revives [*réchauffe*] like Burgundy, it satiates [*lénifie le gosier*] like
Bordeaux . . . it makes us tender like the *lacryma-christi*;[1] finally, above all,
it causes us to dream." So begins "Le bourgmestre en bouteille" or "The
Burgermeister in the Bottle," an immensely popular French tale of adventure from the late nineteenth century. "Le bourgmestre" was a standard
story in the widely circulated, popular anthology *Contes et romans populaires,* by Emile Erckmann and Alexandre Chatrian.[2] The story is about two
Frenchmen who have a chance meeting on the road to Schloss
Johannisberg in the autumn of 1846. Both are wine lovers on their way to
survey the harvest of Germany's Rheingau region. Both men are drawn to
Germany because of an uneasy mix of admiration for the regional wines
and apprehension about the wine's origin.

They travel on horseback through the vineyards of Rheingau, arriving
well into the evening at a modest inn. In the warm, cozy dining area, a
golden baked ham flanked by two bottles of wine—one red and one white—
await the tired travelers. Both men agree to begin the meal with the deeply
pigmented red wine of the region. Both eagerly raise their glasses. Ludwig,
the more temperate of the two travelers, drains his glass, only to be immediately overcome by a profound sadness that seems to reach deep into his
soul. Hippel—who is likened to Silenus, an old, bearded, woodland satyr
who attended Bacchus—enthusiastically depletes his glass, smacking his
lips with pleasure. He swiftly consumes the entire bottle and orders a second. Ludwig, somewhat confused by his melancholy, sips a glass of white
wine and watches the jovial Hippel continue his meal. He isn't quite sure

whether the slowly creeping sadness transforming Hippel's face by the end of the meal is real or simply imagined.

At three in the morning, after a brief, fitful sleep, both Frenchmen awake with an uncontrollable desire to flee. Both have had bizarre dreams. Both sense that something has taken hold of their souls. It is the usually merry Hippel who is the most agitated. As he explains to Ludwig: "I feel that two contrary principles are struggling within me: one black and one white, the principles of good and evil." Ludwig is convinced that the wine is to blame. This conviction becomes stronger as Hippel recounts a dream in which he is transformed into a German *burgermeister* who owns a small vineyard. The miserly *burgermeister* lives to amass more wealth. He appreciates neither the land's treasured beauty nor the rich pleasures of the vine. Indeed, his soul seems detached from both the treasures and the pleasures. The *burgermeister* dies while idly coveting a neighbor's vineyard; few mourn his loss. At the end of the dream, only the flies seem eager to attend to the *burgermeister*'s rotting corpse.

Hippel and Ludwig try to forget the dream at daybreak by setting off into the vineyards. Despite the beauty all around them, the travelers remain deeply troubled by the sense of *déjà vu* that overwhelms Hippel. Several brief conversations reveal that the German *burgermeister* of Hippel's dream was not sheer fantasy. Driven by a mixture of disbelief and nagging fear, Hippel and Ludwig race to the burial plot of the *burgermeister* and at his tomb they discover not only the secret of their currently troubled souls but also the source of the vague, unspecified doubts about the wines of the Rhine that prompted the journey of the two curious Frenchmen. They discover a wall "covered with magnificent vines, so heavy with grapes that one bunch simply toppled over the next." The tomb itself is wrapped with vines so thick that they remind the friends of a "boa gorging on its prey." The roots of the vines are equally impressive, penetrating deep within the tomb. A peasant with a sinister smile approaches to explain that this is the tomb of the *burgermeister*. Brief glances are exchanged between the two compatriots. Abruptly, Hippel hurls himself upon the peasant. "Scoundrel! You made me drink the soul of the burgermeister!" he bellows. Ludwig wraps his arms around Hippel and struggles to restrain him; they tumble backward. Pressing against the hard, cold wall of the tomb, the melancholy of the two Frenchmen lifts. Both understand that their search has ended. Both realize what had made them so dubious about German wines. The lesson is clear: good wine is not the simple product of the soil; it is the product of the soul.

The symbolic and revelatory power of a popular story like "Le bourgmestre en bouteille" made it a basic building block of the French national imagination. Although this tale was intended for adults, it was much like G. Bruno's immensely popular *Le tour de la France par deux enfants*, a classic children's story about two "grown-up" boys who venture alone across France.[3] Historians have studied the travels of the two main characters of *Le tour de la France*, André and Julien, to understand the formation of collective identity at the turn of the century. Intended as a reader for French schoolchildren, the story of the excursion of André and Julien strove to demonstrate that regional differences in France were "gifts to the nation" that come together to create a unique "French temperament."[4] By the time "Le bourgmestre en bouteille" was published, several generations of French men and women had mastered Bruno's primer in school. Readers were familiar with the notion that all the regions of France were linked, trading products as well as their intrinsic qualities.

Hippel's and Ludwig's story, in many ways, continues this earlier journey of André and Julie. The two adult heros pass through territory on foot and horseback, and it is the physical contact with the land that gives the journey its intensity. Unlike their younger counterparts, however, Hippel and Ludwig pass into a foreign land, making this more than a tranquil survey of German territory. The two Frenchmen, through their encounters, instruct the adult reader that wines, much like nations, possess eternal, natural qualities that reveal much about the soul, the guardian of supreme spiritual values. The tale of the passage through German vineyards links wine and its consumption with the quintessentially French concept of *terroir*. A term with no precise equivalent in English, *terroir* has been generally applied as a descriptor for the holistic combination in a vineyard environment of soil, climate, topography, and "the soul" of the wine producer.[5] *Terroir*, as elaborated during this period, was seen as the source of distinctive wine-style characteristics detailed at the beginning of "Le bourgmestre en bouteille." Apart from any specific historical era, political regime, or social structure, wine consumption and *terroir* were fundamental references that the collective "France" elaborated for itself in the late nineteenth century. Stories like "Le bourgmestre en bouteille" were a success in no small part because they identified, articulated, and promoted the connection between France's collective genius and her material world. Historians generally view this late-nineteenth-century period as crucial for both the emergence of a mass, consumer culture and the creation of national consciousness. This was a time of rapid change, the beginnings of a modern revolution in consumption in which social groups and their environments were dramatically transformed.[6] The French, in their search for new social devices to express cohesion and identity amidst this change, developed a complex relationship to food and drink.[7]

This extraordinary relationship between the French and cuisine has not gone unnoticed by scholars. Cultural anthropologists, for example, have traced the spread of the vine and wine as symbols in the Mediterranean.[8] Historians, particularly practitioners of the Annales school, have focused on wine as an element of diet, examining drinking patterns over the centuries.[9] While this research tells us much about conditions of everyday life and the cultural landscape of viticulture, we still understand relatively little about the importance of wine as a means of expressing both social stratification and social solidarity. We understand little about how wine's symbolic power is, in Pierre Bourdieu's words, "a transformed, that is to say unrecognizable, transfigured, and legitimated, form of the other types of power."[10] We understand little about how wine was invoked at the local and national levels as a part of an "an essential, a true France."[11] Hippel's and Ludwig's adventure and the depiction of the "barometers" of the soul—wine and *terroir*—offer one vantage point for exploring these issues, exploring how French wine consumption came to be part of the "rituals of pleasure" that contributed to France's reputation as a "land of treasures."

RITUALS OF PLEASURE

Hippel and Ludwig were not atypical Frenchmen. At least they were not atypical when we regard their consumption patterns: three bottles of wine—two red, one white—with a single meal. Consumption patterns across time, particularly regarding drink, are notoriously difficult to assess. As Michael Marrus noted in his study of social drinking in France, "inebriation in times past becomes quickly blurred in the collective memory," and official statistics of consumption are often inaccurate because of the rich tradition of fraud and tax evasion in the wine and liquor industry.[12] Despite these flaws, which tend to skew any data downward, historians agree that there are some general trends that can be discerned. Official statistics for the nineteenth century suggest that there was a "great collective binge" that took place in France as the century drew to a close. Total alcohol consumption per adult in France increased by 50 percent after 1830; wine consumption, in particular, showed a sharp increase beginning in the 1890s.[13] Historians agree that during this late-nineteenth-century period wine became "a ubiquitous and daily beverage."[14] Hippel and Ludwig were neither drinking generously nor alone. "[T]his is the time," wrote Marrus, "it turns out, in the era sometimes knows as *la belle époque*, that Frenchmen drank the most."[15]

By the 1890s, when "Le bourgmestre" was first published, this liberal consumption was the focus of public concern, and a shrill attack was launched on overindulgence.[16] Complaints about excessive drink, particularly those directed at the lower classes, were neither new to this era nor limited to France.[17] What was new for France, however, was the sense of urgency to the complaints and the public consciousness of drinking within French society. Indeed, the French Senate elevated the discussion to one of national importance with the publication of an intensive study of the problem in 1887.[18] Drink was seen as weakening France's productive and reproductive capacities.[19] Patriotic posters cried, "The Fatherland is in

Danger! Down with Alcohol! Vive la France!"[20] Several temperance organizations were founded in a nation that had long rejected the temperance movement.[21] Throughout the 1890s, as one historian notes, "a flood of pamphlets, articles, lectures, and statements by public personalities began to rain down on a hitherto insouciant public."[22] The prestigious Academy of Medicine admonished the French that excessive drink would assure the decline of the nation.[23]

The fictional Frenchmen, Hippel and Ludwig, of course, were à table in 1846, long before this general alarm regarding drink sounded. Readers of the story in the 1890s, at the peak of the antialcohol fervor, nonetheless would not have been appalled as the two Frenchmen imbibed their favorite libation. Quite the contrary. The chosen beverage, wine, was viewed, in the words of a contemporary, as "good for one's health and good for the nation."[24] The connection between wine and health is probably most vividly revealed in the language of the late nineteenth century. Fermented drinks—wine, cider, beer—were not designated in the French language under the word alcohol (alcool) and thus were not associated with discussions of alcoholism (alcoolisme) or excessive alcoholic consumption. Wine was termed, even among temperance organizers, as a boisson hygiénique, a healthy drink.[25] Commercial interests bolstered the linguistic association through marketing and legislative efforts.[26] The wine industry, for example, marketed specialty wines as a form of hygiene such as "Grand Vin de Santé"[27] or "Vin de Champagne diabetique."[28] Meanwhile, health professionals at the Grande Pharmacie on the boulevard Haussman in Paris sold a house brand of "Médicinal Champagne" for a range of ailments.[29]

Temperance organizations never took a stand for total abstinence, in keeping with this general French view that wine drinking was an essential component of good hygiene.[30] Historians trace the roots of the wine-health connection in France back to the Middle Ages, when knowledge of the physiological effects of wine was an important part of the practice of medicine.[31] This was reinforced during the eighteenth century when philosophers, encyclopedists, and technicians turned their attention to the "science" of food, dining, and drink.[32] An intense interest in the science of gastronomy developed by the 1820s.[33] New taste professionals in France, such as Brillat-Savarin and Alexandre Grimod de La Reynière, enumerated some of the fundamental truths of the "science," as it was termed, in books, pamphlets, and journals.[34] One of those "truths," according to Brillat-Savarin, was that "[t]he fate of nations depends on how they are fed."[35] Romantic-era gastronomy linked the combined contribution of food and wine not only to a diner's health but also to the health of the nation.

Less than half a century later, with the festering sense of shame over the loss of French territory to Prussia in the 1870s, the fate of the nation appeared to depend on drink.[36] Wine as the *boisson hygiénique* emerged as the key to both personal and national health. Scientific and medical studies concluded that the best solution for controlling excessive drinking and alcoholism was to create stricter state controls of distilled beverages, like spirits and absinthe, while *increasing* distribution of wine.[37] A regularly cited study of the French military garrison in Bordeaux, for example, concluded that soldiers who marched after drinking wine were "less tired and went along the road singing and chanting refrains in cadence." This was in sharp contrast to beer-drinking soldiers, who were "sluggish, marched with a heavy step . . . and reached the finishing point worn out, exhausted."[38] In light of this scientific evidence, the Academy of Medicine, the same group which had admonished the French about excessive drink, endorsed the increase in wine consumption.[39] The medicalization of society had given the early "science" of gastronomy new authority. Far from being a cause of decline and social disorder, wine was deemed the source of national renewal.

Hippel and Ludwig, partaking of the chosen beverage, understand that wine is more than fermented grape juice. Even in a nation with a rich democratic tradition, all wines, not all *boissons hygiéniques*, were equal. Indeed, there were two distinct types of wine production in France: one that created expensive wines deemed to be of high quality that had a hierarchical classification system, and another that created cheaper, mass-produced wines that were deemed to be of lesser quality. Ludwig, the narrator of the story, illustrates the importance of these distinctions when he compares "the noble wines of the Rhine" not to a local *pinard* of the peasantry or the liters of ordinary wines consumed by the Parisian working classes, but to the wines of France's prestigious production areas of Champagne, Burgundy, and Bordeaux. The intrinsic, almost sacred qualities of these wines warranted their linkage to no less than the sacrificial tears of Christ. These were the wines of the dominant social and political classes, who were defined "not only in relation to the means of production, but by knowledge and taste."[40] These were the wines that came to be most closely associated with France.

Historians have pointed to the years between 1870 and 1914 as a period of rapid change when social groups and their environments were dramatically transformed, resulting in a search for "new social devices to ensure or express social cohesion and identity and to structure social relations."[41] Knowledge and taste, expressed through wine consumption, were central to this process. Consumption of fine wines was a visible sign of rank and class membership for the aspiring elite in public space. The emergence of restaurants brought formerly private rituals into the public sphere and shifted gastronomy, including fine-wine consumption, to a central place in social life. Gastronomy was concerned not only with classifying wines but also with teaching "how to put them on the table in such an order as to produce for the guests an enjoyment constantly increasing."[42] Fine wine and the rituals surrounding its consumption were a source of solidarity and legitimation, setting apart the wine and those who consumed it from less-affluent consumers of common wines. As Jean-Paul Aron has stated, it was "*à table* that the nineteenth century began to define itself; it is *à table* that business deals are made, ambitions declared, marriages arranged," and in this way, food, drink, and their consumption became a part of emerging nineteenth-century rituals of membership.[43]

The two fictional Frenchmen, with time and money for a leisurely visit to the vineyards, are the embodiment of French knowledge and taste. They are taste experts, connoisseurs, through both temperament and education. "The very principle of connoisseurship," writes ethnographer Robert Ulin, "implies not only a recognition of distinctiveness but an intuitive judgment of qualities thought to be objective."[44] Ludwig is the prototype of this objectivity as he delineates the distinctive style characteristics of French wines. It is ultimately this objectivity in his ability to discern distinctiveness that exposes the flaws in German wine and saves his friend's soul.

Connoisseurship, however, depends also on "intuitive judgment" or good taste. Taste, as Pierre Bourdieu and others remind us, is a term laden with contradictions.[45] Taste can be improved with proper education. Yet taste, as Leora Auslander demonstrates in her excellent examination of the construction of taste in modern France, is also understood to be first and foremost "innate and emotional."[46] With his "large fleshy nose, a unique mouth for *degustation*, [and] a three-story belly," Hippel was born ready to savor wine. His racial characteristics could be read as a visible sign that, as one writer noted, "gastronomic taste is innate in the [French] race."[47] As a descendent of a mythic noble savage—Silenus, an old, bearded, woodland satyr who attended Bacchus—he appears as a link between an ancient Rousseauian past, where sensual pleasures were unthreatened by civilization, and the good life of modern France at the end of the bourgeois century. Taste, as interpreted by the objective yet innately endowed connoisseur, offered a bridge between the hedonism of luxury wines, which were originally associated exclusively with the frivolity and decadence of aristocrats, and the middle-class ethos of frugality, self-denial, and civic responsibility of *la Belle Époque*.

Good taste is both constituted and represented by the two Frenchmen of "Le bourgmestre en bouteille." This is demonstrated by the sharp contrast of their German counterpart, the miserly *burgermeister*. Physically the *burgermeister* is described as large and flabby, with grey eyes, large nose, and thin, tightly pursed lips. He appears "heavy, thick, and dense," attributes assigned equally to "German thought, literature, and art" and "Black Forest meatballs" by one French author.[48] He has none of the physical attributes or sensory skills necessary for the practice of good taste.

This explains why he notices none of the sensual pleasures of his surroundings. Most shocking to the two fictional Frenchmen are his diet and rituals of consumption. The German wakes in the morning and stuffs a crust of bread in his pocket, which he will chew as he surveys his property. "*Une croûte de pain!*" exclaims Hippel, "Is it necessary to be so stingy, so miserly?" Lunch is no better for the burger, who demands that some boiled beef (*bouilli*)[49] and a few potatoes be prepared by his cook. "A wretched dinner!" the exasperated Hippel cries.[50] Not a drop of wine is consumed; not a single ritual of pleasure is a part of the solitary life of the *burgermeister*.

The *burgermeister* has transgressed boundaries of class by transgressing the boundaries of good taste. Good taste was, as Ludwig suggests, learnable. Acquiring good taste meant learning to discern distinctions through studied consumption of quality wines. Certain groups—especially the bourgeoisie of Europe and North America, who could afford quality French wines—were well positioned to improve their knowledge of taste. The prices of Champagne, Burgundy, and Bordeaux wines assured that they were consumed by a limited clientele, but new marketing techniques had broaden this circle of clients and increased demand.[51] The German *burgermeister*, despite his class position, seems to lack some intrinsic quality that could be nurtured or cultivated into good taste. The author suggests that the missing quality was "Frenchness."

The contrast between the two Frenchmen and the German instructs the reader that good taste, at its base, was an "inevitable and natural emanation of national character." Taste could not be purchased or, more important, taught to someone who did not already possess a foundation as part of a national legacy.[52] Appreciation of the pleasures of French wine was a marker of good taste. And good taste, like good wine, as this story instructs, came naturally from French soil. "Doesn't good taste grow spontaneously on French soil?" one French writer queried in 1896. "Yes, it is an indigenous plant, but one which, nevertheless needs cultivation in order to bear its delicate fruit."[53] By the turn of the century, innate, national taste and "authentic" quality wines were so intertwined, so "rooted" in France that it was difficult to invoke one without eliciting the other. Although French luxury wines could serve as symbols of social stratification, the wines of France, more generally, and the unique *terroir* that produced them were encrusted with myths of national genius.

LAND OF TREASURES

"French soil enjoys the privilege of producing naturally and in abundance the best vegetables, the best fruits, the best wines in the world," wrote the famous French chef and gastronome Auguste Escoffier.[54] French wines were regional products associated with the soil, which had an unshakable popular reputation, affirmed by writers, historians, and geographers for being uniquely rich, fertile, and productive—a national treasure. Hippel's and Ludwig's adventure in Germany is, above all, a story about the unique eternal, natural qualities embodied in the term *terroir*. *Terroir* was the source of distinctive wine-style characteristics detailed at the beginning of "Le bourgmestre en bouteille"; *terroir* was the source of the transfer of the "soul" of the *burgermeister*. The sharp contrast with Germany in "Le bourgmestre" elaborates the qualities of French *terroir* and offers reassurance to readers that the "barometers" of the soul—wine and *terroir*—confirm that in the struggle of the "two contrary principles . . . one black and one white, the principles of good and evil," the principles of good ultimately prevail in France.

Terroir is a much-debated term within the wine industry even today. Opinions differ greatly on the reality of *terroir* in determining wine quality. A combination of soil, topography, and climate are said to create a unique *terroir* that, according to the *Oxford Companion to Wine*, "is reflected in its wines more or less consistently from year to year, to some degree regardless of variations in methods of viticulture and wine-making."[55] Each plot of vines, like the one over the tomb of the *burgermeister*, and ultimately each region, like that of the Rhine, has a unique *terroir* that ultimately creates a distinct wine-style characteristic. The precise conditions of each *terroir* cannot be duplicated and, by extension, neither can the wines that each *terroir* produces.

Terroir, as the fictional Hippel and Ludwig demonstrate, has historically been interpreted to extend beyond these natural components. In a recently published work on the influence of geology on wine, Hugh Johnson, the world's best-selling wine author, argues that "*Terroir*, of course, means much more than what goes on below the surface. Properly understood, it means the whole ecology of the vineyard: every aspect of its surroundings from bedrock to late frosts to autumn mists, not excluding the way the vineyard is tended, nor even the soul of the *vigneron*."[56] The science of *terroir* with the study of microclimates and soils, while still the subject of debate, appears to lend credibility to many claims regarding the role of the natural environment in determining wine quality. It is, however, the almost mystical quality—"the soul of the vigneron"—added to the definition of *terroir* that continues to make the subject controversial among viticulturalists, historians, and geographers.

A search for the mystical roots of *terroir* takes us back to the era when the story of Ludwig and Hippel was first published.[57] "Le bourgmestre en bouteille," much like *La tour de la France* and others of this genre, was successful because it both demonstrated and promoted the notion of the "authentic" France as an organic entity. This was firmly grounded in the new science of French geography that emerged at the end of the nineteenth century. Geography in France, as articulated by its most revered practitioner Vidal de la Blache, provided a multifaceted analysis of the "natural" state of France, with its symbiotic relationship between people and landscape. Central to Vidal de la Blache's classic works, most notably *Tableau de la géographie de France* (1903), is the view that environment, shaped by internal and external factors, determines the way of life (*genre de vie*) of a locality and its people. According to this logic, a country can only be understood through its environment as determined by its geomorphology. France's geography, according to Vidal de la Blache, situated it at the crossroads of Europe, the crossroads of "the civilized peoples."[58]

France was more than the historical synthesis of all these civilizations; it was the culmination of civilization. Vidal's formulation of France, one historian has noted, "clearly owned something to nongeographical considerations."[59] Breaking from popular nineteenth-century ideas that linked climate to a theory of natural borders, Vidal de la Blache argued that France was a unity because of its "personality." This French personality, he argued, was a result of its diversity. Within the small area that was France, he noted that geomorphological evolution had created diverse conditions that interacted to create France. It was man, however, that ultimately established the link between the disparate features produced by nature. The diversity of people within France, reflected in regional identities, gave the nation a unique ability to assimiliate and "transform what it received."[60] France was an organic entity with a diversity of related parts, all of which supposedly gave the nation its unique personality.

While other nineteenth-century writers such as Jules Michelet would argue that France's personality emanated from Paris, Vidal de la Blache and his followers emphasized the importance of rural France, the France of *pays*. Throughout his body of work, Vidal de la Blache gave a great deal of attention to detailing local life. He emphasized local names for regions and types of landscape, commenting on the intimate connection between the land and people. Often he contrasted these regional appellations with the sterility of generic labels created by politicians or scholars. Vidal de la Blache looked to the soil and its inhabitants in search of France's personality, the roots of France's genius. Throughout his works are almost lyrical passages describing the rich relations between place and population. Indeed, the real life of France was the world of the people of rural France, who "emodied the *genius loci* that laid the groundwork for our national existence."[61]

Neither Vidal nor his followers attempted to find any scientific explanation or "necessary principle" explicit in nature for the existence of France. For the founder of French geography, there was no doubt that France was a gift, a land of treasures. "It is the abundance of 'goods of the earth,' as old folks say, that for them is identical with the name of France," he wrote at the beginning of *Tableau*. "For the German, Germany is above all an ethnic idea. What the Frenchman sees in France, as his homesickness shows when he is away, is the bounty of the earth and the pleasure of living on it."[62] This indissoluble relation between the French and their natural world was eternal for Vidal de la Blache.

The work of French geographers such as Vidal de la Blache was adopted by the republican government of the Third Republic as part of its standard pedagogy for generations of French schoolchildren. While the geography texts created by Vidal de la Blache and his followers did not explicitly link agricultural products with the French personality, the elevation of the rural world to the center of a transcendent French civilization created a new prestige for regional products emanating from the soil. Wine, in particular, with its importance as the national *boisson hygiénique,* was a material manifestation of the holistic relationship between the people and the natural environment. Indeed, statements found in popular scientific works show a belief in an animating spirit shared by people and wine. It is this notion of the animating spirit that underlies the story of Hippel and Ludwig. The adventures of the two Frenchmen instruct the reader that wine was the realization of a nation's personality, its spirit in the material world. Wine consumption and *terroir* were fundamental references that the collective "France" elaborated for itself in the late nineteenth century. Stories like "Le bourgmestre en bouteille" were a success in no small part because they identified, articulated, and promoted the connection, established by the sciences of gastronomy and geography, between France's collective genius and her material world.

Hippel and Ludwig know that French wines could serve as symbols of social stratification. But as good Frenchmen, they see the wines of France more generally as the centerpiece of Frenchness, the foundation of national genius. Wine, just like the treasured land at the crossroads of civilized peoples, became the common property of all classes of French society in the democratic discourse found in these travel stories of early Third Republic France. References to a particular regional wine might be used to signal social class, but references to French wine in both popular stories and national debates about issues ranging from public health to agricultural legislation were designed to evoke shared national character traits. In this way, wine became a complex symbol, used to delineate class boundaries and yet at the same time evoked as a unifying national patrimony. Good wine and good taste, as Hippel and Ludwig teach their readers, was characteristic of France. Wine was part of an essential "ritual of pleasure" that symbolized the superiority of the French people, blessed with a "land of treasures."

NOTES

1. *Lachryma-christi* has a double meaning here. It refers to both the sacrificial tears of Christ and an excellent wine from the slopes of Vesuvius. Special thanks to my colleague Antonio Calabria for drawing attention to this double meaning. I would also like to take this opportunity to thank William V. Bishel, James McDonald, and Warren Belascoe for their careful reading of this essay.

2. Emile Erkmann and Alexandre Chatrian, *Contes et romans populaires* Series 8 (Paris: Hachette, 1890), pp. 48–57.

3. *Le tour de France par deux enfants* was a reader for elementary school children published in 1877 which sold six million copies by 1901. In their study of the story, Jacques and Mona Ozouf explained that the book was used as "a geography text, an ethics handbook, a primer in the natural sciences, or a basic introduction to French law, with which every citizen was supposed to be familiar." See Jacques and Mona Ozouf, "*Le tour de la France par deux enfants*: The Little Red Book of the Republic," in *Realms of Memory: The Construction of the French Past*, vol. 2 *Traditions*, ed. Pierre Nora (New York: Columbia University Press, 1997), pp. 125–148.

4. Ozouf, p. 129.

5. Quoted from a recently published work on the influence of geology on wine. See the Foreword by Hugh Johnson in James E. Wilson, *Terroir: The Role of Geology, Climate, and Culture in the Making of French Wines* (Berkeley and Los Angeles: University of California Press, 1998), p. 4.

6. For more on this transformation, see Eric Hobsbawm and Terrence Ranger, eds., *The Invention of Tradition* (Cambridge: Cambridge University Press, 1992).

7. Pierre Bourdieu argues that the relation between elite wine and French culture is so intertwined that it is almost impossible to discuss one without the other. See Bourdieu, *Distinction: A Social Critique of the Judgment of Taste* (Cambridge: Harvard University Press, 1984), p. 53.

8. See, for example, D. Stanislawski, *Landscapes of Bacchus: The Vine in Portugal* (Austin, TX: University of Texas Press, 1970); and Robert C. Ulin, *Vintages and Traditions: An Ethnohistory of Southwest French Wine Cooperatives* (Washington, DC: Smithsonian Institution Press, 1996). Cultural anthropology has long recognized the importance of food and drink as a means of exchange and communication. See, for example, Mary Douglas, "Deciphering a Meal," *Daedalus* (Winter, 1972): 61–81; Yvonne Verdier, "Pour une ethnologie culinaire," *L'Homme: Revue française d'anthropologie* 9 (1969): 49–57; Peter Farb and George Armelagos, *Consuming Passions: The Anthropology of Eating* (Boston: Houghton Mifflin, 1980).

9. For a good overview of Annales historiography, see Robert Forster and Orest Ranum, eds., *Food and Drink in History: Selections from the Annales: Economies, Sociétiés, Civilisations* (Baltimore: Johns Hopkins University Press, 1979).

10. Pierre Bourdieu, "Sur le pouvoir symbolique," *Annales, Economies, Sociétés, Civilisations* 32 (1977): 411.

11. Herman Lebovics, "Creating the Authentic France: Struggles over French Identity in the First Half of the Twentieth Century," in John R. Gillis, ed., *Commemorations: The Politics of National Identity* (Princeton: Princeton University Press, 1994), p. 240.

12. See the discussion of the problems with using government statistics and tax records in Michael Marrus, "Social Drinking in the Belle Epoque, *Journal of Social History* 7 (1974): 115–141; and Thomas Brennan, "Towards the Cultural History of Alcohol in France," *Journal of Social History* 23 (1989): 71–92.

13. Michael R. Marrus, "Social Drinking in the Belle Epoque," *Journal of Social History* 7 (1974): 115. This conclusion is supported by Thomas Brennan in "Towards the Cultural History of Alcohol in France," *Journal of Social History* 23 (1989): 71–92.

14. See Scott Haines, *The World of the Paris Café: Sociability among the French Working Class, 1789–1914* (Baltimore: Johns Hopkins University Press, 1996).

15. Marrus, "Social Drinking in the Belle Epoque," 115.

16. For several excellent studies of the polemical nature of these discussions, see Susanna Barrows, "After the Commune: Alcoholism, Temperance, and Literature in the Early Third Republic," in John M. Merriman, ed., *Consciousness and Class Experience in Nineteenth-Century Europe* (New York: Holmes & Meier Publishers, 1979), pp. 205–218; Catherine Kudlick, "Fighting the Internal and External Enemies: Alcoholism in World War I France," *Contemporary Drug Problems* 12 (Spring, 1985): 129–158.

17. See Patricia Prestwich, *Drink and the Politics of Social Reform: Antialcoholism in France since 1870* (Palo Alto, CA: Society for the Promotion of Science and Scholarship, 1988). Concern about alcohol and social disorder were also common in other European nations. See, for example, James Roberts, *Drink, Temperance, and the Working Classes in Nineteenth-Century Germany* (Boston: Allen and Unwin, 1984); Lilian Shimas, *Crusader against Drink in Victorian England* (New York: St. Martin's, 1988).

18. The Senate report is discussed in Marrus, "Social Drinking in the Belle Epoque," 188.

19. Allan Mitchell, "The Unsung Villain: Alcoholism and the Emergence of Public Welfare in France, 1870–1914," in *Contemporary Drug Problems* (Fall, 1986): 453.

20. Quoted in Marrus, "Social Drinking in the Belle Epoque," 199.

21. See Patricia Prestwich, *Drink and the Politics of Social Reform*.
22. Marrus, "Social Drinking in the Belle Epoque," 188.
23. See the discussion of the Académie de Médecine's response to drinking in Mitchell, "The Unsung Villain," 452.
24. Marrus, "Social Drinking in the Belle Epoque," 120.
25. Brennan, "Towards the Cultural History of Alcohol," 78.
26. Brennan, "Towards the Cultural History of Alcohol," 79.
27. Châlons-en-Champagne, Archives départementales de la Marne (hereafter A.D.Ma.) 16U195 Marques de fabrique, label number, 1565.
28. A.D.Ma. 16U195 Marques de fabrique, label number 2124.
29. A.D.Ma. 16U195 Marques de fabrique, label number 1616.
30. See the discussion in Brennan, "Towards the Cultural History of Alcohol," 79.
31. See Roger Dion, *Histoire de la vigne et du vin en France des origines au XIXe siècle* (Paris: Flammarion, 1959), pp. 402–404.
32. For a survey of Enlightenment interest in gastronomy, see chaps. 11 and 12 of Barbara Ketcham Wheaton, *Savoring the Past: The French Kitchen and the Table from 1300 to 1789* (New York: Scribner, 1983).
33. "*Gastronomie*," the term for this new science, appeared in the French language at the very beginning of the nineteenth century. See Pascal Ory, "Gastronomy," in Pierre Nora, ed., *Realms of Memory: The Construction of the French Past*, vol. 2, *Traditions* (New York: Columbia University Press, 1997), p. 452.
34. See, for example, Brillat-Savarin, *Physiologie du goût* (Paris, 1825); Alexandre Grimod de La Reynière, *Almanach des gourmands* (Paris, 1803); and Horace-Napoléon Raisson, *Code gourmand, Manuel complet de gastronomie* (Paris, 1827).
35. Brillat-Savarin, *Physiologie du goût* (New York: Scribners, 1879), p. 3.
36. For more on the memory of the loss of Alsace, see Jean-Marie Mayeur, "Une Mémoire-frontière: L'Alsace," in Pierre Nora, ed., *Les Lieux de mémoire*, vol. 2 (Paris: Gallimard, 1986); Frederic Seager, "The Alsace-Lorraine Question in France, 1871–1915," in Charles K. Warner, ed., *From the Ancien Regime to the Popular France* (New York: Columbia University Press, 1969).
37. Mitchell, "The Unsung Villain," 452.
38. Study cited in Marrus, "Social Drinking in the Belle Epoque," 120.
39. See the discussion of the Académie de Médecine's response to drinking in Mitchell, "The Unsung Villain."
40. Leora Auslander, *Taste and Power: Furnishing Modern France* (Berkeley, CA: University of California Press, 1996), p. 142.
41. Eric Hobsbawm and Terence Ranger, eds., *The Invention of Tradition* (1983; rpt., New York, 1992), p. 5.
42. Brillat-Savarin, *Physiologie du goût* (1879), p. 33.
43. Jean-Paul Aaron, *The Art of Eating in France: Manners and Menus in the Nineteenth Century,* translated by Nina Rootes (London: Peter Owen, 1975), pp. 10–11.
44. Robert C. Ulin, *Vintages and Traditions*, p. 45.
45. See, for example, Bourdieu's analysis in his work *Distinction*.
46. Auslander, *Taste and Power*, p. 1.
47. Marcell Rouff, *La Vie et la passion de Dodin-Bouffant gourmet* (1924; new edition Paris: Stock, 1984), pp. 18–19.
48. See discussion in Ory, "Gastronomy," p. 444.
49. His lack of taste is highlighted by the choice of *bouilli*, which, in its feminine form, is a sulfer-based pasty wash for removing mildew from vines.
50. "Le Bourgmestre en Bouteille," p. 51.
51. For more on these marketing techniques, see my article, "Oiling the Wheels of Social Life: Myths and Marketing in Champagne during the Belle Epoque," in *French Historical Studies* 22 (1999): 211–239.
52. Auslander, *Taste and Power*, p. 386.
53. Henri Noussane, *Le goût dans l'ameublement* (Paris: Frimin-Didot, 1896), pp. 241–242; quoted in Auslander, *Taste and Power*, p. 387.
54. Auguste Escoffier, *Souvenirs inedits: 75 ans au service de l'art culinaire* (Marseille: Editions Jeanne Laffitte, 1985), p. 191.
55. Jancis Robertson, editor, *The Oxford Companion to Wine* (New York: Oxford University Press, 1994), p. 966.
56. See Hugh Johnson's introduction to James E. Wilson, *Terroir: The Role of Geology, Climate, and Culture in the Making of French Wines* (Berkeley and Los Angeles: University of California Press, 1999).

57. The mystical soil-and-wine connection undoubtedly predates this era. I have chosen to focus on the late nineteenth century because it appears to be the moment when the mystical qualities of the soil were given a "scientific" base and then legitimated by laws for appellations promulgated by the French government of the Third Republic.
58. Jean-Yves Guiomar, "Vidal de la Blache's *Geography of France*" in Pierre Nora, ed., *Realms of Memory*, vol. 2, p. 188.
59. Guiomar, "Vidal de la Blache's *Geography*," p. 189.
60. Guiomar, "Vidal de la Blache's *Geography*," p.191.
61. Quoted in Guiomar, "Vidal de la Blache's *Geography*," p. 204.
62. Paul Vidal de la Blache, *La France, tableau geographique* (Paris: Hachette, 1908), p. 50.

Chapter 4

___

"EDDIE SHACK WAS NO TIM HORTON":
DONUTS AND THE FOLKLORE OF MASS CULTURE IN CANADA

STEVE PENFOLD

*E*arly in the morning of February 21, 1974, on the highway between Toronto, Ontario, and Buffalo, New York, legendary defenseman Tim Horton was driving too fast. A few hours before, fresh from a hard-fought National Hockey League (NHL) game, which saw the Toronto Maple Leafs defeat his Buffalo Sabres, Horton had downed a handful of painkillers and headed off into the night in his fancy sports car. After a stop in the Toronto suburb of Oakville to check on his business interests—a chain of forty Tim Horton Donut Shops—Horton pulled back on to the Queen Elizabeth Way and put the pedal down. Less than an hour later, he approached Lake Street in St. Catharines, only fifteen minutes from the U.S. border. At this point, the story gets confusing. Local lore around St. Catharines has it that the Ontario Provincial Police had set up a roadblock to slow him down, which Horton, it is said, swerved to avoid. According to the official version, Horton was alone on the highway that morning. No matter, since the result was the same: at high speed, the great defenseman drove off the Queen Elizabeth Way, was thrown from his car, and died minutes later.

Horton's death marked a turning point in his status as a Canadian icon. To this point, his life had had all the trappings of the classic myth of white Canadian manhood. He was born at the dawn of the Great Depression in the Northern Ontario railway town of Cochrane—a place of hard work, hard winters, and hockey rinks—and traveled south to the big city as a teenager to pursue every "true Canadian" boy's dream of playing professional hockey. Horton patrolled NHL bluelines for 22 years, seventeen of them for the storied Toronto Maple Leafs franchise. And while hockey was known as a brutal and bloody sport, and Horton was renowned for his rock-solid body checks, by all accounts Tim was a true gentleman who always kept his physical talents in proper perspective. Indeed, for Canadian sons of a certain generation, Horton was one of a handful of players who our fathers implored us to be, a kind of archetype of the Canadian man: humble in origins, large in talent, strong in body, and gentle in demeanor. Horton's tragic end, coming just at the closing of what is widely viewed as Canadian hockey's greatest era, ought to have solidified his place in the mythic pantheon of the Canadian man: a northern boy made good on sweat and talent, playing Canada's national pastime in its golden age.[1]

But Horton's death, rather than solidifying his place as a masculine myth, ensured for him a very different, and much quirkier, path to pop culture iconography. Ten years before his death, he and a rather unlikely friend, a semi-pro jazz drummer from Quebec named Jim Charade, had opened the first of many Tim Horton Donut outlets to sell coffee and donuts along the model of U.S. chains like Dunkin' Donuts and Mister Donut. In 1967, Charade was bought out by one of the chain's early franchisees, a former cop named Ron Joyce, who built the chain into a coffee and baked-goods empire. The corporate headquarters of Tim Donut Limited now oversees a mammoth chain by Canadian standards, comprising almost 2,000 outlets nationwide, pulling in approximately $1.6 billion in gross revenues per year. Considering that the Canadian retail market is about one tenth the size of its American cousin, this is an awesome figure. By comparison, there are more Tim Horton shops than McDonald's outlets in Canada, and the chain controls almost 50 percent of the baked-goods segment of the quick-service restaurant sector. While there are other donut chains with impressive regional coverage, Tim Horton shops are ubiquitous on the Canadian landscape.[2] To donut lovers of a certain generation, then, Tim Horton is just a name on a sign that we pass several times every day, no more real than Ronald McDonald.[3]

The theme that unites these two sides of Tim Horton iconography is their connection to the patriotic symbolism of everyday life in Canada—to a kind of folklore of mass culture where commodities are used to express important, if ironic, interpretations of national and local identity. Donuts are a mass-production and mass-consumption product. They are produced in large volumes by chains that parachute standard store designs into communities across the country. Yet donuts are also a quirky receptacle for the politics of identity in Canada. My discussion of this notion will follow two paths of this donut folklore: first, the idea that the donut is a Canadian food, and second, the way the donut expresses local identities for certain Canadian cities.

In Canada, the donut is widely believed to be the unofficial national food. Indeed, the fatty treat is celebrated in song and story as a sort of ironic replacement for the dramatic national symbols found south of the forty-ninth parallel. "If there's one thing that is distinct, that is ours, that Canadians can claim as theirs," Canadian-born comedian Eugene Levy told a half-American audience, "I'd say it's doughnuts."[4] Bill Kennedy of Henry Farms, Ontario, told the Canadian Broadcasting Corporation (CBC) that "the donut has to be Canada's national food. Now of course I know that they're not created here but they've been perfected here, and it's part of our national identity. To criticize the donut is to criticize Canada." This idea is a common bit of lore in the donut shops that seem to populate every corner of Canada's suburbs. "Was there [a time] before Tim Hortons?" asks Steve, of Halifax, Nova Scotia. "They seem to have always been with us. [They're a] kind of a uniquely Canadian thing. . . . It's one thing that the Americans don't have that we have. Lots of coffee, lots of donuts."

Donuts take on a deeper national meaning when linked to other, more established forms of Canadiana. Hockey, for example, is commonly teamed with donuts as a national symbol. In Mississauga (a suburb of Toronto), Debbie pointed to the Tim Hortons sign out the window to make her point. "Donuts and hockey: is there anything more Canadian than that?" These sorts of statements are common, but the connection between donuts, Tim Horton, and hockey is somewhat contradictory. In the early days of Tim Donut Limited, Horton's hockey celebrity was a key part of the chain's marketing strategy: his image was used in advertisements for the shops, and Horton himself often appeared at outlet openings, drawing fans more interested in the man than his donuts. "I was more excited by Tim Horton than the availability of donuts," recalls Ed Mahaj, who met Horton at the opening of an outlet in Hamilton, Ontario, in 1964. It is unlikely, however, that Horton's hockey prowess had much to do with the ultimate growth of the chain. The real success of Tim Hortons (and other donut chains) has been their ability to integrate into the daily routines of Canadians in disparate communities, whether commuting, working, nursing hangovers, or just hanging out. Ron Joyce often reminds interviewers of this fact, making it clear that although Horton might have been an initial draw, customers returned because they had "a good experience."[5] Horton's portrait was removed from the stores in the early 1990s at the request of his widow, and today many Canadians have no idea that he was an actual person, let alone a famous hockey player. Nonetheless, the great defenseman continues to play a key role in cementing the chain's place in national folklore. The donut-hockey nexus rests to a large degree on the dual iconography of Tim Horton, expressed nicely in a song by Toronto bar band "go bimbo go!" which reconnects Horton's status as a masculine myth and pop icon:

Tim, Tim Horton,
More of a man than you'll ever be.
Tim, Tim Horton,
He may be gone, but his donuts, they carry on.[6]

In 1994, former Toronto Maple Leaf Eddie Shack jumped on the donut and hockey player bandwagon, lending his name to a chain of donut shops on the outskirts of Toronto. Contrasting the place of Tim Horton and Eddie Shack in the political economy of the donut and the masculine myth of hockey is common fare in Southern Ontario donut shops. Like Horton, Shack played in hockey's golden age, but Eddie would hardly make any father's list of male role models. More known for a string of comic commercials than any great contribution to patriotic mythmaking, Shack is a real character, much like the goofy uncle who shows up to family reunions and won't stop talking.[7] Nor is Shack a particularly admired donut impresario. His chain never totaled more than a handful of outlets. "Tim Horton was an impressive kind of guy: short and stocky, brush cut, played for the Leafs," sums up John Fitzsimmons of Hamilton, Ontario. "If they'd have had an Eddie Shack Donut back then, I'd have said 'I ain't going in there, the guy's a goof!' But now he's a legend. He was fun to watch, but [Eddie Shack] was no Tim Horton."

Hockey is a winter sport, and Canada is thought to be the great northern nation, so winter is another Canadian theme linked to donuts. Canadians eat more donuts per capita than any other nation on earth, a fact that is often attributed in donut lore to our famous harsh winters. Nutritionists, it is claimed (although they are never named), say our seemingly insatiable craving for donuts is related to our need for fatty foods to fight off the Canadian cold.[8] While this argument is patently illogical—cold winters are no more common in Toronto than they are in, say, Cleveland—it fits nicely into the urban legend motif of folklore, especially its appeal to quasi-scientific authority.[9] Moreover, the idea expresses, albeit in the scientific detachment of the nutritionist, a long-standing and often melodramatic belief that Canada's climate and geography created a distinctive identity. Historian W. L. Morton argued that "Canadian life. . . . is marked by a northern quality. . . . The line which marks off the frontier from the farmstead, the wilderness from the baseland, the hinterland from the metropolis, runs through every Canadian psyche."[10] The relationship of donuts and winter can be equally lyrical: "Winter is the perfect Canadian season," Chad Skelton wrote in one of our national newspapers:

> Summer is too Americanized. We don't really have a Canadian way of doing it. We
> go to air-conditioned multiplexes to watch the latest Hollywood blockbuster, sip
> 7–Eleven Slurpees, play beach volleyball and eat Dairy Queen sundaes. But think
> of defrosting your fingers around an extra-large Tim Hortons coffee on a February
> morning. Now that's Canadian. . . ."[11]

Skelton's association of seasons and consumer products with national experiences—Slurpees and summer with America, Tim Hortons and winter with Canada—is surprisingly rich in its use of national imagery. No discussion of Canadian identity strays very far from nervous references to the economic and cultural influence of the United States. Former prime minister Pierre Trudeau once said that living next to the United States "is in some ways like sleeping with an elephant: No matter how friendly and even-tempered the beast, one is affected by every twitch and grunt."[12] The way Canadians see and understand their southern neighbor—what might be called the Canadian "idea of America"—is complex and multidimensional. Its negative side—anti-Americanism—has been ably studied in terms of politics, trading relationships, cultural policy, and even the products of popular culture,[13] but it is a much more deeply rooted impulse than any of these studies convey. Indeed, anti-Americanism in Canada is a lot like breathing: it is controlled by semivoluntary muscles; you can stop it for a while if you try, but most of the time it just happens. Yet the impulse to pull away coexists with a deep fascination with all things American, especially the products of U.S. mass culture. Skelton's passage nicely encapsulates this odd duality. We consume American products, yet somehow crave a more "genuine" Canadian mass culture experience, like a Tim Hortons coffee on a February morning. A rambling essay scrawled on the back of three Tim Hortons napkins makes the point more explicit:

> Lately, I've been wondering what part of Canadian culture is solely ours. . . .
> Since the 20s, Canada has become Americanized. . . . Everybody says "those igno-
> rant, arrogant Americans" and they're absolutely right, but what people don't real-
> ize is that . . . we ARE Americans. We buy their clothes, watch their TV, and do
> most things exactly the same as them. . . . Why we look up to "big brother" U.S. I
> don't know, but that can't be helped. What we can do is recognize what is ours
> and ours alone. I have found it . . . [it's] Tim Hortons, Timmy's, Horny Tims. . . .
> Seeing a Tim Hortons is just as common as seeing a Canadian flag.[14]

The Canadian "idea of America" often expresses itself in the folkloric figure of the "ignorant American." "People in the United States," argues Rob, whom I encountered one evening in a Coffee Time Donuts in Niagara Falls, ". . . they can't assimilate the difference between the United States and Canada. I've worked with people in the United States that want to bring things into Canada, and I say '*You can't, you're crossing an international border.*' They don't realize that. They just treat it as another state. . . . They also bring their skis up here in the summer." One difference they do notice, he continues, puffing out his chest with ironic pride, is the donut shops: "The U.S. people come over—I have a friend from the U.S. . . . and he says he astonished, he thinks it's a joke, that [on] every corner there's at least one store."

The idea of associating the donut with crossing the border is a surprisingly common piece of folklore, especially among Canadians traveling or living in the United States.[15] "Before we crossed the border at Fort Erie to drive south," Phyllis Keeling told me a few years ago, "we always stopped for our last coffee and donut. As soon as we crossed the border [on the way home], we pulled into Tim Hortons." She didn't have to wait very long. At all three checkpoints along the New York–Ontario border, the Duty Free stores include a donut shop (two Tim Hortons and one Donut Diner).[16] Another piece of border lore is what I call "the immigrant's tale." In this story, a new arrival confesses that at first she didn't understand why Canada had so many donut shops, but eventually found an understanding of the country in these odd national institutions, as with the donut patron who told CBC Radio that he thought "Now I am a Canadian" the first time he bit into a donut.[17]

Canadians living in the United States are especially likely to associate border crossings with donuts. Tales abound of "Canadians abroad" asking relatives to bring them a dozen Tim Horton donuts when they visit. Conversely, expatriate Canadians speak of associating a trip to the donut shop with returning home. Mathew Truch, a Canadian-born physicist now living in Rhode Island, made sure that one of his first stops on a trip back to Canada with some American friends filled his craving for crullers. "Donut shops are more important that one may think from here [the United States]," he wrote to me. "I recently took a short vacation with some [American] friends to Toronto and Montreal, and they were quite impressed with the few Tim Hortons that I made them go to, as I wanted some crullers, darn it." Jonathan Singer, who grew up in Toronto but now lives in California, told me that on returning to Canada, a donut shop is the first stop he makes, even before he goes home to drop off his luggage: "I very much associate donut shops with Canada. . . . Leonard Cohen made a reference to 'the holy places where the races meet' . . . and I think that donut shops, in their humble and occasionally grungy way fit the description nicely." Singer doesn't eat many donuts. Rather, it is the culture of the shops that he associates with Canada, especially what he sees as its more civil political culture relative to the United States:

> . . . I really don't like donuts very much. Asking visitors to bring donuts would be unlikely for me. What I do associate with Canada is the culture of acceptance, conversation, and debate . . . that occurs in Canadian donut shops, and very few other places. I can't think of a single U.S. equivalent. . . .

The rise of these national associations seems curiously disconnected from the origins and the fate of the commodity itself. As with much of twentieth-century Canadian economic history, big-time donut retailers developed in Canada as branch plants or Canadian-owned versions of U.S. mass-production ideas. This process dates back to the invention of the donut machine by New York baker Adolph Levitt in 1920 and the extension of his company—the Donut Corporation of America (DCA)—to Canada in 1935. Under the name the Canadian Doughnut Company (CDC), DCA's Canadian wing manufactured donut mixes and machines for bakeries and wholesalers like Margaret's Donuts in Toronto, which was founded in the late 1940s. CDC also supplied what could have been the first donut shops in Canada, a chain of three Downyflake Donut outlets that dotted Toronto's foodscape at various points in the 1950s. The Downyflake shops had disappeared by the 1960s, but the dynamic of importing American ideas continued with the arrival of U.S. companies like Mister Donut and Dunkin' Donuts and the advent of Canadian-owned chains like Tim Hortons and Country Style, founded by local entrepreneurs who borrowed the model of the American chains. In 1962, Jim Charade started the shop that would become Tim Horton Donuts after touring Mister Donut's Boston operations and deciding he could do it himself. Country Style began in 1963 when its Canadian founder, Alan Lowe, spotted an American shop that he figured he could franchise for the Canadian market.[18] The American colonization of Canada's donutscape continued even in 1995, when Tim Hortons was sold to Wendy's. While Canadians are normally sensitive to the threat of American-owned companies, the sale of this "national institution" to an American hamburger company did not seem to affect Tim Horton's link to national mythology.[19]

Nor has the decline of the donut as a commodity done any harm to the national myth. Since the late 1970s, donut sales have been steadily decreasing as a proportion of donut store revenues, replaced by a succession of supposedly more healthy products, like muffins and, most recently, bagels.[20] Indeed, donuts now make up less than a quarter of the average sales in Canadian donut shops. Tim Hortons even took the word "donut" off its signs more than a decade ago, preferring to tell anyone who asks that the company is in the "Always Fresh" business. The addition of new product lines coincided with a larger process of pulling away from the seedy, masculine, working-class image of the donut shop. This change included banning smoking, pulling out counters, and adopting softer, brighter interior colors, mainly with the aim of attracting a broader clientele.[21] "They say now that the donut stores have turned into restaurants," says Al Stortz of Welland, Ontario, "There's one down the road here near where I used to work. . . . It says 'Donuts and more.' So in other words you can go in and get a hamburg or whatever. . . . I don't think you'll likely find an actual donut shop anymore."

The inverse relationship between the myth and the commodity serves to highlight the folkloric quality of Canada's devotion to donuts. The associations of nation with commodity are not statements of literal truth—we could easily think of several U.S. equivalents of chatting in a donut shop—but as with folklore, the veracity of the claim is less important than the fact that the stories are told enough times to help shape or express an understanding, a "way of seeing" one's environment.[22] In this way, the donut is helped along by its association with other, more established images of Canada. Another folkloric quality of the Canadian myth of the donut is the way it deploys—in quite different communities—a standard cast of characters to express ideas of national characteristics: the goofy, ignorant American who doesn't understand Canada; the immigrant or world traveler who discovered Canada in a donut store; and the world-weary Canadian who finds home in the donut shop.

For a widespread national myth, however, this folklore of the donut is actually quite recent and quite regional in origin. Indeed, it seems to trace its lineage to southern Ontario in the late 1970s. "Doughnuts [sic] are as integral as federal-provincial relations in the Canadian way of life," declared the *Hamilton Spectator* in 1977, staking out a claim to one of the earliest nationalist references to the donut.[23] A few years later, donuts joined beer, back bacon, and toques as Canadian symbols in Bob and Doug MacKenzie's Great White North, a popular comedy sketch on the show *SCTV*, which originally aired in Canada but was eventually picked up by NBC in the United States. Bob's and Doug's movie, *Strange Brew* (1983), featured the duo working in a Toronto brewery, eventually saving the city from Max Von Sydow's evil plot to control the local populace with a concoction of hypnotic beer. They spent much of their time, however, bribing their dog with various treats, driving around Toronto in their van, and scarfing down dozens of Country Style donuts (which dominated the Toronto market at this time). By the late 1980s, the press was starting to notice that the donut shop had become "Canada's answer to Britain's neighborhood pubs."[24] In 1991, Scarborough, Ontario, native and *Saturday Night Live* stalwart Mike Myers linked donuts and Canada in *Wayne's World*, his brilliant cinematic exploration of the suburban dork *mentalité*. The film was based on Myers's experiences growing up in the suburbs of Toronto and included many landmarks of local teenage popular culture transposed to the movie's Chicago setting. Wayne's main hangout was a donut shop named for Chicago Blackhawks legend Stan Mikita, a thinly veiled reference to Tim Hortons.

The rise of these sorts of references coincided with important developments in the donut business. Tim Hortons began to assert its dominance of the Canadian donut market in this period, jumping from 68 outlets in 1977 to 100 in 1978 and 200 by 1984. Meanwhile, other chains typically added fewer than ten outlets a year and crawled into the mid-1980s at least a hundred outlets behind Tim Hortons. Underneath the major chains, Canada's donutscape was becoming much more crowded, with the advent of many new chains and the proliferation of independent shops. In 1975, there were only five donut franchisors and a smattering of unaffiliated shops. Ten years later, there were almost twenty donut franchisors and dozens of independents. In southern Ontario, it seemed that every conceivable geological feature, building type, or royal title was being teamed with donuts in the hope of business success. By 1979, the Greater Toronto Area had a Donut Corner, Cave, Nook, Tree, Hole, Haven,

Place, Shop, Shoppe, Plaza, Centre, Fair, King, Queen, Duke, Master, Hut, Shack, House, Inn, Castle, Factory, City, World, and Galaxy.[25]

The emergence of donut lore also conforms to the regional dynamics of Canadian popular culture. "Canadian culture," wrote literary critic Northrop Frye, "is not a national development but a series of regional ones, what is happening in British Columbia being very different from what is happening in New Brunswick or Ontario."[26] One observer went so far to say that Canada is not a nation-state at all, since it has a federal government that is not anchored to a national cultural foundation.[27] Certainly, ideas of national identity do exist across the country, but they are refracted through regional attachments. Indeed, what passes for "official" nationalism is often simply the regional delusions of southern Ontario, which is the site of much of Canada's "national" cultural production. "Southern Ontario regionalism," a group of literary critics explain, "has been largely successful by being invisible, by resisting precise territorial definition, and by passing itself as Canadian nationalism."[28] Donut folklore follows this pattern. The national claim of the *Hamilton Spectator*, for example, was made at a time when donut stores were quite notably concentrated in southern Ontario. As Tim Hortons established a legitimate national presence through the 1980s and 1990s, the regional dynamics of donut lore became more complicated. The Maritime provinces (Nova Scotia, New Brunswick, and Prince Edward Island) are now a common source of nationalist donut lore, and it occasionally crops up in the west, often focused on Robins Donuts. But this brand of donut lore is notably absent in urban British Columbia, where upscale coffee shops like Starbucks are considered to be bulwarks of local coffee culture. In Vancouver, visitors and new arrivals notice the lack of donut shops as much as the temperate climate and scenic vistas. "Forget flowers in January," *Vancouver* magazine reported in May 1999, "The real shock for inmoving Canadians is Vancouver's lack of doughnuts. . . . Here, muffins, scones, and cinnamon buns take top billing in bakery cases, and biscotti at coffee counters. . . ." Donuts continue to be most deeply rooted in Ontario, and despite its national language, donut folklore remains much less common west of Ontario and in francophone Quebec.[29]

Another regional aspect of donut lore in Canada involves the claim made by some Southern Ontario cities that they are the "donut capital of Canada."[30] This image exists on two levels. On the first level, many people in Southern Ontario simply assert that wherever they live is the donut capital of Canada, usually citing anecdotal evidence about the number of shops compared to other cities. "Gee, I thought Niagara Falls was [the donut capital of Canada]," says Peter, "It seems like there's one on every corner. Just down the street there used to be three. Like, in one little area . . . you got one here, one there, one over there. If you go down Drummond Road I think there's two Tim Hortons right across from each other. They say people in Ontario like these places, but if you go to Quebec . . . I think in Montreal there's only one Tim Hortons." But if pressed, the image in these places doesn't go much deeper than a straightforward observation on cultural geography.

Much more intriguing is the second, deeper level of the donut capital claim. Some cities make quite passionate and even quasi-official claims, citing statistics to prove the point and even linking the prevalence of donut shops to a sense of local identity. "St. Catharines has the most donut shops per capita of any place in Canada," Ben told me half-angrily in a Bakers Dozen Donut outlet, tapping the table that separated us with his finger to emphasize each word. When I smiled in bemusement at the passion of his claim, he ran down some imaginary mental arithmetic to prove his point. Citing statistics about "donut stores per capita" is the most common way to back up claims to donut capital status. The method of calculation varies, but normally involves noting that someone else did the math. "A friend of mine figured it out using the Yellow Pages," one St. Catharines donut store patron told me, insulating the boast from questions about the calculation process, a standard strategy of urban legends.[31] Other claims look to more weighty authorities. Many St. Catharines donut affectionados insist the city was granted this designation by an unnamed edition of the *Guinness Book of World Records*. Indeed, the former mayor, Joe McCaffery, told me as much shortly before his death, adding the other local legend that Johnny Carson had mentioned the city in these terms in a monologue. Citing these sorts of authorities continues unabated by their apparent inaccuracy. "Agent N" of the self-characterized Coffee Crusaders, who write Internet reviews of St. Catharines donut shops, offered me proof of the claim in the fact that "David Letterman once said it on his show!" although the mysterious crusader allowed that it might be "just an urban legend."

West down the Queen Elizabeth Way, Hamilton makes similar claims, even granting the boast a quasi-official status. The first Tim Horton franchise was opened on Ottawa Street in Hamilton in 1964, and the Web page of the Hamilton Public Library, under the heading "Significant Cultural Landmarks in Hamilton," claims that the city is the "coffee and donut capital of Canada." Ed Mahaj, who grew up on Ottawa Street, thinks the claim is just common sense:

> You go through Hamilton, and every second street corner has a donut shop on it. . . . I've been all over the States and . . . it seems very unique to Hamilton. I mean, there's more per square block [than any other city]. . . . You'll never see an empty donut shop in Hamilton. If you drive from one end of the city to the other, the number of donut shops is incredible.

The *Hamilton Spectator*, the city's major newspaper, seems to run an article on the claim at least once a year. A few years ago it sent a reporter out into local donut shops to debunk the claim that Moncton, New Brunswick, was most devoted to the Tim Hortons chain, spending much of the article, headlined "Nice Try Moncton, We're the Tim Hortons Capital of Canada," on the dubious mathematics of per capita donut shop saturation.[32]

But the specific claims are less important than the messages they carry. "To be sure," wrote Robert Blumstock in the *Spectator* a decade ago:

> we in Hamilton are never likely to have the media come in droves to discover us. We may never have anything to compare to the CN Tower or other skyscrapers and landmarks of Toronto. But there is at least one area in which we outpace our provincial capital. We have more doughnut shops per capita. . . . We have a doughnut shop for every 5000 people while Toronto's doughnut availability is one shop for every 2000.

According to Blumstock, the simple, blue-collar nature of the city explains its devotion to donuts: "there are our obvious attributes: a sensible, hard-working bunch who are not easily taken in by the latest food fashions." A similar argument was advanced in St. Catharines by a pair of entrepreneurs hawking "donut capital" T-shirts: "the doughnut title tells everyone in no uncertain terms that St. Catharines citizens are honest, sober and hard-working people."[33] This sense of ironic pride in the lack of cultural alternatives relative to other cities and the pride of being simple, hard-working people underlies most of the donut capital claims I've heard.

This populist impulse draws on a more general belief that the donut is an unpretentious blue-collar food, an idea that seems to have a long history. In 1934, an American traveler used the donut to symbolize social leveling in Toronto, writing in *The Geographic Magazine* that "citizens say 'Sir' to policemen, yet it is a democratic place and any day at Bowle's Quick Lunch you may see knights munching a doughnut beside a taximan."[34] If the donut is a folk food, then the shops must be humble, unassuming places, a notion that has become especially popular in the era of gourmet coffee shops, which began to franchise through Canada in the 1980s. In a donut outlet in Moncton, New Brunswick, Eugene Leblanc provided me a map of the social status of various coffee shops: "It's a real social scale. . . . This is at the bottom, Joe Mocca's [a specialty coffee shop] is in the middle, and Starbuck's is at the top. . . . The bottom of the barrel is here, because . . . it's a little rougher part of town. I don't mind it . . . because I grew up here." In Toronto, Melanie, who works as a physiotherapist, claimed to be "a blue-collar coffee drinker. Sometimes, I go to Starbuck's for a Frappacino, but I'm a Tim's girl through and through." These populist claims continue despite the remaking of donut shops into mass market coffee outlets. Ron Joyce noted as early as 1984 that "[o]ur marketing people try to tell me we cater to the blue collar worker, but I don't believe that," noting that anyone from a bank director to a factory worker could enjoy a donut and coffee.[35]

In the case of donut capital, this populist impulse is turned to specific local purposes, normally to contrast the social life of one place with that of another. "Well, Hamilton's a simple town," Ed Mahaj told me to explain the donut capital claim, using Toronto as a point of reference:

> I used to love playing up on it when I was doing business in Toronto. People would say "where are you from?" and I'd say "I'm from Hamilton . . . down in the east end." . . . That's a rough area, and I'd play up on it. . . . One characteristic that people from Hamilton possess versus people from Toronto, they're much more unpretentious. People from Toronto tend to be much more pretentious—glitz and show forms a much more important part of their life.

In St. Catharines, Floyd explained the claim by informing me that "the donut's just . . . about the only thing in the [city] to be devoted to." In this case, the point of reference is not Toronto so much as an unnamed, imagined place where "something" might actually happen. Our conversation continued on this line:

> **SP:** Isn't there anything else to do around here besides go to [Tim] Hortons?
> **Floyd:** Well, there's [Tim Hortons], or you could start up a band or start up a drug habit.
> **SP:** Which one are you doing?
> **Floyd:** All three.[36]

The connection between the simple life and the donut puts us on perilous analytic ground. In his study of antimodernism and the myth of innocence, historian Ian McKay reminds us that the collection of folklore can be based on politically regressive readings of the "simple life." McKay reconstructs the world view of Nova Scotian folklorists in the middle of the twentieth century, following their travels to fishing outports in search of the Folk: simple people living "authentic" premodern experiences outside the complications of market capitalism, mass culture, modernism, and so on. That folklorists found the Folk, McKay argues, is not to say they existed; rather, folklorists carefully filtered and selected stories, songs, and superstitions to emphasize their ideas about the premodern qualities of outport life.[37]

In donut capitals we are in danger of inventing a kind of industrial Folk for postindustrial times, replacing outport peasants and their songs with unpretentious blue-collar folk and their donuts. It deserves explicit mention, then, that neither Hamilton nor St. Catharines is actually simpler than any other city. If they are "blue-collar" places devoted to donuts as a folk food, then this may be more a question of political economy than it is a cultural choice. Both cities are reliant on heavy industry—steel in Hamilton and automobile production in St. Catharines—which means they are populated by a lot of shift workers seeking all-night hangouts. It helps that donut shops, based as they are on trading small purchases for time, are notoriously recession-proof. "The average cheque in a donut shop is less than two dollars," Country Style Donuts President Garry Macdonald observed some years ago, "It's habitual. People will give up a lot of things during hard times. But they won't give up their morning coffee and doughnut."[38] As such, donut shops often take on decidedly unfolksy roles, serving as magnets for the unemployed, the underemployed, the drunken, the hungover, the homeless, and so on. Floyd made this abundantly clear in his amusing depiction of the cultural options in St. Catharines, as did Tom Busnarda, whose evocative description of the place of the Ottawa Street Tim Hortons in the complex nighttime culture of east end Hamilton bears quoting at length:

> It was a working-class community. When Tim Hortons opened that donut shop it became a hub very quickly. . . . It was open very late hours and one of the things it became associated with was a subculture in the east end of Hamilton that involved . . . the abuse of some substances. . . . Street people tended to congregate at Tim Hortons . . . People would sit for hours over a cup of coffee and cigarettes. There were a lot of what at the time we would call rubbies [chronic alcoholics]. . . . There was some violence. . . . There were some hookers who hung out there. . . There was a whole subculture . . . . a poor working-class subculture that weren't employed in the regular ways at the steel factory. . . .

This is not the kind of description that gets posted on a Web page under "Significant Cultural Landmark," to be sure.

Moreover, even if the donut has become a vehicle for quirky depictions of local and national life, it is a commodity whose production and consumption follow the rhythms of North American capitalism. Indeed, there is much about Canada's donutscape that owes its character to what George Ritzer called the "McDonaldization of society," the relentless drive of large corporations toward efficiency, predictability, calculability, and control.[39] As a commodity, the donut is produced as part of a tightly defined McSystem, where each aspect of the production process is broken down into distinct steps that can be analyzed, reduced to the cheapest and most efficient formula, and codified in easy-to-follow procedures. Average waiting times, for example, are measured and compared against a company-defined standard, a set of formulas that allows, say, 22 seconds to make a sandwich, five seconds to put it in a bag, and so on.[40] Even more striking is the way the logic of mass production is applied to manufacturing the donut shop itself. Operations manuals can codify almost all the decisions associated with running a small business, from locating a site to building the outlet, purchasing supplies, hiring staff, and so on. By extension, the system mass-produces small-businesspeople, harnessing their entrepreneurial ambitions to the corporate philosophy of the chain. "To make the donuts is not [a] big problem," one longtime franchisee told me:

> The problem is: how [are] you gonna learn about the business? . . . I used to work in a factory. . . . Some people [were] carpenters or . . . electricians, and [don't]

know a lot of things [about how] to run a business. A business is not to make the donuts and say "I know I'm a good baker, I'll open a donut shop and tomorrow I'll be fine . . . because people are gonna like my donuts." . . . I believe in the franchise. . . . Because if you open a store "Steve's Donuts," nobody knows you . . . it doesn't mean anything. Country Style, Tim Hortons, [that's] a name, [that's] advertising. Not only that, [the company representatives] come here, they see something from other stores. . . . Somebody is more experienced than me, they bring in business people, . . . who understand what customers want today. . . .

Like the donuts they serve, donut shops and their owners are commodities to be mass produced in standard, interchangeable form across the country.

Donut outlets seem to grow out of every open space in the Canadian ecology of eating out. Each time the market has appeared saturated, donut companies have simply redefined the rules of the game. They have designed new, "nontraditional" outlets (mainly small kiosks) for hospital lobbies, Canadian Tire outlets, and gas stations, as well as compact, "drive-thru"-only outlets for small lots on heavily developed suburban strips. The major companies now also eagerly penetrate markets once thought too small. Journalist John Lorinc relates the story of Tom Wadden, a former sales manager interested in getting into the donut business near his home in Tottenham, a small town perched on the fringe of Toronto's booming suburban belt. In 1992, Wadden tried to interest Country Style and Tim Hortons in coming to the area, but neither company thought the town was large enough to support an outlet. Wadden eventually went with another chain—one of the smaller outfits that started in the mid-1980s' burst of franchisors—only to have Tim Hortons open a shop down the street in early 1995. Apparently, remarks Lorinc, "Tottenham was a good spot for a doughnut store after all."[41] One of the reasons the chains have rethought smaller communities is that traditional markets have become so overcrowded. In the early days, donut chains, like most fast food restaurants, granted territories to their franchisees, but they eventually abandoned this concept. Industry analyst Mat Reime notes that donut chains "realized they were working on a different scale. . . . If your next store is two miles away, so what. Half a mile to a doughnut shop is a huge distance. How far are you going to walk for that?"[42]

Donut folklore cannot be separated from these questions of McDonutization. The structure of the donut business—the efficiency of the system, the harnessing of entrepreneurial ambition, the pinching of territories, the saturation of markets, the seemingly limitless possibility for growth—provides the foundation to build a popular and widespread folklore. A single shop might produce a set of stories and might weave itself into the social life of a neighborhood or town. These local attachments may even be communicated to a wider audience. But the folklore of mass culture is nurtured by social patterns with much greater reach, patterns that are repeated across space and time, that can be observed over multiple visits and extensive travels. Both of the main threads of donut folklore—that the donut is the national food, and that certain cities are donut capitals—are, at base, simply ways to observe and acknowledge the McDonutization of the foodscape. They both grow from an inventory of our own social patterns. Even if, for example, we have long forgotten (or never knew) that Tim Horton was a great hockey player, we constantly observe his iconic status in our daily activities. We drive by "his" donut shop several times a day. We use "his" drive-thru on the way to work. Perhaps we hang out in "his" parking lot after school or bring "his" donuts to work. We can apply this logic to other donut shops, and to their cumulative effect on the Canadian foodscape. Whether the name on the sign is at the top of the donut business, as with Tim Horton, or near the bottom, as with Eddie Shack, the donut shop weaves itself into the everyday practice of community life. But this connection between commodity and community gives Tim Hortons a unique position in Canada's donut lore. Indeed, the dominance of the chain, as much as Tim's own status as a masculine myth, means that the brand name "Tim Hortons" appears in donut lore as often as generic references to "the donut." No other chain enjoys this sort of brand recognition. "People don't say 'coffee shop' anymore," Mr. Mugs franchisee Curtis Mitchell lamented in the *Hamilton Spectator* recently.[43] "They say 'Hortons'."

Donut folklore springs from a phenomenon that is everywhere but expresses definite ideas of place. It is focused on a mass commodity yet announces a kind of imagined community. For Benedict Anderson,[44] almost every community (though he wrote mainly of nations) is essentially an act of imagination. Since most communities are not based on face-to-face relations, they exist because their members make a perceptual leap: they form a mental connection to people whom they might never actually encounter. "[T]he members of even the smallest nation," Anderson argues in an especially powerful passage, "will never know most of their fellow-members, meet them, or even hear of them, yet in the minds of each lives the image of their communion." Anderson is careful to distinguish this sort of imagination from a fiction or a hoax: "[A]ll communities are to be distinguished, not by their falsity/genuineness, but by the style in which they are imagined."[45] In this sense, connections between donuts and Canadian life that seem tenuous when viewed with even the slightest detachment—claims about donut stores per capita or about using fatty foods to survive harsh Canadian winters—seem less important for their relative accuracy than for their rendering of community characteristics. Much of donut folklore plays on a sense of ironic pride in marginal status, poking fun simultaneously at the unsophisticated hinterland and the pretentious metropolis. At the local level, the donut capital claim uses irony to "imagine a community" that stands in opposition to a cultural metropolis—in many cases to the pretensions of Toronto to the status of "world-class" city. Through a broader lens, the national folklore of the donut uses an opposition in much the same way, replacing the populist irony of the donut capital with a nationalist, anti-American variant. Many observers have noted that this sort of double-edged, ironic posture seems endemic to Canadian cultural life, driven by a belief in our status as Other. "Canadian consciousness," writes Andrew Wernick, "is . . . an ironic duality that borrows the clothes but not the spirit of American razzle-dazzle, and . . . knows itself to be rooted in the dull daily experience of living in a [peripheral] region in which nothing really happens."[46] The various threads of donut folklore, then, are neither simple reflections of structure nor folkish cultural givens, but "ways of seeing" a place and its relation to another, ways of understanding how one sleeps next to an elephant, how one is affected by its every twitch and grunt.

If we believe that the dynamic of mass culture is to degrade production on the one hand and to reduce social experience to consumption on the other, then the donut takes on considerable analytic power. In Canada, the donut is mainly produced by large companies, sold in cookie-cutter shops across the country, and served by low-wage workers doing carefully defined, unskilled jobs. Yet the donut is also a vehicle for ironic depictions of Canadian life. Ultimately, the effect of donut folklore—the nature of its mediation of structure and identity, of mass and community—remains ambiguous. On one hand, we construct our relation to mass consumption in local and national terms, endowing the mass commodity with an imagined community. Conversely, we open a space for mass culture in our own lives, allowing its institutions a place in local experience. And so, in Canada, we eat America's fast food yet hunger for the subject position of "Canadian consumer," living the simple life in a donut capital, hoping that when February rolls around, Eddie and Tim will deliver us from multiplexes, Slurpees, and American summers.

NOTES

For comments on earlier drafts, I would like to thank Warren Belasco, Jeet Heer, Gillian Poulter, Jarrett Rudy, Diane Swartz, and the Toronto Mass Consumption Reading Group.

1. On Tim Horton's life, see Douglas Hunter, *Open Ice: The Tim Horton Story* (Toronto: Penguin Books, 1994); and Lori Horton and Tim Griggs, *In Loving Memory: A Tribute to Tim Horton* (Toronto: ECW Press, 1997). Roy MacGregor, *The Home Team: Fathers, Sons and Hockey* (Toronto: Penguin Books, 1995), explores the theme of father-son relations through sports. The masculine and nationalist themes of hockey in Canada are critically analyzed in Richard Gruneau and David Whitson, *Hockey Night in Canada: Sport, Identities, and Cultural Politics* (Toronto: Garamond Press, 1993). See also Paul Rutherford, *When Television Was Young: Primetime Canada, 1952–1967* (Toronto: University of Toronto Press, 1990), pp. 241–255. David Whitson nicely explores some of the issues of identity raised by the marketing of hockey and the globalization of the NHL. See his "Hockey and Canadian Identities: From Frozen Rivers to Revenue Streams," in David Taras and Beverly Rasporich, eds., *A Passion for Identity*, 3rd ed. (Toronto: ITP Nelson, 1997).

2. According to the *Bakers Journal* (Dec. 1999), there were 5,689 donut shops in Canada at the end of 1999. This figure represents about 10 percent of the nation's commercial

restaurants. Tim Hortons is the only chain with any genuine claim to deep national coverage, although some of the other major chains combine strength in one region with a smattering of outlets in other parts of Canada. Other major donut chains in Canada include: Country Style Donuts (founded in Toronto, 1963) with 380 outlets in Canada (100 foreign); Coffee Time Donuts (founded in Bolton, Ontario, 1982), 360 outlets in Canada (4 foreign); Dunkin' Donuts (founded in Massachusetts; first Canadian outlet, Montreal 1961), 240 Canadian outlets; Robin's Donuts (founded in Thunder Bay, Ontario, 1975), 250 outlets; and Bakers Dozen Donuts (founded Mississauga, Ontario, 1977), 75 outlets. See *Bakers Journal* (December 1999); *Foodservice and Hospitality* (July 2000). Below these companies lies a gaggle of smaller chains, usually centred in a particular region or city. There is also an extraordinary number of independent shops. On the political economy of the donut in Canada, see John Lorinc, *Opportunity Knocks: The Truth about Canada's Franchise Industry* (Scarborough: Prentice Hall Canada, 1995).

3. The historian of the donut is continually confronted with two problems of syntax. First, the "apostrophe problem": "Tim Hortons" has no apostrophe to indicate possession. The problem is further compounded by the fact that some Tim Hortons shops, mainly ones opened in the mid-1980s, actually do have an apostrophe ("Tim Horton's") while most outlets simply read "Tim Hortons." The second issue is how to spell donut. In Canada, this question can take on a nationalist slant, since the traditional spelling ("doughnut") has a British feel and therefore fits into the category of "Canadian spellings" like "labour," "favour," "humour," and so on. Indeed, "donut" is often seen as an American bastardization, although it may simply reflect a desire for cheaper and more streamlined signs. No matter, since I have chosen to use "donut" and no apostrophe. This decision no doubt offends the sensibilities of the gramatically correct, but it reflects the most common usage.

4. *Toronto Star* (January 20, 1999). A note on method: this paper blends donut lore culled from newspapers, radio, songs, poems, and my own collection of interviews with donut eaters across Canada. All unreferenced quotations are from my collection of interviews. The interviews were undertaken as part of my in progress Ph.D. thesis (Department of History, York University, Toronto), which examines the history of the donut in Canada. I located interviewees in one of two ways. Some contacted me after my donut research was profiled in local or national media. Most interviewees, however, were encountered simply by visiting donut stores from Vancouver to Halifax. In some cases, interview subjects asked to be referred to by their first names only. Others asked not to be named at all.

5. See, for example, "From Doughnuts to Dollars," *Forever Young* (June 1999).

6. Quoted in *Saturday Night* (September, 1999).

7. On Eddie Shack, see Ross Brewitt, *Clear the Track: The Eddie Shack Story* (Toronto: Stoddart, 1997).

8. See, for example, Betsy Kuller, "Why Fried Dough Is Our National Passion," *Toronto Star* (August 21, 1995). I am often asked to comment on this theory in radio interviews.

9. See Jan Brunvand, *The Vanishing Hitchhiker: American Urban Legends and Their Meaning* (New York: Norton, 1981).

10. Cited in Northrop Frye, "National Consciousness in Canadian Culture," in *Divisions on a Ground: Essays on Canadian Culture* (Toronto: House of Anansi Press, 1982). The northern vision of Canada has a long history, especially in nationalist thought. It is often linked to various forms of antimodernism, although its form, articulation, and political possibilities can shift wildly depending on the era, the medium of communication, and so on. On the origins of the northern vision in Canada, see Daniel Francis, *National Dreams: Myth, Memory and Canadian History* (Vancouver: Arsenal Pulp Press, 1997); Carl Berger, "The True North Strong and Free," in *Imperialism and Nationalism: A Conflict in Canadian Thought* (Toronto: Copp Clark Ltd., 1969).

11. Chad Skelton "Winters 'R' Us," *Globe & Mail* (November 19, 1996): A18.

12. This was part of an address given to the National Press Club in Washington in March 1969. See *Globe & Mail* (October 16, 1999): A10.

13. See, for example, Jack Granatstein, *Yankee Go Home: Canadians and Anti-Americanism* (Toronto: HarperCollins, 1996); and especially the various essays in David Flaherty and Frank Manning, eds., *The Beaver Bites Back? American Popular Culture in Canada* (Montreal: McGill-Queens University Press, 1993).

14. "A Slice of Canadiana," by Kirsten of Brantford, Ontario. This is one of the increasing number of examples of donut lore being posted on the Web; online at www.tvo.org/eh/users/Je96ep. The use of colloquialisms like "Horny Tims" is quite common. The adoption of such nicknames is surely a test of iconic status. The suburban-nationalist icon, Canadian Tire, a national chain of hardware stores, is affectionately called "Crappy Tire" by most Canadians. Only my father, who was perhaps the final holdout

of dignified Victorian formalism in language, insisted on calling it "The Canadian Tire Corporation" in everyday conversation.

15. For a discussion of ideas of border crossings, see Patrick McGreevy, *The Wall of Mirrors: Nationalism and Perceptions of the Border at Niagara Falls* (Orono, Maine: Borderlands, 1991).

16. Thanks to Daniel Robinson for this point. Donut Diner (founded 1988) is a chain of about thirty shops located in the Niagara Peninsula of Southern Ontario. This sort of association of product with "home" has some equivalents, especially Canadian beer, which is routinely believed to be better than the American counterpart.

17. Metro Morning, CBC Radio, January 22, 1997. See also "An Englishman Falls in Love," the story of a culture-shocked English visitor who "decided to move to Canada [based] solely on the fact that it's the place you find Tim Horton's coffeeshops"; online at www.jungleweb.net/vanguard/coffeeshop.

18. DCA actually moved into the Canadian market in 1931, but did not set up a branch plant in Canada until 1935. On the origins of DCA, see Susan Levitt Steinberg, *The Donut Book* (New York: Alfred A. Knopf, 1987). On its Canadian operations, see *Canadian Baker* (March 1957): 28 *Canadian Baker* (April 1957): 54; "DCA Canada Ltd. Celebrates 50 Years," *Bakers Journal* (December 1985): 26; "Margaret's: 2800 More Doughnuts in Five Years," *Canadian Baker* (October 1957): 36–37. Jim Charade's trajectory into the donut business is from Hunter, *Open Ice,* and an interview I conducted with him. The information on the founding of Country Style Donuts is taken from an interview I did with Kevin Watson, the son of one of the early directors of the company and now the executive vice president. As early as 1897, the donut was used as a symbol of the way the American influence creeped into Toronto's British traditions. Beckles Willson wrote in the Toronto-based *Saturday Night* magazine that "Toronto . . . [is] the sole British city where the inroads of ice-water and doughnuts are most manifest—at once the most English and the most American of Canadian cities," *Saturday Night* (May 8, 1897). Thanks to David Kimmel for this reference.

19. The sale to Wendy's was big news in Canada, with many press reports calling Tim Hortons "a national institution." See *Toronto Star* (August 9, 1995): B1, 3; (August 21, 1995): B3; *Globe and Mail* (July 4, 1995): B10; (March 15, 1995): B21; (August 10, 1995).

20. Most major donut chains started adding such products in the early 1980s. For a discussion of these trends, see the epilogue ("How Bagels Became White Bread: Tim Horton Meets the Yuppie") of my thesis.

21. Interview, Patti Jameson, Director of Marketing, Tim Donut Limited; Cathy Mauro, Director of Marketing, Country Style Donuts.

22. John Berger, *Ways of Seeing* (London, 1972).

23. *Hamilton Spectator*, (March 6, 1977).

24. See, for example, *London Free Press,* May 16, 1987.

25. I discuss the historical development of the donut business in my thesis.

26. Northrup Frye, "Sharing the Continent," in *Divisions on a Ground,* p. 63.

27. Robert Collins, *Culture, Communication and National Identity: The Case of Canadian Television* (Toronto: University of Toronto Press, 1990).

28. Christian Riegal, Herb Wyile, et al., *A Sense of Place: Re-Evaluating Regionalism in Canadian and American Writing* (Edmonton: University of Alberta Press, 1998).

29. Tim Hortons opened its first shop west of Ontario in Richmond, British Columbia, in the mid-1970s. Robin's Donuts, founded in Thunder Bay in 1975, dominated the western market until quite recently, when Hortons began expanding its operations there.

30. There are other local varieties of donut lore. For example, the Tim Horton chain sells "donut holes" (small round clumps of donut batter in several flavors) under the trade name "Timbits." In St. Catharines, where Tim Horton drove his car off the road, it is common to point to the spot where he went off the road and say: "That's where they invented Timbits." A sick, morbid joke, to be sure, but morbidity has a place of honor in folklore.

31. Brunvand, *The Vanishing Hitchhiker.*

32. See Mark Higgins, "Forget B.C. or Brazil: For Real Coffee, Try Moncton," *Globe and Mail* (May 18, 1994); Paul Benedetti, "Nice Try Moncton, We're the Tim Hortons Capital of Canada," *Hamilton Spectator* (May 24, 1994). Moncton, now most known for its bilingual workforce and telemarketing call centers, is one of the few cities outside Southern Ontario that makes any claim to donut capital status. The claim is always brand specific—citing Tim Hortons per capita, never donut shops more generally. In the parking lot of the Mountain Road Tim Hortons, one Canadian sailor shook his head dismissively and told me that "there used to be a Mr. Donut down the street, but it went out of business fast. . . . This is a Tim's town."

33. Robert Blumstock, "Doughnut Lovers Give Hamilton Its Unique Flavor," *Hamilton Spectator* (August 10, 1988); Rob McConnell, quoted in "Duo Celebrates Donuts," *St. Catharines Standard* (May 14, 1994).
34. Cited in *Historic Toronto—A Look at the History of the Corporation of the City of Toronto* (City of Toronto, n.d.). Thanks to Charlene Kish for this reference.
35. *Hamilton Spectator* (January 22, 1985).
36. See also Michael Collins, "What Have They Got That We Don't?" *What's Up Niagara* (July 1988).
37. Ian McKay, *The Quest of the Folk: Antimodernism and Cultural Selection in Twentieth-Century Nova Scotia* (Montreal: McGill-Queens University Press, 1994). McKay capitalizes the word "Folk" to highlight its constructed quality.
38. "Who's Eating All Those Doughnuts?" *Financial Times of Canada* (March 2–8, 1992). In a Roger and Me moment born of desperation, the former mayor of St. Catharines once told me that donut stores were good for the economy because they brought jobs.
39. George Ritzer, *The McDonaldization of Society* (Thousand Oaks, CA: Pine Forge Press, 1993). See also the various critiques in Mark Alfino, John S. Caputo, and Robin Wynyard, eds., *McDonaldization Revisited: Critical Essays on Consumer Culture* (Westport, CT: Praeger Books, 1998).
40. For a discussion of fast-food labor processes, see Ester Reiter, *Making Fast Food: From the Frying Pan into the Fryer* (Kingston-Montreal: McGill-Queens University Press, 1991).
41. Lorinc, *Opportunity Knocks*, p. 168.
42. Quoted in *Halifax Daily News* (January 15, 1995).
43. *Hamilton Spectator,* July 22, 2001.
44. Benedict Anderson, *Imagined Communities: Reflections on the Origin and Spread of Nationalism* (London: Verso, 1991).
45. Anderson, *Imagined Communities*, p. 6.
46. Andrew Wernick, "American Popular Culture in Canada: Trends and Reflections," in Flaherty and Manning, eds., *The Beaver Bites Back?* p. 297. On Canadian identity and irony, see also Linda Hutcheon, *Splitting Images: Contemporary Canadian Ironies* (Toronton: Oxford University Press, 1991).

Chapter 5

FOOD AND NATIONALISM: THE ORIGINS OF "BELIZEAN FOOD"

RICHARD R. WILK

INTRODUCTION: DEFINING THE NATIONAL

*I*n this time at the beginning of the new millennium it is not unusual to hear intelligent people say that the era of the nation state and national culture is ending and a brave new world of global consumer culture, multinational economies, and transnational migration is upon us. Even those who are more sanguine about the future survival of the nation and of local culture tend to see the forces of globalization locked in opposition to the autonomy and continued vitality of national and subnational cultures.[1] The idea that national culture is on the verge of death or terminal dilution through globalization is itself globally distributed: part of high and low culture, political debate, academic theorizing, and popular outrage in many parts of the world. In almost any country, from the smallest village to the biggest city, it is possible to have the same conversation about how local or national culture is rapidly being lost or destroyed by imported goods, ideas, practices, and languages. Its not just a few scholars who think that national cultures are "withering away" or "on their last legs."[2]

In Belize, where I have been doing anthropological research since 1973, many people would agree wholeheartedly that national culture is disappearing quickly. This is one of the few issues that both political parties and the full spectrum of political opinion, from the far right to the far left, would agree on. Whatever made Belize a special and unique place is rapidly being destroyed, not just by American television, tourists, and supermarkets, but also by an influx of Central American low-wage workers, cheap Chinese bakeries and fried chicken stands, and rude Jamaican dance-hall music. "Globalization," said a local scholar, "is killing us."

Of course there is another side to the story. Some scholars argue that on the contrary, existing nations, or aspiring nations based on religion or ethnicity, are being revitalized through their opposition to the forces of globalization.[3] Others say that rather than fading away, new forms of nationhood are emerging that are creolized, deterritorialized, reimagined, or commodified.[4]

Despite these differences, both sides in the debate start from the same assumption: that national, regional, or ethnic cultures are fundamentally different from mobile, market-based, mass-mediated, global cultural forms, so they represent different and basically antithetical processes. The two may not annihilate each other right away, but there is no question that they are opposed, one pushing for a world of local distinctions, and the other aiming to wipe those distinctions away and homogenize everything.

In many ways this makes for a satisfying story. But in this paper I want to build on recent scholarship that suggests that it is very deceptive, if not downright wrong, especially in the parts of the world so often labeled "developing."[5] A longer historical perspective shows, for example, that there have been many different periods of globalization in world history; the current phase may be different in degree rather than in kind from what has come before. With hindsight, it is easy to see that the nation-state and various forms of nationalism are actually the products of global political and cultural processes that began centuries ago.[6] The role of the nation-state is certainly *changing* in the most recent stages of globalization. While the economic role of the state has been challenged, national and subnational cultural expressions have not lost their power or attraction. Instead, like the nation, national culture is itself changing as new forms of cultural production, often highly self-conscious, performative, contentious, and highly charged with emotion and meaning, are appearing all over the world.[7]

In this paper I explore the ways that globalization and local identity are closely related processes that depend intimately upon each other. The research for this paper did not begin on the topic of food at all, though I have sporadically been taking notes on Belizean foodways since I first began doing fieldwork there in 1972. My research on consumption in the Belizean middle class began formally in 1990, but a good deal of my time and attention was spent on gathering data on clothing, housing, jewelrys, and music and in describing the events where they were consumed. As the research progressed, I began more intensive projects on beauty pageantry, television viewing, shopping, and tastes and preferences for different foods. With Belizean colleagues I conducted large-scale surveys of food preferences, collected recipes and lists of ingredients, and engaged in structured interviews on likes and dislikes, family meals, festive meals, and judgments of food quality. After finishing this fieldwork and publishing material on television and beauty pageants, I continued historical and documentary research on Belizean food, drawing mostly on nineteenth century newspapers and other contemporary documents.[8]

Why should such a story about such a tiny and unique place as Belize be relevant to other cases or to broader issues? While in many ways Belize is an oddity, the processes taking place there that shape cuisine and identity are exactly the same as those existing in many other places in the world. Rather than being just about Belize, this paper is about the tension between local and global, the processes of migration, travel, mass-mediated communication, creolization and mixture, and the development of new identities out of old ones. I use the history of Belizean foodways to show how the global and the local have actually been intimate partners rather than contending forces. First, historical information will show that the antecedents of Belizean food were completely global. Second, I argue that the recent development of Belizean national cuisine has also been a thoroughly global process.

Belize is a particularly interesting place to look at food, globalization, and nationalism because it is among the least likely places where you would expect to find a national cuisine. Like the United States, it is a polyglot place populated entirely by immigrants, many of whom have shed their traditional ethnic and national identities. The indigenous Mayan culture of Belize was largely exterminated before the colony was established, so there was no existing tradition to refer back to, and the slaves did not have provision grounds on which to base a reconstructed African diet. From early in its history, Belize has been an unusually global society, with open borders, a mobile population, and close connections with international commerce. Indeed the only reason the country exists is because of the global trade in exotic tropical products, mainly timber. From the time of its first settlement, Belize has also been a multiethnic polyglot place, which poses particular problems for the emergence of national culture, a process that is still ongoing as new immigrant groups enter and large parts of the population leave for the United States. Also, Belize has legally been a nation only since independence in 1981, an event followed quickly by the arrival of satellite television, offshore banking, and hundreds of thousands of foreign tourists. How could there ever be a national cuisine when there was no national culture? To answer this question, we have to be more precise about what we mean by a national cuisine.

WHAT ARE NATIONAL CULTURE AND BELIZEAN FOOD?

A number of scholars have drawn a distinction between the habitual, daily, lived practices shared among a group of people, as one form of shared identity, and those explicit, self-conscious, symbolic, and performative displays that are often given the public label "national culture."[9] It is tempting to treat this polarity archaeologically, as if they were two separate strata of culture; so that on the surface, for example, you have the public official banquet version of cuisine, but beneath there is a deeper layer of real unself-conscious home cooking. Or you can treat one as the

Table 1. Polarities of Food Culture

Lived Practice	Public Performance
Cooking	**Cuisine**
Meals at home	**Public banquet**
Ancient tradition	**Modern artifice**
Working class	**Elite class**
Regional	**National**
Local	**Cosmopolitan**

ancient and primordial authentic practice and the other as some artificial product of modernity, or even the playfully mass-mediated reflexive post-modernity. Others say that the strata are divided by class, with the daily subsistence diet representing the authentic pole, and the lavish meals of the elite, the performative. And then there is the popular perception in Belize and many other places, that new globalized forms are superseding the "real" and "authentic" local foods. In Table 1 I have lined up these various interpretations to show how the polarities are related. These distinctions are clearly related to those drawn by Sidney Mintz between the "inside" and "outside" meanings of food.[10]

There is an important set of distinctions here between cuisine as an unself-conscious, nonreflective aspect, "habitus" of food that is deeply embodied through many cultural and social practices, and cuisine as part of the national imagination, as a set of public, political, performative, symbolic discourses. But there is no evidence that these two aspects of food can ever be separated from each other or that either can be treated as more real or authentic; they exist in every place, culture, class, and time. You can find them at every level of the global system, from the family meal up to McDonald's. As Jeffrey Pilcher shows in the genesis of Mexican national food, the national emerges from the interaction between practice and performance, domestic and public, high and low, local and foreign, rather than from the dominance of one over the other.[11]

Nevertheless, the dynamics of the relationship between national food as daily practice and food as public symbol have changed over time in Belize. In particular, the audience for the public aspects of national food has changed dramatically. Under the colonial regime, food was a class and ethnic symbol that maintained firm social boundaries. Today the symbolic and social consumption of food has much more diverse audience, including increasing numbers of Belizeans living abroad and foreign expatriates and tourists living in and visiting Belize. The result is a series of contending versions of Belizean national cuisine rather than a single accepted code. This diversity of public notions of national food, however, remains in tension with daily culinary practices and tastes that have become remarkably uniform.[12]

To show how the relationship between public and private versions of Belizean food has changed over time, I will distinguish two main periods, colonial and postcolonial.

THE COLONIAL MELTING POT

Belize was called "The Bay" or "Honduras Bay" in the seventeenth century, when English-speaking Europeans first visited. The initial settlers, the "Baymen," included buccaneers, outcasts, and merchants, many of English origins, along with their African and Indian slaves. They paddled up rivers in search of logwood, sarsaparilla, and fustic for export. Later, mahogany became the principal export while agriculture remained almost absent, creating an enclave economy producing entirely for export and consuming few local products.

The cooking of the early settlers was probably derived from the preserved rations of sailors, supplemented by wild game, fish, and turtles (buccaneers were known for the large amount of meat in their diet).[13] To feed their slaves while working in the forest, they imported flour and salt fish or meat from North America and the Antilles, and sugar from the Caribbean. Visiting in 1675, Captain William Dampier found that logwood cutters ate "Pig and Pork, and pease, or beef and dough-boys (dumplings)." They drank coffee, rum, and rum punch. Sometimes wheat flour and rum were directly bartered for logwood.[14] By all evidence, both the slaves and their masters ate the same imported staples; the masters ate more meat, especially game, and much larger and more varied rations of alcoholic drinks and condiments.[15]

During the nineteenth century, and especially after the end of slavery, the ethnic composition of the colony diversified. Besides the local white settlers, a mixed group of "Creole" and free colored emerged as a small middle class of functionaries and merchants, always subordinated to British expatriates and local whites. The top rank of the social scale consisted of foreign-born or -educated staff who expected to retire to their home country. Immigration from neighboring countries provided both a small Hispanic mercantile and managerial group from Mexico and Honduras, and a rural Mayan agricultural class employed on sugar plantations that started up in the 1840s. Small groups of Garifuna (Afro-Amerindians from the island of St. Vincent, also called Black Caribs) and Maya also entered the country from neighboring Guatemala, the former settling along the seashore. The majority of the population was still an urban-based African-descended working class engaged through debt-servitude in forest extraction and other manual labor.

While Hispanic and Maya farmers did produce much of their own food and clothing, everyone else relied on imports. According to customs

FOR PUBLIC SALE.

On WEDNESDAY next the 27th inst. at 12 o'clock precisely, an assortment of Goods, property of the late I. B. EVERETT, Esq. deceased, at his late vendue-room.

J. ARMSTRONG, Executor.

ALSO

COGNAC BRANDY, CHERRY DITTO, RATAFIA. WHITE LISBON, VIN de GRAVE, OLD PORT. BRANDY FRUITS assorted, FRENCH OLIVES & CAPERS, & FLORENCE OIL.

Persons having property in the vendue room, are requested to take it away previous to the day of sale, or it will be sold.

JUST IMPORTED.

PER BRIG JANET DUNLOP AND FOR SALE BY,

CAMPBELL &CO,

Bales —Best Strelitz Oznaburgs, 148 yards, ditto. ditto. in half pieces.
Ditto—Brown and bleach'd Flax, and low Sheeting, 35 yards.
Cases—White and brown Linen Platillas.
Ditto—Gentlemen's superfine black and drab beaver Hats.
Ditto—Men's oval shaped tine plated Hats.
Bales—Men's blue cloth Jackets, checked and striped cotton Shirts.
Ditto—Men's oznaburg Shirts and Trowsers.
Kegs—6 dy. 8 dy. 10 dy. 20 dy. and 30 dy. nails.
Cases—Cross cut and hand Saws, and Mincheat Blades.
Casks—Hoes, falling and squaring Axes, and Carpenter's Tools.
Tin Cases—Whitechapel Needles. *Crates.* - earthenware.
Barrels half and quarter barrels—GUNPOWDER. *Kegs*—Patent Shot.
Firkins—Tongues, best Loch fine Herrings. *One tierce*—Yorkshire Hams.
Kegs—Bristol Tripe. *Hampers*—Potatoes.
Barrels—Madeira Wine in bottles. (of superior quality.)
Ditto.—Claret, ditto. ditto. Pink and White Noyeau.
Ditto.—Orange Wine. A few doz. Jamaica Bitters, and Valerian Wine in pint bottles.
Cases—Jamaica Pickles, preserved Tamarinds, green Sweetmeats, preserved Ginger, and Guava Jelly in pots.
Mushroom and Walnut Ketchup, Essence of Anchovies, French Capers, Cayenne Pepper, and Currie Powder.

In addition to their previous large stock, a very extensive and well selected assortment of British and German DRY GOODS.

ALSO Just landed ex. Deveron from London; Superfine blue Cloth. Military Surtout Coats.
Ditto. ditto. Shell Jackets braided and lined with silk.

AND of former *late* Importations,

Trunks—Youths and Ladies Shoes. A small assortment of Hair, Cloth, and Shoe Brushes.
Ditto.—Rich needle-worked mull and jaconett muslin Ladies' Dresses.
Ditto.————ditto. Flounces and Trimmings.
Cases—Linen Thread No. 12 to 24. *Ditto.*—Cotton ditto. in balls No. 16 to 40 and 20 to 70. &c. &c. &c.

Figure 1. Two advertisements for the sale of imported cargoes in Belize, from the *Honduras Gazette and Commercial Advertiser,* December 23, 1826.

records, in the early nineteenth century food accounted for more than 80 percent of all imports by value. Advertisements from the early nineteenth century show a remarkable range of luxury imported food and drink, often identified with a place of origin in Europe, along with the staple casks of flour and salted meat. By the end of the nineteenth century, much wider varieties of canned and preserved foods were imported, allowing expatriates to reproduce many aspects of familiar British meals, though by no means the entire range. Branding became increasingly important throughout the nineteenth century, culminating in the 1890s when merchants began advertising particular lines of branded goods with advertisements created by the manufacturer.

Local foods in the elite diet usually had close analogs back at home, so a local fish was called "mountain mullet," and local geese, deer, and ducks were avidly sought. The local fauna were almost always domesticated by covering them in imported sauces or wrapping them in dough. A newspaper article from 1866 reports that sportsmen looked forward to a "parrot's tongue pie."[16]

In the colonial system of selling imports, in markets where quality was often poor and hard to monitor, consumers came to depend on the reputations of merchants and brands and on price signals as guides to quality. Because the local market was so small, novelty was also highly valued. During most of the nineteenth century, local merchants began their advertisements with "Just Arrived," "Landed This Week," or "Just Imported." They associated products with brand and place names from home or other countries with reputations for quality; thereby tying elite consumers to their "home" and excluding the uneducated and poor, who might not distinguish English from Dutch cheese. Brands or products were often associated with specific places (often British counties), and advertising for elite and middle-class consumer goods became a cultural geography of the empire. Advertisers asserted the quality of their goods by assuring that they were the same products sold "at home" in Britain.

Elite consumption helped create a colonial enclave that combined the familiar and the exotic in complex ways; consumption was a barrier between the culture of the distant home and the reality of the tropics beyond the front gate, as well as an emotional and social link back to a cultural source. At the bottom of the social scale, in contrast, cheap generic imported goods were a matter of daily survival. Laborers were often paid partly in scrip negotiable only at the company store, where only low-quality, unbranded imported goods were sold. Many employees in agriculture and forestry were bound to their employers through advances of imported food and other goods at Christmas time. They often went on a "spree" at the beginning and end of their contracts, during which they spent their cash on rum, clothing, and other consumables. At this time, consuming name-brand items and luxuries became a matter of public pride and social display; foreign visitors and the educated elite constantly criticized what they saw as "wasteful" spending of money on luxury food, drink, and household goods at Christmas.

A growing free rural and urban population throughout the nineteenth century crafted a diet like that of many Caribbean peasantries. A contemporary account stated that:

> Their dwellings are little better than outhouses, even in the towns; their food coarse and ill-prepared, consisting for the most part of salt-fish, and plantains or yams, flour, pork, tropical fruits, vegetables and fresh fish, with rice or cornflour; clothing light and inexpensive as a rule, although they spend a good portion of their wages on cheap finery and dressy but not costly clothes. They raise poultry and pigs, but buy nearly every other article of food. Tea they use but little, but must have coffee and consume large quantities of sugar in one form or another.[17]

Caught between the extremes of this hierarchy was a thin and precarious middle class of local petty bourgeoisie. They were ethnically quite mixed, and increasingly identified themselves as Creoles rather than as European, Hispanic, or Colored. They worked as small merchants, petty officials, tradespeople, and clerical workers. Their continuing membership in the middle class, their jobs, and their status depended on maintaining respectability as the British elite defined it. Their dependence on the favors and approval of the elite was reflected in their consumption, which was often hypercorrect and conservative, with a limited range of stews and roasted meats complemented by bread, potatoes, and rice. For example, they frowned on many local foods such as fresh fish, tropical produce, and game meat that were often a necessity among the rural poor (for whom they were part of a subsistence lifestyle) and were also eaten by the upper elite, for whom selected varieties were considered exotic delicacies. Lobster is a good example of a "class sandwich" eaten by the poor because it was abundant and by the elite because it was a delicacy in Europe, but shunned by the middle class as a "trash fish." Older Belizeans from respectable middle-class backgrounds told me their parents would not allow lobster or game meat in the house. Men of that generation would rarely appear in public dressed in anything but a black wool suit. Their standard of consumption was very difficult to maintain on limited salaries, requiring all kinds of compromises and accommodations during recessions and inflation.

This middle class composed the audience at all the "enlightening" public entertainment sponsored by the elite: the cakewalks, tea dances, recitals, and garden parties, always announced in the newspaper, where high European culture was retailed and performed for a local audience. The social strongholds of this middle class were the lodges and friendly societies that sponsored dances and social events of exaggerated respectability and gentility, where high-status, respectable foods like ham and turkey were eaten, defining the line between middle class and underclass.

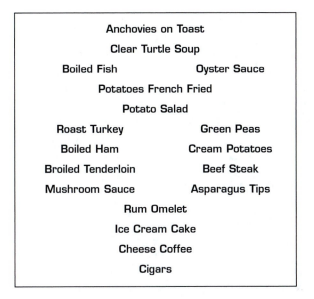

Figure 2. Menu for dinner held at Wagner's Hotel on the occasion of Mr. R. Wilkins's Departure for England. Note that potatoes do not grow in Belize. From *The Clarion*, Belize City, 5 June 1902.

One solution they found to the problem of distancing themselves on an inadequate budget from the poor freed slaves was an extensive borrowing of food items from the Mexican/Mestizo culture in the northern district of the country. This "Spanish" food, especially festive dishes like *tamales, relleno* (a stuffed chicken stew), *escabeche* (stewed chicken with onions and vinegar), and *tacos* entered the middle-class diet as a safe option, associated neither with the class below or the class above. *Tamales* were absorbed into the middle-class Creole diet along with flour *tortillas*, but the foods of poor and rural Creoles were avoided.

This is not to say there was no recognition of or resistance to the tyranny of European standards, which were presented and maintained with all the arrogance of empire, just that there were no legitimate alternatives, no models of alternative indigenous practice as in the neighboring Hispanic republics. Kinship networks bound the local population together in ways that often confounded class barriers. As gifts, local products "from the bush," such as fruit wines, game meat, and fruit, moved into middle-class homes, where they were often cherished with an almost guilty nostalgia for the simplicity of country life. But they were also a source of social embarrassment and danger.

The events where class lines were most strictly drawn were the private gatherings of the expatriate elite, where the consumption and display of imports—always in a context defined as a European enclave—were the central activity. Menus for formal dinners, such as that in Figure 2, were published in the newspapers, and imported dishes (including live oysters from New Orleans) were always prominently featured. The other arena where foreign consumption was modeled for the local audience was elite weddings and funerals. It was not unusual for local newspapers to publish long lists of all the wedding gifts. Many of the items were related to the preparation, consumption, and display of imported food in social settings. The new family was outfitted for the kinds of consumption expected of the colonial elite and for eventual return to the mother country. None of the items on these wedding lists could have originated in Belize.

NATIONAL CUISINE UNDER COLONIALISM

By the early twentieth century, with the arrival of Garifuna migrants, Chinese and East Indian laborers, three different groups of Mayan Indians from Guatemala, and a host of Europeans from at least eight different countries, Belize was one of the most diverse places in the Caribbean. Alongside this mosaic of imported cuisines, a publicly recognized Creole cuisine could not develop because of class divisions. When writing about local food habits, the British interpreted everything through their own concept of race, so diet was a characteristic of each separate group within the colony. Each "race" had characteristic foods that distinguished them; *tortillas* for the Maya, fish and yams for the Garifuna, and so on. On top of this was a model of empire in which culture originated in England and percolated down, through education and the process of civilization, to the various subject groups. This left virtually no space for public recognition of something uniquely local and Belizean. The only local distinction the British could offer in public was to praise the abundance and variety of local fish and game, which they often compared favorably to those at home.[18]

Does the absence of a public, performative national cuisine mean that there was none? I would argue instead that the colonial period saw a great deal of nationalizing *practice* when it came to cooking and eating. In other words, the foundation of a common lexicon of ingredients and condiments, a common set of cooking practices, and a shared repertoire of dishes was being forged in markets, kitchens, mess halls, restaurants, and clubs during colonial times. But it passed almost completely unremarked, unnoticed, and unrecorded by historians, travelers, or journalists. Its traces emerge only in the common lexicon of all the different "ethnic" cuisines of the country as they appeared at the end of the colonial period.

Some of the elements of this common lexicon include the valences of different ingredients. Throughout all Belizean cooking, the most valued items are packaged, preserved, branded imports, and specific wild game meats. Local meats, fruits, and vegetables always have a lower rank. This is especially clear at holidays and festivities, where imports or local game are always required elements of the meal. Even in everyday meals,

Richard R. Wilk

canned or preserved meat or fish is almost always preferred to the local product, just as potatoes outrank cassava or yams.

Another common characteristic that emerged from the colonial period is a strong preference for highly processed ingredients and an equation of whiteness with purity. Thus brown sugar produced in Belize was exported to England, refined to whiteness, and shipped back for consumption. Wheat-flour breads and *tortillas* were preferred to corn, canned condensed milk to the local fresh product.

This convergence was not necessarily voluntary. All the class and ethnic communities of colonial Belize worked within a common set of constraints on the variety of ingredients they had to work with. Market channels were firmly controlled by a small number of Belize City merchant houses, run by white Belizeans or expatriates, which simply did not import the ingredients that Chinese, East Indian, or Hispanic cooks needed to maintain their cuisines. They had to simplify and substitute. Shops throughout the colony stocked the same narrow ranges of products, so all cooks except the richest had the same narrow set of ingredients to work with. Worse, the merchant houses systematically refused to carry local products and drove local producers out of business through price competition. Thus, by the end of the nineteenth century, imported red kidney beans had driven the local black beans out of the market, and the red beans became the foundation of most urban dishes (though black beans remained popular in the countryside, where they were grown and traded informally).

Given the small size of the colony (the population did not exceed 50,000 until 1931) and the degree of interethnic mating, it would be surprising if there was not a lot of sharing of specific recipes and cooking techniques during the late colonial period. Hired working-class Creole, Garifuna, and Hispanic women ran the kitchens in all the elite households and in many respectable middle-class households as well. Professional cooks were also hired by timber companies, sawmills, chicle camps, and sugar mills to feed an often multiethnic workforce. These cooks, and others working across cultures and classes, engaged in various kinds of creolization that led to convergence.[19]

MIXING

The most obvious form of creolization is mixing of ingredients, methods, and dishes. A good example is the practice of marinating ("seasoning") all meat and fish with a packaged Yucatecan spice mix called *recado rojo* (which contains achiote and oregano), lime juice, and seasoned salt mix. This method is today widespread among cooks of all ethnic groups and probably dates back to the early 1900s, when seasoned salt mixtures were first imported. Mixing also occurs within meals, where dishes of different ethnic origins are served together: *conch ceviche* followed by a hamburger, for example.

SUBSTITUTION

A special form of mixing occurs when an item that is normally part of a dish or meal is substituted by one of different origin. The Garifuna fish-and-coconut stew with plantain dumplings (*hudut*) was adapted by substituting flour dumplings for the mashed plantain. Local game meats and vegetables were substituted for European ones on the tables of the elite, who continued until quite recently to serve callaloo in cream sauce and call it "spinach." Similarly, Hispanic cooks sometimes substituted oatmeal for cornmeal in preparing thick breakfast drinks (*atole*).

WRAPPING

Sometimes creolization is accomplished by enclosing something foreign within a familiar wrapping, or vice versa. One of my first rural meals in Belize was fried Danish lunch meat wrapped in a homemade flour *tortilla* (itself an original product of substitution). A similar kind of process occurs through *submersion*, when one ingredient is literally submerged and absorbed inside another; macaroni is broken into pieces and mixed into peppery cowfoot soup.

COMPRESSION

With distance from the source, it is possible to compress a whole variety of dishes and modes of preparation into a single category, and a few emblematic dishes stand for the whole. Thus a small selection of Ethiopian dishes becomes "African food," more readily adapted and absorbed. In Belize two main forms of compression took place, first as elements of French, North American, and English cookery became a generalized "European" food, and second as a varied set of borrowings from neighboring Hispanic republics and from several Mayan cultures were compressed into the category "Spanish food."

ALTERNATION

One of the most subtle ways that creolization took place was by giving foods of different origins their own time and place within the total dietary system. New or different foods are associated with particular events, days, or periods, on one level keeping them separate but at another level incorporating them into a regular rhythm of consumption. The black Christmas cake is a good example in Belize; carefully assembled from expensive imported ingredients, it remains distinctly English in form but has become an inextricable part of the yearly cycle of Belizean cuisine among most ethnic groups. Similarly, Spanish foods first entered many Creole middle-class diets not as courses in the main noontime meal but as light dishes eaten as part of evening "tea." Alternation was often the entry point for dishes to become a more general part of everyday practice. Rice and beans cooked with coconut milk was a common "Sunday dinner" dish in the early part of the twentieth century; from there it became associated with almost every kind of public event and then it finally acquired the status of a daily staple.

The net effect of these processes has not been an even mixture or homogenization of national food practices. Each ethnic group and class continues to maintain distinct dishes and practices, especially in rural communities that still produce much of their own food and do not have to rely on the market. Overall the nation's food practices appear to be heterogeneous, polyglot, disorderly, and even incoherent. On one level it appears that urban Creole food has been the most syncretic, absorbing elements from different ethnic groups as well as British and other foreign traditions. But the ethnic cuisines, with the exception of Chinese cooking, have also steadily creolized too; and outside of ethnic communities, Creole food became a kind of "lingua franca," an accepted common dialect in which everyone could take part and partake (just as Kriol as a language has become the common medium of communication for all ethnic groups). This laid the groundwork for the later emergence of Creole food as the self-conscious "national" cuisine of Belize.

THE TRANSFORMATION OF COLONIALISM

The early years of the twentieth century saw a number of economic and social changes in Belize. Perhaps the most important was a long-term decline in forestry as timber was exhausted and mechanization replaced much of the workforce. Agriculture took up little of the slack, though chicle gathering in the rain forest (for the North American chewing gum industry) provided cash income for subsistence farmers. The colonial government became a larger employer, but foreign corporations, which profited from both imports and exports, still tightly controlled the economy.

Class structure also changed. The local elite began to make common cause with the local mixed Creole group and claimed a common Creole identity, in contrast to and sometimes in conflict with expatriates and colonial officials.[20] The boundaries between the local elite and the middle class became less distinct; a few Hispanic families acquired wealth and elite status, and Hispanics came to dominate the middle class in some parts of the country. The labor and Garveyite movements during the period after World War I emphasized the conflict between the interests of the local working classes and the governmental and mercantile middle class and elites, though within the umbrella of a common Creole ethnic identity.[21]

The economy dramatically changed again in the 1960s, when sugar, citrus, and banana exports began to increase. There was some distribution of land to small farmers in the 1970s, and the number of subsistence and small mixed farms increased somewhat, though the bulk of land remained in foreign hands or government reserves. In the 1980s several clothing assembly plants were built with Taiwanese capital, and garments now account for almost one fourth of export value.

More recently, Belize has seen some drastic demographic change. Warfare in neighboring republics led to a major influx of Hispanic refugees, who have settled mostly in the countryside.[22] Emigration to the United States increased, drawing disproportionately from the urban Creole population. The ethnic balance of the country changed as a result, and Hispanics emerged as the majority in the 1990 census.[23] A major tourist influx in the 1980s took place at the same that the Belizean middle class began to visit the United States and neighboring countries more frequently. Satellite television also had a major effect on a growing sense of Belizean nationhood.[24] Television and the wide availability of consumer goods of all kinds have provided a diversity of cultural models; the result is that the cultural hegemony of the elite as the arbiters and models of civilization and conduct has been undercut. Fashion and cultural knowledge flow inwards into the country at all levels of the social scale through channels as diverse as *Cosmopolitan* magazine and MTV's *Real World*.

The result is a social hierarchy that still has extremes of wealth and poverty, and where color and ethnicity still make a difference. But there are also multiple social distinctions that crosscut wealth and education, and ties of kinship, neighborhood, and political faction link people together across both class and ethnic lines. There is also a wider variety of pathways for both upward and downward mobility, many of which lead Belizeans for sojourns in the growing Belizean communities in the United States. In last century, imported consumer goods served mainly to separate and regulate class relationships. While they remain ubiquitous, imported goods and new foods play many more roles today. They are used to make many kinds of social distinction and they are embroiled in new forms of political contest, where they have acquired new meanings.

BELIZEAN NATIONAL FOOD

Above I have argued that as daily practice, Belizean food had acquired a distinctive national character during the colonial era, but nobody paid public attention to it. Only in the last few decades have there been public debate and discourse about national food. Unlike many other countries, the arena for this emergence of the national has not been in the pages of cookbooks, government nutritional policies, or local politics. Instead the transnational setting of the Belizean migration has been a particularly important setting, as has the marketing of Belizean culture to increasing streams of foreign tourists, the production of public festivals and cultural performances, and the local use of media such as music cassettes and videotape, and now the Internet. Here I will discuss only a few examples of the ways these complex developments have combined to produce new forms of public national cuisine.

The first published mention I have been able to find of national food is in the early 1960s, when an American expatriate called rice and beans

Richard R. Wilk

the "national dish" and noted that it was usually served with potato salad made with imported ingredients.[25] Throughout the 1960s and early 1970s, while the government took several measures to develop a national flag, anthem, and other symbols, there was no clear official policy on national foods or diet. There were several attempts to formulate an import-substitution policy, particularly encouraging local farmers to produce more rice, beans, chicken, and pork through price supports, subsidies, and import restrictions of various kinds. This had the effect of keeping prices for these products low, furthering the reliance of urban consumers on rice and beans as a staple, and cementing their position as "the national dish." Yet officially all the government had to say was that local foods were healthy and better for the economy; there was no explicit public policy to promote local cuisine. Only in the 1980s did the government actively promote some kinds of local food through school gardening programs.

At the same time, another import public arena for the definition of Belizean national food had opened in the United States among the growing expatriate Belizean community in New York, Chicago, and Los Angeles. By 1972, there was a "Belize Bar and Grill" in Brooklyn, New York, where you could drink imported Belizean Belikin beer and have a plate of rice and beans along with several generic Caribbean dishes such as fried plantains, barbecued chicken, and hibiscus (sorrel) tea. Belizean migrants found that it was easy to get the ingredients they needed to cook familiar foods in Hispanic and Caribbean markets, but they also resisted being lumped together with other Caribbean migrants. They kept personal networks open with other migrant Belizeans as well as their homeland, connections that were kept vital through a constant flow of videotapes, audiocassettes, photos, letters, gifts, and other supplies.

The development of Belizean food in the United States was in many ways similar to the processes that have characterized the development of other expatriate cuisines in this country.[26] At a distance from the home country, ethnic or national cooking tends first to become simplified and compressed, with a focus on a few prominent, emblematic dishes such as chow mein, tacos, or spaghetti. Cheaper and more easily available ingredients may be substituted for the original ones. In American Belizean restaurants, rice and beans became the single central dish, accompanied not by a variety of stews, meats, or sauces as in Belize, but always with stewed chicken, fried plantain, and potato salad (coleslaw was sometimes substituted for the latter). In Belize the complementary dish, beans and rice, cooked and served separately instead of together, is equally popular but it does not appear often in restaurants in the United States. From the wide variety of Belizean desserts, restaurants tended to serve only two or three, usually sweet potato "pound" and lemon or coconut pie. They often substituted coconut oil for harder-to-find coconut milk, and used pork hocks instead of salted pigtail in the beans. As time has passed, more

The QuikPages
NATIONAL BUSINESS WEB SITE DIRECTORY

Flowers Por Belizean Style
7328 N Clark Street
Chicago, IL 60626

Phone: (773) 761-4388

The Best of Belize!

Flowers Por Belizean Style is a taste of the best of South of the Border flavor right here in Chicago. One bite and you'll swear the Windy City is basking in a tropical breeze. Everything is made fresh from our own authentic recipes.

- **Chicken Tamales**
- **Pawades**
- **Cowfoot Soup**
- **Conch Soup**
- **Red Snapper**
- **Fish Balls**

Featuring Different Style Dishes
Every Friday & Saturday

Open Monday to Friday 9 a.m. - 5 p.m.

Family Owned & Operated

Mention you saw us on the Internet!

Figure 3. Advertisement for Flowers restaurant in Chicago from the Internet. Original is located at http://www.flowerstyle.qpg.com.

Belizean restaurants have opened, and their menus have tended to become more diverse, as shown in the Internet advertisement for a Chicago Belizean restaurant in Figure 3.

While the few Belizean restaurants presented Belizean cooking to the wider public and became emblematic of the whole nation, festival cooking asserted a special place for Belize among other Caribbean migrant cultures in the United States. In Chicago, for example, many kinds of Belizean food and drink appear at the booths at Belize Day every August. The display and serving of Belizean food at this and similar festivities in New York and Los Angeles are a matter of public pride and emotion for the Belizean expatriate community. Many Belizean women in the United States work as domestics and make it a point to introduce their hosts to Belizean cooking. And no gathering of Belizean kin in the United States, for a party, wedding, or funeral, is complete without tamales, *escabeche*, and rice and beans. Cooking rare and/or expensive foods like venison or the root crop, fish, and salt pork stew called "boil-up" is often the excuse for a party.

As in many other migrant communities, among expatriate Belizean Americans food remains a central source of national identity and a focus of intense nostalgia for home. It also reflects some of the ambivalence that migrants have for a home that they often do not really want to go back to. Migrants from rural areas are particularly nostalgic about freshwater fish (generally much preferred to ocean fish in Belize), turtles, and special deserts. They say that the salted pigtail you buy in Belize tastes better than that you can get in the States (even though the Belize item is itself imported from Canada). The mangoes in the United States are never as nice as the ones on the tree in Granny's yard. And trips home or visits from Belize often involve an extensive "suitcase trade" in frozen river fish and turtles, jars of pickled craboo fruit or coconut oil, *recado* seasoning, Creole buns from favorite bakeries, and hard-to-find items such as the black coloring for Christmas cakes. Entrepreneurs may carry a large quantity of particular foods to sell for holiday meals, when they are required on the menu. Rural Creole people, for example, pay very high prices for *hicatee* (a freshwater turtle) at Easter.

Karen Olwig reports that on the Caribbean island of Nevis the farmers mostly eat imported frozen chicken but keep a few goats around for the holidays, when their families come home from the States and want to eat the curry goat they remember so well.[27] In a similar way, the public, self-conscious version of Belizean national food owes more to the Belizeans living in the United States than it does to Belize itself. People in Belize continued to cook and eat Belizean food, but the idea that it was unique, special, and part of a national identity was largely prompted by the processes of migration and tourism. Belizean restaurants in the United States were the first to portray their food as part of the national character. Migrants returned to Belize from the United States and carried the idea of a national cuisine home. In 1990 the first self-proclaimed Belizean restaurant in Belize was opened by a couple that had just returned from living in Los Angeles for twenty years. At first the local diners were a bit perplexed by the idea that the same dishes they had always eaten were now Belizean food. Then the restaurant found abundant new customers: tourists and foreign residents in search of the authentic "local" experience.

A wide variety of visitors to Belize from the United States played a role in defining and nationalizing Belizean cuisine. In 1977 the local newsmagazine *Brukdown* included a long feature article extolling the cultural importance of rice and beans, submitting ten local restaurants to a taste test. The article was inspired and written by the expatriate American owner of the magazine, a strong promoter of nationalist issues who wanted to see more local cultural pride. One of the highest-rated of the "local" restaurants was actually run by another longtime American expatriate. In those days it was common to hear Peace Corps volunteers, diplomats, anthropologists, and other members of the foreign community lamenting that Belizeans did not value, present, or preserve their traditions or culture. The implication was that if Belize wanted to be a real nation, it needed to have some decent handicrafts, some rhythmic and loud ethnic music and dance, a national costume, and a national cuisine. Development meant finding and formalizing Belizean food as quickly as possible. Two of the three cookbooks published in Belize were the result of projects funded by international aid organizations with the intention of filling this gap.

To summarize, one version of national food was developed in America by Belizeans for Americans; another was developed partly by Americans in Belize, for Belizeans; but a third version of Belizean food is the one that attracts the most attention: the version developed by Belizean and foreign entrepreneurs to feed foreign tourists with a taste for something authentically Belizean.

For many years before independence, the official government policies in Belize were cautious or hostile to tourism development, and tourists were rare. The few hotels tended to serve bland American or European dishes or Chinese food, since nobody thought visitors would want to eat local food. When tourism began to develop in the late 1970s, it was confined to the offshore islands (the Cays) which had a predominately Hispanic population; they cooked mostly American, European, or Mexican dishes for the tourists.

But a change in the ruling party in 1984 led to active tourism promotion, and by that time the trend was all in the direction of ecological and cultural tourism. In order to compete, Belize needed those ethnic costumes, that loud and rhythmic music, and the somewhat exotic and thoroughly authentic national cuisine. The first signs of its appearance outside the Cays was in the most expensive restaurants in Belize City, where chefs

Belizean Dish of the Day

Sunday......   Tender Baked Chicken
                Spanish Style Vegetable
                    Rice
                Fried Plantain

Monday......   Villa Special Conch Soup
                White Rice
                Hot Rolls and Butter

Tuesday.....   Spanish Style Relleno
                Hot Corn Tortillas

Wednesday...   Fried Fish Steak
                White Rice and Stewed
                    Beans
                Coleslaw
                Fried Plantain

Thursday....   Stewed Chicken
                Rice and Beans
                Potato Salad

Friday......   Stewed Gibnut
                Rice and Beans
                Potato Salad
                Fried Plantain

Saturday....   Fried Whole Fish
                Rice and Stewed Beans
                Coleslaw
                Fried Plantain

Big on Friendly Service

Figure 4. Menu for the "Belizean Dish of the Day" from The Villa restaurant, 1989. At the time this was one of the best hotels in the city, and the restaurant was frequented by expatriates and tourists.

began to include a "Belizean Dish of the Day" on their menus, both for the benefit of tourists with a taste for local dishes and to attract some local lunch trade. Figure 4 is one such menu from the Villa Hotel in Belize City, when it was the second most expensive hotel in the City. Some dishes are hardly recognizable as Belizean at all. They all form a particular subset of bland and generic local foods with familiar ingredients, unlikely to offend the visitor or the high-status local. There was no pigtail, cowfoot soup, or canned corn beef and eggs in this version of Belizean food.

With the flowering of tourism in the 1990s, the tourist industry has become an endless source of innovation in the promotion of new Belizean culinary traditions. The country still lags far behind its neighbors, however, and several popular travel guidebooks warn the traveler not to expect great or original food.[28] In words remarkably similar to those of the original British colonists of the nineteenth century, many of the current tourist guides choose nature, rather than culture, as the high point of local food; come to Belize and eat armadillos, pacas, iguanas, conch, turtle, and shark. The other main theme of the tourist version of Belizean food is the richness and diversity of Belizean culture: Belize as the land of a mosaic of "myriad cultures and cuisines."[29] While the government has been working for the last thirty years to ease ethnic tensions and build a national consensus, the tourist industry eagerly decomposes Belize into national and ethnic parts, each of which can be sold or promoted separately.

As tourism has become one of the two largest industries in Belize, the trade of feeding tourists has led to dramatic changes in Belizean food practices. On one hand, tourists demand a highly international diet, requiring Belizean cooks to learn much more about international standards and recipes; and this knowledge has diffused through the country. Providing the familiar foods that tourists like has required new, elaborate supply chains, new distribution systems, and massive amounts of imports of processed foods from the United States and elsewhere, not to mention a huge investment in food preparation equipment and technology. On the other hand, the tourist's endless taste for the exotic has led to entire fishing, hunting, and extractive industries oriented solely to keeping shrimp, venison, and fresh papaya flowing onto the table.

CONCLUSIONS

The irony of these recent developments in "Belizean food," as a self-conscious and public phenomenon, is that despite all the noise and publicity, most Belizeans unself-consciously go about their daily business of cooking and eating food. While different national cuisines contend in public, vying for attention and legitimacy from tourists, scholars, and chefs, in their kitchens and dining rooms, Belizeans of different ethnic groups have forged a remarkable degree of consensus on what they like to eat and how it should be prepared.

To give just one example, in 1990 I surveyed over 1,100 students of all different ethnic groups and classes in six high schools, and asked each one to describe their favorite meal. Over 60 percent said rice and beans, stewed chicken, and potato salad, and another 22 percent gave a minor variation of the same meal. In surveys of adults I found a similar consensus: across ethnic groups and regardless of age or education, Belizeans share a preference for a series of main dishes and desserts, which they prefer to pizza, hamburgers, or any other recent import. The surveys reveal a robust consensus not just on rice and beans, but on "Spanish" dishes such as *tamales* and *panades* (fried corn turnovers stuffed with shark) and *garnachas*, on "Creole" or "Carib" foods such as cowfoot soup, *serre, dukunu*, and boil-up, and on a whole series of pies, cakes, and puddings whose main ingredient is often canned, sweetened, condensed milk.

Those who live for more than a few days in a Belizean community will hear a gentle call outside the door in the evening. If they go outside, they will find a child with a plastic bowl of something warm on his or her head, offering creole bun, *panades*, or something else for "a shilling" (25 cents). As the evening passes, children carry plates of food across the village from house to house, as families share what they have. This is certainly where part of Belize's national cuisine comes from, but as I have argued, it is hardly the only place. The Belizean village now includes close relatives in Chicago, the local ecotourism lodge, and at least one eager Peace Corps volunteer. The food people eat every day cannot be separated from their ideas and images of food, from the notions of cuisine on the cooking programs they watch on their satellite TV, or even the musings of the visiting anthropologist eating at their table.

NOTES

1. Research for this paper was conducted with the support of a Grant In Aid from the Wenner Gren Foundation for Anthropological Research and a Fulbright Fellowship. I want to thank Melissa Johnson, my field assistant for much of the project and now herself a member of the Belizean culinary diaspora, the fine staff of the Belize Archives, Coleville Young, Evan X Hyde, Sylvan Roberts, Inez Sanchez, Joseph Palacio, Dacia, Gloria, Glenn and Rudolph Crawford, and all of the other people who helped me gather data for this project. I also thank Ben Orlove for comments on various stages of this paper, and Anne Pyburn for continuing inspiration, editorial contributions, and stimulating ideas. I thank Elvia Pyburn-Wilk for help in finding crucial reference sources in the library. On globalization, see Benjamin Barber, *Jihad vs. McWorld* (New York: Times Books, 1995); and Daniel Korten, *When Corporations Rule the World* (West Hartford CT: Kumarian, 1995).
2. Arjun Appadurai, *Modernity at Large: Cultural Dimensions of Globalization* (Minneapolis: University of Minnesota Press, 1996), pp. 18–22; Ulf Hannerz, "The Withering Away of the Nation," *Ethnos* 58 (1993): 377–391; Helena Norberg-Hodge, "Consumer Monoculture: The Destruction of Tradition," *Global Dialogue* 1 (1999): 70–77.
3. Samuel Huntington, *The Clash of Civilizations and the Remaking of World Order* (New York: Simon & Schuster, 1996).
4. Robert Foster, "Making National Cultures in the Global Ecumene," *Annual Review of Anthropology* 20 (1991): 235–260; Linda Basch, Nina Schiller, and Cristina Blanc, eds., *Nations Unbound* (Langhorne, PA: Gordon & Breach, 1994); Saskia Sassen, *Losing Control? Sovereignty in an Age of Globalization* (New York: Columbia University Press, 1996).
5. Christoph Brumann, "The Anthropological Study of Globalization: Towards an Agenda for

the Second Phase," *Anthropos* 93 (1998): 495–506; Karen Fog Olwig, *Global Culture, Island Identity* (Chur, Switzerland: Harwood, 1993); Richard Wilk, "The Local and the Global in the Political Economy of Beauty: From Miss Belize to Miss World," *Review of International Political Economy* 2 (1995): 117–134.

6. New forms of nationalism: Joel Kahn, *Culture, Multiculture, Postculture* (London: Sage, 1995). Production of nationalism in the past: Benedict Anderson, *Imagined Communities*, 2nd ed. (London: Verso, 1991); Eric Hobsbawm and Terrence Ranger, eds., *The Invention of Tradition* (Cambridge: Cambridge University Press, 1983).

7. Foster, "Making National Cultures," 235–245; Ulf Hannerz, *Transnational Connections: Cultures, People, Places* (New York: Routledge, 1996); Jonathan Friedman, "The Past in the Future: History and the Politics of Identity," *American Anthropologist* 94 (1992): 837–859.

8. Richard Wilk, "Colonial Time and TV Time," *Visual Anthropology Review* 10 (1994): 94–102; Richard Wilk, "Connections and Contradictions: From the Crooked Tree Cashew Queen to Miss World Belize," in *Beauty Queens on the Global Stage*, Colleen Cohen, Richard Wilk, and Beverley Stoeltje, eds. (New York: Routledge, 1995), 217–233; Richard Wilk, "'Real Belizean Food': Building Local Identity in the Transnational Caribbean," *American Anthropologist* 101 (1999): 244–255.

9. Pierre Bourdieu, *Outline of a Theory of Practice* (Cambridge: Cambridge University Press, 1977); Orvar Lofgren, " Materializing the Nation in Sweden and America," *Ethnos* 58 (1993): 161–196.

10. Sidney Mintz, *Tasting Food, Tasting Freedom* (Boston: Beacon Press, 1996), pp. 20–24.

11. Jeffrey Pilcher, *Que vivan los tamales! Food and the Making of Mexican Identity* (Albuquerque: University of New Mexico Press, 1998).

12. For recent discussion of competing ethnic and national identity in Belize, see Laurie Medina, "Defining Difference, Forging Unity: The Construction of Race, Ethnicity and Nation in Belize," *Ethnic and Racial Studies* 20 (1997): 757–780.

13. Alexandre Exquemelin, *The Buccaneers of America: A True Account of the Most Remarkable Assaults* (London: Routledge, 1924).

14. William Dampier, *Captain Dampier's Voyages: Voyage to the Bay of Campeachy*, vol 2., John Masefield, ed. (London: E. Grant Richards, 1906), pp. 123, 186.

15. Because slaves worked in logging instead of farming in Belize, they had many opportunities to hunt and fish, had free time and the right to work for wages during the rainy season, and were generally given a ration of rum and adequate food. Some slaves were allowed to cultivate small "provision grounds" near towns, and free people of color also did some farming and full-time fishing, though these activities are poorly documented. We do not know very much about the diet of slave women and children who remained in town while men were in the forest cutting wood. But it is clear from ration lists that male slaves did subsist almost exclusively on salt pork, flour, and rum for months at a time, as documented in the accounts of exploratory expeditions. See for example Edward Despard, "Documents Relating to the Exploration of British Honduras in 1787," Manuscripts in the Bancroft Library, University of California, Berkeley.

16. *The Colonist* (Belize City) (June 13, 1866).

17. Archibald Gibbs, *British Honduras: An Historical and Descriptive Account of the Colony from its Settlement, 1670, Compiled from Original and Authentic Sources* (London: Sampson Low, Marston, Searle, and Rivington, 1883), p. 171.

18. Fowler, for example, hunted and fished his way through the jungle while exploring, and found the "mountain mullet, surpassing, I thought, the trout in the delicacy of its flavour." See Henry Fowler, *A Narrative of a Journey Across the Unexplored Portion of British Honduras, with a Short Sketch of the History and Resources* (Belize: Government Press, 1879), p. 25. Gibbs calls one local fish the "West Indian Salmon"; Gibbs, *British Honduras*, p. 187. Similar praise for the local brocket deer can be found in newspaper articles about local hunting: *Honduras Gazette and Commercial Advertiser* (Belize City) (December 9, 1826).

19. I have based these types on a close reading of James Tobin, ed., *Re-Made in Japan: Everyday Life and Consumer Taste in a Changing Society* (New Haven: Yale University Press, 1992). The articles in this book describe a number of ways that Japanese consumers have appropriated foreign objects, foods, and practices to make them Japanese. I do not use the full range of possibilities in this discussion.

20. Karen Judd, "Cultural Synthesis or Ethnic Struggle? Creolization in Belize," *Cimarron* 1–2 (1989): 103–118.

21. Nigel Bolland, *Colonialism and Resistance in Belize* (Belize City: Cubola Productions, 1988).

22. Michael Stone, "Backabush: Settlement on the Belmopan Periphery and the Challenge to Rural Development," in *Third Annual Studies on Belize Conference, Proceedings, Belize City, 1989*, the Society for the Promotion of Education and Research (Belize City: SPEAR, 1990), pp. 82–134.

23. Laurie Medina, "Immigration, Labor, and Government Policy: Class Conflict and Alternative Paths Towards Development," in *Independence Ten Years After, Proceedings of a Conference, Belize City, 1991*, the Society for the Promotion of Education and Research (Belize City: SPEAR, 1992), pp. 144–158; Dylan Vernon, "Belize Exodus to the United States: For Better or for Worse," in *Third Annual Studies on Belize Conference, Proceedings, Belize City, 1989*, the Society for the Promotion of Education and Research (Belize City: SPEAR, 1990), pp. 6–28.
24. On television and national identity in Belize: Wilk, "Colonial Time," 98–102.
25. Helen Critchlow, *It's Crazy, I Love It! Life in British Honduras* (New York: Exposition Press, 1968), p. 87; see also several scattered references to rice and beans in Algar Gregg, *British Honduras* (London: Her Majesty's Stationary Office, 1968).
26. Richard Pilsbury, *No Foreign Food: The American Diet in Time and Place* (Boulder, CO: Westview Press, 1998).
27. Olwig, *Global Culture*, p. 198.
28. Most of the popular guidebooks to Belize take something like this position. For an online example, see "Destination Belize," in Lonely Planet (online travel information); available at http://www.lonelyplanet.com/dest/cam/belize.htm#cult; Internet; accessed July 4, 2000. This guide states that "Belize has never really developed a national cuisine. Its cooking borrows elements from the UK, the USA, Mexico and the Caribbean."
29. "Belize: What to Eat," in Global Gourmet (online food information); available at http://www.globalgourmet.com/destinations/belize/belzwhat.html; Internet; accessed July 4, 2000.

Part Three

THE BUSINESS OF TASTE

Chapter 6

INVENTING BABY FOOD: GERBER AND THE DISCOURSE
OF INFANCY IN THE UNITED STATES

AMY BENTLEY

*T*he consumption of food is an extraordinarily social activity laden
with complex and shifting layers of meaning. Not only what we eat,
but how and why we eat, tell us much about society, history, cultural
change, and humans' views of themselves. What, when, and how we
choose to feed infants and toddlers—the notion of "baby food" as opposed
to "adult food," and whether these foods are nourishing and satisfying—
reveal how mass production, consumption, and advertising have shaped
our thinking about infancy and corresponding parenting philosophies and
practices. This essay explores the naturalization of mass-marketed baby
food through an examination of the origins, development, and early marketing of the Gerber Products Company. Specifically, it relates how in one
generation, from Gerber's beginning in the late 1920s to the 1950s' postwar
baby-boom years, mass-produced solid infant food, especially fruits and
vegetables, shifted from being an item of rarity into a rite of passage—a
normal, naturalized part of an infant's diet in the United States.

While scholars have amply researched and analyzed the shift from
breast- to bottle-feeding in the United States and elsewhere, the important
historical, cultural, and nutritional implications of solid infant food in this
change have not been adequately explored.[1] An in-depth historical examination of the subject is important, as late-twentieth-century studies show
that before the age of four months, an infant's gastrointestinal system is
ill equipped to receive anything but breast milk or its equivalent (though
there is much debate over the adequacy of formula substitutes as well).
Too early an introduction of solids can put undue stress on kidney func-
tioning. Foods displacing breast milk (solid food as well as formula) limit
the ingestion of important antibodies, enzymes, hormones, and other substances that assist in a child's optimal development. Moreover, studies

show that children who are breast-fed develop fewer bacterial and viral ill-nesses, food allergies, incidences of diarrhea, ear infections, and perhaps even cancer. Thus prevailing wisdom at the turn of the twentieth century exhorts breast-feeding to the age of twelve months—with the American Academy of Pediatrics advocating the nursing of infants to two years of age if possible—and the introduction of foods at four to six months.[2]

In the space of about a hundred years (from the mid-nineteenth to mid-twentieth centuries) normal feeding patterns of infants in the United States changed from near-exclusive provision of breast milk (whether by mother or by wet nurse) and an introduction to solids later in the infant's first year, to bottle-feeding and the introduction of solids at six weeks post-partum. These interrelated changes from breast to bottle and from late to early introduction of solids were both products of many well-known social and economic components of the late nineteenth and early twentieth cen-turies: industrialization, mass production, and advertising of the food sup-ply; changing consumption patterns; the discovery and promotion of vitamins; evolving notions of the body and health; the promotion of sci-ence as the ultimate authority; and the medicalization of childbirth and infancy, yielding the medical establishment's increased prominence and power. While mothers and health professionals alike welcomed commer-cially mass-produced baby food as a convenient, affordable way to provide more fruits and vegetables year round for American babies, the creation and marketing of Gerber baby food, which from its inception has domi-nated the U.S. market, helped spur the introduction of solid foods into babies' diets at increasingly earlier and earlier ages. Gerber baby food thus functioned as not only a supplement to but also a substitute for breast milk, playing an important role in the dramatic decline of breast-feeding in the twentieth century. To explore these issues, I will examine the dis-course of late-nineteenth- and early-twentieth-century "pre-Gerber" infant feeding patterns, detail the origins and development of Gerber baby food, and analyze early marketing campaigns in the 1930s directed toward women as both professional dietitians and mothers.

A word about sources and their interpretation: the following ideas and arguments rest largely on close readings of (among other types of data) over two dozen household and child-care advice manuals. These materi-als, as well as Gerber's advertising campaigns and corporate literature, are documents largely prescriptive in nature, and thus problematic. While they divulge much about the ideas of the "experts," they are less success-ful in helping us understand what and how women actually fed their infants: how they used the foods, what meanings women inscribed upon them, and how women received and made use of the advertising informa-tion and images. Historian Jay Mechling rightly views with skepticism any demonstratable connection between advice manuals and actual practice. Arguing that people gain most of their notions of "correct" child-rearing from their parents as well as the larger culture in which they were raised, he regards any instruction through child-care manuals as supplemental at best. "Childrearing manuals are the consequents not of childrearing values," Mechling argues, "but of childrearing manual-writing values,"[3] which is to say, the values of those people writing the manuals, embedded in the existing culture and patterns of behavior. During the period explored here, Mechling notes, the "source of advice is connected with the rise of a specialized subuniverse of knowledge, language, and power [and] communicates quite clearly that childrearing knowledge was specialized knowledge" held by a growing number of "experts," whether in home economics, nutrition, or the medical profession.[4] Thus, "to whatever extent there appears to be a sharing or at least a complementarity of these internal states across several authors," Mechling concedes, "the historian can generalize further about some sector of the belief system of a historical American society."[5]

While this belief system may not directly coincide with mothers' actual infant feeding practices, it is possible to tease out some information from the experts' publications regarding how, what, and when mothers fed their infants.[6] Fortunately, for our purposes we can use these sources of information for what they do best—to uncover a newly emerging discourse regarding infant food and feeding practices from such "experts." While the manners in which women actually did feed their infants become visible here through a limited number of primary documents, a full understanding of actual practices, a crucial part of the larger historical dynamic, must be saved mostly for another day. Nevertheless, a focused examination of the "expert" discourse becomes the first step in unfolding the very important story of women and solid infant feeding practices in the United States.

"ARTIFICIAL" INFANT FEEDING IN THE NINETEENTH CENTURY

To understand fully the effects of mass-produced baby food it is important to revisit the development of artificial infant formulas, the forerunners of mass-produced solids such as Gerber. Existing scholarship indicates that in the preindustrial Western World, 95 percent of children were breast-fed, either by their mothers or wet nurses. Breast-feeding, often called "wet-nursing" whether performed by the infant's biological mother or by another woman, contrasted with the remaining small percentage of infants who were "dry-nursed," or "brought up by hand," that is, fed mixtures of boiled flour and water or animal milk, variously called pap or panada.[7] While the earliest-known infant feeding devices date back to the second or third centuries, we know little about how they were used.[8] Cross-cultural research as well as common sense, however, indicates that the weaning process took place over a period of months or years. Preindustrial-era infants were at some point introduced to pap mixtures as a supplement to breast milk, which then gradually became a more prominent part of their diet.[9] Until the early twentieth century, however, infants *exclusively* dry-nursed or fed artificially usually failed to thrive, because of either inadequate nutrition or contaminated animal milk or water.[10]

In the mid-nineteenth century, experts admonished (and there is evidence to suggest at least that it was mainstream practice) that infants live on a liquid diet of breast milk or modified cow's milk for most of their first year.[11] Women passed around home recipes for breast milk substitutes or, for those with the means or access, found them in the published household advice manuals common to the period. A pediatrician writing in the twentieth century described the practice as "the grandmothers' aphorism, 'only milk until the eruption of molars' (12–16 months)."[12] According to one researcher, "Milk alone was believed sufficient until the baby showed signs of failure, and often the young child's diet was confined to little more than milk until he or she was two years of age. Meat was considered damaging."[13]

Advice manuals recommended that cereals or meats (not necessarily in that order) be introduced when teeth began to appear, between six and nine months of age, but only as thin gruel mixtures, beef broth, or juices. Such "foods," as they were characterized, over a century later would be constructed as "liquids." "The food for children should be light and simple," advised Mrs. Sarah Josepha Hale in 1857, "gruel alone, or mixed with cow's milk; mutton broth, or beef tea; stale bread, rusks, or biscuits, boiled in water to a proper consistence, and a little sugar added."[14] Hale recommended that weaning could take place as early as seven months but more commonly after twelve months.[15]

While mothers fed infants the "strength-producing" meats and cereals in the first year, advice manuals recommended that children not be given fruits and vegetables until two or three years of age. This was in part the result of Americans' wary attitude in general toward fruits and vegetables. Medical opinion, as well as folk practice in the United States, was still influenced by the centuries-old Galenic theories of health and disease, which dictated that eating fruit made people, especially children, susceptible to fevers.[16] Properties inherent in the fruits and vegetables were thought to cause severe diarrhea and dysentery, especially in the summer. An 1880s' newspaper illustration, for example, depicted a skeleton disguised as a fruit seller offering produce to little children, indicating that raw, unboiled fruits and vegetables led to cholera.[17] While there is no question that fruits and vegetables could cause harm, especially in such turn-of-the-century urban metropolises as New York City, with its inadequate, overloaded water and sewer systems, the actual culprit was most likely bacteria residing on the outside of the produce or contaminated water or milk that happened to be ingested, rather than anything innate in the produce itself.[18] Given the laxative effect of fruits and vegetables if consumed in excess, however, it is easy to understand how people made the assumption. Moreover, in this era before the discovery of vitamins, most people felt that fruits and vegetables provided excessive bulk and roughage, and contributed little in the way of nourishment helpful to infants.[19] Advice manuals of the mid-nineteenth century reflected while even attempting to modify this prevailing ideology. "[T]he growing creature requires food that contains the elements of the body . . . food that abounds in albumen, fibrine, gelatine, and the earthy salts," said Joseph B. Lyman and Laura E. Lyman in their 1867 guide. "[W]hat substances do we find richest in the constituents of perfect food? *Flesh, milk, eggs* and *wheat bread*."[20] However, they noted, "There is in the minds of thousands of anxious mothers a great dread of fruits of all kinds as being dangerous for the young."[21] Attempting to dispel these commonly held notions, the Lymans advised that the problem was children's consumption of fruits to excess, not the produce itself.

By the late nineteenth century, the industrialization and advertising of the food supply laid important groundwork for changing recommendations concerning infant care and feeding. Before 1900, most Americans' diets were monotonous regimes of soups, stews, bread, dairy products, fresh meat when available, salted or smoked when not, and fruits and vegetables only when seasonal unless preserved through pickling, jams, and preserves, drying, and some home canning. Improvements in stoves and kitchen devices made food preparation easier; iceboxes and refrigerators kept foods fresher; all, in many ways, made cooking a less arduous task for women—although there were most certainly trade-offs, as many scholars have pointed out. Canned goods, especially canned produce, though commonly available in the late 1800s, were too expensive for most. By the 1920s, however, manufacturers produced canned goods in sufficient quantity to present more affordable prices, allowing Americans to consume (among other things) more fruits and vegetables year-round. With this industrialization of the food supply, Americans' diets became more varied and their nutrition subsequently improved, though it can be argued that canned goods and other processed foods diminished taste and nutrients, leading to Americans' acclimation to salt and sugar in heavy quantities.[22] To sell these mass-produced items, major enterprises engaged the proliferating advertising firms to create increasingly sophisticated appeals. The increased number and circulation of magazines and newspapers and the growth in population and literacy rates ensured audiences for corporate advertising.[23]

Moreover, *fin de siècle* Americans turned increasingly to science as the ultimate authority, including in matters of health and the human life cycle.[24] An effect of this was the increased stature, whether self-generated or not, of the medical community. Doctors supplanted midwives in delivering babies, who now entered the world more often in hospitals than in homes. Employing wet nurses as an alternative to mothers' breast-feeding, a common practice among wealthier women, became less common as wet-nursing, most often performed by poor women, immigrants, and women of color, became more stigmatized, and as safer non-breast-milk alternatives became available.[25] Instead, during this "chemical period" in infant feeding, medical authorities took charge, partially by devising complicated "percentage" formulas only they could administer as breast milk replacements.[26] As Rima Apple and others have amply demonstrated, the result was the medicalization of motherhood. Profoundly influenced by prevailing behaviorist theories of psychology, authorities advised that parenting instincts and common sense must take a backseat to science. Infants were to be fed on strict schedules, for example, and were not to be picked up when crying, which would only reward their negative behavior, experts told women.[27]

Doctors and child-care experts still considered breast-feeding best if a woman's breast milk supply was adequate, no doubt in part because of the high infant mortality rates occurring in the burgeoning cities that had limited access to fresh, clean cow's milk. Marion Mills Miller in 1910 advocated that "no other milk, however skillfully modulated, no 'infant's food,' however scientifically prepared," could fully replace mother's milk.[28] In their 1920 manual, Martha Van Rensselaer, Flora Rose, and Helen Cannon, eminent Cornell University home economists, gave recipes for artificial formula but called it "the next best thing" if a "baby cannot be fed by its own mother."[29]

As the medicalization of motherhood developed, child specialists offered more and more reasons why breast-feeding was inadequate. Improved technology helped artificial formulas and cow's milk to become regarded as safer and more healthful alternatives for infants. Optimistic faith in science required little reasoning about why formula feeding was equal to—if not better than—breast milk. Formula feeding was easier for doctors to measure and regulate, allowing them to tinker with the makeup of artificial formulas when necessary. Anxious mothers, becoming less and less confident of their parenting abilities and common sense, wanted what was best for baby and voluntarily relinquished their authority. Hospital deliveries that whisked babies away to the nursery fostered a sterile and awkward climate for mother-infant bonding and discouraged breast-feeding. Taking their cues from the medical community, home economics experts recommended not only that an infant's mouth be swabbed and rinsed with fresh water after every feeding, but that a woman's breast be cleaned with a boric acid solution before and after nursing as well.[30]

Thus an unintended consequence of the medicalization of motherhood was the decline of breast-feeding. Mothers became more and more convinced that they did not have sufficient milk to nurse their newborns. Although most certainly some women could not physically breast-feed, and the new mothers who performed paid employment outside the home found it logistically difficult to do so, it is not surprising that around the turn of the century the numbers of women breast-feeding their infants declined (though they would still remain relatively high through the 1930s when compared to the numbers just two decades later).[31] No doubt many simply did not want the bother of nursing their infants. Wealthier women, who had always breast-fed less often than other women, now turned to using artificial formulas instead of employing wet nurses. Middle-class women followed suit, with working-class women and women of color gradually ceasing to breast-feed accordingly.[32]

By the late 1880s several brands of "proprietary foods," mass-produced, mostly grain mixtures to be added to milk or water—the forerunners of today's infant formulas—appeared on the market, including Leibeg's Food; Nestle's Milk Food; Carnrick's Soluble Food; Eskay's Albumenized Food; Imperial Granum; Wells, Richardson, and Company's Lactated Food; Wagner's Infant Food; Mellin's Food; as well as Borden's Eagle Brand condensed milk.[33] Most included cereal grains as part of their "formulas," some included dried cow's milk as well, but nearly all designated their products as "food" rather than "liquid," as formulas later were characterized. Brightly colored and elaborately etched trade cards, the popular turn-of-the-century advertising medium which women and children in particular delighted in collecting and trading, illustrate this demarcation of infant formula as food. Advertising slogans included: "Nestle's Milk Food: Baby's Friend"; "Imperial Granum: The Incomparable Food for the Growth and Protection of Infants and Children"; "Wells, Richardson, and Company's Lactated Food: A Scientific Food for Infants and Invalids"; "Wagner's Infant Food: Infants and Children fed on Wagner's Infant Food are remarkable for muscular strength, firmness of flesh, and a lively and intelligent appearance"; and "Mellin's Food for Infants and Invalids: The only perfect substitute for Mother's Milk."[34]

Home economists and nutritionists, women in these newly emerging fields that employed the latest scientific discoveries about food and nutrition, did not much like proprietary, or patent, foods. "They cannot compete successfully with carefully made milk mixtures in substitute or artificial feeding," advised Flora Rose of Cornell University's recently established Home Economics Department:

> Perhaps the strongest case against the patent foods is their lack of the food-stuff known as mineral matter or salts, which is so essential to healthy growth and development. Many cases of malnutrition result directly from the use of such of these foods as are deficient in fat and mineral matter. A common ailment among babies thus fed is rickets, an ailment that is serious and may be lasting in its effects.[35]

What Rose called "mineral salts" were indeed important. Confirming what many chemists and nutritionists suspected, within the next decade researchers discovered vitamins in foods, including vitamin D, which prevents rickets. Some evidence indicates that most mothers, at least in rural areas, did not feed their infants mass-produced proprietary foods. While

Cornell University home economics students in the 1920s added a small amount of Mellin's Food to their month-old charges' formula, a 1933 study of over seven hundred infants in upstate New York indicated that only 6 percent of mothers had ever fed their babies patent foods, half using brands which were to be mixed with milk and half those to be mixed with water; most stuck to the well-known and trusted Holt's formula of cow's milk diluted with water and with sugar added.[36] Still, the increasing availability and promotion of such products, along with the rise in safer, cleaner cow's milk thanks to certification programs and pasteurization, contributed to the number of women who bottle-fed their infants.

It makes sense that manufacturers and advertisers constructed these liquid formulas as "solid" rather than "liquid." This was the infant "food" of the time, after all, the nourishment on which babies survived, as there was not yet a tradition of feeding infants under nine months real solids, especially fruits and vegetables. While a very small supply of canned fruits and vegetables for infants was available, these were sold at apothecaries and used as medicine. They were clearly not designed for everyday use.[37] Without a mass-produced baby food such as Gerber (or Heinz or Beech-Nut) there was no solid commodity known as "food" with which to contrast the infant formula, the second generation (such as Nestle's Lactogen) of which was being developed in the 1920s.[38] As parents and doctors became more acclimated to artificial infant formulas, however, it was only a small step to the earlier and earlier introduction of solid foods. In just a few short decades, authorities' opinions about the subject changed dramatically.

WOMEN AND INFANT FEEDING IN THE PRE-GERBER TWENTIETH CENTURY

The first three decades of the twentieth century, a time characterized by the arrival of the culture of modernity, were a period of great change not only for women but also in the realms of economics, politics, the arts, science, and social and religious thought. In the 1910s and 1920s, still before Gerber's era, infant feeding practices had begun to change noticeably, most prominently in the larger role fruits and vegetables were to have in an infant's diet. Still, experts recommended a relatively late introduction of solids, and grassroots evidence indicates that most mothers still began their infants on solids at relatively later ages, after six months of age or older.

During these decades scientists had begun to identify as "vitamines" (the spelling was later modified) the specific nutrients in foods that were previously called "mineral salts." Vitamins, scientists learned, existed not only in meat, grains, and dairy products, foods they had always considered vital to nourishment and growth, but also in fruits and vegetables, which had previously been regarded as benign at best and as suspicious by many, although several nineteenth-century groups did espouse the virtues of a vegetarian diet.[39] The promotion of fruits and vegetables as vital to human growth and nourishment was heightened during the Great War, as the federal government found it difficult to recruit able-bodied young men and maintain their health while in the service. Government officials and military physicians immediately employed and propagated the new knowledge of vitamins to help solve this problem of recruits' poor health.[40] By the 1920s, home economists and dietitians were introducing Americans to the notion of vitamins and advising them not only to consume more fruits and vegetables themselves, but also to feed more such foods to their children as well.

Early-twentieth-century household advice manuals, though at times contradictory, reveal this increased emphasis on fruits and vegetables while still recommending the introduction of solids in the second half of the infant's first year. A 1914 advice manual, with the delightfully straightforward title, *How to Cook and Why*, by Elizabeth Condit and Jessie A. Long, for the first time enthusiastically endorsed fruits and vegetables specifically for their "mineral matter." "As in all questions of feeding," related the authors, "it is the food given the children which is of the greatest importance. Serious results follow in the unhealthy development of their bodies when their food lacks mineral matter and the acids found in fruits."[41] They recommended introducing a barley-flour-and-water mixture and strained, diluted orange juice at between six and nine months of age, but still did not advocate the introduction of solids until between nine and twelve months. Cornell's Flora Rose recognized the importance of vitamins, referring to them as "fat-soluble" and "water-soluble growth-promoting substances."[42]

In 1928, on the eve of Gerber baby food's introduction, Carlotta C. Greer, in her *Foods and Home Making*, gave both vitamins and vegetables a prominent place in advice for infant feeding. Experts advocated orange juice for infants, Greer informed, "because it contains vitamins and minerals."[43] "Scientists working on the effect of food on the body are proving that fresh vegetables are needed to make us healthy."[44] "Both babies that are fed on mother's milk and those that are fed on modified cow's milk should have certain food other than milk," Greer advised, although "the young baby must not be given solid foods."[45] Greer recommended a teaspoonful of orange juice introduced at three weeks of age, cereals at five to six months, vegetables at six months, toast or zwieback at seven months, and egg yolk at twelve months.[46] While she advocated the introduction of certain foods, fruits, and vegetables much earlier than previous advice givers, she still recommended the relatively later introduction of cereals and meat (the latter which Greer did not recommend during the first year at all). Indeed, while some well-known authorities in the 1920s advocated that a one-year-old should consume a diet almost entirely of liquids—whole milk or whole milk with a cereal dilutant, orange juice, and perhaps simple cereal gruels and beef juices—increasingly these recommendations were viewed as "conservative" or "old-fashioned." More usually experts advocated a diet similar to Greer's: the early introduction of orange juice and cod-liver oil, and solids, specifically egg yolk and cereal, at five to six months of age.[47]

Grassroots evidence—what and how women were actually feeding their babies in the pre-Gerber decades of the twentieth century—seems to indicate that while some women no doubt introduced solids at an early age, the mainstream consensus and practice was not to rush their introduction, especially fruits and vegetables. For example, a collection of letters written in the 1910s to Cornell Home Economics Department professor Martha Van Rensselaer reveals glimpses of both early and later introduction of solids. The letters were written mostly in response to Flora Rose's *The Care and Feeding of Children* series of pamphlets. The pamphlets, part of the Cornell Farmers' Wives Reading Courses (later called the Cornell Study Clubs), contained study questions which women were to fill out and send back to the home economics department. While most of the letter writers praise the courses and the information, and some are testimonials to the good advice contained in the pamphlets, a few take stern issue with the information.[48]

Mr. W. J. Gilchrist's January 30, 1911, letter, for example, indicates that he and his wife followed Flora Rose's advice to breast-feed exclusively until at least nine months: "We have now a fine healthy child of 9 months. No little credit is due to the information contained in the above mentioned tract. As the baby is about to start on artificial foods, would you kindly inform me where we can procure part 2 of [*The Care and Feeding of Children*]?" Another 1911 letter from a German immigrant whose English is self-taught reveals the opposite.[49] "Dear Miss Van Rensselear," begins Mrs. Marie Christ. "I [raised] 6 babies myself and have got them all. 3 strong boys, and 2 girls, one girl got drowned, 7 years old." Responding to the study question "Is it as common as it used to be for mothers to nurse their infants?" Christ replied, "I think no and these is lots of reasons for it":

> Some have to work to hard, and that was my reason, because I could not nurse a one. Some are to[o] [weak] in their whole system and some do not want the bother. . . . I think there is not hardly a one among thousands in the european country who thinks that just the nursing of the mother should be enough after a babie is 3 months old, and some start earlyer than that, to feed them something besides the nursing. The[y] look at they nursing just as we do, to the tea and coffee given to a five year old one. Nobody would think that would be enough for a whole meal. The[y] all feed them something besides the nursing, thousands of mothers just simple[y] cook a porridge from half watter, half milk and sugar and god wreath flour. The older the[y] get, the less water the[y] put in. I know babies and my oldest boy never got a drop of water after he was 4 months old.

"What the american babies needs," Christ concluded, "is more nourishing food, less [waking], less candy, and cookies, and [cakes], and a little toughening."[50]

While the letters indicate that women introduced solids to their infants at various ages, a 1933 Cornell study (still in the early years of mass-produced baby food) of the feeding practices of over seven hundred infants in upstate New York revealed on average the late introduction of solids. While sixty percent of infants were fed orange juice during their first three months and infants received cod-liver oil at 5.2 months on average, the average age at which solids were introduced included: cereal at 7.5 months; vegetables at 9.4 months; fruit at 8.1 months; egg at 10 months; meat, 11.6 months; and fish, 12.1 months—much later than the practices that occurred only a couple of decades later.[51]

GERBER: CREATION NARRATIVES AND ICON

In the late 1920s, with changing attitudes toward fruits and vegetables and the discovery and promotion of vitamins, the market was ripe for the introduction of industrialized canned food for babies, especially produce, and Gerber stepped up to fill the niche. According to company legend, a narrative prominently featured in late-1990s Gerber public relations, the Gerber Products Company grew not out of a corporate-driven search to develop a new product and generate a consuming public, but out of the genuine need and inventiveness of a mother trying to prepare mashed peas for her seven-month-old child. Those canned fruits and vegetables for infants previously brought to market were expensive, manufactured in limited quantities, and available only at drugstores. Now that fruits and vegetables were a recommended part of a six-to-twelve-month-old's diet, women largely cooked and strained fruits and vegetables for their toddlers, an often onerous process. Thus, in the summer of 1927, Mrs. Dan Gerber, wife of the Fremont Canning Company's owner Dan Gerber, "following the advice of a pediatrician," we are told, was trying to strain peas for her infant daughter. Finding the job tedious and time-consuming, she asked her husband to try his hand at the task. According to the company history, "After watching him make several attempts, she pointed out that the work could be easily done at the Fremont Canning Company, where the Gerber family produced a line of canned fruits and vegetables. Daniel Gerber, covered in strained peas, thought his wife had a good point." From this, we are told, came the idea to market strained vegetables and fruits along with the company's regular line of canned produce. By late 1928, strained peas, prunes, carrots, spinach, and beef vegetable soup were ready for the national market.[52]

We do not know whether this creation narrative is "true," especially since in its 1930s advertising Gerber related a very different version (discussed later). However, the facts could most certainly be accurate. Since women at the time performed most of the work surrounding child-rearing, it makes sense that one mother, frustrated at the time it took and messes it created to prepare the now-vital fruits and vegetables for infants, would seek time- and labor-saving methods. That the husband of "Mrs. Dan Gerber"—we never learn *her* given name—processed canned fruits and vegetables already makes it more plausible. Whether accurate or not, the story creates a compelling, personalized portrait of the beginnings of Gerber—a homey, "authentic" happening far removed from the cacophony of noise and the mire of produce by-products of the industrial canning factory. The story of a woman's ingenuity transforming child-rearing in the United States enhances the purity and trustworthiness of the product, a key factor to Gerber's success, and also mutes the profit motive of the company.

The new baby food products were so successful that within a matter of years the Fremont Canning Company changed its name to the Gerber Products Company, and abandoned its line of regular vegetables to become the exclusive makers of baby foods. Part of the canned goods industry, which in general experienced solid growth during the Depression years, Gerber baby food did extremely well.[53] First producing pureed vegetables and fruits (the process was termed "strained " at the time), it soon added a line of cereals and within a few years introduced chopped produce and dinner combinations for older toddlers. While in 1930 the company produced 842,000 cans of baby food, by 1931 the number had risen to 1,311,500 cans; one year later, in 1932, Gerber manufactured 2,259,818 cans of baby food.[54] Despite competitors' quick development of their own mass-produced strained baby foods—only one "drugstore" baby food, Clapp's, began selling in the supermarkets, while by 1935 Gerber's biggest competitors, Beech-Nut, Heinz, and Libby's, had entered the baby food market—Gerber managed to maintain its dominance of this new market.[55]

Evidently Gerber had hit a chord with consumers, mothers, and health professionals. Conditions were such that commercially canned baby food provided mass quantities of preprepared strained fruits and vegetables to a public primed to accept them: canned goods were becoming more affordable and familiar to more Americans; advertising was hitting its stride; fruits and vegetables were more commonly recommended for infants; and doctors and health professionals were becoming more and more involved in (and controlling of) infant health and everyday care. Women at home full-time or part of the considerable number of working mothers—employed as domestics, factory workers, seamstresses, teachers, secretaries, clerks, or telephone operators—no doubt embraced and benefited from already-prepared solid infant food. Moreover, Gerber baby food was not the only new phenomenon emerging at the time that significantly altered child-rearing. Commercial diaper services, more homes wired for electricity, washing machines, refrigerators, and other innovations of technology in the home altered women's work in general as well as child care in particular.[56]

Few Americans today are unfamiliar with the winsome, compelling Gerber baby who has graced the labeling and advertising of the Gerber Products Company since the early 1930s. Indeed, since its first full-scale production and marketing of commercially canned solid baby food, Gerber has dominated such competitors as Clapp's, Stokeley, Libby, Heinz, and

Beech-Nut in U.S. market share.[57] The Gerber name is synonymous with baby food, and the icon of the Gerber baby has traditionally symbolized quality and trustworthiness (so much so that a 1998 survey found Gerber to have the highest consumer loyalty of any commercial brand in the United States).[58] In 1928 the Fremont Canning Company solicited illustrations of a baby face for the advertising campaign to introduce its newly developed baby food. Dorothy Hope Smith, an artist who specialized in drawing children, submitted a simple, unfinished, charcoal sketch, indicating she could finish the sketch if it were accepted. Again, according to the company narrative, Gerber executives were so taken with the simple line drawing of an infant's head that they acquired it as it was. The illustration proved so popular that Gerber adopted it as its official trademark in 1931, and offered consumers copies for 10 cents.[59]

THE NATURALIZATION OF GERBER: DECLINE OF BREAST-FEEDING, EARLIER INTRODUCTION OF SOLIDS

In the 1920s, food corporations and pharmaceutical companies developed such second-generation commercial infant formulas as Nestle's Lactogen and S.M.A. These formulas (many of which were packaged without directions, making it necessary for a woman to consult a pediatrician in order to use them), as well as the several brands of canned evaporated milk that were popular breast milk substitutes, helped augment the dramatic decline in the number of women breast-feeding their infants, as well as the duration of breast-feeding. By the 1950s, the vast majority of mothers were bypassing nursing altogether and starting out their infants on mass-produced formula.[60] As evidence of the completeness of this transformation, it was during the 1950s that "artificial food" and "proprietary food," terms commonly used in all child-care and pediatians' manuals to refer to infant formula, were dropped, indicating that the use of such breast milk substitutes was now entrenched, if not the norm.[61]

During approximately the same time period, the average age at which infants were first fed fruits and vegetables decreased dramatically. In the late 1920s, just as Gerber began its national advertising and distribution of canned baby foods, prevailing wisdom advocated introducing strained fruits and vegetables at around seven months. By the next decade, however, pediatricians advocated the introduction of fruits and vegetables at between four to six months of age. Adhering to the "if a little is good, a lot must be better" school of thought, by the 1950s the average age at which doctors recommended these foods be first fed to infants was four to six weeks, with some doctors advocating—and women feeding—infants strained cereals and vegetables within days of birth.[62] While there is not necessarily a causal connection between the decline of breast-feeding and the earlier introduction of solid baby food, it makes sense that the widespread acceptance of artificial formulas acclimated mothers and doctors alike to infants' ingestion of non-breast-milk substances. Thus it may have felt more comfortable and seemed more customary to introduce solid baby food into infants' diets at earlier and earlier ages. As this early introduction of solids became standard advice and practice, Gerber baby food (as well as other brands) functioned not only as a supplement to but as a substitute for breast milk.[63]

One way of documenting the emergence of the idea of introducing solids at such early ages is by turning to early advertising campaigns of the 1930s. Shortly after the Fremont Canning Company began to manufacture its baby food, it began to advertise. Mass-producing any industrial product, especially in the Great Depression of the 1930s, as consumer purchasing slowed to a minimum, meant establishing and expanding a steady market of buyers by acquainting the public with products through advertising campaigns. Gerber, like other manufacturers of new products, found it necessary not only to educate and persuade the public to feel comfortable enough to buy and use baby food, but to acclimate and familiarize people with the manner in which baby food was packaged and presented—the metal cans as well as the labeling. Since fully automated canning factories had been in operation for only a relatively short time, allowing foodstuffs to be canned and sold to consumers for reasonable prices, Americans still held lingering suspicious about the quality of canned goods. Though it had been two decades since Congress had passed the Pure Food and Drug Law, some well remembered the days of adulterated and spoiled foods concealed by opaque packaging.[64] Further, Americans in the first part of the twentieth century were still becoming acquainted with mass advertising designed to create new needs where none had existed before, or to promote products, such as Gerber baby food, which responded to and allowed for a more fast-paced life brought on by technological innovation.[65] With the mass production and advertising of goods, memorable packaging and branding became an essential part of the product, "an integral part of the commodity itself."[66] The Gerber baby from early on became just that: an indivisible part of the commodity, allowing the Gerber Products Company to bypass such traditional middlemen as grocers and through advertising to appeal directly to women as dieticians or as mothers.

By playing on parents', especially mothers', guilt, presenting medical doctors as the ultimate baby experts, and positing the uncontested assumption that commercially prepared foods are superior to those cooked at home, Gerber advertising in the 1930s successfully imbued its products with qualities of exceptional purity and wholesomeness, convenience and modernity, and scientific efficiency. While by no means an exhaustive study of Gerber promotion pitches, a survey of 1930s' issues of the *Journal of the American Dietetic Association* and the *Ladies Home Journal* helps reveal how Gerber quickly undertook an ambitious national campaign to convert health professionals and consumers to its baby foods. In its earliest years of advertising, Gerber focused on helping consumers and dieticians become comfortable with the idea of using canned goods in general and Gerber products in particular, and persuading women that it was in their best interest, and in their babies' interest, to use Gerber baby foods.

CONVINCING THE DIETICIANS

In the late 1920s and well into the 1930s Gerber placed full-page advertisements in each monthly issue of the *Journal of the American Dietetics Association*, the official publication of the American Dietetics Association (ADA). The ADA, founded in 1917, was the professional organization for the fast-growing, overwhelmingly female field of dietetics and nutrition. Whereas there were 660 ADA members in 1925, for example, by 1938 the number had grown to 3,800. The ADA in the 1920s and 1930s became influential in coordinating and promoting dietary policy and guidelines for optimal health and nutrition.[67] Promoting Gerber baby food as scientifically prepared and thus free of contaminants, vitamin-filled, healthy and wholesome food for infants was clearly the primary goal of the company's ADA journal advertising. "Care in every detail makes the Gerber products better for Baby," began one 1932 advertisement.[68] Two 1934 advertisements, each complete with photos of workers dressed in white operating sparkling clean machinery, began respectively, "Oxygen is excluded in the Gerber straining process [to conserve vitamins],"[69] and "Careful sorting—rigid inspection, another reason why Gerber's are better for Baby."[70] In the same issues the American Canning Company ran regular advertisements designed to resemble scholarly articles on the safety and healthfulness of canned foods. "The Canning Procedure,"[71] "Vitamins in Canned Foods: Vitamin A,"[72] and "Canned Foods for Infant and Early Child Feeding"[73] were three such ads, each providing scientific information on the benefits of canned foods. Such ads, along with the Gerber ads, were attempting to combat suspicion toward canned foods.

While many middle-class women in the United States were using commercially canned goods with some regularity by this time, food professionals in particular still held some justifiable suspicion as to whether canned produce was nutritious and safe as well as fresh. In what would become standard practice, some 1930s ADA journal issues also included bona fide research, funded by Gerber, touting the safety, healthiness, and full vitamin content of canned baby foods. Flora Manning, in the Division of Home Economics at Michigan State College, published two such articles in the 1930s, "Canned Strained Vegetables as Sources of Vitamin A," and "Further Studies of the Content of Vitamins A and B in Canned Strained Vegetables."[74] In both Manning found a minimal difference between the vitamin content of (Gerber) canned, strained vegetables and (noncanned) fresh (a slightly lower vitamin content in the former), but whether intentionally or not, minimized this difference through opaque, indirect language.

Another set of Gerber ADA journal advertisements situated dieticians as the intermediary between women and their children's doctors. Revealing its faith in the power of persuasion through advertising, ads began with such openings as "Gerber advertises . . . so that mothers will cooperate with you";[75] "Yes, Doctor, we do talk to your patients . . . and we tell them facts which help you and help us";[76] and "Thanks, Doctor, this helps me carry out your instructions."[77] The copy situated the reader, as female dietician, conversing with the (male) medical doctor about how to persuade women to feed their children Gerber baby food. The ads and articles functioned to advance the idea that Gerber's canned fruits and vegetables for baby are just as nutritious as fresh as home prepared foods and even more appropriate since they are so scientifically prepared.

CONVINCING THE MOTHERS

Like many new mass-produced and advertised products in the early twentieth century, Gerber's first advertising campaign in 1929 focused on selling its products directly to women, since many grocers did not carry Gerber baby foods.[78] The ads were placed in such leading women's magazines as *Ladies Home Journal*, subscribed to by over a million women.[79] In what was common practice at the time, the advertisement urged women to send in one dollar for a set of Gerber foods, and asked them to provide the name of their grocer, whom Gerber would then persuade to carry their products. Doctors, however, could request the products free of charge. Emphasizing its products as scientifically prepared and thus trustworthy, Gerber informed women that its foods "Provid[ed] in a scientific, wholesome manner . . . the important vegetable supplement to baby's milk diet." It also focused on the products' ability to impart to women freedom and mobility, a notably modern concept: "[T]he new Gerber Products make Mother and Baby alike independent of the kitchen's restrictions. Baby can really travel now."[80]

Later advertising focused on this theme of freedom for mother and baby. Not only did Gerber provide freedom from kitchen drudgery, but ads asserted that preparing baby foods by hand was essentially a disservice to the woman herself, her baby, and her husband. "For Baby's Sake, Stay Out of the Kitchen!" read the headline of one 1933 advertisement. "It isn't fair to baby—really—to spend long hours in the kitchen. . . . For baby's sake and for your own—learn what doctors tell young mothers just like you."[81] Moreover, the ads argued that women could not provide the same quality no matter how hard they tried: "You can't, with ordinary home equipment, prepare vegetables as safe, as rich in natural food values, as reliably uniform as ready-to-serve Gerber products!"[82] The opening of another Gerber ad read, "Square Meals for Baby . . . and better for him than vegetables you could prepare yourself with ten times the work!" "Don't serve Gerber's for your sake," the ad went on, "*serve them for Baby's sake!*" "They're the finest vegetables Baby can eat—and Baby deserves the best!"[83]

Most strikingly, the advertisements focused on a woman's relationship with her husband. An early Gerber ad in *Ladies Home Journal* opened with a photo of a concerned-looking man's face. Surrounding the male face was the text: "To puzzled fathers of rather young children. If you've had to exchange a charming wife for a tired mother who spends endless hours in the kitchen dutifully scraping, stewing and straining vegetables for your child—you'll be glad to read this story." It continued with a version of the Gerber creation story different from the late-twentieth-century one mentioned earlier, one that focused on a male persona entirely. "Five years ago, Mr. Dan Gerber faced the same situation, and knowing a great deal about vegetables he set out to solve this problem."[84] Although an accompanying photo depicted a woman feeding a baby identified once more as "Mrs. Dan Gerber," there was no mention whatsoever of her involvement in the creation. The narrative implied that Dan Gerber's frustration and dissatisfaction (at "having to exchange" his once-charming wife for a now-tired and haggard-looking spouse) led to Gerber baby food being invented. Although the advertisement carried a masculine persona, it was clearly designed for women's consumption, appearing as almost an ominous warning to mothers of small children. Gerber advertising as a whole appeared aimed not only at increasing women's confidence in the wholesomeness of the product but also at reducing their confidence in their ability to care for their infants—and also that hardworking provider—without the help of these experts and these products.

In addition, both sets of advertising indirectly or directly advocated the earlier and earlier introduction of these foods. Many ads referred to the use of solids at three months or earlier. Under the above mentioned photo of "Mrs. Dan Gerber" and her daughter Paula, for example, the caption notes that "Paula began to eat Gerber Strained Cereal at 3 months, and had her first Gerber's Strained Vegetables at 3 1/2 months" (again, this is in contrast to the 1990s creation story that mentions that the mother is feeding peas to her "seven-month-old," an age no doubt assigned in light of our contemporary standards of introducing fruits and vegetables only after four to six months of age).[85] Gerber's competitors contributed to this trend as well. A 1937 ad for Clapp's baby food included photos of three-month-old baby John Curlett being fed his Clapp's Baby Cereal. "At 4 months," the copy informed women, "he'll be introduced to all of Clapp's Strained Vegetables." The final photo showed John at eleven months of age, "flourish[ing]" because of his Clapp's diet.[86] The most blatant ad, however, was a 1938 Libby's baby food ad picturing a baby barely able to hold up its head. The caption reads: "Hurry, Mother, it's Libby time! Tiny babies love the vegetables that Libby prepares so carefully."[87]

Not only did specific ad copy and photographs encourage the notion that infants under four months need solid food, but the icon of the Gerber Baby itself contributed. The drawing that graces every Gerber product and advertisement since 1931 looks, according to those nongovernmental agencies monitoring the World Health Organization International Code of Marketing of Breastmilk Substitutes, younger than the six months WHO guidelines deem the appropriate age at which infants should begin receiving solids.[88] The Gerber baby itself, then, gave (and gives) the implicit impression that babies this young should be eating solid foods.[89]

In conclusion, it makes sense that Gerber and other baby food manufacturers would advocate the early introduction of their foods. They sought to create and expand the market share of this new product that fitted right into a society increasingly shaped by technology and modernity. Once the idea of "baby food" in general, and Gerber baby food in particular, became a common part of American infant feeding practices, it is not hard to see how mothers and health and nutrition experts could assume that when it came to fruits and vegetables, the more the better and (devoid of substantial scientific research indicating otherwise) the earlier the better. By 1960, one doctor felt compelled to argue that the medical community's allowance/approval of early solids was neither due to infant food companies seeking to expand market share nor to pushy mothers seeking permission to feed their newborns solids:

> The concept that the [infant food] manufacturers . . . should have been influential in formulating the opinions or feeding customs of modern physicians is highly improbable. . . . Equally specious is the argument that many physicians are influenced by the pressures, hopes, or ambitions of the mothers in competing with their neighbor's babies.[90]

Clearly, this doctor assumed that the "fault" lay with mothers. Mothers or not, it would take a later generation of mothers and health professionals to question significantly this prevailing wisdom—which had gained credence during the mid-twentieth century—that while the early introduction of solids might not necessarily help infants, neither would it harm them.

NOTES

1. Some of the scholarship on breast- to bottle-feeding include Rima Apple, *Mothers and Medicine: A Social History of Infant Feeding, 1890–1950* (Madison: University of Wisconsin Press, 1987); Penny van Esterik, *Beyond the Breast-Bottle Controversy* (Rutgers University Press, 1989); Valerie Fildes, *Breasts, Bottles, and Babies: A History of Infant Feeding* (Edinburgh: Edinburgh University Press, 1986); Janet Golden, *A Social History of Wet Nursing in America: From Breast to Bottle* (Cambridge: Cambridge University Press, 1996); Patricia Stuart-Macadam and Katherine A. Dettwyler, eds., *Breastfeeding: Biocultural Perspectives* (New York: Aldine de Gruyter, 1995); Marilyn Yalom, *A History of the Breast* (New York: Alfred A. Knopf, 1997); Meredith F. Small, *Our Babies, Ourselves: How Biology and Culture Shape the Way We Parent* (New York: Anchor Books, 1998); Linda M. Blum, *At the Breast: Ideologies of Breastfeeding and Motherhood in the Contemporary United States* (Boston: Beacon Press, 1999).
2. Jane E. Brody, "Breast Is Best for Babies, But Sometimes Mom Needs Help," *New York Times* (March 30, 1999); Elizabeth Cohen, "New Two-Year Breast-Feeding Guideline Irks Busy NYC Moms," *New York Post* (October 1, 1998): 29; Frances J. Rohr and Judith A. Lothian, "Feeding Throughout the First Year of Life," in Howard and Winter, eds., *Nutrition and Feeding of Infant and Toddlers* (Boston: Little, Brown, and Co., 1984), pp.

65–130; Lewis A. Parness, ed., *Pediatric Nutrition Handbook,* 3rd ed. (Elk Grove Village, IL: American Academy of Pediatrics, 1993). See also Michael C. Latham, "Breast Feeding Reduces Morbidity," *British Medical Journal* (May 15, 1999): 1303–1304; Michael C. Latham, "Breastfeeding—A Human Rights Issue?" *International Journal of Children's Rights* 18:56, v. 6 (1998): 1–21.

3. Jay E. Mechling, "Advice to Historians on Advice to Mothers," *Journal of Social History,* 9, 1 (Fall 1975): 55.

4. Mechling, "Advice to Historians," 55.

5. Mechling, "Advice to Historians," 56.

6. And further, I might disagree a little with Mechling and argue that, at least in the post–World War II era, most new middle-class parents are far enough removed from extended family, and thus inexperienced enough with infants (especially when it comes to the post-1970s return to breast-feeding) that the manuals do reflect practice more than they might otherwise. Many first-time middle-class parents would report that they purchase such texts as the popular *What to Expect* books and regard them as holy writ.

7. Fred T. Sai, "The Infant Food Industry as a Partner in Health," in Frank Falkner, ed., *Infant and Child Nutrition Worldwide: Issues and Perspectives* (Boca Raton: CRC Press, 1991), p. 247.

8. Valerie Fildes, "The Culture and Biology of Breastfeeding," in Patricia Stuart-Macadam and Katherine A. Dettwyler, eds., *Breastfeeding: Biocultural Perspectives* (New York: Aldine de Gruyter, 1995), pp. 101–126; Thomas E. Cone, Jr., "Infant Feeding: A Historical Perspective," in Howard and Winter, eds., *Nutrition and Feeding of Infant and Toddlers* (Boston: Little, Brown, and Company, 1984), 1–7. In fact, until the late eighteenth century, dry-nursed infants were more likely to be fed thin gruel mixtures, as using animal milk was regarded with some suspicion.

9. Van Esterick, *Beyond the Breast-Bottle,* chap. 5, esp. pp. 172–173; see also Jun Jing, "Introduction: Food, Children, and Social Change in Contemporary China," in *Feeding China's Little Emperors* (Stanford: Stanford University Press, 2000), p. 9.

10. Catherine E. Beecher and Harriet Beecher Stowe, *The American Woman's Home Companion* (New York: J. B. Ford and Company, 1869), p. 268. "Artifical" is the term in the literature used for foods other than breast milk given to infants. This includes prepared liquid formulas and "beikost," a term meaning any nonmilk food. See Sara A. Quandt, "The Effect of Beikost on the Diet of Breast-Fed Infants," *Journal of the American Dietetic Association* 84 (1984): 47–51; see also S. J. Fomon, *Infant Nutrition,* 2nd. ed. (Philadelphia: W. B. Saunders, Co., 1974); Felisa J. Bracken, "Infant Feeding in the American Colonies," *Journal of the American Dietetic Association* (1953): 1–10.

11. Interestingly, not until the nineteenth century did cow's milk, usually diluted with water and sweetened with sugar, become the breast milk substitute of choice. See Alice L. Wood, "The History of Artificial Feeding of Infants," *Journal of the American Dietetic Association* (1955): 21–29.

12. Herman Frederic Meyer, *Infant Foods and Feeding Practice* (Springfield, IL: C. C. Thomas, 1952), 143.

13. Wood, "History of Artificial Feeding," 24.

14. Mrs. Sarah Josepha Hale, *Mrs. Hale's Receipts for the Million* (Philadelphia: T. B. Peterson and Brothers, 1857), p. 219.

15. Hale, *Mrs. Hale's Receipts,* p. 220.

16. Patricia M. Tice, *Gardening in America, 1830–1910* (Rochester, NY: The Strong Museum, 1984), pp. 53–54; Sidney Mintz, *Sweetness and Power: The Place of Sugar in Modern History* (New York: Viking, 1985), pp. 75–76; J. C. Drummond and Anne Wilbraham, *The Englishman's Food: A History of Five Centuries of the English Diet* (London: Pimlico, 1939, 1991), p. 68; Wood, "History of Artificial Feeding," 22.

17. Tice, *Gardening in America,* pp. 53–54.

18. See, for example, Edwin G. Burrows and Mike Wallace, *Gotham: A History of New York to 1898* (Oxford University Press, 1999), ch. 67; Cone, "Infant Feeding," 12.

19. Cone, "Infant Feeding," 14; Suzanne F. Adams, "Use of Vegetables in Infant Feeding through the Ages," *Journal of the American Dietetic Association,* 35 (July 1959): 692–703.

20. Joseph B. Lyman and Laura E. Lyman, *The Philosophy of House-Keeping: A Scientific and Practical Manual* (Hartford: Goodwin and Betts, 1867), p. 303. Italics in original.

21. Lyman and Lyman, 304.

22. Susan Strasser, *Never Done: A History of American Housework* (New York: Pantheon, 1982); Ruth Schwartz Cowan, *More Work for Mother* (New York: Basic Books, 1983).

23. See, for example, Roland Marchand, *Advertising the American Dream* (Berkeley: University of California Press, 1985); Stuart Ewen, *Captains of Consciousness: Advertising and the Social Roots of Consumer Culture* (New York: McGraw-Hill, 1976); Jackson Lears, *Fables of Abundance: A Cultural History of Advertising in America* (New York: Basic Books, 1994).

110   *Amy Bentley*

24. Charles Rosenberg, *No Other Gods: On Science and American Social Thought* (Baltimore: Johns Hopkins University Press, 1997); Susan Reverby and David Rosner, eds., *Health Care in America: Essays in Social History* (Philadelphia: Temple University Press, 1979).
25. Yalom, *History of the Breast,* pp. 123–124; Blum, *At the Breast,* pp. 20–22; Golden, *Social History of Wet Nursing.*
26. Wood, "History of Artificial Feeding," 25.
27. Katharine K. Merritt, "Feeding the Normal Infant and Child," *Journal of the American Dietetic Association,* 14 (April 1938): 264–268; Apple, *Mothers and Medicine*; van Esterik, *Beyond the Breast-Bottle.*
28. Marion Mills Miller, *Practical Suggestions for Mother and Housewife,* ed. Theodore Waters (New York: The Christian Herald Bible House, 1910), p. 89.
29. Martha Van Rensselaer, Flora Rose, and Helen Cannon, *A Manual of Home-Making* (New York: Macmillan Company, 1920), p. 435.
30. Flora Rose, "The Care and Feeding of Children: Part 1" (October 1, 1911): 15 (Kroch Library Archives and Manuscripts, Cornell University, Ithaca, NY).
31. Apple, *Mothers and Medicine,* pp. 152–154.
32. Sarah A. Quandt, "Sociocultural Aspects of the Lactation Process," in Stuart-Macadam and Dettwyler, *Breastfeeding: Biocultural Perspectives,* p. 134; Valerie Fildes, "The Culture and Biology of Breastfeeding," in Stuart-Macadam and Dettwyler, *Breastfeeding: Biocultural Perspectives,* pp. 108–109.
33. Apple, *Mothers and Medicine,* chap. 1.
34. Trade card collection, Winterthur Museum and Library, Winterthur, DE; article on trade cards, Ellen Gruber Garvey, *The Adman in the Parlor: Magazines and the Gendering of Consumer Culture, 1880s to 1910s* (New York: Oxford University Press, 1996), chap. 1; See also Susan Strasser, *Satisfaction Guaranteed: The Making of the American Mass Market* (New York: Pantheon Books), pp. 164–166; Harvey Levenstein, *Revolution at the Table: The Transformation of the American Diet* (New York: Oxford University Press, 1988), chap. 10; Apple, *Mothers and Medicine,* chap. 1.
35. Rose, "Care and Feeding," 24–25. "When a patent food is made with milk," conceded Rose, "its bad effects are minimized and it may serve a useful purpose."
36. "Report of Richard, April 15 to June 15, 1920," Records of the Home Economics Department, Cornell University, Collection #23/2/749, Box 19, Folder 44. Rachel Sanders Bizel, "A Study of Infant Feeding Practices as Found by a Survey of 702 New York State Babies," Ph.D. dissertation, Cornell University, March 1933, pp. 66–68.
37. Stephen S. Nisbet, *Contribution to Human Nutrition: Gerber Products Since 1928* (New York: The Newcomen Society in North America, 1954), p. 10.
38. Apple, *Mothers and Medicine,* chap. 3.
39. Harvey Levenstein, *Revolution at the Table,* ch. 7.
40. Levenstein, chap. 9.
41. Elizabeth Condit and Jessie A. Long, *How to Cook and Why* (New York and London: Harper and Brothers Publishers, 1914), p. 102.
42. Rose, in Van Rensselaer, Rose, and Cannon, *Manual of Home-Making,* p. 412.
43. Carlotta C. Greer, *Foods and Home Making* (Boston: Allyn and Bacon, 1928), p. 34.
44. Greer, *Food and Home Making,* p. 265.
45. Greer, *Food and Home Making,* p. 501.
46. Greer, *Food and Home Making,* p. 501.
47. Nancy Lee Seger, "A Study of Infant Feeding Practices as Used with Cornell's 45 'Practice House' Babies from 1920–1944," Master's thesis, February 1945, Cornell University, pp. 115–117.
48. Collection of letters to Martha Van Rensselaer (MVR) in the 1910s, found in the Home Economics Records 23/2/749, Box 24, Kroch Library, Cornell University.
49. 4/3/1911 letter to MVR from Mrs. Marie Christ.
50. Ibid.
51. Bizel, "Study of Infant Feeding Pracices," pp. 137, 160.
52. Gerber Company History, Gerber Web site. A similar version, one that gives Mrs. Gerber's name as Dorothy, is recounted in Ellen Shapiro, "The Consultant Trap," *Inc.,* 17 (December 1995): 31–32.
53. "Food Industries Buy," *Business Week* (December 15, 1934): 14, 16.
54. *History of the Fremont Canning Company and Gerber Products Company, 1901–1984* (Fremont, Michigan: Gerber Products Company, 1986). Publication found in the Gerber corporate archives, which are closed to the public. (This specific information was supplied by Ms. Sherri Harris, Gerber archivist.)
55. Nisbet, *Contribution to Human Nutrition,* p. 15.
56. Cowan, *More Works for Mother.*

57. Judson Knight, "Gerber Products Company," in *Encyclopedia of Major Marketing Campaigns,* Thomas Riggs, ed. (Farmington, MI: The Gale Group, 2000), p. 667.
58. Mercedes M. Cardona, "WPP Brand Study Ranks Gerber 1st in U.S. Market," *Advertising Age* (October 5, 1998): 3.
59. At the start of the twenty-first century, the Gerber baby continues to appear on all company packaging and advertising, including in its recently redesigned labels and new line of organic foods. Judann Pollack, "Gerber Starts New Ads as Agency Review Narrows," *Advertising Age* (December 16, 1996): 6.
60. Apple, *Mothers and Medicine,* chaps. 3 and 5, esp. pp. 81–90; Blum, *At the Breast,* pp. 38.
61. For example, the terms were used in the 1952 edition of Herman Frederic Meyer's *Infant Foods and Feeding Practice: A Rapid Reference Text of Practical Infant Feeding for Physicians and Nutritionists* (Springfield, IL: C. C. Thomas), but by the next edition, in 1960, the terms had been dropped.
62. Meyer (1952), p. 143; Walter W. Sackett Jr., *Bringing Up Babies: A Family Doctor's Practical Approach to Child Care* (New York: Harper and Row, 1962), chap. 6. See also Cone, "Infant Feeding," p. 17; Adams, "Use of Vegetables"; Nisbet, *Contribution,* pp. 11, 19.
63. Cone, "Infant Feeding," p. 18.
64. Strasser, *Satisfaction,* pp. 33–35.
65. Ibid., pp. 89, 95.
66. Gerald B. Wadsworth, "Principles and Practice of Advertising," *A&S* (January 1913): 55; quoted in Strasser, *Satisfaction,* p. 32.
67. Lynn K. Nyhart, "Home Economists in the Hospital, 1900–1930," in *Rethinking Home Economics,* Sarah Stage and Virginia B. Vincenti, eds. (Ithaca: Cornell University Press, 1997), pp. 125–144. Reference on p. 128.
68. *Journal of the American Dietetic Association,* 8 (July 1932): 199.
69. Ibid., 10 (July 1934): 183.
70. Ibid., 10 (May 1934): 79.
71. Ibid., 11 (January 1936): 493.
72. Ibid., 12 (September 1936): 271.
73. Ibid., 15 (April 1939): 305.
74. Flora Manning, "Canned Strained Vegetables as Sources of Vitamin A," *Journal of the American Dietetic Association,* 9, 4 (November 1933): 295–305; Flora Manning, "Further Studies of the Content of Vitamins A and B in Canned Strained Vegetables," *Journal of the American Dietetic Association,* 12 (September 1936): 231–236.
75. *Journal of the American Dietetic Association,* 11 (September 1935): 293.
76. Ellipses in original. *Journal of the American Dietetic Association,* 15 (June-July 1939): 513.
77. Ibid., 16 (January 1940): 85.
78. Strasser, *Satisfaction,* pp. 11, 126.
79. Ibid., p. 91.
80. *Ladies Home Journal,* 46 (July 1929).
81. Ellipses in original.
82. *Ladies Home Journal,* 50 (August 1933): 77.
83. Italics and ellipses in original. *Ladies Home Journal,* 50 (October 1933): 127.
84. *Ladies Home Journal,* 50 (July 1933): 51.
85. Elsewhere I have seen the baby's name given as "Sally." See Shapiro, "The Consultant Trap."
86. *Ladies Home Journal,* 54 (September 1937): 60.
87. *Ladies Home Journal,* 55 (December 1938): 99.
88. World Health Organization, *International Code of Marketing of Breastmilk Substances* (Geneva: WHO, 1981).
89. In 1992 Gerber, seeking to enter the infant food market in Guatemala, was told by the government it could not use the Gerber baby on its products or in its advertising, as the baby looked too young to pass the International Code of Marketing of Breastmilk Substitutes set up in 1977 by the World Health Organization in conjunction with UNICEF. One very clear rule of the code prohibits advertising of foods with pictures of very young babies, who give the appearance (especially to illiterate women) that such products are acceptable substitutes for breast milk. *Cracking the Code: Monitoring the International Code of Marketing of Breast-Milk Substitutes* (London: World Health Organization, 1977). See also June 13, 1997, correspondence from David Clark, Legal Officer, UNICEF, in author's possession.
90. Meyer (1960), p. 172.

Chapter 7

HOW THE FRENCH LEARNED TO EAT CANNED FOOD, 1809–1930s

MARTIN BRUEGEL

*7*he editor of the *Journal d'agriculture pratique* was frustrated in 1905. Of course, we know that French peasants hardly ever lack things to complain about, and their representatives had already perfected the ways in which to voice discontent over the nineteenth century. Yet neither tariffs nor consumption taxes agitated the spokesman. Overproduction was on his mind, or rather, the waste it brought about. His distress resulted from the knowledge that a solution to spoiling agricultural produce and butchery meat was at hand. Food sterilization was the answer to the problem, a technique that was about to celebrate its centenary. Yet the revolutionary invention of boiling comestibles in completely sealed containers to prevent their decay had experienced great difficulty in catching on in France. That it was the Parisian confectioner Nicolas Appert (1749–1841) who had discovered the preservation procedure made matters even more irksome to the *Journal*. Glancing beyond the hexagonal frontiers, the journalist noted the growth of canning industries in the United States, Germany, and England. Then he concluded, "We cannot rely on France to develop such industries. . . . We would have to overcome the irrational as well as instinctive repugnance [for canned food] among a large part of the population. It would be an arduous task. Just look to the army, where it is difficult to enjoin the men to eat canned meat."[1] The majority of the French had not yet learned how to consume sterilized foods, and it seemed clear to the writer that the lack of a taste for these conditioned victuals impeded their introduction in the everyday food repertory and the full commercialization of the agricultural surplus.

The almost secular resistance to canned foodstuffs is puzzling in the face of the hope that Appert's breakthrough raised at the beginning of the nineteenth century. The instant government-sponsored publication of

Appert's do-it-yourself manual in 1810—with a second edition to follow in 1811 and a third in 1813—bespoke the authorities' pressing interest in a rapid diffusion of the inventor's knowledge. They wished to encourage emulation on an artisanal as well as a domestic scale. Indeed, Appertizing (as it was then called) promised a steady supply of victuals. In an age when subsistence crises still haunted people's minds, threatened to upset the social order, and preoccupied governments, canning seemed capable of vanquishing the irregularities of agricultural production. Its potential was to allow transport of excess crops through space and time and thus satisfy demand in other places and at later periods. The *Journal de Paris* rhapsodized in 1810, "henceforth, everybody will be able to preserve the treasures nature bestows on us in one season and enjoy them in the sterile season when she refuses them." Hence, too, the flourishing of metaphors to express the deseasonalization of foodways. Appert's method "succeeds in inverting the order of the seasons," "naturalizes spring and summer in winter," and "fixes the seasons, so much so that spring, summer and autumn live in bottles." In short, Appertization was a step in humanity's emancipation from the fetters of nature.[2]

The selfsame argument in favor of Appertizing surfaced repeatedly in the nineteenth century and thus adds to the conundrum of the sluggish acceptation of canned food in France. By 1841, the editors of the fifth edition of Appert's *Art de conserver* noted: "it happens every year that many places of our country abound in quality goods like fruit, vegetables, fish, meats, etc. that are squandered or sold at next to nothing whereas elsewhere and at another moment in time, their prices double or quadruple and sometimes they're even hard to come by; we would not suffer such inefficiency if we employed preservation techniques to prolong the life of perishable comestibles and augment their uses." The development of food preservation, the trade journal *La Sardine* explained in 1900, "helped remedy the shortcomings of nature because it does not produce at a steady pace and, moreover, needs to rest in winter after the crops of the summer. Nowadays it is possible to lay up excess production, thus palliate insufficiency and even prevent famines," a reasoning with which a contemporary grocer's handbook, concerned about permanently full shelves, agreed.[3]

With so much support from opinion makers, the uphill battle of sterilized foods brings to mind Joseph Schumpeter's adage that innovations seldom find profitable markets automatically. Or, to reverse the perspective: consumers hardly ever take spontaneously to new commodities. The case of canned foods in France presents the opportunity to track the itinerary of the new product so as to examine the lag between discovery and use, and to trace the thresholds over which it had to step to enter French households. The focus of this analysis is on quotidian routines and its emphasis as much on the novel object as on the work it took to devise modes of handling it. If such an approach seems to correspond to the consumer equivalent of "learning by using" a new technology, often encountered in economic studies of the diffusion of innovations or new technological standards in manufacturing and service industries, the mirror effect comes with an important twist. The social-historical research design conceives of institutions rather than individuals as carriers of information about new commodities and sponsors of their uses. Economic and sociological explanations of the path of innovations rely on the transmission of knowledge of a thing's practical usefulness by word of mouth from the experienced owner of the object to the novice and possible buyer (with geometrically cumulative effects on the number of users). The assumption seems unlikely to present operational value for historical study because evidence to document its workings is hard to come by; it is reductionist in its presupposition of a device's uniform utility and technical potential, a premise that eliminates the user's capacity for creative handling and differentiated appropriations; and it is unrealistic because of its abstraction from the very often time-consuming and costly acquisition of skills required to sustain the diffusion of new items that it aims to explain. The following pages, then, offer an investigation of the processes by which French women and men got to know about sterilized foods, learned to trust their reliability, and acquired the technique to use them. Attention to the transmission of practical information on new goods puts the focus on consumers who are all too often absent from discussion of the rise of so-called consumer societies.[4]

THE PRICE OF CONSPICUOUS CONSUMPTION

Little is known about the adoption of innovations in everyday life, and few historians have turned to canned food to learn about the adaptation of new commodities to common uses. Relying entirely on the writings of proselytes, Jean-Paul Aron inferred that sterilized victuals encountered "an extraordinary favor" among consumers during the nineteenth century. Aron failed to look at production volumes and consumption practices in his approach to foodways and inadvertently wrote a history of gastronomy and rules of good taste rather than of eating habits. More alert to social reality, Alberto Capatti located the roots of the modernization of foodways among single men in the Paris of the 1880s, where they subsisted on one of the early convenience foods—canned sardines. According to Capatti, this consumption was the spark to ignite their diffusion. Supposedly the process ushered in the popularization of canned foods and also led to "the democratization of the table" because hitherto expensive sardines were now available to smaller purses, too. However, the few cookbooks aimed at single men at the turn of the twentieth century cautioned their readers about the dangers to avoid when opening cans and eating their contents. Both cost (which remained high, as shown below) and directions for use

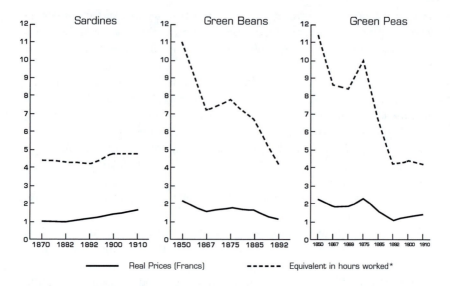

Figure. 1. Real Prices of Canned Foods 1850s–1910.

* Equivalent = Nominal price divided by hourly wage of a provincial laborer. Half cans for sardines, cans for vegetables.

Sources: *Exposition universelle de 1867 à Paris; Catalogue général, Aliments* (Paris, E. Dentu, 1867), 225; Armand Husson, *Les consommations de Paris*, 2nd ed. (Paris, Hachette, 1875), 469–471; *Le coopérateur*, Oct. 1869, Jan. 1885, Jan. 1892; "Résumé rétrospectif," *Annuaire statistique 1937* (Paris, Imprimerie Nationale, 1938); Jean Fourastié et al., *Documents pour l'histoire et la théorie des prix* (Paris, A. Colin, 1958), t. 2, vi–xxi.

discouraged rather than invited consumption. It comes as no surprise, then, to read the comment of a logistics officer who wrote in 1911: "sterilized victuals produced for the civilian element, whether they be meat, fish, game, vegetables, etc., can under no circumstances be considered of common use." The absence of easy, routine consumption of canned foods proved a problem for army supplies. While Capatti intuits an incipient, if insufficiently grounded delineation of their integration into French foodways, he is certainly wrong when claiming their "indisputable legitimacy" among everyday foodstuffs at the beginning of the twentieth century. The social mechanisms that structured and organized their introduction remain in search of a description and an explanation.[5]

Price, of course, had something to do with the prolonged indifference that characterized the popular French attitude toward canned food throughout the years before World War I. Figure 1 indicates that on the one hand, retail prices of the most readily available sterilized vegetables dropped substantially over the second half of the nineteenth century. The much-touted sardines, on the other hand, tended to cost slightly more in real terms on the eve of 1914 than in the 1870s, a stinging disavowal of man's domain over sea life. In comparison, the purchase of basic food-stuffs consumed in French working-class households required far less work: a kilogram of bread cost about an hour's, a kilogram of potatoes roughly half an hour's work by a provincial craftsman around 1910.

However, while high prices may explain the small market for canned foods in France, they cannot account for the popular rejection of sterilized foodstuffs. They also obscure the coexistence of different modes of con-sumption. Indeed, after the mid-nineteenth century, the French leisure class revelled in the countercyclical potential of Appertized vegetables and fruit. To serve green peas or pears out of glass jars during their fashionable dinners amused the rich, who delighted in the rarity of the produce in win-ter and spring. Baron de Brisse included three artisanally produced veg-etable preserves in his *Gastronomic Calendar* of 1868. Culinary historian Louis Bourdeau insisted that Appertization made sense only for the finest, most expensive vegetables that would grace the table of wealthy urbanites. A can of sardines or artichoke hearts proved a welcome addition to the bas-ket of fine foods taken along on a leisurely automobile trip of women or a hike of men in the Alps, pastimes of the social elite in *fin de siècle* France. Thorsten Veblen's concept of conspicuous consumption exactly captures the essence and the function of this behavior and also catches its social limits. For the lavish display of material possessions and indulgence in leisure time, with their concomitant squandering of wealth, exerted no dis-cernible effect on conduct beyond the confines of the select few.[6]

REASONS FOR POPULAR RESISTANCE TO CANNED FOOD

The cost of canned foods was likely to dissuade members of the popular classes from purchasing them. But from skepticism to defiance, the very novelty and the concomitant mystery about the preserving principle gen-erated resistance to sterilized foodstuffs. Unlike members of the leisure class, who relished their capacity to offer Appertized, conditioned prod-ucts out of season, lower-class people appeared to insist on the direct and timely provenance of foodstuffs on their tables. Although historians must be cautious when observers naturalize popular tastes, there seems to pre-vail a concordance about the predilection for fresh foodstuffs among the laboring people. "The private is by principle opposed to every innovation in foodways," military physician Kirn commented in 1884. "He mistrusts by instinct the inventions of modern science [especially chemistry]; he likes to eat his customary food." The fondness for "natural" products turned the case of meat, one of the most prestigious items in the hierar-chy of foods, into a riddle for observers of the French working class at the end of the nineteenth century. Indeed, commentators were mystified when they discovered the habit of blue-collar households in larger and smaller cities to forgo affordable cuts at the butcher's and to substitute bread and vegetables for butchery meat so as to purchase sausages, bacon, stew, and roast on the farm even when the provisioning cost (measured in time and money) exceeded the market price. Commercial mediation, let alone artisanal and industrial transformation of food products, triggered suspicion among French consumers, who appeared to cherish the direct connection with the land as the source of production.[7]

The imperfect mastery of the production process inflicted aberrations on canned preserves that justified popular circumspection about industrially conditioned food. When insufficiently controlled, Appert's technique altered the texture, the appearance, and the flavor of victuals. A popular idiom quickly baptized these unpleasant, unintended transformations with the label of *"le goût de conserve."* The phrase expressed discomfort with canned foods whose smell and taste, so the descriptions went, offensively and disturbingly reeked of smoke, straw, or metal. But the rejection of canned food originated in more than a distaste for its organoleptic qualities. Danger lurked in tin cans because defective soldering could cause lead poisoning or botulism. Most of the publicized accidents occurred in the army, where one survey of territorial troops found 1,804 cases of intoxication between 1886 and 1904 (or about one hundred per year), a sizeable part of which were ascribed to the consumption of spoiled cans. These incidents resonated through the printed media and medical journals. Needless to say, such reports sustained popular uneasiness, and the preoccupation with public health prompted the government to appoint a commission of experts whose task it was to propose guidelines for the inspection of the industrial production of canned foods.[8] Precaution had roots in observed experience, the very same experience that induced industrialists to improve their technical proficiency and warrant food security in order to offset misgivings about food sterilization.

THE GENDERED PATHS OF LEARNING: WOMEN AS PRODUCERS . . .

Newness and health hazards caused suspicion among French consumers. And yet the French learned to eat canned foods. Their resistance did not diminish as a consequence of enhanced product safety only, for increased confidence precisely required experience to build on. The abatement of distrust and resistance resulted neither from a hypothetical word-of-mouth persuasion between individuals, nor from the enticement of chimerical status considerations. Because consumption is an eminently social phenomenon, social institutions and processes must suffice to explain the effects of new commodities in people's lives. The acquisition of a new taste requires the intervention of social groups physically to acquaint the newcomer with the merchandise and the technique required to manipulate it, to instigate and organize the first trial, to keep on pressure after the initial rejection, with explanations on the appropriate use of the good, and eventually to sustain routine consumption.[9]

In France, the institutions to assure these steps toward the integration of canned food in the average food basket were the public school and the army. Military service was second, after free and compulsory education, to reach a majority of the French for an extended period of their lives after the 1870s, when the newly minted Third Republic conceived of public instruction and the army as agencies of change. The link between the two vectors of republican order appeared self-evident. "The army is the continuation of the school," Officer Gerardin declared in 1907, and the defense of French society hinged as much on women's education as on men's military preparedness. Women, after all, were responsible for the primary socialization of children in families. The efforts of public education "to form accomplished housewives, model women, who would save many a man from falling into misery" appeared trifling to philanthropist and educator Charles Driessens, who advocated the consequential teaching "of notions of home economics to girls" in 1891. For, so he argued, "in her, I see the wife, as in the boy, we see the soldier." Both military circles and school reformers subscribed to the promotion of instruction on household affairs because, in the last instance, tidy households run by efficient wives were "the real safeguard of the child, the family, indeed the whole society." This was a tall order given the social tensions that characterized France after the defeat against Germany and the upheaval of the Commune. Nevertheless, the public school and the army were tools to integrate French society around the values of the emerging middle classes: merit based on self-discipline and orderly conduct was to lead to upward mobility and respectability.[10]

Food and foodways figured prominently among the tools as well as the targets of reform. The army exposed every generation of young men to new ways of organizing their daily routine, and one of its projects was to "apply to the soldier's provisioning, the method commonly called *cuisine bourgeoise*." Working-class privates were to see vegetables, fruit, and fish in meals composed of several dishes instead of their ordinary stews and soups accompanied by dark bread.[11] The same impulse transpired in efforts directed at young and adolescent girls. Special programs were necessary because mothers had not kept up with progress and could no longer pass on sufficient knowledge to their daughters. The diffusion of "simple notions of domestic economy"—hygiene, efficiency, thrift—constituted an admittedly limited mission of primary schools after 1882. Only in 1907 did the French government issue a "Program of social hygiene and home economics" which implemented compulsory courses at all levels of public schools. A well-designed education in home economics would, so its promoters claimed, elevate women to the position of "the most precious allies in the fight against the ravages that devastate humanity: tuberculosis, alcoholism, infant mortality," whose origins reformers located in individual recklessness rather than general living conditions.[12]

Young women learned new techniques of householding before World War I. While teaching home economics aimed at enhancing women's efficiency and productivity in homes, it added manual to managerial know-how. To be sure, many a lesson conveyed advice to sharpen the alertness of women in the market, where they had to confront an increasing supply of industrially transformed goods. But classes on "Keeping a household budget" and "How to recognize food falsification" accompanied introductions and exercises in "Homemade preserves—their preparation, their dangers" and "Provisioning households with self-made preserves." Renée Raymond exulted that the organization of programs on food preservation was "a severe blow to old rural ways [that] will replace salted goods and other, more primitive recipes." The privately run *Ecole des Mères* taught a section on the hygiene of food preparation and sterilization. The preservation industry's trade journal supported demonstrations of "the mysteries of putting up food according to Nicolas Appert's method" at agricultural fairs. The public school gave a key position to preservation procedures in the practical instruction of women, who were to acquire the virtues of order, economy, and foresight. Food preservation embodied all the objectives of household education: it required method, prevented wastage of produce which, in turn, led to savings during winter and spring, and contributed to a varied diet throughout the year.[13]

Inclusive instruction propagated the technical know-how of food sterilization, but utensils (glass jars, rubber bands to ensure airtight sealing) remained quite expensive at the turn of the twentieth century. Then, too, handbooks addressed urban mistresses, who hired domestics to do the work. Renée Raymond recommended close supervision of the staff "because of the sustained attention Appertizing demands." Such spare time was rare in the countryside in an era when the mechanization of farming was barely stammering in France. Harvests required women to labor in the fields precisely when vegetables, fruit, and berries were ready for preservation. Schools, however, acquainted rural women with Appertizing gestures and taught them tricks like putting cloth between completely immersed containers and tying a particular kind of safety knot on wires. Women may not have found much time to practice food sterilization once their pupils' career was behind them. But home economics exposed them to modern appliances and taught them skills that fostered the transformation of the farm kitchen from a place whose main purpose it was to feed the men into a site of production where female artisanal proficiency in summer and fall led to savings in winter and spring.[14]

. . . AND MEN AS CONSUMERS

The educational project in the military had the use of discipline, and the captive population of privates risked a series of sanctions when shirking obligations and commands. While political and military authorities recognized the advantages that canned food provided to modern armies and so contributed to the efforts of perfecting it, industrialists saw army logistics as a vast and lucrative market for their product as well as a testing ground to evaluate consumer reaction. Army service was more than instruction in national defense: it operated as a school of taste formation for a majority of French men before World War I and so helped to accustom them to industrially transformed foodstuffs.

Military command had been aware of Appert's discovery early on, and Napoleon I awarded an important prize to the inventor. But it took the defeat of 1871 against the German army to put an end to the eclipse of canned food in army supplies. "We pretend to have a mobile army," an indignant *Bulletin de la réunion des officiers* exclaimed in 1875. "Yes, of course, if we forget the soldier's well-being. He who feeds on dry bread, biscuits, and only drinks water even though his back pack weighs sixty [French] pounds." A badly nourished man was tantamount to a demoralized soldier. The *Bulletin* concluded that it was absolutely necessary to include sterilized foodstuffs in the soldiers' rations. Four reasons induced army experts to experiment with the supply of canned foods. Obviously, preservation prevented the decay of food and hence limited costly losses. The packaging made transport relatively easy. Because containers could vary in size, they contributed to the individual soldier's mobility, eliminating the necessity of centrally located field cuisines from which to fetch supplies during campaigns. The cans provided, so to speak, fast-food meals to the soldier in the field because they could be eaten cold or hot depending on the imperatives of the circumstances. The net effect of these advantages was, so the preserved-food advocates promised, a healthier, more valiant soldier. After 1872, then, the army's provisioning service was instructed to keep on hand enough canned food to supply 1.2 million men for fifteen days.[15]

One quarter of the cans on hand were to be consumed every year. Military rules mandated canned food to be on a unit's menu every fourth day, but units appeared to enjoy a certain latitude in carrying out the disposal of their stocks. Some army divisions diminished the ratio of cans to fresh food per meal and so offered sterilized foodstuffs three times a week, while others increased the portions but put more space between the days on which sterilized victuals were served. The variations around the prescription and experiments with daily fare were the creative responses of logistics officers and army cooks to their men's distaste for canned foods. "Too many cans, and you disgust the private," Captain Kirn noted in 1885, while Commander Thiébaut, author of a guide to varied food preparations in the army, commented in 1899 that "the day when the main meal contains canned food is not much appreciated by our soldiers."[16]

With supply assured and renewal of the inventory compulsory, effective consumption still required prior instruction. The army, Physician Lux declared without circumvolution, was the place where Frenchmen were given the opportunity of sampling foods hitherto unknown to them. Preserves figured prominently among the newly available comestibles. Part of the campaign was pedagogical. It pertained to teaching soldiers about the benefits of canned food in military provisioning and combat strategies. The emphasis was on the diversification in a meal plan, augmented by the addition of sterilized victuals. Varied menus contributed to the troops' health, even if the introduction of variety required the staging of something akin to celebrations and entertainment to heave mealtimes out of the ordinary routine, because privates scorned cans. During the early military engagements in World War I, when supplies of canned food became vital to the soldiers in the trenches, the trade journal *Industrie française de la conserve* insisted that "it is absolutely necessary to accustom the draftees to eat the new blend of beef and vegetables with pleasure, which requires an introductory lesson on its contribution to general health." In the late nineteenth century, however, bare numbers spoke in favor of a better cuisine: by far the most important cause of hospitalization in the military was food-related, whether it was because of inadequate provisioning and exhaustion by under- or malfeeding, or intestinal trouble caused by careless preparation.[17]

Indoctrination about the sanitary rewards of canned food contributed to lowering the rejection threshold. But soldiers had to acquire the technique of handling cans in the field. It proved necessary to teach them how to distinguish between damaged and innocuous cans by inspecting the integrity of the tin and soldered seams. To gain access to the contents entailed the risk of injury from knives in the absence of can openers, and thus required calm coaching first and practice in the terrain second to assure safety. As a matter of fact, military authorities published brochures and handbooks on "the distribution, preparation and consumption of canned foods" in which they explained, for example, the series of operations necessary to "unmold" canned beef. They conceded that "the semicylindric form of the cans does not permit an easy unseating of its contents, and it is therefore necessary to operate with caution." In true military fashion, step-by-step directions were given, from the cleaning or degreasing of the container to the hole a soldier sometimes needed to carve into the compressed meat to get it out in the open. If the most rational, because speediest, method was to ingurgitate the corned beef or sardines cold, recipes that required cooking times from forty minutes to an hour and three-quarters suggested more appetizing formulae. Unit cooks had fourteen recipes using canned meat out of 189 at their disposal, yet no constraints but time and utensils seemed to have limited their imagination.[18]

Both pedagogy and practice aimed at diminishing the prejudice toward cans among the draftees. Instructors had to insist, one piece of advice imported from Switzerland suggested, that contrary to popular belief, only the best of raw materials went into the preserves distributed in the military. Although innovation in the content's composition proved arduous because military authorities worried about the weight of cans and their resistance to oxidation, industrialists observed reactions in the army closely enough to suggest ameliorations and increase the chances of canned foods reaching general acceptance. So carrots were added to beef to mask both the *"goût de conserve"* and the unappetizing sight of a "lonely piece of meat swimming in a tasteless sauce generally lost when the can is opened." The army's social constitution was so close to social representativity, and certainly close enough to those social groups the industry wanted to reach, that soldiers functioned both as a test population for new products and as the targeted vectors to carry the acquired taste back to their private lives.[19]

NECESSITY MAKES VIRTUE: WORLD WAR I

The efforts to improve the organoleptic and visual aspects of canned food accelerated with the onset of World War I. Necessity made virtue then, and awareness that soldiers survived on cans doubled with the conviction that "the vital questions of the national defense are to a large extent bound up with canned food." This recognition had come as a shock to strategists, for Commander Mada had already disclosed by 1916 that "the invasion of Belgium and France by German armies was without a doubt greatly facilitated by their efficient provisioning with canned foods." Hyperbole apart, the beginning of the war vindicated the use of sterilized cans among mobile units.[20]

Yet even warfare in trenches fostered the consumption of canned food. Army and firms launched a publicity campaign in which they exhorted civilians "to add a few cans of food to every parcel" sent to the front line. Industrialists shared the faith in the nation as a whole, but they did not lose sight of their own interest, either. To provide discounts on cans when dispatched to troops "certainly amounts to a true service to our soldiers; but even if we think about it from the sole point of view of our material interests, we are creating a clientele that is going to be loyal to us when peace reigns again." The incentive of a trip to the grocer's shelf proved the last threshold on the way to the quotidian purchase of sterilized comestibles. The growing demand generated entrepreneurial verve: according to industry accounts, the number of canneries in France had skyrocketed from 1,443 to 7,340 between 1914 and the end of 1918.[21]

In an unanticipated turn, the appeal also activated the theoretical knowledge of home canning that women had acquired in the schools of the Third Republic. Hard times popularized the practice. "The war has greatly influenced the production of preserves in homes," the correspondent from Menetou-Salon in the centrally located department of the Cher reported to the scholars who were undertaking a vast inquiry into popular food habits in 1936. "It was necessary to send food to prisoners or soldiers on the front to improve their meager lot. Mothers, wives sterilized meat." In the departments of the Oise and the Loire, women put up vegetables and fruits during the hostilities to dispatch them to their troops. If the additional calories did indeed contribute to the soldiers' physical well-being, the cans also became vectors of sociability. One war memorialist recalled the eating of cold corned beef as moments of sharing during which hitherto scorned, if vital, cans allowed soldiers to trade stories and jokes, and to relax before the battle returned.[22]

Wartime intensified but did not alter the industry's reliance on the army as a school of taste. And if the army united different age cohorts and first-time draftees who either brushed up on or got initiated to canned food, instructors applied their accumulated peacetime experience to bring along the process smoothly. When yet another combination of meat and vegetables in a can was included in army supplies, the State Secretary of Supply and Intendance received a letter advising that "the introduction of this type of can be preceded by a detailed description of its contents in front of our troops, of its appearance when the can is opened, and by the wide distribution of recipes for its preparation to avoid both premature rejections after superficial examination and bungling attempts at preparations that are always prejudicial to their acceptance." Taste makers had learned their lesson: it took patient perseverance to get consumers to appreciate a new, industrially produced food.[23]

CONSUMPTION ROUTINES AND STANDARDIZED PRODUCTION AFTER WORLD WAR I

The equation worked. The intensification of didactic efforts benefited from the rise in patriotic zeal to lift cans into the consumer basket. With all the necessary conditions present, the war added the last—and sufficient—ingredient to generate a taste for sterilized foodstuffs. The 1936 survey into popular food habits prompted one informant from the department of the Doubs to remark, "after 1914, chocolate and canned foods were bought for the soldiers in the field and slowly entered our alimentation." Another pollster turned the proposition around: "Our soldiers brought back recipes from other regions and the habit of eating canned food." Some correspondents breathed a spectacular tone into their account: "During the war, many a man left the country [le pays], saw new parts of the world, ate differently. Upon returning, they noticed that 'le pays' lacks some goods to make life more comfortable—wine, white bread, canned foods—and so they do not hesitate to order a barrel of wine, to purchase a crate of pasta or to make ample provisions of canned sardines." To some observers the transformation of dietary habits was overwhelming. "Since the Great War groceries have invaded the countryside: sugar, coffee, chocolate, pasta. Canned fish, canned vegetables used to be rare, today they appear even in the humblest families," the report from Lescure in the department of the Ariège read. The war was not simply a parenthesis to be closed to effect a return to prior modes of consumption. Cans had become a routine presence in French households.[24]

Canned foods form, however, a somewhat special category of consumer items: they are neither entirely durable nor quite perishable goods. Purchase (as well as home production that, incidentally, also experienced expansion after the Great War) aimed at constituting a stock of preserves whose purpose was to relieve unanticipated temporary needs or to upgrade a meal on short notice. Advertisements and consumer advice in ladies' magazines during the 1930s precisely emphasized the economy of time that cans helped to realize. The advantage was not lost on women in the countryside where, as one school teacher from the department of Doubs testified in 1936, "during the season of great labor, the housewife comes home from the fields and throws together a meal in which eggs have an important part. She also uses cans: green peas, fish, corned beef." "Makeshift" defined the application and main utility of canned foods in urban and rural homes after World War I. Another correspondent put it rather more bluntly. After listing the gamut of canned goods from meat to vegetables and fish (but without mentioning fruit), he noted, "the housewives increasingly use these products because they permit an economy of time, if not money."[25]

The ubiquity of canned foods notwithstanding, their turnover in French kitchen cupboards and pantries never reached the velocity with which working-class families in Detroit consumed them in the late 1920s. Comparisons suffer from the notorious shortcomings of French industrial censuses and the absence of consumer or budget surveys. But disparate data about production, exportation, and importation of canned goods permit a general evaluation. While yearly per capita consumption around 1900 stood at an estimated 220 grams (or half an American pound) of canned sardines and about 118 grams (or about a quarter of an American pound) of canned meat in France, in the 1930s it reached 1.4 kilograms (or somewhat over 3 American pounds) of canned tuna and sardines, and 2.6 kilograms (or about 6 pounds) of canned tomatoes, green peas, and green beans. A member of a Detroit working-class family disposed of 1.2 kilograms (or 2.6 American pounds) of canned fish and 7.4 kilograms (or over 16 pounds) of canned beans, tomatoes, and green peas in addition to 1.5 kilograms (or a good 3 pounds) of canned soup in 1927 to 1928. When checked against its European neighbors, however, France barely lagged behind, even if the increasingly popular canned mushrooms and asparagus are lacking in the comparison. Figures from the International Labor Bureau indicate that a member of the German middle or lower classes (civil servants, employees, workers) consumed approximately 4.7 kilograms (or 10 American pounds) of canned vegetables and fruit, while workers in the Belgian city of Anvers reached just about 5 kilograms of canned food (fish, vegetables, fruit). By the late 1920s, average French consumption of Appertized victuals had as good as caught up—or kept up—with comparable industrial nations.[26]

The familiarity of French consumers with their products pleased the representatives of the canning industry. They recognized that the Great War "had accustomed the urban population to consume cans regularly" and had helped promote the skills to distinguish safe from corrupted products. But now that the consumers were making educated choices, other problems surfaced and called for attention. Industrialists anticipated an expansion of the domestic demand because "the conditions of modern life develop, in an extraordinary manner, the utilization of canned food." This very growth required changes in supply. Gone were the times when artisanal production would be enough to satisfy a privileged fringe of the French population. While Portuguese sardines, Italian tomatoes, or American corned beef seemed to threaten indigenous production and motivated the implementation of protectionist trade policies, the leaders of the canning lobby advocated "the standardization of French canned foods." Inspiration proceeded from across the Atlantic, and the trade journal made no secret of its goal to "Americanize" production and distribution.[27]

"Normalization" amounted to the marketing of a small number of uniform containers. Economies of scale saved on machines, tools, and labor. Engineers and industrialists forecast reduced production costs, improved international competitiveness, and expanding sales. Norms, however, also aimed at disciplining the domestic market. They established the benchmarks or conventions of competition. Sanctions punished deceitful behavior: merchandise whose geographic origin was proven fraudulent lost access to the grocer's shelves; spoiled products, even if discovered long after they had left the factory, remained the canner's legal responsibility. These measures endeavored to sustain consumer confidence and loyalty to a product whose industrial transformation continued to stain its reputation. Canneries regularly had to fight off assaults on the sanitary integrity of their goods. It was surely no coincidence that the institution of norms on sizes and labels of tin cans and glass jars followed the debates on the effects of conditioning and heating on the vitamin contents of sterilized foods. However much standardization responded to imperatives of profit-making by simplifying production, industrywide and legally binding norms also installed a playing field—a market—in which consumers, their (perceived) concerns, and their protection had a role to play.[28]

CONCLUSION

The explanation of how the French learned to eat canned foods moves the focus of historical investigation onto consumers and the formation of their tastes. The emphasis on the genesis of consumption practices steers clear of the misleading equation between mass production and a progressive convergence of lifestyles in so-called consumer societies. Indeed, assertions about the socially integrative capacity of goods follow and confirm advertising claims or discourses on the benefits of consumption without losing any time looking at the uses of things.[29] An analysis of the ways in which people became users of Appertized comestibles demonstrates the importance of institutions in the dissemination of information. Thus the acquisition of tastes and the ensuing willingness to buy imply a social transfer. Neither producers nor the "mass" of individual consumers paid the full monetary price to obtain knowledge of new merchandise and its applications. The cost of becoming a consumer was spread through society. While the case of French canneries until the 1930s may be peculiar, it is likely that other industries (bicycles, automobiles, electric household appliances) succeeded in transferring a taste for their products through social institutions that imparted experience and practice to individual women and men who then carried the acquired skills into private households and families. These institutions not only initiated novices to new goods; they also assured valuable feedback to manufacturers on improvements to apply or desirable characteristics to add to commodities so as to satisfy specific needs or desires. In other words, institutions like the public school and the army constituted the return link between users and producers, endowing consumers with the capacity to affect product innovation and the long-term supply of goods in the market.[30] Finally, the effects of mass production incited industrialists to call for the institution of product norms to regulate competition (and maybe exclude foreign rivals who did not live up to these legally enforceable conditions). French entrepreneurs recognized the advantages of standardization as embodied by the American model. They easily combined this admiration with the (transnational) business sense that well-publicized, visible commercial standards were a cornerstone of consumer society: norms and classifications functioned as guarantees reassuring customers about product integrity and safety, a certification that, as recent history suggests, proved all the more necessary when the commodities were industrially transformed foods.

NOTES

I wish to thank Clare Crowston, Arwen Mohun, Pierre Saunier, Warren Belasco, and Philip Scranton for their comments, strictures, and suggestions.

1. *Journal d'agriculture pratique,* 2 (1905): 140. On the canning industry in the United States, see Mark William Wilde, "Industrialization of Food Processing in the United States, 1860–1960," Ph. D. dissertation, University of Delaware, 1988, pp. 28–69; in Germany, see Uwe Spiekermann, "Zeitensprünge: Lebensmittelkonservierung zwischen Industrie und Haushalt, 1880–1940," in *Ernährungskultur im Wandel der Zeiten. Tagungsreader,* ed. Katalyse/Buntstift (Köln: Katalyse/Buntstift, 1997), pp. 30–42; in Great Britain, see James P. Johnson, "The Development of the Food-Canning Industry in Britain during the Interwar Period," in *The Making of the Modern British Diet,* ed. Derek Oddy and Derek Miller (London: Rowman and Littlefield, 1976), esp. pp. 73–74.
2. *Journal de Paris* (May 21, 1810): 1003; A. B. L. Grimod de la Reynière, *Almanach des gour-*

mands, 4th year (1806): 180–181, and 5th year (1807): 275, 291; *Le courrier de l'Europe* 601 (Feb. 10, 1809): 3–4. *L'Art de conserver pendant plusieurs années toutes les substances animales et végétales* (Paris: Patris, 1810) went through four French editions during Appert's life.

3. Nicolas Appert, *Le livre de tous les ménages*, 5th ed. by MM. Prieur-Appert and Gannal (Paris: E. Dentu, 1842), p. 169; *La Sardine* (July 1900): 4; see also J. B. Fournier and Louis-Sébastien Le Normand, *Essai sur la préparation, la conservation et la désinfection des substances alimentaires* (Paris: Chaignieau aîné, 1818), p. 123; P. Faucheux, *Traité de conserves alimentaires à l'usage des ménages* (Nantes: V. Mangin, 1851), p. iv; Léon Arnoud, *Manuel de l'épicier* (Paris: J. B. Baillière, 1904), p. 64.

4. Joseph Schumpeter, *Theorie der wirtschaftlichen Entwicklung* (Leipzig: Duncker und Humboldt, 1912), pp. 119, 133–134. "Learning by using" in Nathan Rosenberg, *Inside the Black Box: Technology and Economics* (New York: Cambridge University Press, 1982); "word of mouth" in Everett M. Rogers, *Diffusion of Innovations*, 4th ed. (New York: The Free Press, 1995), pp. 68–69.

5. On the lack of histories relating the fate of innovations, see Rosenberg, *Inside*, pp. 19, 55, and 109–111. Jean-Paul Aron, *Essai sur la sensibilité alimentaire à Paris au 19e siècle* (Paris: A. Colin, 1967), p. 69; Alberto Capatti, *Le goût du nouveau; origines de la modernité alimentaire* (Paris: A. Michel, 1989), pp. 19–20, 42, 81, 124; Jenny Touzin, *La cuisine chez soi. Cuisine des célibataires* (Paris: F. Brossier, 1889), pp. 164, 455; Charles Driessens, *Alphabet de la ménagère* (Paris: chez l'auteur, 1891), p. 70; G. Blanc, "Les conserves de viande," *Revue du service de l'intendance militaire,* 24 (March 1911): 199.

6. Baron de Brisse, *Calendrier gastronomique* (Paris: E. Bonnaud, 1868), pp. 22, 25, 36; Louis Bourdeau, *Histoire de l'alimentation* (Paris: F. Alcan, 1893), p. 78; see also Paul Gaubert, *Etude sur les vins et les conserves* (Paris: Mme Croissant, 1857), pp. 407–465, and Xavier Rocques, *Les industries de la conservation des aliments* (Paris: Gauthier-Villars, 1906), esp. p. 73; *La Sardine* (July 1900): 3; *Le Conseil des femmes* (Nov. 15, 1903): 274; *La Conserve alimentaire* (Sept. 1907): 131; and ibid. (Feb. 1908): 19; Antonin Rolet, *Conserves de fruits et légumes* (Paris: J. B. Baillière, 1912), pp. 10, 56; Thorsten Veblen, *The Theory of the Leisure Class* (New York: Penguin, 1994 [1899]), pp. 68–101.

7. For popular resistance, see Grimod de la Reynière, *Almanach*, 7th year (1810): 165; *Bulletin de pharmacie* 2 (July 1811): 334; Faucheux, *Traité*, p. iv; Antoine Ronna, *Les industries agricoles* (Paris: Librairie agricole, 1869), p. 294; Louis-Guillaume Figuier, *Les merveilles de l'industrie*, t. 4: "Industries agricoles et alimentaires" (Paris: Furne, Jouvet & Cie, 1877), p. 635; J. Talayrach, "Contribution à l'étude de la congélation de la viande," *Archives de médecine et de pharmacie militaires,* 36 (1900): 294. On the popular predilection for fresh produce, see Louis Kirn, "L'alimentation du soldat," *Journal des sciences militaires*, 9th ser., 16 (Oct. 1884): 136; see also *Archives de médecine et de pharmacie militaires* 4 (1884): 488; "L'alimentation du soldat," in *Encyclopédie d'hygiène et de médecine publique* (Paris: Lecrosnier et Babé, 1895), 7, pp. 188–89. On the fondness for "natural" meat, see Pierre Saunier, *L'évolution du coût de l'alimentation depuis le début du siècle* (Paris: INRA, 1975), pp. 41–44.

8. On "Goût de conserve," see Louis Kirn, *L'alimentation du soldat* (Paris: L. Baudoin, 1885), p. 120; Ernest Sacquépée, *Les empoisonnements alimentaires* (Paris: J. B. Baillière, 1909), pp. 6–7, 76–81; *Le coopérateur; Journal de l'épicerie*, (Oct. 20, 1889): 663; *Journal de l'épicerie* (Aug. 23, 1893): 1; Antonin Rolet, *Les conserves de légumes, de viandes, des produits de la basse-cour et de la laiterie* (Paris: J. B. Baillière, 1913), p. 421; *Journal de l'épicerie*, (August 23, 1893): 1; Angel Marvaud, *Les maladies du soldat étude étiologique, épidémiologique, clinique et prophylactique* (Paris: F. Alcan, 1894), p. 818; Baudoin, "Accidents graves d'intoxication par ingestion de sardines à l'huile, observés à l'Ecole militaire préparatoire d'infanterie des Anderlys," *Archives de médecine et de pharmacie militaires* 37 (1901): 423–430; Brouardel, "Rapport de la commission chargée de déterminer les causes des accidents d'intoxication produits par les conserves de viande et les moyens d'y remédier," *Revue du service de l'intendance militaire* (Jan. 1902): 1–20; for the effects of inspection and a call to tighten it, see *Revue d'hygiène* (1909): 254.

9. This approach parallels Howard S. Becker's description of the development of a marijuana habit among Americans in the 1940s; see his *Outsiders. Studies in the Sociology of Deviance* (New York: The Free Press, 1973 [1963]), pp. 41–58.

10. L. Gerardin, "La ration du soldat. Manuel pratique d'éducation alimentaire," *Revue du service de l'intendance militaire* (May 1907): 397; see also "L'armée et l'école," *Revue du cercle militaire* 32 (May 10 and 17, 1907): 501–505, 535–536; Driessens, *Alphabet*, pp. v–xiii; *Bulletin du cercle militaire*, 21 (Nov. 22, 1891): 1237; Augusta Moll-Weiss, *Les écoles ménagères à l'étranger et en France* (Paris: A. Rousseau, 1908), p. 1.

11. For *Cuisine bourgeoise* in the army, see Ch. A. Schindler, "L'alimentation variée à l'armée," *Archives de médecine et de pharmacie militaire,* 5 (1885): 461; see also Antony, "Etude pra-

tique de l'alimentation dans le corps de troupe," ibid., 4 (1884): 363; E. Haeffelé, *Nouvelle cuisine militaire en garnison, en manœuvres et en campagne* (Nancy: Sidot Frères, 1892); there is some evidence that the Civil War was a boost in the development of a taste for canned food in the United States; see James H. Collins, *The Story of Canned Food* (New York: E.P. Dutton & Co., 1924), p. 239.

12. Marie-Ernestine Wirth, E. Bret, *Premières leçons d'économie domestique* (Paris: Hachette, 1907), p. 2; Moll-Weiss, *Ecoles*, pp. vii, 198, 298–317.

13. Moll-Weiss, *Ecoles*, pp. 211–222, 318–324; Renée Raymond, *La conserve à la maison* (Paris: Hachette, 1913), vol. 1, 6; *La conserve alimentaire* (June 1905), 469–470; J.-M. Guillon, *Les écoles ambulantes d'agriculture pour jeunes filles et pour jeunes gens* (Paris: Imprimerie nationale, 1911), pp. 10–21; R. Leblanc, *L'enseignement ménager* (Paris: Larousse, 1913).

14. Raymond, *Conserve*, vol. 3, p. 5.

15. For evidence of early explorations and attempts to provide canned food to sailors and soldiers, see Appert, *L'art*, 4th ed. (1831), p. viii; Gilbert Urbain Guillaumin, *Encyclopédie du commerçant. Dictionnaire du commerce et des marchandises* (Paris: Guillaumin, 1837), vol. 1, p. 649; Jules Bonhomme-Colin, *Notice sur les conserves alimentaires et sur leur application possible à la nutrition de la marine, l'armée, les classes ouvrières, les hôpitaux et les prisons* (Nantes: Merson, 1843), pp. 40–41; Jean-Baptiste Fonssagrives, *Traité d'hygiène navale* (Paris: J. B. Baillière, 1856), p. 600; "Des préparations modernes de conserves alimentaires et de leur importance pour les armées," *Bulletin de la réunion des officiers* 5 (Aug. 7, 1875): 740; "Conserves," *Dictionnaire militaire: Encyclopédie des sciences militaires* (Paris: Berger-Levrault, 1894), vol. 1, p. 703; "L'alimentation du soldat," *Encyclopédie d'hygiène*, vol. 7, p. 188; "Note sur les approvisionnements pour le service des subsistances," Oct. 5, 1872, Xs 114, Subsistances, Section Historique de l'Armée de Terre (Vincennes).

16. For instructions and variations on frequency of use, see "Des préparations," *Bulletin* 5 (April 7, 1875): 741; "La fabrication des conserves pour l'armée française," *Revue du service de l'intendance militaire,* 25 (March 1912): 275–280; "Le ministre de la Guerre à M. le général commandant en chef," April 9, 1915, and "Circulaire du ministre de la Guerre," Dec. 12, 1915, 6N46, Section Historique de l'Armée de Terre; Rocques, *Industries*, pp. 166–167. For soldiers' reactions, see: Kirn, "Alimentation," *Journal*, 9th ser., 15 (July 1884): 291, 448; Thiébaut, *Guide pratique d'alimentation variée dans les corps de troupe* (Paris: R. Chapelot, 1899), p. 59; intervention of Senator Viseur, March 28, 1898, *Annales du Sénat*, vol. 51, 500; *Revue du cercle militaire,* 28 (July 16, 1898): 63; Branlière, "Causerie sur l'alimentation des troupes pendant les campagnes lointaines," *Revue du service de l'intendance militaire,* 17 (March 1904): 209.

17. E. Lux, *De l'alimentation rationnelle et pratique des armées en campagne et à l'intérieur; transformation du mode alimentaire actuel* (Paris: C. Tanera, 1881), p. 18; see also *Revue d'hygiène* (1888): 347; *Industrie française de la conserve* 3 (May 1915): 100; "La cuisine du soldat," *Bulletin* 3 (April 19, 1873): 367; Kirn, "L'alimentation," *Journal*, 9th ser., 14 (April 1884): 419–439; these concerns were part of the debate on the relation between food, health, and performance connected with the rising European science of work; see Anson Rabinbach, "The European Science of Work: The Economy of the Body at the End of the Nineteenth Century," in Steven L. Kaplan and Cynthia J. Koepp, eds., *Work in France: Representations, Meaning, Organization, and Practice* (Ithaca, NY: Cornell University Press, 1986), pp. 475–513.

18. *Administration et comptabilité intérieure des corps de troupes ordinaires, Livre de cuisine militaire en garnison* (Paris, H. Charles-Laveuzelle, 1908), pp. 18, 94–96, 158; *Revue du cercle militaire* 35 (June 3, 1905): 560; Ch. Viry, "Notes sur l'amélioration du régime alimentaire des troupes en garnison," *Archives de médecine et de pharmacie militaires,* 32 (1898): 83–87; "Editorial," *La conserve alimentaire,* 1 (Jan. 1903): n.p.; ibid., 17 (May 1904): 257.

19. "Recommandations faites en Suisse pour la préparation et la consommation des conserves," *Revue du service de l'intendance militaire* 12 (July-Aug. 1899): 623; Cahiers des charges pour la fabrication et la fourniture des conserves de viande cuite sur le territoire français en cas de mobilisation (1894), fol. 16, Ravitaillement des armées, 7N24, Section Historique de l'Armée de Terre; Auguste Corthay, *La conserve alimentaire; traité de fabrication* (Paris: A. Rety, 1902), pp. 354–358; *La Conserve alimentaire* 5 (May 17, 1904): 270; Rolet, *Conserves de légumes*, p. 421; H. Copeaux and A. Kling, "La fabrication des conserves de viandes pour le ravitaillement du camp retranché de Paris," *Génie civil* (April 3 and 10, 1915): 7 (authors' offprint at the Bibliothèque Nationale de France); Victor-Simon Laurent, *Résumé du fonctionnement des services de l'alimentation et du ravitaillement des troupes en campagne* (Paris: H. Charles-Lavauzelle, 1912).

20. *Industrie française de la conserve* 3 (May 1, 1915): 136; *L'information* Aug. 7, 1916): 3, 6N2646, Section Historique de l'Armée de Terre; Maurice Piettre, *L'industrialisation de l'élevage et de la fabrication des conserves de viandes* (Paris: J.-B. Baillière, 1920), pp. 8, 374.

21. *Industrie française de la conserve* (May 1, 1915): 100–102; for a wartime brochure, see *Conserves: légumes, fruits, œufs, viandes* (Paris: Larousse, 1917); for canneries, see *Industrie française de la conserve* 27 (April 1919): 73.

22. Commission de recherches collectives, Enquête 3 sur l'alimentation populaire quotidienne (1936), microfilm 2, Menetou-Salons, Cher; microfilm 9, Fournaeux, Loire; microfilm 11, Beauvais, Oise, Musée national des arts et traditions populaires, Paris (henceforth CRC 3, microfilm, village, department); Roland Dorgeles, *Les croix de bois* (Paris: A. Michel, 1923), pp. 31, 122, 211, 229.

23. *Industrie française de la conserve* 3 (May 1, 1915): 1; Raguenau to M. le Sous-secrétaire d'Etat du ravitaillement et de l'intendance, (March 9, 1916), 6N2646.

24. CRC 3, microfilm 6, Exincourt and Avoudray, Doubs; microfilm 12, Vallée des Arves, Savoie; microfilm 13, Giroussens, Tarn; microfilm 1, Lescure, Ariège; microfilm 2, Dozulé, Calvados.

25. *L'art ménager* (March 1930): 82; ibid. (Aug. 1930), 298; *Le journal de la femme*, Feb. 18, 1933): 15; *Marie-Claire* 9 (April 30, 1937): 34; CRC 3, microfilm 6, Varée-le-Grand, Doubs, and microfilm 9, Souvignargues, Gard.

26. Calculations based on Rocques, *Industries*, p. 65; Osman Jones and T. W. Jones, *Fabrication des conserves*, trans. and adapted by Georges Genin (Paris: Dunod, 1941), pp. 2–7; France, Douanes (Direction général), *Tableau général du commerce de la France* (Paris: Imprimerie Nationale, 1895–1904, 1929–1935). No data are available on canned fruit in France. Bureau international du travail, *Contribution à l'étude de la comparaison internationale du coût de la vie* (Geneva: BIT, 1932), pp. 51–52, 104; id., *L'alimentation des travailleurs et la politique sociale* (Geneva: BIT, 1936), pp. 214–223. These data should not dissimulate wide discrepancies between consumers and nonconsumers of canned foods. In Detroit, for example, only 17 families out of 100 actually bought corned beef; their family consumption stood at 14 pounds per year, while the average figure indicates a yearly 2.4 pounds per family; 1993 figures for French family consumption are 10.3 kilograms (or 23 American pounds) of canned vegetables and roughly 1 pound of canned fish per person per year; see Patrice Bertail, Christine Boizot, and Pierre Combris, *La consommation alimentaire en 1993* (Paris: INRA-OCA, 1997).

27. *Industrie française de la conserve* 22 (June 1918): 179, ibid. 24 (Oct. 1918): 301, ibid. 32 (Feb. 1920): 2; ibid. 78 (Feb. 1932): 9; René Legendre, *Alimentation et ravitaillement* (Paris: Masson, 1920), p. 306.

28. *Industrie française de la conserve* 34 (July 1921): 76; ibid. 62 (June 1928): 189–199; ibid. 74 (April 1931): 32–35; *Bulletin du comité technique de l'alimentation* 181 (Oct. 15, 1934): 281.

29. Among numerous examples, see Victoria de Grazia, "Amerikanisierung und wechselnde Leitbilder der Konsum-Moderne (*consumer-modernity*) in Europa," in *Europäische Konsumgeschichte*, ed. Hannes Siegriest, Hartmut Kaelble, and Jürgen Kocka (Frankfurt a. M.: Campus Verlag, 1997), esp. pp. 117–118.

30. A recent review of the historiography on marketing regrets the absence of considerations on "the specific role of consumers in the development of consumer culture"; see Roy Church, "New Perspectives on the History of Products, Firms, Marketing, and Consumers in Britain and the United States since the Mid-Nineteenth Century," *Economic History Review* 52 (Aug. 1999): 431.

Chapter 8

SEARCHING FOR GOLD IN GUACAMOLE: CALIFORNIA GROWERS MARKET THE AVOCADO, 1910–1994

JEFFREY CHARLES

"The cold fact of the matter is that the avocado does not sell itself."
—M. L. McMahan, sales representative,
Calavo Growers of California, 1953[1]

*M*ost North Americans are now familiar with the avocado, if only in its pureed form, spooned on a taco or scooped up by a tortilla chip. If they give the green mush any thought, they might link it with the recent popularity of "Mexican" food. Yet the avocado became a significant crop in Southern California in the 1910s, and efforts to market it nationwide have been ongoing since the 1920s. Cultivated in Mexico, Latin America, and the Caribbean since the beginning of human civilization, the fruit had failed to catch on in Europe and in North America through the nineteenth century. In the early twentieth century, it was "discovered" by agricultural speculators, who hoped that this foodstuff would bring them riches and easy living on lush Southern California estates. In order to realize these dreams, however, a market for the fruit had to be created in the United States. This the industry undertook with mixed results, successfully building an avocado market in California and the Southwest, where menus already showed the influence of Mexico and Latin America, but failing to win broad acceptance at tables outside these regions. Only with the Latino migration beginning in the late 1970s did the fruit became a regular item in groceries of the Eastern and Midwestern United States.

By itself, this story does not seem very remarkable. As a specialty fruit, the avocado is an early exemplar of the contemporary proliferation of grocery produce that makes it possible, in my local supermarket, to buy six different kind of mushrooms, organic broccoli sprouts, kiwi fruits, star fruits, and pluots (a hybrid of plums and apricots). The enormous and superfluous range of commodities available for sale is one of the hallmarks of an advanced consumer society, representing the freedom of choice so valued by its celebrants or the waste and exploitation condemned by its detractors. Why, then, should it be different for agricultural food products?

Behind the production of this speciality fruit, however, is a significant and revealing history. As sociologists and anthropologists have pointed out, food is different from run-of-the-mill commodities, both in the depth of meanings ascribed to it and in the complexity of the system that produces it.[2] Some of the more centrally consumed foodstuffs, such as sugar, even helped create the system of political institutions, economic forces, and cultural constraints that govern us to this day.[3] In the case of the avocado, it was the system that "manufactured" the sale of the fruit in the United States. From the beginning, the influence of marketing in the twentieth-century history of the avocado in the United States shows itself as much on the side of its production as on the fruit's consumption, given that real estate promoters sold tracts based on wild promises of the fruit's profitability. In plucking the avocado from the peasants of Mexico and Latin America to develop it in the United States, California growers exploited the power and reach of their nation's colonial enterprises. Through the twentieth century they have used government assistance to prevent the emergence of south-of-the-border competition, even as their sales benefit from Latino immigrant influence. The extent of resources expended on this minor industry was extraordinary but not unique in the annals of the consumer economy. If this were a matter of shoes or clothing, successful domestic marketing would complete the story, and we would, as early growers boastfully predicted, be dining regularly on avocados as a main course.

Unfortunately for its early boosters, the avocado is not clothing. As an agricultural crop it proved maddeningly inconsistent in its production, while as a food new to U.S. palates, it ran into the tangle of various messages "encoded" into our culinary tastes.[4] Some of these problems come with the avocado's anomalies according to a European perspective. It is a fruit, but it is not sweet. It contains high levels of fat. The fruit never ripens on the tree but only after it has been picked. When it is ripe (and when it is properly ripe is really the only time it can be eaten) it is overly soft in comparison to other ripe fruit. It cannot be cooked, stewed, or baked, or it turns rancid.

Other complications in marketing the avocado had to do with the impact of consumer culture on the middle and upper classes. These women and men were experiencing increasing anxiety surrounding food in the twentieth century, created in part by the increasing choice available to the prosperous consumer, the diminishing formal rules governing dining, and an obsession with health and fitness.[5] On the one hand, its exotic qualities, its nutritional value, its association with the social innovations of California helped advertisers shape a positive image for the fruit. On the other hand, its limited range in cooked dishes, its richness, and its ethnic associations inhibited its appeal. Defined as a salad ingredient, the avocado thereby entered the province of women and dieters, and had to battle the fat it contained. Marketers also downplayed the avocado's south-of-the-border associations, probably correctly estimating the prejudices of U.S. consumers in the mid-twentieth century, but also restricting the fruit's culinary uses.

Thus, for avocado marketers, changing the diet of the U.S. eater proved far more difficult and complicated than early boosters imagined. In fact, from the perspective of avocado growing, that most grounded of activities, farming, was subject to airy flights of consumerist fancy, while the supposedly capricious consumers, at least when it came to their consumption of the fruit, remained stuck in the ruts of the tried and true.

THE ORIGINS OF THE AVOCADO INDUSTRY IN CALIFORNIA

The avocado first appeared in U.S. markets in the late nineteenth century, simultaneously with the emergence of the United States as a full-fledged imperial power in Latin America and the Caribbean. Though it would play a much smaller role in agricultural history, the avocado's arrival was linked with the U.S. role in banana growing and in the coffee trade. By the turn of the century, the U.S. Department of Agriculture (USDA), inspired by U.S. success in these tropical commodities, was sending down botanists and "agricultural explorers" on "expeditions" to Mexico, Central America, and the West Indies to see if they could uncover new tropical products which might be adapted to growing in the United States.[6] On one such trip, to Mexico and Central America, USDA researcher G. N. Collins "discovered" several varieties of avocados which exhibited a hardiness and thick skin that appeared to make U.S. production and shipping feasible, and publicized his research in a 1905 government pamphlet, *The Avocado, A Salad Fruit from the Tropics.* Collins's work was the first in a series of investigations in Mexico and Latin America designed to further the prospects for avocado growing in the United States.[7]

The U.S. market had received increasing numbers of avocados from Cuba after the Spanish-American War, and, according to Collins, the "New York Cuban and Spanish populations are always ready to purchase avocados," while the fruit was enjoying a minor vogue on "the tables of the rich and fashionable." He quoted from an October 1904 *Cooking School Magazine* directions for "aquacate salad" which must have been the first recipe for guacamole published in the United States.[8] Still, the avocado, as Collins recognized, needed extensive introduction to U.S. palates.

This "butter fruit" had been first observed and described by sixteenth-century Spanish colonizers in the West Indies. Though it was grown throughout the Caribbean, Latin America, and Mexico, it never became a full participant in the Columbian horticultural exchange, despite its adaptability to Mediterranean climates.[9] Perhaps because of difficulties in shipping sample fruit across the Atlantic, or because its texture and taste, always noted as unusual by early observers, confounded European expectations of a fruit, the avocado remained an oddity in Europe well into the twentieth century.[10]

A fruit that, as Collins described it, was "unfamiliar to our fathers" and whose taste was "seldom accepted at the first trial" hardly seems the basis for a remunerative industry in the United States. Indeed, it is unlikely that avocado growing, had it been confined to Florida and Eastern market conditions, would have made much headway in the United States. But the avocado found root in the speculative hothouse that was early-twentieth-century Southern California, and soon an avocado planting boom was on.

Southern California at the turn of the century was in the midst of two dramatic land-based economic transformations. The first was based on the buying and selling of real estate, a process which required the continuous infusion of migrants and outside capital. The real estate economy generated the incessant boosting of Southern California's natural advantages—its climate and scenery—but also helped bring about the manipulation of nature to supply the region with the essential water it lacked (water which also would allow the avocado industry to take root).[11]

At the same time, partly because of the same natural climatic advantages that were trumpeted by real estate boosters, and partly because of the fortuitous timing of its economic development, California emerged on the forefront of a national agricultural revolution that was bringing corporate methods of specialization, organization, and marketing to farming. Soon Californian lettuce, peppers, onions, apricots, peaches, plums, raisins, walnuts, and almonds would be available for daily consumption across the nation. In Southern California, the citrus industry led the way in agricultural and economic transformation, making use of USDA scientific expertise, employing new methods of cooperative packing and shipping, and above all, skillfully advertising its product using the Sunkist brand name. "Oranges for health, California for wealth" went the famous slogan, advertising both the fruit and the state as commodities.[12]

Given the boosting of its climate and the extraordinary success of the citrus industry, it is little wonder that California found itself prone to speculative frenzy surrounding land and horticulture. That anything might grow in such a climate, that an easy living could be had with even a backyard garden—this promise appeared in every real estate ad that offered at least a quarter acre to accompany its suburban bungalow. In their publications and pronouncements, California horticulturalists promised to elevate the moral character of the state and improve the health of the nation while restoring farming as an arena of egalitarian opportunity.[13] Citrus proved that it was indeed possible to make a great deal of money as a "gentleman planter," but rapidly rising prices of good citrus land and the high costs of bringing such land into bearing soon closed out all but the wealthiest.[14] A number of alternatives, many of them tropical fruits, were sold by promoters as the next "can't miss" agricultural product. The lichee, the loquat, the kumquat, the cherimoya, the feijoa, and the sapote were all announced with great fanfare as potential moneymakers for anyone who could plant a tree.[15] The avocado appeared in the context of this hype and hucksterism surrounding agricultural products in early-twentieth-century California. In fact, early promoters of the avocado felt they had to separate themselves from the empty promises of previous agricultural promoters by claiming that they too had "thought of avocados in the same light as we did a few years ago of the Belgian hares, spineless cactus and eucalyptus" until they realized the true virtues of the avocado.[16]

What were those virtues, as defined by the avocado's early promoters, that encouraged the proliferation of avocado planting where other tropical fruits had failed to take hold? Early USDA reports talked vaguely of the "food value" of the avocado and suggested from its use in Latin America that it could become a staple of the American diet.[17] Later, promoters would pick up on those reports and inflate them beyond recognition, but whatever demand there was for a new staple was not reflected in the avocado market prior to 1915. Avocado trees had been growing here and there in Southern California since the 1850s, and the late-nineteenth-century market from groceries and restaurants was easily satisfied by imports from Mexico. In the early twentieth century, California would narrow the opening for shipping fruit into the state, due to fear of pests and crop diseases, and the turmoil surrounding the Mexican Revolution would further cut imports from south of the border, but demand levels in California did not justify a full scale industry. Nor could California growers anticipate a national market, as imports from Cuba and a small group of domestic growers in Florida easily satisfied the East Coast demand.[18] Instead, the boom in avocado planting arose not from the intrinsic food virtues of the fruit, but from the public relations skills of a group of growers and nurserymen, the enthusiasms of a few scientists and hobbyists, the support of the USDA and the University of California, and, above all, the indefatigable boosting of real estate firms selling avocado acreage.

The first public relations salvo came from the highly profitable sales of a few crates of extra large California avocados early in the teens, much publicized in the Southern California atmosphere of agricultural speculation. As investors' interest increased, the lucky owners of the few producing trees in Southern California were able to sell small branches of their tree, referred to as "budwood," at great profit. (These branches could be grafted unto seedlings, and would bear fruit much more quickly than a tree grown only from seed.) Of course, the fortunate owners of bearing avocado trees in the early twentieth century, several of whom were already "orchardists" growing citrus, such as Jacob Miller of Hollywood and C. P. Taft of Santa Ana, shrewdly played their role in building publicity surrounding the fruit, widely advertising their small crop at inflated prices. Much additional attention resulted when grower William Woodworth insured his avocado tree in 1913 for $30,000, making it, a local newspaper claimed, "the most valuable tree in existence."[19]

However, this type of publicity alone would not have sustained the boom. In 1915, a small group of early growers formed the California Avocado Society, an organization crucial to the further growth of the avocado industry. Made up largely of well-to-do hobbyists, nurserymen, botanists, and entrepreneurs, the California Avocado Society took the first steps to organize the avocado industry and would play a key role in sponsoring early marketing efforts. In particular, two members, a father and son, would be of central importance to the development of the early industry. Fred O. Popenoe was a horticultural pioneer who moved to Altadena, California, in 1904. With a number of investments in Mexico and Latin America, and a hobbyist's enthusiasm for gardening, he made the decision to combine the two in a business. A few years after his California arrival, he founded the West India Gardens, dedicated to the introduction of tropical plants to California. Having been intrigued by the avocado when he first encountered it, in 1911 Popenoe employed the son of Santa Fe Railroad's representative in Mexico, Carl Schmidt, to travel the main avocado-growing regions and send back promising budwood for California cultivation. (One of the samples that Schmidt sent back was named "Fuerte" ["strong"] by Popenoe, because it survived a frost that killed others. The Fuerte became, for a time, the dominant strain in the California industry, and is still one of the more commonly marketed avocados.)[20]

As Fred Popenoe advertised the profit potential of avocados via his nursery, his son, Wilson, who had caught the horticultural bug from his father and was trained as a botanist, became a USDA employee. Avocados were his special love; just as an orchid fancier becomes utterly absorbed in the discovery and crossbreeding of new varieties of the exotic flower, so did the younger Popenoe relish investigating the botanical qualities and eating potential of the myriad wild and domesticated strains of the Latin American fruit. Thanks primarily to the Popenoes' efforts, the nascent California avocado industry caught the attention of both the USDA and the University of California system. When the California Avocado Society petitioned the USDA for research support, the department agreed to send young Popenoe to Latin America as a plant explorer, to build on the earlier work of G. N. Collins and hunt for more strains of avocados suitable for California cultivation.[21]

Thus for nine years, from 1916 through 1924, Wilson Popenoe roamed Central and South America, periodically sending reports and avocado budwood to Southern California. He became well known outside the avocado industry as well, reporting on his adventures as an agricultural explorer in

National Geographic magazine, eventually becoming employed by the United Fruit Company as chief agronomist, and having his life in Guatemala chronicled in a book by Louis Adamic, *The House in Antigua*.[22]

Wilson Popenoe's reports, published in the *Yearbook of the California Avocado Society*, overflow with the boyish enthusiasm of a true avocado fanatic: "Here they were," he wrote in a 1920 report, "the gardens of Atlixco. Somewhere among all those trees below me, I thought to myself, must be the parent Fuerte, and the parent Puebla and many other trees I had come so a far to see."[23] Nonetheless, in Popenoe's explorations, and in the subsequent growth of the California industry, there was an undeniable element of colonial exploitation. Popenoe was sending budwood from Mexico, Guatemala, and Nicaragua to help California avocado trees develop resistance to disease and cold at the same time that federal legislation, passed in 1914, prohibited the importation of actual avocados from Mexico and Central America in the name of pest and disease control. (This prohibition still restricts the importation of avocados into the Southern California market.)

Popenoe himself was a great admirer of Latin Americans, and, in general, California avocado growers paid due homage to the south-of-the-border origins of their industry. In the 1930s members of the Avocado Society went on a pilgrimage to the original Fuerte tree and presented its owner with a plaque, "in testimony of our gratitude and appreciation."[24] Even those Californians most respectful of the Latin American people fitted the mold of the romantic sympathizers described by historian Frederic Pike— they paid homage to the noble simplicity, gracious traditions, and ancient ceremonies of its natives, but felt that way of life must yield to the cultivating energy of the progressive, development-oriented United States.[25] To the growers the avocado was a natural bounty of the tropics, a simple food which would benefit our overcivilized palates: "the Guatemalan porter does not offend his stomach by covering his avocado with condiments of all sorts. He breaks off a small piece of his tortilla and scoops out a bite of fruit, eating them together. I envy him," claimed grower Lester Keller in 1918. Nonetheless, as Wilson Popenoe argued, because of the inclination of "primitive races of people to devote their attention in the main to crops which give quick returns," the avocado remained "horticulturally speaking, a new fruit," and it was up to California to take the lead in proper application of plant science to place the avocado in the "position which ultimately it must occupy—that of staple foodstuff."[26]

The California avocado industry did take the lead in scientific development, but in congruence with its origins, it did so with an unprecedented amount of government support and during an era of rapidly rising prestige for scientific inquiry. Some of this support, again, came from propitious timing—the avocado emerged as a new crop just as the USDA was establishing agricultural experiment stations and the University of California was moving into applied research. Perhaps, too, the wealth of early avocado investors meant special attention from the government. Whatever the reason, in addition to the funding of Popenoe's expeditions, avocado growers would benefit from University of California and USDA studies on the nutritive value of the avocado, as well as chemical analyses to help establish standards of ripeness for marketing purposes. University of California scientists would also help in cataloging and standardizing various strains of the fruit, determining which would be most productive. Later, growers would receive assistance from university agronomists in establishing the cooperative marketing program that became Calavo. "Probably no other horticultural industry," the faculty of the College of Agriculture at Davis concluded in a 1946, " has had a similar advantage in its infancy."[27]

Even without the imprimatur of government support, the real estate industry would have oversold the commercial possibilities of avocado acreage. Now, armed with government-sponsored scientific and economic studies, their rhetoric took flight. From the late teens to the late 1920s, realtors advertised avocado lands from north of Santa Barbara to south of San Diego. As a *Business Week* article recalled in 1935:

> Visitors to southern California in 1927–29 remember that only the most elusive could dodge a free special train or sightseeing bus excursion trip which brought Iowans, Kansans, and not a few native sons to a tent where Judge or Senator Somebody, commission orator, would offer his sandwich munching audience a chance at independent incomes with enormous profits from a few acres of land suitable for avocados.[28]

These pitchmen's sales brochures, some of which were circulated as far as New York, combined pseudoscientific analyses of the avocado with more familiar real estate palaver. Of the many such examples of sales pamphlets, the work of realtor Edwin Hart, selling lands southeast of Los Angeles, might stand as typical example. Hart's brochure started, as did all of them, reciting the California dream of a leisurely suburban life in an ideal climate:

> Perhaps you have dreaming for years of a few acres out in God's big wide outdoors: a home perennially bathed in sunshine; trees studded with golden ripe fruit; and perhaps a few chickens too! A few acres of land—the basis of all wealth—upon which you could not only enjoy life but from which you could derive a greater income in order to further contribute to the happiness of your loved ones.

Hart, and the other brochures, then shifted into a plain-talking, hard-headed consideration of the financial possibilities (utterly ignoring the start-up costs, the uncertainties of agricultural production, and the fluctuations in the market):

> A good Avocado tree ten years old or more should produce 200 pounds on average and planted 60 trees to the acre would mean 12,000 pounds to the acre; at

only 10 cents per pound the return to the grower would be $1,200 gross. If all expenses connected with the growing amounted to as much as $400 per acre, it would still leave a net profit of $800 per acre. By 1940 these lands with producing avocado trees should be valued at from $3000 per acre up. Long before 1940 you should be on easy street.

Hart's brochure at least offered land; still another brochure dispensed with the necessity of owning the land altogether, and offered "annuities" in the avocado production of acreage in Ventura county:

Mr. Brown subscribes for an acre of avocados in the Calavoado estates tract for his son Jimmie . . . by the time he is seven years old the income begins. When he is ten the income has increased to $10,000 a year, more or less. When he is 17 the income should have doubled and should increase a little each year until he is 25 years old then continue at about the same rate for life.

But regardless of the financial terms they offered, all these ads, to clinch the deal, turned to product itself, equating nutritive value with market value. As Hart's brochure put it:

The Avocado is more than a dessert fruit or a relish—it is a Health fruit possessing unusual Vitalizing and Rejuvenating properties. It is a food of incomparable value for people with stomach or kidney trouble or for people who are debilitated. The avocado is the most complete natural product of the vegetable kingdom—it ranks with eggs and milk in its ability to sustain life. It has by analysis from 1.14 to 4.39% of protein, and from 9 to 31.6% of oil and is an excellent source of indispensable vitamines. Its fuel value will vary from 783–1376 calories per pound, which is far in excess of the fuel value of lean meat. The high oil content makes it a natural internal lubricant.

Or, as one other brochure neatly combined the appeals: "A heritage of Health to your Children in a cluster of Green Gold."[29]

Whether or not as a direct result of these brochures, an enormous expansion of acreage planted with avocados occurred during the teens and twenties. What had been at most a few acres in 1913, the beginning of the avocado boom, extended to 1,300 by 1920, and passed 7,000 by 1930. The result of this new acreage meant that the forty or so avocado growers who had shipped at most 1,000 pounds to local markets in 1915 had expanded to several hundred searching for national markets for over 100,000 pounds in 1925. By the end of the 1920s, the avocado crop was nearing a million pounds and still growing.[30] (See Table 1.) Consumer desire generated this phenomenal crop expansion, but it was a desire originating on the side of production, lured by dreams of pleasant country living amidst green gold. To sustain the vision, however, appeared to require what proved a much tougher marketing job—North Americans had to be convinced that the avocado deserved a place at their tables.

Table 1. Avocado Acreage, Production, and Average Price per Pound Received by Californian Farmers, 1925–1940[31]

Year	California Bearing Acreage	Californian Production in Pounds	Price per Pound to Californian Growers	Acreage outside California	Florida Production
1925	600	193,800	.36	800	200,000
1926	1,000	351,630	.30	1,100	300,000
1927	1,500	754,322	.30	1,300	500,000
1928	1,600	955,575	.35	1,500	800,000
1929	1,800	800,000	.32	1,500	840,000
1930	2,300	4,220,000	.13	1,500	1,240,000
1931	3,000	5,040,000	.08	1,600	1,640,000
1932	4,200	3,300,000	.09	1,600	2,800,000
1933	5,600	4,900,000	.08	1,600	4,400,000
1934	7,300	18,600,000	.05	1,600	4,000,000
1935	8,600	10,400,000	.09	1,600	2,000,000
1936	10,200	12,220,000	.07	1,700	1,200,000
1937	11,600	10,600,000	.08	1,700	4,000,000
1938	12,500	28,200,000	.05	1,700	4,200,000
1939	13,100	15,600,000	.07	1,700	4,400,000
1940	15,300	29,200,000	.05	1,900	1,660,000

THE ARISTOCRAT OF SALAD FRUITS: EARLY MARKETING EFFORTS

Moved by a sense of urgency spurred by the burgeoning number of growers and the increasing tonnage available to ship, the leaders of the California Avocado Society combined to support a cooperative marketing organization in 1924 that they named, as a result of a contest among members, Calavo. The cooperative was a familiar form of agricultural organization by the 1920s, designed to give farmers some control over the market for their goods. Those who joined packed and shipped their product under a single label and shared the costs and the profits according to the size of their crop. If enough growers joined, shippers and retailers, the middlemen in the consumer food chain, would be forced to deal with the cooperative as the sole representative of the growers, and the cooperative could then have a strong voice in setting prices, subject, of course, to variables such as supply and consumer demand.[32]

In forming Calavo, growers could draw on past experience. Both the citrus industry and the raisin industry had formed successful cooperatives in the decade before. They could also woo growers to their cooperative without fear of restraint-of-trade litigation. In 1923, the state of California had passed the Cooperative Marketing Act, "to encourage the intelligent and orderly marketing of agricultural products." Growers who joined Calavo agreed to ship all their crop through the organization's packing houses, with expenses deducted from the fruit's selling prices. They also agreed to pay a cent-per-pound tariff to support advertising the fruit. By the end of the 1920s, Calavo had signed up nearly 95 percent of the growers, giving the organization virtual control of the trade. The responsibility then fell to Calavo to advertise the fruit to national markets.[33]

Calavo marketers, while not innovators, were reasonably savvy in the culture of advertising. The director of Calavo, George Hodgkin, had worked for Sunkist, one of the great agricultural marketing successes, and Calavo in addition received the advice of the advertising agency Lord and Thomas. These professionals believed that in introducing a new fruit, especially one as unusual as the avocado, they not only had to suggest culinary uses for the fruit, they also had to associate values with the avocado that were not necessarily related to the avocado as a food.[34] Supply of avocados was steadily increasing, but availability on the national market was still limited, so high retail prices (from 50 to 85 cents apiece in the late twenties) were the norm. Marketers understood that at those prices, they needed to appeal to the "the type of hostess who, regardless of cost would serve Calavos" and they believed that, as Lord and Thomas advertiser Don Francisco told the California Avocado Society:

> If you can make people think it is the proper thing to have an Calavo cocktail or salad, it is a mighty important influence . . . for instance it got around that broccoli was a smart thing to serve for all menus. It suddenly appeared on the menus of fashionable restaurants. Few people knew just what it was or where it came from, but thousands of people began wanting broccoli because it was the new and proper thing to serve.[35]

Pursuing this "top-down" strategy, for its first national advertising campaign in 1928 Calavo placed ads in upper-crust magazines *Vogue* and *The New Yorker.* The pitch was to make Calavo avocados the "aristocrat of salad fruits," to be served in elegant surroundings at special occasions. The 1930 *New Yorker* ad, for example, straining to match the arch wit of the magazine itself, promoted the serving of avocados for those occasions: "When the bridge unbeatable come for dinner. But first we will serve Calavos, my dear, and crack their hauteur." "Their chagrin at your coupe cuisine will do weird things to their game."[36]

Some complications arose in the decision to position the fruit as an item of aristocratic fashion. As part of that process, the advertisers attempted to distinguish their product from avocados grown in Florida and

Cuba by referring to all their fruit as "Calavos" rather than avocados, as in "blend three Calavos with chili sauce."[37] As Calavo head George Hodgkin explained the strategy, "Calavo, The Aristocrat of Salad Fruits is not only superior, but distinct and apart from ordinary avocados."[38] Yet this was the fourth name used for the fruit in the United States. In the Eastern United States, Americans were accustomed to calling avocados "alligator pears." Early on, Californian growers after a brief debate on whether to use the more "authentic" "aguacate," the Mexican word for avocado, had decided to campaign for the anglicized version of the name.[39] Calavo marketers were hoping, however, to build high-class associations with their fruit and accomplish what is known in today's marketing parlance as "building the brand." This strategy was already a time tested one for basic necessity such as soap. It was not necessarily the most effective in introducing a fruit unfamiliar to the majority of potential customers. Through the thirties some confusion occurred over terminology, as recipes appearing in newspapers and cookbooks might refer to an avocado cocktail, or alligator pear cocktail, or Calavo cocktail. As the *Vista Press* grumbled in an editorial, "avocados should be avocados, avocado trees should be avocado trees, . . . and there are reasons why the adoption of such a name is confusing and will become of lessening value as the avocado becomes a greater problem from which to derive profits."[40]

In fact, the attempt to substitute Calavo for avocado did not last, but the "top-down" approach to marketing continued through the Great Depression. Beginning in the late 1920s, to "teach consumers just how to use Calavos in order to take full advantage of the flavor and food value," Calavo employed a "group of famous home economics writers" many of them syndicated columnists, to prepare recipes using avocados, which they then featured in their columns, distributed by Calavo to grocery stores or sent by request. The suggested recipes they chose to feature were those of fancy salads, suitable for ladies' luncheons or dinners with guests. These recipes included avocado with grapefruit salad and french dressing (judging by cookbooks, perhaps the most commonly recommended way to serve avocados through the 1950s); Calavo cocktail, with a dressing made of mayonnaise, cream, catsup, and lemon juice; Calavo cardinale, an avocado stuffed with cold lobster and mayonnaise; and Calavo Omelet A La Reine, a cheese omelet topped with avocado. Missing entirely was anything that suggested the fruit's Latin American origins—not even something close to guacamole.[41]

There was nothing surprising in this neglect of the food's origins. The 1930s was not a period where ethnic food had any consumer appeal, especially in the upper-class markets at which Calavo was aiming. Further, as Harvey Levenstein has pointed out, it is generally true that when dominant nations adopt the food of subordinate ones, they try to disassociate the food from its "inferior" origins.[42] Ironically, many of the pickers and most of the packers of avocados were Mexican-American. Though on the whole the avocado industry did not have the labor troubles experienced by the citrus and other farming industries, still, no matter how quiescent the workers, the growers' perception of Mexican-Americans as cheap labor would have rendered them undesirable as consumers.[43]

In fact, however, it was precisely in those regions where south-of-the-border influences prevailed that the avocado sales had their greatest success. On the whole Calavo did a remarkable job of moving the fruit in conditions of economic depression, winning the plaudits of *Business Week* in 1935 in an article entitled "Calavo Growers Star as Sellers." Prices were low, ranging from 5 to 9 cents a pound, but gross returns per acre were high enough that few growers went out of business. Over 75 percent of the avocados, however, were sold in California and the Southwestern states, suggesting that no matter how hard Calavo pushed elegant recipes for hostesses searching for something new to impress their guests, those influenced by Latin American culinary traditions and already aware of the avocado were doing the bulk of the buying.

In striving to reach a national, upper-class market, Calavo growers also retreated from earlier hopes about avocados in the American diet. Growers before World War I had talked of the "food value" of the fruit, meaning its nutritive qualities, and argued that the avocado might become a staple in North American diets as a "substitute for meat" because of its high natural fat content. "A pound of avocados equals a pound of beef-steak" asserted grower William Spinks.[44] USDA researcher Collins had called the avocado a "salad fruit" in 1904, but this designation hardly seemed adequate to establish avocados as a culinary gold mine. Further, judging from the California Avocado Society membership and rough grower censuses, the overwhelming majority of avocado growers were men, and it is clear that talk of a salad fruit offended the gender sensibilities of some of the growers, who associated salad with effete aristocratic society. As grower Lester Keller put it:

> I believe the word "Salad" has done more to injure the introduction of the avocado than most anything else. We are not a salad eating race, like the French for instance. The impression has seemingly gotten well established that avocados are only eaten in salads by the idle rich who have cultivated a taste for the things.

Subsequent avocado marketing occasionally showed the heritage of this male concern, running ads into the 1940s that the avocado helped create a salad that "even husbands can love."[45]

By this time, the salad, still associated strongly with women, was now understood by nutritionists to be part of a healthy and lean regimen. Calavo advertisers thus hoped to position the avocado as an important auxiliary to a culinary trend. Horticulturist and avocado grower J. Eliot Coit described the new circumstances:

> The American citizen is giving more thought to the effect of different foods on his complexion, his digestion, his elimination. The science of dietetics is booming. . . . The avocado being the aristocrat of salad fruits, fits precisely into this trend of the times. Rest assured that from now on the citizen is going to have a fresh salad with his hog hominy. The remarkable rise of the lettuce industry proves that. The point for us is to decide is whether that lettuce leaf on his salad dish will support diced avocados or sliced cucumbers.[46]

The salad emerged as a crucial part of the meal in part because fashionable society had declared war on fat, and "dieting" had become part of the popular lexicon. By the 1920s women were the primary targets of the stress on slimness, and since the American housewife presumably made the decisions about what appeared on the table, it was to women that Calavo directed its advertising campaigns.[47]

Unfortunately, in assigning the avocado to that part of the menu that was so associated with dieting, advertisers ran into difficulties with the high natural fat content that early growers had been convinced made avocados the staple food of the future. Aware from the beginning that this was a problem, Calavo advertisers attempted to confront the problem of the avocado's "richness" by describing its nutritives as "stored in natural fruit oil." They also suggested that the avocado's fat made a healthy substitution for other types of fats; among the recipes suggested in the Calavo recipe book was Calavonnaise, a "slenderizing alternative" to regular mayonnaise, and by the earlier thirties, ads appeared suggesting that half an avocado as lunch would "streamline your salads." After World War II, what writer Michelle Stacy calls the "tyranny of the calorie" only intensified, and ads through the fifties into the 1980s assured consumers that the avocado was not "fattening," each half of an avocado containing slightly under 150 calories.[48]

AVOCADOS FOR THE MASSES: POSTWAR MARKETING

Whether it was caloric qualities of the fruit, the culinary conservatism of the Depression, or the limitations of Calavo's ad campaign, the national market failed to develop even into the forties. In response to accusations of neglecting the national market, Calavo officials pointed to the fragmented nature of avocado growing in California. The bulk of avocado growers remained wealthy hobbyists and small producers. "The avocado is rich and nutty and so are those who grow it" one grower had quipped in the 1920s, and through the immediate postwar era, avocado growing remained an avocation for many growers. Well into the 1950s, two thirds of Calavo members produced less than 50 percent of the crop. This allowed for some remarkable individual stories, including Jennie Gano, a "plucky seamstress from Indiana" as the *Los Angeles Times* characterized her in 1936, who was one of the few women growers of the fruit. She "used to lug a suitcase full of avocados on a twice a week round of Los Angeles markets and hotels" but she eventually made herself comfortably wealthy and produced a hybrid which won a place in markets. Another amateur-made-good story was that of Rudolph G. Hass, a Pasadena mail carrier whose patented summer bearing hybrid, the Hass, became after World War II the most commonly planted avocado.[49] Still, the number of small producers and the different varieties emerging from their groves inhibited the type of mass marketing based on systematized production that was the norm even for goods like lettuce, a notoriously unpredictable crop. To make matters more difficult, avocado trees revealed a disturbing tendency to alternate bearing—heavy one year, and little the next. As Calavo marketers complained, new customers gained with low prices and heavy advertising one year would be lost with high prices the next. Without an orderly supply, how could they build demand?[50]

Growers who still harbored fantasies of green gold were in no mood for such excuses, no matter how justified they might be. Supply was steadily increasing and then took a sudden jump upward when, as prosperity returned after the war, there was a new boom in avocado planting. Avocado groves had remained marginally profitable during the thirties, based on developing regional markets, but investors again seemed to be using criteria other than rational calculation in deciding that avocados equaled prosperity. As in the 1920s, new growers seemed driven as much by visions of a Southern California lifestyle as by hopes of avocado profits. *The Saturday Evening Post*, *Look*, and the important Western regional magazine *Sunset* carried features on the avocado-growing life in the late forties and fifties, with pictures of the bucolic avocado estates of film director Frank Capra and baseball great Duke Snider. *The Saturday Evening Post* story asserted that "supply just can't seem to keep up with ever increasing demand," and was illustrated with pictures of joyful families picking together in their groves. A columnist for the *Santa Ana Register* complained that in these stories:

> [I]t was made to appear that almost anyone out of the East could come to
> Southern California, collect an avocado tree or two, pitch a hammock between
> them and wait for the fruit to ripen. When it did ripen, it immediately turned to
> gold. Security, prosperity, and happiness ever after.[51]

Despite warnings from the Orange County Farm Bureau chief that "the avocado industry needs to be deglamourized," acreage rapidly increased. From 1949 to 1954, over 800 acres a year were planted with avocados, most in an area north and east of San Diego. By 1960, total plantings stood at over 20,000 acres. The number of pounds of avocados sent to market in good years now numbered in the tens of millions, and by the early sixties, in the hundreds of millions. With such production, prices rarely rose above 20 cents a pound through the 1950s and 1960s, dropping well below that figure in high-yield years. At these prices, farm advisors reported to the Avocado Society, only acreage that bore over 5,000 pounds a year could make a profit, but the average production per acre was often below that figure, bearing from 2,000 to 3,000 pounds a year. Little wonder that a survey of San Diego growers done in the late 1960s found that only five of 345 growers depended on avocados for their entire income. Most were retirees or absentee farmers who paid managers to cultivate their groves and who made only occasional appearances at their estates.[52]

Nonetheless, even hobbyists and retirees chafed at losing money year after year, and Calavo faced new imperatives to develop national consumer demand. Wartime advertising had continued with themes developed in the late 1920s: "Many V-gardners have made their salads more delightful and richer in food value with an addition of purchased avocados. . . . People like new foods, especially if the foods have goodness and glamour. Avocados are veritable grenades of glamour."[53] But with avocado prices dropping down to 10 cents a piece at the retail level, it was no longer adequate to aim at upper-class gourmets with grenades of glamour. Furthermore, Calavo was facing increasing dissension from the ranks of the growers, who complained that Calavo had failed to develop the national market. Calavo still remained the largest marketing organization, but the percentage of growers who belonged to the cooperative fell to under 60 percent in the mid-1950s.[54]

As production continued to increase and prices continued to drop through the 1950s, grower disaffection led to a dramatic change in the organizational basis of avocado marketing. With the support of a law that allowed the formation of a marketing association funded by mandatory contributions of all directly associated with the industry, growers voted to form the California Avocado Advisory Board in 1961. This board then assumed the bulk of the responsibility for advertising California-grown avocados to a consumer market, with Calavo working only for its members and concentrating on retailers. (The board, now called the California Avocado Commission and no longer funded by mandatory grower fees, still had most of the marketing responsibility in the late 1990s.)[55]

Later, growers would credit this shift in marketing organization with increasing the demand for avocados, but the board's main contribution seemed to be continuing old themes with more money and a more ads. They continued to use women's magazines as their primary promotional platform, and they continued to fight the perception of avocados as fattening while beginning to develop a countercampaign on the healthfulness of avocados. They also sought tie-ins with national food manufacturers such as Kraft, but a general reluctance to recognize the fruit's role in ethnically derived regional cuisine remained. Avocado marketers understood, as William F. Cowan, vice president of Calavo put it in 1966, that "this generation's homemakers like to prepare exciting and daringly different meals. It's a swinging generation whose demands we intend to serve," but that still did not include advertising the avocado's place in Latin American–influenced foods.[56] The first recipes for guacamole, along with pronunciation aids, "Say Huakamole," had appeared in the late 1940s, suggesting a greater willingness to play up the exotic character of the avocado. But marketers tried harder in the two decades following World War II to link the avocado with the processed food of the mass market than with a zesty south-of-the-border menu.

As Donna Gabaccia has noted, the processed-food industry did not necessarily require a denial of ethnic associations, as the decades after World War II saw a new partnership between ethnic foodways and national corporations, with products Chef Boyardee Spaghetti, Gebhardt Chili, and, most significant for the avocado's future, Frito Lay's chips.[57] For a time in the 1960s, Calavo tried to market its avocados with a "luau" promotion, almost suggesting that the avocado as a tropical fruit came from the Pacific rather than south of the border. Even as late as 1975 the California Avocado Advisory Board published a cookbook, *Avocado Bravo: Spain's Legacy to California Cuisine,* which offered recipes for a refined serving of avocado "Spanish style"—garnished with "fresh mint and lemon juice, with a tulip of sherry by the side," juxtaposed with "the time honored Mexican way; a little tequila, a lick of the salt from the back of the hand, a squeeze of the lime . . . then the avocado. With a tortilla or two this is a Mexican meal." Plainly this cookbook was as condescending toward south-of-the-border culture as the most benighted grower of the early twentieth century. In its attempt to deemphasize Mexico, it even suggested at one point that guacamole was "Mediterranean" in origin: "Every crook and corner of the Mediterranean has its own ancestral and hotly defended recipes for the spicy sauces and relishes called salsas. California towns and cites, north and south, are now a source of such salsas—savory and redolent of the mother dishes from the Mediterranean."[58]

Fortunately, the end of such mission-era fantasies was in sight, for the cultural climate had changed, and the market for avocados was carried along with it. Guacamole received an official coming-out recognition in 1970, at least in the Western region, when *Sunset* magazine put avocados on the cover for its article "Guacamole: Sauce of the Americas": "It's endlessly versatile. It's a dip, a sauce, a dressing, a spread. It's guacamole." From the mid-seventies on, the avocado industry acknowledged, even if it did not embrace, the "sauce of the Americas" in its ads and in its products. In the 1960s Calavo had mastered the technique of quick-freezing avocado pulp so that it would not discolor or turn rancid when thawed. It sold the frozen pulp primarily to restaurants and food service chains, but by the mid-1970s it was also selling its own brand of guacamole, something it continues to do today. Though the California Avocado Commission only reluctantly celebrated guacamole, it fully recognized the value of the image of the California lifestyle. Well into the eighties, the commission linked the avocado with an image of California as being informal, "natural," and, well, swinging, with its "Love Fruit from California" campaign. Even as suburbanites stocked their kitchen with appliances in "Avocado Green," the avocado as food finally seemed to be reaching the mass market.[59] "The public interest in avocado seems insatiable," Calavo reported in 1976.[60]

Meanwhile, interest in avocados was extending elsewhere in the world. In Israel, growers used U.S. techniques of cooperative marketing and state support to expand a European market for the fruit.[61] In the motherland of the Californian avocado industry, Mexico, growers were increasing their production to over a billion pounds, eight times what California's industry produced. Partly under the influence of this expanded production, and partly because of a postwar celebration of "authentic" Mestizo cuisine, avocado consumption in Mexico nearly tripled from 1970 to 1989; its per capita consumption, at 8 kilograms, was also eight times that of the United States. What Wilson Popenoe had paternalistically argued, that U.S. scientific expertise could benefit the less-developed south, had indeed occurred in the avocado industry, as Mexico profited from U.S. growing techniques and the Hass hybridization. At the same time, a Mexican reaction against U.S. influences generated a new celebration of the pre-Columbian fruit of the Aztecs.[62]

Meanwhile, in the United States the influence of Latino culture via immigration brought increasing sales, which led to another surge in avocado acreage. Between 1979 and 1984, planting tripled, with total acreage peaking in 1987 at nearly 80,000. What made this most recent boom more remarkable is that it occurred exclusively in Ventura and Northern San Diego counties, north and south of Los Angeles, respectively, while Los Angeles and Orange County, meanwhile, were losing most of their orchards to residential development. Though the market was undeniably expanding, once again, this boom in planting seems due to factors tangential to the demand for the fruit. Calavo officials cited "developers, syndicators, and tax-shelters" as responsible for the expansion. Numerically the industry continued to be dominated by small planters, with 58 percent of the orchards less than 5 acres, suggesting the continuing allure of an avocado ranch in Southern California to retirees and prosperous corporate managers.[63]

But this most recent boom in California avocado acreage may have been the last. In the 1980s, troubles beset the industry. High production led to low prices in the early eighties, at a time when water costs were increasing. Then, later in the decade, bad weather cut supplies so severely that all growers lost money. The early 1990s brought some highly profitable years, but water costs remained high. Irregularities in supply combined with troubling indications that a national market still was not fully developed. In fact through the early 1990s, 75 percent of avocados produced were consumed in California and the Southwest, a percentage little changed from the Great Depression. Fortunately for the growers, the number of people living in that region had increased dramatically, as did the influence of Latinos on the culture of the region—so the avocado industry remained afloat on the demographic shift to the Sunbelt.[64]

For the first time in its history, however, the California industry faced a threatening political environment. Since the 1970s, Mexican growers had petitioned for entry to the U.S. retail market, arguing that the pest problems that had presumably prevented their avocados' entry into the U.S. market had been eliminated. The clout of California growers had long kept them at bay. But in the late 1980s and 1990s, an inexorable ideological momentum toward "free trade" began to undermine growers' defenses. Such was the political influence of these generally wealthy Southern Californians that even the passage of the North American Free Trade Agreement (NAFTA) in 1994 did not mean the end of the avocado ban, as growers won a special exemption on the basis of protection against pests. The Mexican avocado industry, however, was now virtually pest-free—so much so that California packers Calavo and Mission Produce had opened plants in Mexico for packing and shipping the Mexican fruit to Europe and Japan.[65] The Californians' arguments were so clearly based on attempts to protect their closed market that even usually sympathetic Washington officials were forced to recognize the validity of Mexican protests about this violation of NAFTA principles. The USDA also came under pressure from other domestic fruit industries, which saw themselves as being held out of Mexican markets because of the avocado controversy. Also siding with the Mexican industry against the California growers, in an ironic echo of ads run by the California Avocado Commission, was the Consumers Union. "Avocados are a great food," the Consumers Union San Francisco representative, Bryan Silberman, argued as a reason for doing away with the ban. "This is a test of USDA's intent to improve the lot of consumers."[66]

Finally, in early 1997, the USDA lifted the ban on Mexican avocado imports, albeit with strict provisions that limited the regions and periods in which they were shipped. On the basis of the pest-control issue, California growers had been able temporarily to protect their own key markets in the Southwest. Long-term worries remained that once through the door, Mexican avocados would be able to expand their access into the Southwest markets, where their lower labor and water costs would give them an unbeatable price advantage.[67]

Whether cheaper Mexican fruit will have any more luck in expanding the Eastern U.S. market remains to be seen. The avocado is now firmly associated with guacamole and with Latino cuisine, so much so that its consumption peaks at over 30 million pounds on two specific days of the year, the day of the Super Bowl and Cinco de Mayo. California marketers have now launched a campaign, "Blazing Avocados," to help "shed the guacamole-only image."[68] In some respects, this is an unwitting acknowledgment of marketing failure, since California marketers have never stressed guacamole as the main use of the avocado, and the "guacamole-only image" arose independently of any industry efforts. Nonetheless it is true, as Mark Affleck, head of the California Avocado Commission, points out, that "in California consumers also use avocados in everything from sandwiches and avocado sorbet to facial cream," and for the extent of this regional use, the state avocado industry deserves full credit.[69]

CONCLUSION

The avocado's place in the national diet is now well established, if predictable: it occasionally appears in salads and sandwiches but most often it will be pureed and consumed with salty snacks. However ambivalent their role in its current use, California marketers successfully familiarized North Americans with an unusual fruit. Prosperous, white, predominantly male growers from the 1920s through the 1950s appropriated the avocado from south of the border and, with sophisticated marketing, did their best to divorce it of its ethnic connotations and to expand its upscale appeal. They never quite succeeded in either attempt, though some of the more manly early growers would undoubtedly be gratified that in contemporary America, football games and corn chips, and not fancy dinners and salad-making, generate peak avocado consumption. Still, on a regional level, the recipes encouraged by marketers and published in *Sunset* and local newspapers did help demarcate a post–World War II California cuisine.[70] To the degree that the development of the California industry supplied expertise and entrepreneurial stimulus to growers in other countries, including Israel and even, indirectly, Mexico, Californians also played a role in whetting appetites for the fruit worldwide. Thus California growers might not have shaped palates as they planned, but they did help create conditions that allowed guacamole to circle the globe.

NOTES

1. M.L. McMahan, "The Last Thirty Inches," *California Avocado Society 1954 Yearbook* (Santa Ana, 1954), p. 135.
2. Roland Barthes discusses food as "a system of communication, a body of images, a protocol of usages, situations and behavior" in "Toward a Psychosociology of Conemporary Food Consumption," excerpted in Carole Counihan and Penny Van Esterik, *Food and Culture: A Reader* (New York: Routledge, 1997), pp. 20–27.
3. Sidney Mintz, *Sweetness and Power: The Place of Sugar in Modern History* (New York: Viking Press, 1985).
4. The term is from Mary Douglas, "Deciphering a Meal," in *Implicit Meanings* (Boston: Routledge, 1975).
5. Alan Ward, *Consumption, Food and Taste: Culinary Antinomies and Commodity Culture* (London: Sage Publications, 1997), p. 29. Ward identifies "culinary antinomies" that he feels emerge from twentieth-century anxieties surrounding food. He focuses on the wavering between novelty and tradition, health and indulgence, economy and extravagance, and care and convenience. All these "antinomies" are visible in avocado marketing.
6. Revealingly, these explorers worked in the division of "plant industry," indicating thinking about the economic purpose of their work, to assist the U.S. agricultural "industry." Lester D. Langley and Thomas Schoonover, *The Banana Men: American Mercenaries and*

Entrepreneurs in Central America, 1880–1930 (Lexington, KY: University Press of Kentucky, 1995); Michael F. Jiménez, "From Plantation to Cup": Coffee and Capitalism in the United States, 1830–1930," in William Roseberry, Lowell Gudmundson, and Mario Samper Kutschbach, *Coffee, Society, and Power in Latin America* (Baltimore: Johns Hopkins University Press, 1995).

7. G. N. Collins, *The Avocado, A Salad Fruit from the Tropics* (Washington, DC: Government Printing Office, 1905).

8. "Three ripe aquacates in halves, take out the stone or seed and scoop the pulp from the skin, add tomatoes, half a green pepper pod, crush and pound the whole, add onion juice, salt, lemon juice. Suitable for breakfast, lunch or dinner." *Cooking School Magazine* 9 (Oct., 1904): 153, cited in Collins, *The Avocado, A Salad Fruit from the Tropics*, p. 44.

9. Charles B. Heiser, "Origins of Some Cultivated New World Plants," *Annual Review of Ecology and Systematics* 10 (1979): 309–326; Wilson Popenoe, *Manual of Tropical and Subtropical Fruits* (New York: The Macmillan Company, 1920), pp. 14–20.

10. One might add another, highly speculative point that the avocado's discovery coincided with a period in European aristocratic cooking which stressed elaborate preparation, not something that suited the avocado's culinary qualities well. Stephen Mennell, *All Manners of Food: Eating and Taste in England and France from the Middle Ages to the Present* (Oxford: Basil Blackwell, 1985), pp. 62–101.

11. Carey McWilliams, *Southern California: An Island on the Land* (Santa Barbara: Peregrine Smith, 1973); Norris Hundley, *The Great Thirst: Californians and Water, 1770s–1990s* (Berkeley: University of California Press, 1992); Norman Klein, *The History of Forgetting: Los Angeles and the Erasure of Memory* (New York: Verso, 1997), pp. 27–38.

12. On the Californian agricultural "revolution," see Stephen Stoll, *The Fruits of Natural Advantage: Making the Industrial Countryside in California* (Berkeley: University of California Press, 1998); on the citrus industry, the articles in the special issue of *California History*, LXXIV (Spring, 1995), esp. Ronald Tobey and Charles Wetherell, "The Citrus Industry and the Revolution of Corporate Capitalism in Southern California, 1887–1944," 6–21; and Douglas Cazaux Sackman, "'By Their Fruits Ye Shall Know Them': 'Nature Cross Culture Hybridization' and the California Citrus Industry," 1893–1939," 82–99.

13. Ian Tyrrell, *True Gardens of the Gods: Californian-Australian Environmental Reform, 1860–1930* (Berkeley: University of California Press 1999), pp. 36–55; David Vaught, *Cultivating California: Growers, Specialty Crops, and Labor, 1875–1920* (Baltimore: The Johns Hopkins University Press, 1999), pp. 11–53.

14. Ronald Tobey and Charles Wetherell, "The Citrus Industry," 14.

15. P. H. Rolfs, "New Opportunities in Subtropical Fruit Growing," in *U.S. Agriculture Yearbook* (Washington, DC: U.S. Government Printing Office, 1905), pp. 439–444. Wilson Popenoe, *Manual of Tropical and Subtropical Fruits*, published later, in 1920, was in part a guidebook to those considering the economic feasibility of the various fruits listed here.

16. Quote from Dana C. King, "Marketing Obstacles and Problems," Proceedings of the California Avocado Society, Second Semi-Annual Meeting, Los Angeles, April 29, 1916, pp. 32–34; similar sentiments are expressed in C. P. Taft, "Things to Be Expected," Proceedings of the California Avocado Society, First Semi-Annual Meeting, Los Angeles, Oct. 23, 1915, pp. 72–73; and William A. Spinks, "The Avocado: Fruit that Will Feed the Hungry Millions and Tickle the Palates of Kings," *Monrovia Independent* (Feb. 2, 1915), clipping in Avocado Scrapbooks, vol. 3, Special Collections, University of California, Riverside (hearafter AS, UCR).

17. P. H. Rolfe, "New Opportunities in Subtropical Fruit Growing," p. 441; Collins, "The Avocado, A Salad Fruit from the Tropics," p. 44; James Edgar Higgins, et. al., "The Avocado in Hawaii" Bulletin no. 25, Hawaii Agricultural Experiment Station, 1911.

18. On the Florida industry, see Clyde B. Markeson, "Economic Aspects of Marketing Florida Avocados," Marketing Research Report 614, USDA, August, 1963.

19. "A Valuable Tree," *Whittier News* (Dec. 17, 1913) (AS, vol. 4, UCR.); Harold Kegley, "Famous California Pear Tree," *Overland* 65 (January, 1915): 70–72. On the origins of avocado growing in California, see Claude B. Hutchison, ed., *California Agriculture: By Members of the Faculty of the College of Agriculture University of California* (Berkeley and Los Angeles: University of California Press, 1946), pp. 214–216.

20. Ira J. Condit, "History of the Avocado and Its Varieties in California with a Check List of All Named Varieties," in Proceedings of the California Avocado Society, Third Semi-Annual Meeting, San Diego, California, October 30 and 31, 1916, pp. 105–122; Joyce Bertoldi, *Avocados: Growing, Harvesting, Marketing* (Las Vegas: Observational Research Publications, 1989), pp. 5–10; C. A. Schroeder, "A Historical Document in California Avocado History," and Don Gustafson, "World Avocado Production," in *California Avocado Society 1976 Yearbook*, 60, pp. 34–76.

21. Wilson Popenoe, *The Development of the Avocado Industry* (Los Angeles: California Avocado Society, 1948); Claude Hutchison, ed., *California Agriculture*, 215.
22. R.B. Swain, "In Search of the Mangosteen," *Horticulture* 69 (December, 1991): 54–58; Louis Adamic's *The House in Antigua: A Restoration* (New York: Harper and Brothers, 1937) is an odd book, partly a homage to Wilson Popenoe ("Pop") and his wife Dorothy, who was also a botanist and who died tragically early when she consumed too much of a toxic fruit, and partly a meditation on the house they restored, which Adamic sees as a romantic representation of Latin American civilization.
23. Wilson Popenoe, "Atlixco," Proceedings of the Semi-Annual Meeting, California Avocado Society, Santa Barbara, October 24, 25, 1919, pp. 24–43.
24. *California Avocado Society Yearbook, 1938* (Los Angeles: Citragraph Printing, 1938), pp. 49–53.
25. Frederick B. Pike, *The United States and Latin America: Myths and Stereotypes of Civilization and Nature* (Austin: University of Texas Press, 1992), esp. pp. 195–285.
26. Lester Keller, "How Far Can We Go with the Avocado as a Food?" Proceedings, California Avocado Society, Third Annual Meeting, Los Angeles, May 18 and 19, 1918, pp. 26–31; Wilson Popenoe, *Manual of Tropical and Subtropical Fruits* (New York: The Macmillan Co., 1920), p. 10.
27. Claude Hutchison, ed., *California Agriculture*, pp. 215–216. Warren Belasco has suggested to me that the government support might have come as result of a "major Malthusian scare" that spurred the U.S. government to develop new tropical foods to meet the predicted worldwide food crisis. This general concern would also help explain Wilson Popenoe's employment as a USDA "plant explorer."
28. "Calavo Growers Star as Sellers," *Business Week* (August 31, 1935): 20.
29. Volume 4 of the Avocado scrapbooks, housed in the Special Collections Library of the University of California Riverside, contains fifteen of these brochures, focusing on land in Ventura County, north San Diego County, and south San Diego. The brochure featured was entitled "Growth" and was put out by Edwin G. Hart and Co. in 1924.
30. Statistics from *Annual Report*, Calavo Growers, Inc., 1934.
31. From Edward Rada, "Mainland Market for Hawaiian Avocados," Agricultural Economics Report no. 18, USDA, September, 1953, p. 12.
32. On the formation of Calavo, see William H. Sallmon, "Marketing Avocados," in *Annual Report of the California Avocado Association for the Years 1923 and 1924* (Los Angeles, 1924), pp. 33–35; on agricultural cooperatives, see Victoria Saker Woeste, *The Farmer's Benevolent Trust: Law and Agricultural Cooperation in Industrial America, 1865–1945* (Chapel Hill: The University of North Carolina Press, 1998).
33. John H. Hart, "The California Avocado Growers Exchange and the Cooperative Marketing Act," *Annual Report of the California Avocado Society for the Years 1923 and 1924*, pp. 55–57.
34. Although here, as their cooperative organizations, avocado marketers drew extensively on the earlier examples of California citrus and other fruits, they departed in some ways from these fruits' success. Advertisers of oranges, pears, and raisins had carefully constructed a set of associations with California sunshine and an invigorating outdoor life. Avocado sellers in more recent times have skillfully exploited these connections, but early on chose an alternate strategy of stressing the fruit's "elegance." Of course, as Steven Stoll pointed out, fruits such as oranges and pears "needed little consumer education" to be appealing. This perhaps was not the case with the avocado. On marketing pears and stone fruit, see Stoll, *The Fruits of Natural Advantage*, pp. 63–93; on citrus advertising, see Douglas Sackman, "By Their Fruits Ye Shall Know Them."
35. Don Francisco, "On Marketing," *Yearbook, 1929* (Los Angeles: California Avocado Society 1929),p. 68.
36. Ad appearing in the *New Yorker* (Dec 20, 1930) AS, v. 5, UCR.
37. Florida and Cuban avocados, of a different "West Indian" variety, tended to ripen in the summer and fall, while most California varieties ripened in the winter and spring, so competition between them was not direct. In fact, beginning in the late thirties through the 1960s, Calavo did some marketing for a few Florida avocado farms. Nonetheless, California growers were anxious to protect their product from even potential competitive threats, and in addition to supporting the "renaming" of their fruit, got legislation passed in the late 1920s that barred Florida avocados from being sold in California, a prohibition that remained until the U.S. Supreme Court declared it unconstitutional in 1961. Markeson, "Economic Aspects of Marketing Florida Avocados," pp. 16–25.
38. George Hodgkin, "Third Annual Report, California Avocado Growers Exchange, January 1, 1927," in *Yearbook of the California Avocado Society, 1927*, p. 145.
39. "Report of the First Semi-Annual Meeting of the California Avocado Association, Los Angeles, May 15, 1915," in *Annual Report of the California Avocado Society, 1915* (Riverside,

CA, 1915), pp. 79–84; Thomas H. Shesdden, "How Shall We Eliminate the Alligator Pear," in *Annual Report of the California Avocado Society, 1917* (Riverside, CA, 1917), p. 42.

40. "Cooperative Marketing and Harmony Necessary," *Vista Press* (January 19, 1929), clipping in AS, v. 7 UCR.

41. *Calavo Book for Chefs* (Calavo Growers of California, 1932).

42. Harvey Levenstein, *Paradox of Plenty: A Social History of Eating in Modern America* (New York: Oxford University Press, 1993), pp. 216–217.

43. Avocados can be picked over a period of several months, alleviating labor pressures on the harvest season; further, groves were on the whole relatively small, not needing large labor gangs, and Calavo ran only one packing plant during the thirties, which was unionized in 1936. (The plant experienced a strike in 1944, but it seemed to be more associated with the Teamster takeover of the Packer's Union than with strong antimanagement sentiment). Strike described in *Annual Report 1946*, Calavo Growers, Inc.; Sidney E. Saunby, "A Glimpse of Union Against Union" clipping from the *Los Angeles Times* ca. 1945, AS, v. 7, UCR.

44. William A. Spinks, "The Avocado: Fruit that Will Feed the Hungry Millions and Tickle the Palates of Kings," *Los Angeles Times* (Feb. 2, 1915), clipping in AS, v. 3, UCR; Wilson Popenoe, "Avocados as Food in Guatemala," *Journal of Heredity*, vol. ix (March 1918): 1–17.

45. Lester Keller, "How Far Can We Go with the Avocado as Food," 27; Ad clipping from *Twin Falls Idaho News* (Jan. 6, 1934), AS, v. 7 UCR, and ad from the 1940s reprinted in *Annual Report, Calavo Inc.*, 1985.

46. Eliot Coit, "The Avocado: Retrospect and Prospect," Report of the Annual Meeting of the California Avocado Society, Whittier, May 19, 1928, in *Yearbook of the California Avocado Society, 1928*, p. 73.

47. On the rise of salads and concern with nutrition in the 1920s, see Harvey Levenstein, *Paradox of Plenty*, pp. 9–39; on changing attitudes toward fat and dieting, see Peter N. Stearns, *Fat History: Bodies and Beauty in the Modern West* (New York: New York University Press, 1997), pp. 3–97; and Hillel Schwartz, *Never Satisfied: A Cultural History of Diets, Fantasies and Fat* (New York: The Free Press, 1986) pp. 77–187.

48. Michelle Stacy, *Consumed: Why Americans Love Hate and Fear Food* (New York: Simon and Schuster, 1994), pp. 28–35. From the 1940s on, Calavo ran periodic ads that reassured consumers that half an avocado had "under 150 calories."

49. Mary June Burton, "Avocados Made to Order," *Los Angeles Times* (August 30, 1936); "Pasadena Mail Carrier Receives Patent," *Pasadena Post-Gazette* (September 20, 1935), clippings in AS, v. 1 UCR.

50. This complaint first appeared in the late 1920s *Calavo Annual Reports*, 1927; and a postwar version, J. S. Shepard, "Through the Looking Glass," *California Avocado Society 1952 Yearbook* (Santa Ana, 1952), pp. 141–143.

51. Bill Allen, "Avocado-Growing Isn't Life of Ease and Riches, Survey Shows," *Santa Ana Register* (March 16, 1949); "New Ways with Avocados," *Sunset Magazine* (February, 1944), clippings in AS, v. 8, UCR; W. Smitter, "The Mysterious Avocado," *Saturday Evening Post*, 221 (February 26, 1949): 30–31; "Avocados' Big Year," *Look* 19 (April 5, 1955): 90–91.

52. Don Gustafson, "Acreage Yields in San Diego County," *Avocado Society Yearbook*, 1976, pp. 22–23; William Sterling Kerr, "The Avocado Industry in Southern California: A Study of Location, Perception, and Prospect," Ph.D. Dissertation, University of Oklahoma, 1970, p. 174.

53. Ad dated 1943, in AS, v. 1 UCR.

54. Kerr, "The Avocado Industry in Southern California," 74–76; This controversy, driven in part by independent packers who resented Calavo's hold on the shipping market, as well as a sense that Calavo, located near Los Angeles, was neglecting San Diego County growers, is well described in a lengthy editorial appearing in the *Fallbrook Enterprise*, "Go Peel an Avocado" (Feb. 23, 1959).

55. Walter R. Beck, "California Avocado Marketing Order," *California Avocado Society 1962 Yearbook*, pp. 17–20.

56. "Kay Berger, Home Economist Appointed to Calavo," *Packer* (May 7, 1966), clipping in AS, v. 14 UCR. B. Bergh, "Some Heretical Thoughts Concerning the Ideal Commercial Avocado," *California Avocado Society 1968 Yearbook* (Santa Ana, 1968), pp. 27–36.

57. Donna R. Gabaccia, *We Are What We Eat: Ethnic Food and the Making of Americans* (Cambridge, MA: Harvard University Press, 1998), pp. 161–174.

58. California Avocado Advisory Board, *The Avocado Bravo: Spain's Legacy to California Cuisine* (1973), 3–5. "Fiesta Fare" ad in *Sunset* 138 (April, 1967): 111; "Luau" promotion discussed in *Annual Report of Calavo Growers* 1967.

59. As the story goes, in the mid-1960s the Color Mangement Group, a consortium of designers for consumer appliance industry, which still meets regularly to ensure that appliances of

different brands coordinate in the kitchen, designated "avocado green" along with "harvest gold" and "coppertone" as one of three official colors of the appliance industry, creating a familiar association with avocados for anyone who grew up in late-sixties/early-seventies suburbia. Lauren Goldstein, "Inside the Color Conspiracy," *Fortune* 138 (July 20, 1998): 30.

60. *Annual Report, Calavo Growers, 1976,* p. 2.

61. "To Market, to Market," *The Economist* (June 25, 1983): 89; Galit Beck, "Agrexco Expects Increase in Exports of Avocados This Year to 60,000 Tons," *The Jerusalem Post* (Oct. 23, 1995): 8.

62. Hoy Carman and Roberta Cook, "An Assessment of Potential Economic Impacts of Mexican Avocado Imports on the California Avocado Industry," in Proceedings of the ISHS XIIIth International Symposium on Horitucltural Economics (August, 1996) and available at on the Internet at http://www.agecon.ucdavis.edu/faculty/roberta.c/usmbt/avocado.htm; on postwar Mexican cuisine, see Jeffrey Pilcher, *Que vivan los tamales! Food and the Making of Mexican Identity* (University of New Mexico Press, 1998), pp. 123–142.

63. *Annual Report, Calavo Growers,* 1984; Brian Alexander "Going for the Green through Avocados," *Los Angeles Times* (January 30, 1992): 3. Statistics from Hoy Carman and Roberta Cook, "An Assessment of Potential Economic Impacts of Mexican Avocado Imports on the California Avocado Industry," p. 2. In an econometric analysis of the impact of CAAB advertising on the industry, Carman and Richard D. Green have found that in addition to consumer demand, a somewhat ironic response to increased consumer advertising was increased planting by growers. Hoy Carman and Richard D. Green, "Commodity Supply Response to a Producer-Financed Advertising Program: the California Avocado Industry," *Agribusiness* 9 (1993): 605–621.

64. *Annual Reports Calavo Growers,* p. 1991; Tara Weingarten "Had Been the Pits, but Avocados Mean Green Again," *San Diego Union-Tribune* (October 24, 1985): Sec. II, 1.

65. John Behrhman, "Avocado Firms Called Inconsistent in Opposing Imports," *San Diego Union-Tribune* (August 30, 1995): Sec. B, 1.

66. Chris Kraul, "Farmers Fight Import of Mexican Avocados," *Los Angeles Times* (August 14, 1995): Sec. D, 1.

67. Dean Calbreath, "Bittersweet Harvest: Local Avocado Growers Facing New Pressures," *San Diego Union-Tribune* (December 17, 1997): Sec. A, 1.

68. California Avocado Commission Web site, http://www.avoinfo.com/tradenews/. Though the recipes listed as part of this campaign have some familiar echoes from the past—an avocado crab dip using cream cheese could have appeared in the original recipe book from the early 1930s—they also frankly acknowledge a Southwestern and Mexican heritage, with heavy use of cumin and chiles. Recipes such as the "avocado flan with oysters and corn" show a sophisticated integration of the Mexican influence into a "California cuisine" that is itself evidence of the hyperrefinement of consumer tastes.

69. Carole Sugarman, "Holy Guacamole! Mexican Avocados Finally Cross the Border," *Washington Post* (January 21, 1998): Sec. 3, 1.

70. Chef and food scholar Mark Hartstein has reminded me that sushi containing avocado is known as the "California roll," an example of how avocados represent the ethnic blending and fresh ingredients that food marketers and restauranteurs now identify with the state.

Part Four

ETHNICITY, CLASS, AND THE FOOD INDUSTRY

Chapter 9

UNTANGLING ALLIANCES: SOCIAL TENSIONS SURROUNDING INDEPENDENT GROCERY STORES AND THE RISE OF MASS RETAILING

TRACEY DEUTSCH

*I*n the years surrounding World War I, chain grocery stores remade Chicago's retailing landscape. It is difficult to overestimate the importance or the suddenness of the change. Neighborhoods that had been dominated by small, locally owned stores were transformed into strongholds of national and regional chains. Concentration reached the point where single firms often operated several stores on the same block. Even nominally independent grocers had adopted many of the techniques of chain stores, joining "voluntary chains" of similarly named stores, all of which carried the same brands of merchandise. Moreover, the techniques popularized by grocery stores were important features of other fields of retailing, too. Hotels, restaurants and cafeterias, candy stores, tobacco stores, variety stores, clothing stores—each field offered its own example of a prominent chain. While urban areas supported more chains than did rural areas, and not all kinds of retailing fully adopted chain-style organization, there was no denying that mass distribution had joined mass production as a distinctive feature of American society. Chains transformed shopping and distribution, defining mass retailing and supplying both necessities and luxuries for many Americans.

These broad changes were made meaningful, indeed were made possible, by changes in people's everyday shopping. Nowhere was this clearer than in grocery stores. This essay connects increasing antipathy toward local grocers to the rise of chain stores and addresses the complicated question of why Americans, and women in particular, sustained the growth of stores that, in Victoria de Grazia's words, were a "hallmark of modern commerce."[1]

I focus on Chicago, where thriving ethnic neighborhoods sustained a bevy of small grocers and where chains were making dramatic inroads by the end of the decade. I argue that the increasingly stormy relationships between grocers and their customers contributed to the rise of chain stores. Furthermore, gender was the framework in which participants understood these conflicts. Chain groceries' emphasis on price was certainly part of their appeal, but it was not all. They also, intentionally or not, responded to long-standing tensions surrounding food buying. Issues that had long frustrated grocers and shoppers came to a head in the 1920s and fueled a move away from conventional, small, independent grocery stores. Chain stores succeeded not only because of low prices but also because of their ability to defuse the tense and often time-consuming negotiations between grocers and customers. Chains promised, in particular, to remake the gender norms and gender relations which had placed such pressure on grocers and their customers. In this early moment of mass retailing, social politics mattered as much as economic rationality.

This argument challenges and builds on recent scholarship on mass consumption. Scholars have long acknowledged the importance of chains as harbingers of a new age in distribution and consumption.[2] This was especially true for grocery stores, in which chains came to dominate very quickly. But scholars have been less forthcoming on the question of why chains triumphed so decisively or why independent stores suddenly seemed so undesirable to customers. This has been true even as new research has produced sophisticated and nuanced studies of other developments for which chain stores were crucial—elaborate advertising campaigns, the development of national brands, the discourse that equated consumption with citizenship, and, especially evident in this volume, changing foodways.[3] The question of why chains and mass marketing triumphed so decisively in the 1920s and 1930s is often lost in the attention to the effects and implications of mass retailing. I argue, however, that this is an important question, requiring attention to how stores actually worked. The answer sheds light on the political nature of consumption, suggesting that stores and their sales resulted from contention and struggle as much as unmediated demand and communal solidarity.

Shopping in small, neighborhood stores was a complicated, politicized process. Especially in white working-class and African American areas, the issues at stake in food shopping could go far beyond concern with low prices and immediate economic gain. In grocery stores in the interwar era, anger over high prices easily became anger over "profiteers" and monopoly. Anger over ill-treatment easily became calls for economic autonomy and solidarity or expressions of anti-Semitism and xenophobia. Finally, every transaction meant implicit and explicit statements of women's fitness as wives, mothers, shoppers, and homemakers. Grocers and customers wrangled with each other, arguing over equitable treatment as often as price. The result was a system of retailing that could be exhausting to participants, even though it was crucial to urban life.

The fight against high food prices in the early 1920s illustrates the politicized nature of shopping. One of Chicagoans' most common complaints during and after World War I was that the cost of living, especially the cost of food, had skyrocketed.[4] The problem was undeniable; the cost of living exploded in the World War I era, growing by nearly 40 percent over the course of the war.[5] In Chicago, still home to the nation's largest meatpacking houses and food wholesalers, the food price index doubled between 1914 and 1920.[6] Concern over rapid inflation, especially of food prices, was a catalyst for government action. The federal government extended its wartime powers to create a "High Cost of Living Division" in 1919 and distributed excess foods at below-market prices in Chicago and other large cities across the country.[7] Chicago's mayor issued a "food shortage warning" and made the high cost of living an issue in the 1919 mayoral election.[8] City Council members also felt considerable pressure to confront food costs. Between 1919 and 1926, they created several committees to deal with the problem of high prices.[9]

As food prices rose, Chicagoans voiced their anger, portraying grocers not as community pillars but as extortionists and profiteers. A 1917 Slovak paper asked: "Of what use is it if we raise vegetables in our back yards to help agricultural production—of what use are all the appeals to the public to support our food administration, if the war profiteers, unconscionable speculators, and other parasites hoard food, only to let it rot rather than accept lower prices?"[10] The mainstream press followed suit. In one dramatic but not atypical presentation, the *Chicago Tribune* put an editorial cartoon on the subject of high prices on its front page. The cartoon featured carloads of young couples being held up at gunpoint. All of the victims made it clear that they had already given all of their money to their grocer or butcher.[11]

However, prices were not the only issue bothering Chicagoans. Throughout the 1920s a number of other issues were flash points for pent-up tensions and resentments. Customers accused grocers of relatively mundane transgressions (charging high prices for low-quality goods) and outright fraud (refusing to credit a customer with a payment made on their account).[12] Politics was as much a presence in these stores as was the food they sold.

At the basis of the personalized politics of shopping was the fact that stores were very small. Even the "model" grocery store of the era's prescriptive trade literature occupied only 1,134 square feet; the first chains, designed for efficiency and rapid stock turnover, often occupied only five or six hundred square feet.[13] Moreover, sales were notoriously low in these small stores. *Average* annual sales for independent grocery stores in Chicago in 1929 were only $13,285.[14] Business was so limited that grocers could keep close track of changing habits. The son of one Chicago grocer remembered: "If my dad had 50 customers, that's all he had, 50. If he got

51 one day, it would be an odd thing. Somebody from the next block was passing by or got mad at his butcher that day."[15]

In these small stores, customers developed personal relationships with their grocers. Grocers offered a range of services that could include letter writing or translating for customers who did not speak English, advice about which foods would store well, and information about neighborhood goings-on.[16] One observer described the way that a neighborhood grocer was drawn into personal relationships with his customers: "He knows their family troubles and family joys. He knows when a child is born, when a boy or girl has married. He is often solicited to help influence certain relatives who also patronize the store." She characterized these relationships as being "primary contact."[17] Using a more scientific approach, a University of Chicago sociologist categorized grocery stores, butcher shops, insurance agencies, and banks as comprising the "town and unit store" category. In these stores, he reported, "the relationship between the store proprietor and the customers is very intimate.[18]

But personal relationships did not guarantee smooth interactions. Instead, they meant that buying and selling was the result of individual bargaining and haggling. Because these were "service stores," meaning clerks retrieved the items from which customers chose, shoppers often held clerks responsible for the quality of goods which they purchased. Customers approached clerks or proprietors about what they wanted to buy and store staff helped customers choose from the bulk and brand-named goods that were kept behind the counter or in a back room. Because prices were not posted, clerks also determined how much customers paid for an item. Stores also filled "phone orders," so that customers could call in their orders for delivery later that day. In all of these transactions, clerks used their knowledge of the customer and of their own bottom line to advise customers. Store workers frequently pushed certain goods and steered customers away from others. Indeed, grocers and clerks so influenced customers' ultimate purchases that early distributors of branded foods considered small, independent grocers crucial allies in attempts to win customers over to their brands.[19]

The result was extensive discussion of whether a good was worth the price being asked. A middle-class observer of one working-class Italian grocery described the scene this way: "The counter is often a scene of bargaining and haggling. Often a visitor feels that the grocer and customer are most unfriendly to one another, as this bargaining goes on. It is with great surprise that the stranger observes the very intimate conversation between the grocer and his bargaining customer after the haggling has been dispensed with."[20] Such behavior was common in middle- and upper-class stores as well. Home economist and business consultant Christine Frederick explained that grocers would have to accustom themselves to what she took as women's natural proclivity to discuss their purchases endlessly: "Watch the average woman shopper as she goes about shopping. . . . She perhaps likes to haggle a bit, or ask questions, or just rid herself of a few irritations over some piece of merchandise that wasn't just right, or which she had no luck in cooking."[21] The act of shopping was enmeshed in personal interactions and shaped by never-ending negotiation.

Personal credit was a special catalyst for the negotiation. Credit bound grocers and customers to each other, whether or not they liked it. Small stores made many of their sales on credit—anywhere from one half to two thirds, according to a 1928 government survey.[22] But that statistic does not do justice to the poverty and emotional appeals that lay behind extensions of credit. In hard times customers could be desperate, and grocers frequently granted credit even when it was not financially wise. A University of Chicago student reported that grocers in working-class Bridgeport granted credit during strikes and layoffs, knowing full well that they would never see their money. One woman grocer recalled that in the early 1930s: "They come, kneel down . . . just like to the Lord, you know. Please give me. My children are starving. . . . So we gave."[23]

Both in spite and because of the difficulty of getting paid back, grocers pressured customers to do so. They were not always successful, and, not surprisingly, collection rates fell dramatically in stores that were the smallest. A store with annual sales of under $10,000 collected, on average, only 34.3 percent of the debts due it every month.[24] The pages of trade journals were filled with advice about how to collect on debt, and editors often advised grocers to limit the credit they offered.[25] In spite of oft-articulated concern with credit, grocers wrote off only a small proportion of their debts as uncollectible and frequently refused to cut off customers, maintaining that it was only by offering credit that they could ensure regular purchases.[26] Meanwhile customers, though they complained about the terms and resented the embarrassment of needing credit, continued to make use of it.[27] However many problems it caused, credit allowed customers to continue to buy food through hard times and tight budgets, and was crucial in grocers' attempts to win purchases from customers. Surrounding the often messy account books of grocers stood the social pressure and economic necessities that shaped everyday acts of food shopping.[28]

The presence of grocers of races and ethnicities different from those of their customers exacerbated underlying tensions. Group solidarity, popular prejudice, and a desire for economic autonomy played out in food stores, complicating shopping and raising the stakes of transactions.

Ethnic and racial politics permeated food shopping. Not only were the foods one bought a sign of communal loyalty, but so too was the grocer from whom one bought. The ethnic press kept up constant pressure on its readers to shop in stores owned by members of their ethnic group. One Slovakian paper noted that Slovak-owned stores were especially likely to help their own during hard times and to give good advice about which foods to buy. More important, supporting Slovakian stores would help the community in general. "Our patronage," the paper maintained, "helps their business to grow and consequently our ideals become a reality."[29] Similarly, a Lithuanian article celebrated and perhaps meant to engender ethnic loyalty: "The time has gone when the Jews or Germans could carry on a thriving business among the Lithuanians of America: our people like to buy from Lithuanians."[30]

Just as grocers from within a community were portrayed as helping consumers, would-be customers were warned away from "outsiders." Rhetoric about supporting a community often shaded into negative portrayals of other ethnic groups. The same article that urged readers to support Slovak stores menacingly pointed out that non-Slovaks "may be your enemy."[31] Most Chicagoans were more specific about the ethnic and religious identities of potential enemies. The secretary of the Yugoslavian Woman's Club claimed that Yugoslavians resented Jews "because the Jewish people don't patronize Jugoslavian stores when the Jugoslavians still patronize their store." Jewish merchants were especially resented, the author claimed, for their unethical practices. "Jugoslav businessmen know the Jewish merchants steal on the weight, therefore, charge a little less to make more business. . . . "[32]

For African Americans, in particular, food shopping was a site of contention. African Americans shared many white Americans' resentment of grocers who were not from their community, but two facts made grocery stores in African American neighborhoods especially politicized. First, African Americans owned very few stores of any kind.[33] Second, the stores they did own tended to be grocery stores.[34] Thus, resentment of outsiders and calls for solidarity often centered on food shopping.

Neighborhood stores were seen as being important arenas for racialized fear, resentment, and anger. In the wake of the especially violent 1919 riot in Chicago, the city council passed a resolution requiring retailers to mark prices clearly, and several Jewish merchants located in African American neighborhoods formed a "protective association."[35] The newly articulated collective outrage of many African Americans, coupled with a general faith in business in the 1920s, reenergized long-standing campaigns to support black-owned businesses. The Chicago Whip, a militant African American newspaper that began publishing just before the riots, frequently called on its readers to shop in black-owned businesses.[36] Both the Whip and the Chicago Defender went on to organize boycotts of white-owned stores throughout the hard times of the early 1920s.[37]

In that decade they were joined by numerous national organizations which also began encouraging African Americans to support African American businesses. Marcus Garvey's United Negro Improvement Association (UNIA) had as one of its primary goals economic self-reliance and urged members to support UNIA-owned "Universal" stores and laundromats. The Colored Merchants' Association, a national trade group begun in 1928, tried to stir up support for its members by organizing "Housewives' Leagues."[38]

While both the UNIA and the Colored Merchants' Association found only limited success, calls for organized, politicized consumption continued throughout the 1930s. "Double duty dollars"—spending that procured needed goods and also went to black-owned businesses—were a theme of sermons, editorials, and daily conversation.[39] Street preachers, churches, and numerous local newspapers organized "Don't Buy Where You Can't Work" campaigns.[40] Groups like the Young Negro's Cooperative League worked to create consumer-run stores which would bring African American customers high-quality goods and bring the community new economic leverage. George Schuyler, the founder of the league, echoed the words of other African Americans who had noted the tremendous potential of organized, politically aware purchasing. "The white man invented the color line, we didn't," Schuyler said, "but we are going to take advantage of it in organizing this vast army of working people."[41]

Ethnic and racial tensions, then, exacerbated the always-present contentiousness of food shopping. Simply getting credit or quality goods required intensely personalized negotiation. Distrust and resentment by grocers and customers could make the negotiation that much more difficult. Another layer of social tension sheds light on the reasons for the rise of chain stores. Behind all of the tensions surrounding grocery stores stood profound anxiety over gender norms and gender relations. Spokespeople of all races and ethnicities, among middle-class and working-class shoppers, in churches and in the City Council, looked to women to solve the problems of consumption. Thus many women were under enormous pressure, political as well as economic, when they shopped.

The "anti-high-cost-of-living" movement of the late 1910s and early 1920s exemplified the difficulties of shopping and the pressure placed on women consumers. Federal and municipal government programs failed to bring immediate relief, and Chicagoans did not hold out much hope for governmental solutions.[42] But if the state was helpless, consumers— women in particular—were not. In spring 1922, the *Chicago Jewish Courier* had warned its readers not to expect much from the city's Committee on the High Cost of Living. Rather, women themselves must collectively take up new burdens. Using stark language, the newspaper warned: "There is only one way to fight the high cost of bread and that is, the housewife must do her own baking. If the Jewish women would begin to bake their own bread, they would get good nourishing bread at small cost and they would help reduce the price of bread at the stores."[43] Later that same month, another Chicago Yiddish-language paper, the *Forward*, urged Jewish women to join the "Mother's League," an organization dedicated to uniting women around issues of consumption:

Women speak singularly, they are dissatisfied, they criticize the landlord, the butcher, the baker, the laundry collector, but, as an organized body of united working women, they do nothing. This is the main task of the Mother's League. It tries to unite all the working women in an organization, through which the scattered minds of individual working women shall be united. Through instruction and education, they will become a force, a factor, in the social, economic, and political life of modern society.[44]

More middle-class and less incendiary women's organizations shared similar views of their responsibilities as shoppers. The newly organized Housewives' League and the "housewifely thrift committee" of the Chicago Women's Club both met regularly throughout the early 1920s.[45] Even Russell Poole, head of the city's Committee on the High Cost of Living, looked to women for the answers to high prices. For instance, when turkey prices rose just before Thanksgiving of 1922 Poole urged women to wait until Christmas to buy turkeys and thus force the price down.[46]

Just as women were expected to solve the problem of high prices, so too were they held accountable for the success of businesses within a community. One Yugoslavian community leader explained that Jewish merchants were only able to fool customers into thinking they were saving money because "more of the buyers—women—are quite ignorant."[47] Similarly, African American merchants often looked to women, in particular, to support their stores. "I would say without fear of contradiction that Negro women are responsible for the success or failure of Negroes in business," asserted one confident merchant.[48] Echoing his suggestion that African Americans were responsible for the demise of locally owned stores, one woman explained: "I try to spend as much as I can with Negro stores, but most of them don't have what you want, or they are too high. That may be our fault for not trading with them more, but we are too poor and have to count pennies."[49] Women were placed under enormous pressure by their communities, by watchful grocers, and sometimes by themselves.

Grocers, also, were disatisfied with this state of affairs. Constantly proving their goodwill and haggling with customers was time-consuming and tiring. Storekeepers saw women as the most important consumers and therefore at the root of the long and difficult negotiations that accompanied any sales. This is not to say that all of a grocer's customers were women. Indeed, trade journals occasionally urged grocers to make men more comfortable in their stores.[50] Moreover, there is significant anecdotal evidence from working-class neighborhoods that stores could sometimes be male spaces.[51] Nonetheless, men's shopping seemed far less problematic to most grocers. Commentators never complained about male customers as a group and almost never ascribed the challenges of storekeeping to men's demanding natures. Rather, it was women's natures that seemed to determine grocers' policies and, therefore, grocers' problems.

Thus the haggling, bargaining, conversation, and negotiation that marked grocery stores was almost always discussed in gendered terms. Trade journals and advice literature frequently mentioned the impossibility of grocers' ever asserting control over women customers. A Commerce Department study warned small grocers about the dangers of insulting women. Researchers explained: "[Grocers] will not wisely attempt to control the time, and consequently the cost, of the service. This lies within the province of the customer only, and she may resent any evident effort to hurry her."[52] Similarly, one monthly column in the trade journal *Progressive Grocer* advised small grocers to accede to women who asked for donations to neighborhood organizations. The motivation was not altruistic but purely practical. Women simply would not be satisfied with rational arguments about shopkeepers' costs and might well organize their peers to boycott a store. "When women get together and pass resolutions," the article reminded grocers, "reason and logic sink through the floor."[53]

Individual grocers also keenly felt that women customers in Chicago were too demanding. One grocer signing himself "the Hebrew slave" complained in a newspaper editorial that Jewish women would not allow their grocers to close the store for the Sabbath. Suggesting force be met with force, he encouraged his retail colleagues to join together and "demand" that women observe posted opening and closing hours.[54] Not surprisingly, when Jewish grocers did attempt to unite and close early (though on Sunday, not on the Jewish Sabbath), they felt compelled to address women specifically. "We request that all women do their shopping early, and permit dealers a few hours of rest," read the notice in a local Yiddish-language newspaper.[55] A store serving a very different market—the upper-class, native-born population of Morgan Park—shared similar concerns about women, even if their methods were more genteel. The owners of Hoyt & Sauer explained a recent remodeling by referring to the ongoing need to please women. They wrote: "Our beauty-conscious women now do 85 percent of the food buying. No longer can we afford to arrange a food store to suit the whims or fancy of some one man—it must have the open display arrangement, pleasing color, beauty, and the charm that appeal to the American woman."[56] The depression of the early 1920s evoked similar concern about women's ability to disrupt grocers' sales. Chicago's Retail Grocers Association published numerous full-page ads in the women's pages of the *Chicago Tribune* to assure women that grocers were working to lower prices.[57]

Accounts like these explicate the exhausting social encounters that occurred in food stores. The tides of personal preferences and communal pressures buffeted both grocers and customers. The very mechanics of grocery stores—the constant pressure to keep prices low, the dependence on credit, and the personal negotiation—made for difficult interactions. Often these tensions were exacerbated by preexisting ethnic and racial antagonism. Customers were expected to demand personal attention and quality foods, but were also expected to work for fair treatment and communal advancement. Grocers, too, felt the pressure of communal expectations, especially around issues of credit and the necessity of daily, personal interactions. Women in particular were placed under enormous pressure by their communities, and the difficulties of pleasing women were seen by many grocers to be the root of their problem. The tumult and drama that often accompanied purchases must have been wearying as often as rewarding.

Into this setting came chains and mass retailers. Chain stores and the techniques they engineered responded to the tensions that permeated food shopping and especially to the difficult gender relations that permeated grocery stores. As chain stores grew, they appealed to women with promises of low prices, trustworthy foods, and more freedom from grocers' and communities' oversight.

Chains grew dramatically in the late 1910s and early 1920s, both nationally and in Chicago. By the end of the 1920s, Kroger's owned 5,575 stores across the country.[58] Safeway owned 2,020 stores, most on the East and West coasts.[59] National Tea, a relatively modest regional chain centered in Chicago and the upper Midwest, owned 1,627 stores, a dramatic increase from the 143 stores it had owned when the decade began.[60] All of these already-large firms were dwarfed by the stunning growth of A&P, which by the end of the decade operated over 15,000 stores nationally.[61] Over the course of the decade, it became the first retailer to have over $1 billion in annual sales[62] and the fifth largest industrial corporation in the United States.[63] By 1929, chains were making 50 percent of all grocery sales in the city of Chicago and operating nearly a quarter of all grocery stores.[64]

Chains promised, and seem to have delivered, lower prices. This was their most obvious difference from smaller independents, which rarely posted prices, let alone competed solely on the basis of price. Chains tried to lower prices by taking advantage of economies of scale, an idea long practiced in manufacturing. Producing goods on a grand scale made possible lower production costs per item. Retail chains adapted this strategy by buying items in very large lots and, at least ideally, selling those items as quickly as possible through as many stores as possible. Chains were able to lower their per-item cost through discounts from processors and suppliers and by operating their own processing and wholesale subsidiaries. It is impossible to estimate how much the average family saved, but virtually every study of chain store operations found significant differences in prices.[65] One study of Chicago grocery stores found that self-service chains had lower prices on nationally branded items than did both service and self-service independent stores. Investigators concluded that chains undersold independents by anywhere from 8.82 percent to 11.54 percent.[66]

Chains also defused many of the causes of tension in food stores by working to eliminate specialized goods and services and personalized attention. Chains sold standardized, often mass-produced goods in standardized settings. That standardization allowed one central office to oversee vast networks of stores—in much the same way that an assembly line could be overseen by one foreman.[67] They also eliminated many of the policies over which customers and clerks had bargained and negotiated; "self-help" and "cash and carry" became synonymous with chain stores. Chains generally refused to grant credit, thus eliminating a notoriously expensive and time-consuming part of grocery store operations. Moreover, prices were set by district or regional authorities and posted in stores, so that customers and clerks no longer bargained over the cost of goods.[68] A member of the Piggly Wiggly chain celebrated and catalogued the areas of standardization when he wrote: "uniformity is the first principle of Piggly Wiggly. Every store must do everything in exactly the same manner, and to my mind this is one of the greatest advantages of our systems. Clerks, goods, fixtures are interchangeable."[69] By excising many services and limiting clerks' ability to bargain with customers, chains also eliminated the causes and focus of customers' anger and animosity.

While the system certainly limited the range of customers' choices, it also allowed them to make choices for themselves. Stock was often kept on open shelving within customers' reach. Shoppers then chose what they wanted and carried it to the front of the store. In this "self-help" system shoppers could look over items and choose the ones they wanted, free from the pressure that a clerk might exert. Grocery store analysts noted that self-help and little interaction with clerks was especially attractive to women shoppers: "A woman does not like to run a gauntlet of clerks looking her over when she enters a store. This is sometimes the case in stores where the clerks are not busy and loll over the counter sizing up the ladies," noted one Piggly Wiggly manager. He went on to proudly assert that "in Piggly Wiggly stores, this cannot happen for no one but the checker is in front and his back is usually to the door."[70]

If the self-help features of chains promised individual autonomy, their very nature defused the racially and ethnically charged atmospheres of food stores. Lizabeth Cohen has documented African Americans' willingness to shop in chains,[71] and that was true for many white, first- and second-generation Americans as well. Of course, chain owners were at least as likely to differ from customers in terms of race and ethnicity as were owners of independent stores. Chain store owners, however, were far removed from the daily operations of chains. Morever, unlike the family-run independents, chains needed outside workers for jobs. They were willing to hire African Americans and white, first-generation Americans to fill positions, especially when stores were in African American or white ethnic neighborhoods.[72] Thus, however indirectly, chains could be seen by wary Chicagoans as supporting an ethnic or racial community.

At the very least, chains offered respite from the communal norms and tensions that permeated neighborhood grocery stores. Neighbors simply would not be as likely to know what a newly married woman served her in-laws or whether or not a family paid its bills on time if people shopped in chain stores. At the most, chains allowed people to meet family budgets while not shopping in the stores of people who, as the Slovakian paper put it, "may be your enemy." Since chains were less personalized, their profits did not benefit rival racial or ethnic groups. They allowed people to avoid the guilt of supporting outsiders.

Chains' advertising reinforced the promises of low price and individual autonomy, especially for women. The straightforward lists of items and prices which constituted most ads implied that women were willing and able to choose goods for themselves with little interference or social pressure at the point of purchase. The "institutional" advertisements of chain grocery firms reinforced the autonomy, efficiency, and distinctive benefits chain stores offered women.[73] Many of these ads explicitly reminded both women and men of women's important role in the family and that chains supplied women with the "scientific" information required for modern-minded housekeeping. A&P, for instance, ran a series of ads in the *Saturday Evening Post* designed to convince men that their wives' difficulties with shopping were as challenging as the problems they encountered in the workplace: "Daily the wife must purchase the family food needs. Countless brands, grades, and prices are confusing, yet she must decide. And she does, wisely and profitably. Give her credit," advised the caption to one advertisement. Other ads in the campaign portrayed the brands that chain stores stocked as an aid to women seeking high-quality foods with which to impress their husband's boss.[74] More bombastic ads came from Piggly Wiggly. One 1922 advertisement in the *Chicago Tribune* extolled the independence and the acumen women would be able to express in their stores: "Piggly Wiggly fosters the spirit of independence—the Soul of Democratic Institutions, teaching men, women and children to do for themselves." The advertisement went on to make an implicit comparison between Piggly Wiggly's self-service stores and their stocks of national brands, and what customers could expect at smaller, independent stores. "In PIGGLY WIGGLY [sic] stores you will find only well-known, established brands of unquestionable quality, and there will be no one there to try to get you to buy 'something just as good.'"[75]

The techniques engineered at chain stores were adopted and adapted by almost all grocers, including smaller neighborhood stores. The real success of chains was that they offered all grocers, whether they identified as chain or independent, a model for defusing social tensions and selling at lower prices. Throughout the 1920s independent grocers often mimicked and adapted the techniques of chains. By the end of the decade, it seemed clear to observers that the techniques of chain stores had come to define mass retailing and had redefined the nature of *all* food retailing.

Throughout the 1920s, independent stores were urged to join chains in limiting the credit they offered, in buying "efficiently" (that is, in large quantities), in moving toward self-service, and in emphasizing low price in their marketing. Even the Department of Commerce urged independent grocers to use chain store techniques. Julius Klein of the Bureau of Foreign and Domestic Commerce assured small merchants that they could succeed in the new world of mass retailing as long as they had "a willingness to work, to utilize new methods, and to take advantage of new conditions."[76] Similarly, many firms involved in the grocery business saw the advantages of centralization and standardization in smoothing retail operations. Wholesalers and the trade press urged independents to mark prices on items and to price uniformly.[77]

Self-service and the independence it promised were seen as especially important advantages in attracting women customers. Although smaller grocers could not always eliminate credit and personal attention, they generally joined chains in moving toward self-service operations. *Progressive Grocer,* a popular trade journal, described the success of shopkeepers who made the transition to self-service. The editors assured their readers that: "Every grocer . . . reports that his customers commend him on the change, and the fact is well established that women prefer to shop at a store arranged with open stock and display—and a large number of them prefer to wait on themselves."[78] When the Department of Commerce and the editors of *Progressive Grocer* worked together to built a model grocery store, the *PG* editor explained that "the store was so planned that every item sold in the store can be seen by the shopper, without the assistance of the clerk" and so took advantage of women's "highly developed shopping instinct."[79]

Voluntary chains, first developed in the 1920s, indicate the extent to which standardization and centralized management had spread throughout the grocery store industry. These were associations of independently owned stores which agreed to buy from the same wholesaler, and which often operated under the same name and imposed similar rules on customers. IGA stores were the most prominent of these kinds of stores, but any number of other voluntary chains—Red & White stores, Royal Blue Stores, and Certified Stores—extended the use of self-service, cash and carry, and standardization. By the end of the decade, nearly 60,000 stores across the country—3,151 of them in Illinois—operated as members of voluntary chains.[80]

Chains held such promise that even people who openly fought for social and political autonomy looked to build on mass retailing's techniques. In the early 1920s, Americans supported a new wave of community-owned stores and consumer cooperatives. Many of these stores, however, were modeled on chains. For instance, the most successful and popular consumer cooperative in Chicago was a centrally managed chain of stores. Building on the labor movement and activism of the post–World War I era, the Cooperative Society of America operated nearly two hundred Chicago stores at the firm's height in 1922. It was not only the largest cooperative but the largest chain in the city.[81] While CSA was the most successful working-class chain in Chicago, it was not the only attempt at such an organization. Similar promises of economic autonomy were held out by Lithuanian community leaders, who worked to persuade would-be entrepreneurs to open a Lithuanian-owned chain of stores, and by African Americans, who worked through the Colored Merchants Association to forge collective purchasing agreements by African American–owned stores.[82] While scholars often see chains as undermining community, in the 1920s, many Chicagoans also saw them as a way of making their communities stronger.

Of course, the promises of autonomy did not materialize in mass retailing. The Cooperative Society of America went bankrupt in 1923. There never was a successful Lithuanian or African American grocery chain. In the 1930s and in subsequent decades, grocery stores gradually adopted a more overtly feminized selling space and worked to restrict customers' ability to demand personalized attention. Over time, even the previously conventional acts of individual assertiveness—bargaining for lower prices, complaining openly about poor-quality goods—were difficult, ineffective, and seen by many shoppers and retailers as being unfeminine. Indeed, to a present-day reader, it is difficult to imagine a time when mass retailing seemed to promise liberation.

And yet few Americans in the 1920s believed that chain stores would undermine their individual or collective power. Institutions from outside the community promised a refreshing anonymity, a chance to escape sometimes-stifling relationships and unsatisfying shopping. They seemed, at least at this time, to disrupt gender roles rather than to reinforce them.

The hopes that many Americans had for chains and the marketing techniques chains used suggest that both consumption and retailing were more political processes than we have imagined. When people made choices about where to shop and what to buy, they took into account their social relationships, their resources, and their desire for autonomy. Retailers knew that. Chains sold self-service as a route to independence, and smaller stores adopted chain store techniques because they also eased negotiations and relations with customers. Authority in the store was a precious commodity, just as important as the food the store sold. Stores were about power as much as price.

NOTES

1. Victoria de Grazia, "Changing Consumption Regimes in Europe, 1930–1970: Comparative Perspectives on the Distribution Problem," in *Getting and Spending: European and American Consumer Societies in the Twentieth Century,* ed. Susan Strasser, Charles McGovern, and Matthias Judt (Washington, DC: The German Historical Institute and Cambridge University Press, 1998), p. 59.
2. Alfred Chandler, *The Visible Hand: The Managerial Revolution in American Business* (The

Belknap Press of Harvard University Press, 1977), pp. 233–235; Richard Tedlow, *New and Improved: The Story of Mass Marketing in America* (New York: Basic Books, 1990); Lizabeth Cohen, *Making a New Deal: Industrial Workers in Chicago, 1919–1939* (New York: Cambridge University Press, 1990).

3. See, for instance, Roland Marchand, *Advertising the American Dream: Making Way for Modernity, 1920–1940* (Berkeley: University of California Press, 1985); Susan Strasser, *Satisfaction Guaranteed: The Making of the American Mass Market* (Washington, DC: Smithsonian Institution Press, 1989); Andrew Hurley, "From Hash House to Family Restaurant: The Transformation of Diner and Post–World War II Consumer Culture," *Journal of American History,* 83 (March 1997): 1282–1308; Lizabeth Cohen, "The New Deal and the Making of Citizen Consumers," in *Getting and Spending: European and American Consumer Societies in the Twentieth Century,* ed. Susan Strasser, Charles McGovern, and Matthias Judt (Washington, DC: The German Historical Institute and Cambridge University Press, 1998), pp. 111–125.

4. For examples of the new discourse about the "high cost of living" see, for instance, "Force Food Prices Down: H.C.L. Rebels Under United Attack Here," and "Wife, Caught in H.C.L. Trap of Death, Vanishes," *Chicago Daily Tribune* (August 12, 1919): 1–2; "Chicago Stockyard Workers Appearing before Judge Alschuler with Demands for Increased Wages Show Estimate of $1,918 a Year for Family of 5," *New York Times* (August 13, 1919): 20; M. D. Shelby, "Housewife and the High Cost of Living," *Outlook,* 123 (September 3, 1919): 13–15; "Cost of Living," *Ladies' Home Journal,* 37 (March 1920): 123–124; L. Wolman, "Cost of Living and Wage Cuts," *New Republic,* 27 (July 27, 1921): 237–239; Neil A. Wynn, *From Progressivism to Prosperity: World War I and American Society* (New York: Holmes and Meier, 1986), pp. 202–203.

5. Ellis Hawley, *The Great War and the Search for Modern Order: A History of the American People and their Institutions, 1917–1933* (New York: St. Martin's Press, 1979), p. 27.

6. "Changes in the Cost of Living in the United States," *Monthly Labor Review* 11 (February 1921): 93.

7. Hawley, p. 47.

8. *Journal of the Proceedings of the City Council of Chicago for the Council Year 1919–20, Being from April 18, 1919 to April 7, 1920* (April 26, 1919): 788.

9. For the creation of the Bureau of Food and Markets, see *Journal of the Proceedings of the City Council of the City of Chicago for the Council Year 1919–20,* 698–700. On the difficulties of the bureau and the rocky transition to the Committee on High Costs, see *Journal of the Proceedings of the City Council of the City of Chicago for the Council Year 1920–21, Being from April 15, 1920 to April 11, 1921,* 110, 210, 525, 531, 1414, 1472.

10. "War Profiteers" (Editorial), *Denni Hlasatel* (November 10, 1917), File ID1a, Box 1, Bohemian, Chicago Foreign Language Press Survey, University of Chicago Special Collections, Joseph Regenstein Library, Chicago, Illinois (hereafter CFLPS). For similar anger from Chicago's Polish community, see "Hunger and Poverty in Chicago," *Dziennik Zwiazkowy* (February 23, 1917), ID1a, Box 32, Polish, CFLPS. Here editors noted that speculators manipulated prices "with the cleverness of a fox." All CFLPS documents were translated by the Works Progress Administration workers who assembled them from Chicago's foreign language newspapers.

11. "The Harvest Moon," *Chicago Tribune* (August 12, 1919): 1. This suspicion of retail grocers, and organized protest of high prices, was a common aspect of post–World War I society. Post–World War I inflation caused protests far beyond Chicago. Angry urban residents launched violent attacks on peddlers and grocers in New York and Boston. Dana Frank, "Housewives, Socialists, and the Politics of Food: The 1917 New York Cost-of-Living Protests," *Feminist Studies* 11 (Summer 1985): 255–286; Harvey Levenstein, *Revolution at the Table: The Transformation of the American Diet* (New York: Oxford University Press, 1988), pp. 109–110. Inflation, political activism, and food protests were even more dramatic in war-ravaged Europe. See, for instance, Tyler Stovall, trans., Colette Friedlander, "Du Vieux et du Neuf: Economie Morale et Militantisme Ouvrier dan les Luttes contre la Vie Chere à Paris en 1919," *Mouvement Social* 1995 (170): 85–113; Belinda Davis, *Home Fires Burning: Food, Politics, and Everyday Life in World War I Berlin* (Chapel Hill: University of North Carolina Press, 2000).

12. See, for instance, "Friend of the People," *Chicago Tribune* (January 2, 1922): 8. Chicagoans often voiced general distrust of their grocers. In 1917, for instance, the *Skandinaven* reported that "the Norwegian Women's Federation has an excellent department for the study of home economics. Food stuffs are being investigated; deputies are being sent to watch the places of sale for groceries and meats." "The Norwegian Women's Federation," *Skandinaven* (August 5, 1917), IK, Box 30, Norwegian, CFLPS.

13. Richard S. Tedlow, *New and Improved: The Story of Mass Marketing in America* (New York:

Basic Books, 1990), p. 230; James M. Mayo, *The American Grocery Store: The Business Evolution of an Architectural Space,* Contributions in American History, no. 150 (Westport, CT: Greenwood Press, 1993), pp. 86, 140. Safeway wanted only 2,100 square feet for its prime locations. H. S. Wright, "Locating Grocery Stores," *Chain Store Age,* 1 (August 1925): 10. As late as 1930, Kroger's "standard store" was only 3,000 square feet. George Laycock, *The Kroger Story: A Century of Innovation* (Cincinnati: The Kroger Company,1983), p. 37.

14. Department of Commerce, U.S. Bureau of the Census, *Fifteenth Census of the United States,* vol. 1, *Distribution: Retail Distribution,* part 2, *Reports by States, Alabama to New Hampshire* (Washington, DC: U.S. Government Printing Office, 1934), p. 633.

15. Quoted in Lizabeth Cohen, *Making a New Deal: Industrial Workers in Chicago, 1919–1929* (New York: Cambridge University Press, 1990), pp. 109–110. Analysts at Harvard's Bureau of Business Research described the same conditions, albeit in drier language: "The retail grocery business is essentially a trade with families. The bulk of the sales of almost every grocery store are made to regular customers who buy constantly, in fact many of them daily." *Management Problems in Retail Grocery Stores,* Bulletin no. 13 (Cambridge, MA: Bureau of Business Research, Harvard University Press, 1919), p. 19.

16. See, for instance, Strasser, p. 67.

17. Jean Brichke, "Report on Term Paper Under Miss Nesbitt's Direction (Standard Budget for Dependent Families) Sociology 264," Box 156, folder 2, Burgess Papers, Department of Special Collections, Joseph Regenstein Library, University of Chicago, Chicago, IL (hereafter Burgess Papers) pp. 13–14.

18. Ernest Hugh Shideler, "The Chain Store: A Study of the Ecological Organization of a Modern City" (Ph.D. diss., University of Chicago, 1927), chap. 2, pp. 8–9.

19. Strasser, pp. 84–88, pp. 187–195.

20. Brichke, p. 14.

21. Mrs. Christine Frederick, "My Idea of a Good Storekeeper," *Chain Store Age* 1 (August 1925): 16.

22. U.S. Department of Commerce, Bureau of Foreign and Domestic Commerce, *Louisville Grocery Survey, Part I, Census of Food Distribution,* Distribution Cost Studies no. 6 (Washington, DC: 1930), p. 14. This finding was very similar to the findings of a national study conducted in 1924 by the Harvard Bureau of Business Research; that study found that the average retail grocer made 61 percent of its sales on credit. *Operating Expenses in Retail Grocery Stores in 1924,* Bulletin no. 52 (Cambridge, MA: Bureau of Business Research, Harvard University Press), p. 11.

23. Oral history interview with Anna Blazewich, November 11, 1977, Oral History Archives of Chicago Polonia, Chicago Historical Society, Chicago, IL, p. 95; For more accounts of grocers who felt pressured into granting credit, see Strasser, p. 69.

24. "Tendency of Grocers Is Toward More Credit," *Progressive Grocer* 9 (December 1930): 34, 102.

25. See, for instance, "Are Outstanding Bills Eating Up Your Profits?" *Progressive Grocer,* 1 (December 1922): 32–34; "Collect Your Bills—and Keep the Friendship of Your Customers," *Progressive Grocer* 3 (April 1924): 27–29, 68; Pop Keener, "Educate Credit Customers to Pay Promptly," *Progressive Grocer* 8 (January 1929): 16–18, 88, 92; Department of Commerce, Bureau of Foreign and Domestic Commerce, *Credit Extension and Business Failures: A Study of Credit Conditions and Causes of Failure among Grocery Retailers in Louisville, KY,* Trade Information Bulletin no. 627 (Washington, DC: U.S. Government Printing Office, 1929), p. 1.

26. Estimates ranged from 10 percent to less than one half of one percent. "Tendency of Grocers Is Toward More Credit," *Progressive Grocer* 9 (December 1930): 34, 102; *Operating Expenses in Retail Grocery Stores in 1924,* Bulletin no. 52 (Cambridge, MA: Bureau of Business Research, Harvard University Press), pp. 47–48.

27. On customers' resentment of the terms of credit arrangements and their reliance on credit, see Strasser, p. 69; Cohen, *Making a New Deal,* pp. 112, 234–235.

28. Independent grocers were notorious for keeping records poorly, if at all. Researchers at the Harvard Bureau of Business Research noted somewhat disdainfully that "a surprisingly large proportion of the retail grocers of the country . . . do not keep records that are even approximately accurate . . . records are [either] inadequate for their needs or none at all." *Management Problems in Retail Grocery Stores,* Bulletin no. 13 (Cambridge: Harvard University Press, 1919), p. 16. See also Strasser, pp. 231–235.

29. "Patronize the Stores of Your Countrymen," *Osadne Hlasy* (December 9, 1932), ID1b, Box 40, Slovak, CFLPS.

30. "An Unexploited Branch of Commerce," *Lietuva* (Lithuanian) (September 6, 1918), CFLPS. ID26, Box 28.

31. Ibid.

32. Mrs. Kushar, not titled, c. 1934, File 3, Box 130, Burgess Papers. Prejudice was, of course, not the sole property of working-class or immigrant groups. Writing in 1925, consumer analyst Christine Frederick described her resentment of local grocers this way: "To be perfectly blunt, the independent merchant is often a dirty, illiterate, short-sighted, half-Americanized foreigner; or a sleepy, narrow-minded, dead-from-the-neck-up American. It irritates and annoys me to trade with such people." Christine Frederick, "Listen to This Sophisticated Shopper!" *Chain Store Age* 1 (June 1925): 36.

33. African Americans owned only 1.4% of all retail stores nationally, according to the 1935 Census of Business. Department of Commerce, U.S. Bureau of the Census, *Census of Business: 1935, Retail Distribution*, vol. 1, *United States Summary* (Washington, DC: U.S. Government Printing Office, 1937), p. I-42. In Chicago there was one black-owned store for every 287 African Americans, as opposed to a ratio of 1:37 for Polish-owned stores and Poles, and 1:40 for Italian-owned stores and Italians. Lizabeth Cohen, *Making a New Deal*, p. 152.

34. Grocery stores and restaurants accounted for nearly half of all sales by African American–owned businesses in 1935. Department of Commerce, U.S. Bureau of the Census, *Census of Business: 1935, Retail Distribution*, vol. 1, *United States Summary* (Washington, DC: U.S. Government Printing Office, 1937), p. I-42.

35. *Journal of the Proceedings of the City Council of the City of Chicago for the Council Year 1919–20, Being from April 18, 1919 to April 7, 1920*, Special Meeting August 5, 1919, p. 1112; "Important Meeting of Jewish Storekeepers on the South Side," *Daily Jewish Courier*, August 13, 1919, ID1b, Box 23, Jewish, CFLPS; untitled, *Forward*, August 9, 1919, ID1b, Box 23, Jewish, CFLPS.

36. Donald Tingley, *The Structuring of a State: The History of Illinois, 1899–1928* (Urbana: University of Illinois Press, 1980), p. 310; Gary Hunter, "'Don't Buy From Where You Can't Work': Black Urban Boycott Movements during the Depression, 1929–1941," Ph.D. Dissertation, University of Michigan, 1977, p. 81.

37. Hunter, ibid; see also Cohen, pp. 153–154.

38. Hunter, pp. 53–55.

39. St. Clair Drake and Horace Cayton, *Black Metropolis: A Study of Negro Life in a Northern City* (New York: Harper and Row, 1945, rev. ed. 1962).

40. For a fuller description of these campaigns in Chicago and elsewhere, see Gary Hunter, "Don't Buy From Where You Can't Work" and Cheryl Lynn Greenburg, *"Or Does It Explode?" Black Harlem in the Great Depression* (New York: Oxford University Press, 1991).

41. "George Schuyler, "Consumers' Cooperation, the American Negro's Salvation," *Cooperation* 17 (August 1931): 145. Consumer cooperatives were an important part of African American struggles for economic autonomy, providing economic leverage and political education to their members. For example, J. L. Reddix founded an African American cooperative in Gary, Indiana. By 1935 it was the largest African American–owned retail operation in the United States. He contrasted the revolutionary potential of co-ops with more conventional salves of the current political economy, noting: "The capitalist system has been benevolent to the Negro. It has given him YMCAs, schools, and education. It has given him his dole during business depressions and has left him poor for the next one." J. L. Reddix, "The Negro Finds a Way to Economic Equality," *Consumers' Cooperation*, 21 (October 1935): 175. No less a personage than A. Philip Randolph remarked that consumer cooperatives were "the best mechanism yet devised to bring about economic democracy." "Brotherhood Consumers Cooperative Buying Rally" [sic] January 1944, Brotherhood of Sleeping Car Porters Papers, Chicago Historical Society, Chicago, IL.

42. In 1917, one Polish-language paper reported that "the people of Chicago are suffering as a result of the exorbitant prices of foodstuffs. . . . Investigations by the municipal, county and Federal authorities in the matter of the high cost of living have produced so far no results at all." "Hunger and Poverty in Chicago," *Dziennik Zwiazkowy* (Feb. 23, 1917), ID1a, Box 32, Polish, CFLPS. The *Chicago Jewish Courier* put the matter succinctly when it wrote: "Democracy apparently sometimes defeats the will of the majority." "Meditation of the Day" (In English), *Sunday Jewish Courier* (May 13, 1923), ID1a, Box 23, Jewish, CFLPS.

43. Sol Posner, "Why Was the Price of Bread Raised?" *Daily Jewish Courier* (March 9, 1922), ID16, Box 23, Jewish CFLPS. Russell Poole apparently agreed with the newspaper, since he threatened bakers with a "bake-your-own-bread" campaign among Chicago housewives if they did not lower the price of bread. "Bakers Propose Employes' Wage Cut; Union Kicks," *Chicago Sunday Tribune* (March 5, 1922), pt. 1, p. 2.

44. The Problems and Aims of the Mother's League," *Forward* (March 12, 1922), ID2b, Box 23 CFLPS.

45. "Women's Club Page," *Chicago Sunday Tribune* (October 9, 1921), pt. 8, p. 5; "Women's Club Page," *Chicago Sunday Tribune* (November 13, 1921), pt. 8, p. 5; "Women's Club Page," *Chicago Sunday Tribune* (January 8, 1922), pt. 8, pp. 5–8.
46. "Don't Eat Turk Till Christmas, Poole's Advice," *Chicago Tribune* (November 22, 1921), p. 3.
47. Mrs. Kushar, untitled, c. 1934, File 3, Box 130, Burgess Papers.
48. Drake and Cayton, p. 441.
49. Drake and Cayton, p. 444.
50. R. L. Hobart, "Rubbing a Sophisticated Male Shopper the Wrong Way," *Chain Store Age* 1 (December 1925): 20–21, 43–44; "It Was a Great Saturday Night at the Empire Grocery," *Progressive Grocer* 3 (July 1924): 29–30; N. Mitchell, "The Kind of Showcard that Brings Results," *Progressive Grocer* 1 (September 1922): 10–12, 53, 54, 56, 58, 60; F. S. Clark, "Does Tobacco Belong in the Grocery Store?" *Progressive Grocer* 1 (June 1922): 7–10, 46, 50, 52.
51. Working-class Chinese and Sicilian grocery stores were both described as sites of men's clubs and social gatherings. One member of a Sicilian men's club in Bridgeport, which met in the back of a store, explained that "Home is for the women to cook and take care of the kids. This is our home." Henry B. Steele, "Bridgeport, no. 60, Organizations, Bridgeport area west side of Halsted to east limit," File 60, Box 87, Federal Writers' Project Papers, Illinois State Historical Library, Manuscripts Division, Springfield, IL. On stores in Chinatown, see "Chinese Families in Chicago," n.d. but c. 1930, Burgess Papers, box 136 file 7; Paul R. Sui, "Family Matters," c. 1930, Box 136, File 7, Burgess Papers.
52. Bureau of Foreign and Domestic Commerce, Department of Commerce, *Louisville Grocery Survey,* Part II, *Costs, Markets, and Methods in Grocery Retailing,* Distribution Cost Studies no. 8 (Washington, DC: U.S. Government Printing Office, 1931), p. 4.
53. Emmett F. Harte, "Honk and Horace Hit a Boycott but Horace Saves the Day," *Progressive Grocer* 1 (December 1922): 43.
54. "The *Eved-Ivri* (Hebrew Slave)—The Grocer," *Daily Jewish Courier* (June 12, 1918), ID1b, Box 23, Jewish, CFLPS.
55. No title, *Forward* (February 6, 1921), Box 23, ID1b, Jewish, Chicago Foreign Language Press Survey.
56. "Charm . . . a Quality of Growing Importance in Grocery Stores," *Progressive Grocer,* 9 (March 1930): 26.
57. Advertisement, "Grocers Want to Help Lower Food Costs," *Chicago Sunday Tribune* (October 23, 1921), pt. 7, p. 2. See also a similar ad from the same trade organization in *Chicago Tribune* (October 5, 1921), p. 15.
58. George Laycock, *The Kroger Story: A Century of Innovation* (Cincinnati: The Kroger Company, 1983), p. 37.
59. "Investors' Aid: Information Service to Subscribers," *Chicago Journal of Commerce and LaSalle Street Journal* (March 24, 1929), p. 8.
60. *Annual Report: National Tea Company,* December 31, 1919; *Annual Report: National Tea Company,* December 31, 1929.
61. Godfrey Lebhar, "Editorially Speaking," *Chain Store Age* 7 (September, 1931): 36.
62. Edwin P. Hoyt, *That Wonderful A&P!* (New York: Hawthorn Books, 1969), p. 130; Richard Tedlow, *New and Improved: The Story of Mass Marketing in America* (New York: Basic Books, 1990), Table 4–1, p. 194.
63. Tedlow, p. 193.
64. Lizabeth Cohen, *Making a New Deal,* p. 108.
65. Einar Bjorklund and James L. Palmer, *A Study of the Prices of Chain and Independent Groceries in Chicago,* vol. 1. *Studies in Business Administration* (Chicago: University of Chicago Press, 1930), p. vii; Tedlow, Table 4–5, pp. 200–201.
66. Bjorklund and Palmer, pp. 2, 14.
67. For a fuller discussion of chain store techniques, see Tedlow, pp. 188–214.
68. The extension of the one-price system outside of the department stores was one of chains' most important innovations. See Strasser, pp. 204–205.
69. A. C. Jones, "An Analysis of Piggly Wiggly Progress," *Chain Store Age* 2 (January 1926): 44.
70. A. C. Jones, "An Analysis of Piggly Wiggly Progress," *Chain Store Age* 2 (January 1926): 39.
71. Cohen, *Making a New Deal,* pp. 152–153.
72. Cohen, *Making a New Deal,* p. 154; Cherly Lynn Greenberg, *'Or Does It Explode?'* pp. 122–123, 134; "History of District '40'" File 40 Box 86, Federal Writers' Project, Illinois State Historical Library, p. 30. Several civil court cases provide evidence that Chicago chains hired African American employees. See Grant Hayes, Administrator of the estate of Robert Hayes, deceased, vs. National Tea Company, Case B213587, Clerk of the Circuit

Court of Cook County Archives, Chicago, IL, and Kroger Grocery and Baking Company vs. Retail Clerks International Protective Association, etc., et al., Case 42C13019, Clerk of the Circuit Court of Cook County Archives.

73. Institutional advertisements attempted to convince customers of the high tone and status of stores themselves, rather than inform them of that week's specials. They were meant to maintain loyalty among customers, and so are especially good sources for getting at the values which chain groceries wanted people to associate with their stores.

74. "The A&P Takes the Woman's Side in a New Advertising Campaign," *Chain Store Age* 4 (April 1928): 62–64.

75. Advertisement, *Chicago Tribune* (September 30, 1921), 26.

76. "Says Independent Is Indispensable," *Progressive Grocer* 7 (November 1928): 96.

77. See, for instance, "A Live Grocer Can Beat Any Chain," *Progressive Grocer* 7 (November 1929): 34–36, 102, 104, 106, 108; Carl Dipman, "Chain Store Problems as Seen by the Owners Themselves," *Progressive Grocer* 3 (November 1924): 25–27, 76, 78, 80; Paul Findlay, "Sell 'em by the Box—a Chain Store 'Secret,'" *Progressive Grocer* 2 (December 1923): 28–30, 66–70; "Charm . . . a Quality of Growing Importance in Grocery Stores," *Progressive Grocer* 9 (March 1930): 26–29, 104, 106; See also Strasser, pp. 229–242.

78. Carl Dipman, "What Happens to Sales When You Modernize," *Progressive Grocer* 8 (August 1929): 39.

79. "Uncle Sam Builds a Model Grocery Store," *Progressive Grocer* 8 (April 1929): 18–25.

80. Godfrey Lebhar, "Editorially Speaking," *Chain Store Age* 6 (March 1930): 44; "New Book Out on Voluntary Chains," *Progressive Grocer* 9 (November 1930): 44; Cohen, *Making a New Deal*, pp. 118–119.

81. Colston Estey Warne, *The Consumers' Co-Operative Movement in Illinois* (Chicago: University of Chicago Press, 1926), p. 176, Table 14, p. 188. For more on postwar consumer cooperatives, see Dana Frank, *Purchasing Power: Consumer Organizing, Gender, and the Seattle Labor Movement, 1919–1929* (New York: Cambridge University Press, 1994).

82. Vaclvas Karuza, "An Unexploited Branch of Commerce," *Lietuva* (September 6, 1918), CFLPS; Gary Hunter, *Don't Buy from Where You Can't Work*, pp. 52–53.

Chapter 10

AS AMERICAN AS BUDWEISER AND PICKLES? NATION-BUILDING IN AMERICAN FOOD INDUSTRIES

Donna R. Gabaccia

*B*eyond the proverbial (but how widely eaten?) "apple pie," Americans lack much sense of having a national cuisine that unites them across ethnic and regional boundaries. Yet consumers in other parts of the world have few doubts about what constitutes American food. Mass-produced foods intended to be prepared or eaten quickly are considered "American" around the globe.[1] What makes foods American—at least to outsiders—is how they are produced, packaged, and served, not who manufactures or eats them or how they taste.

Americans, too, have sometimes viewed foods processed or manufactured on a large scale as icons of democratic and national "American" eating.[2] The culinary icons of the American nation have changed over time, of course. In the nineteenth century, barrels of salt pork emerging from porcine disassembly plants gave way to hygienically sealed containers of preserved fruits, vegetables, condensed milk and soups, and breakfast cereals as symbols of the United States. White Wonder Bread and colorful Jell-O enjoyed iconic moments before fatty hamburgers and sugary Cokes replaced them. For better or worse, American foods have more often been products of American industry than of American kitchens.

Is it significant that only with the formation of a national food marketplace and industrialization did foods and drinks "become American"? In recent years, scholars have enthusiastically accepted food as an important marker and creator of ethnic and racial diversity among consumers.[3] This essay assumes it can tell us something as well about the role of business and industry in nation-building.

Surprisingly little is known about cultural diversity in American business history.[4] Most foreign- and native-born minorities in American industry—including its food industries—were ordinary wage laborers—butcher workmen, brewery workers, and migrant harvesters—not successful entrepreneurs.[5] Students of immigration and ethnicity have established that foreigners were more likely than other Americans to operate small businesses.[6] But far more than manual labor or petty enterprise, it was big business—understood to encompass mass production through technical innovation, public ownership through incorporation, bureaucratic management, and enormous capital—that, rightly or wrongly, defined Americans' sense of their distinctive, national, American genius.[7]

To explore the linkage of industrial production and "American" foods, this chapter focuses on the nativity and lives of leaders of American food industries in the nineteenth and twentieth centuries. Were food industries and American foods in fact native creations? Multicultural histories of the United States have usually suggested instead that European immigrants—as whites—easily became American through upward mobility and citizenship, redefining the national American mainstream (including its culinary habits) as they joined the nation. Attention to the biographies of industry leaders suggests a more complex picture.

This study focuses on businessmen who pioneered the mass production of food and drink for national markets, comparing patterns of enterprise among the native- and foreign-born (and their children, the second generation). Biography may be a controversial method for this undertaking. Business historians dislike the moralizing tone of histories of wealthy robber barons, while social historians find the equally repugnant moral lessons of Horatio Alger lurking in any business biography. But with few archives for the study of business, alternatives are surprisingly limited for historians of business culture. This study draws on 17,000 biographies included in the 24-volume compendium, *American National Biography* (ANB), supplemented by census material and by published biographies and oral histories of four particularly well-documented industry leaders of foreign origin (Agoston Haraszthy, Adolphus Busch, H. J. Heinz, and Giuseppe Di Giorgio).[8]

The 79 business leaders included in this study are by no means a random or scientific sample.[9] At best they raise issues that require further exploration. For one, they point to the fact that foreigners were more likely to become leaders in food industries than in American business generally. But if business leadership was itself no expression of a peculiarly American national genius for industrializing production of food and drink, nativity nevertheless shaped businessmen's lives in the nineteenth and early twentieth century in significant ways. Many commestibles produced on a large scale never became icons of American eating. On the contrary, the formation of a consumer society and a national food marketplace by 1900 sparked intense controversies—veritable food fights—over the definition of American food, drink, and diet.[10] Coke and corn flakes, but not beer or pickles, "became American." Packed and processed

Donna R. Gabaccia

meats and wine, but not condensed milk, white flour, or canned peaches, became the focus of intense consumer scrutiny, distrust, and regulation. Xenophobia significantly influenced which mass-produced foods would "become American," which consumer choices defined membership in the American nation, and how businessmen organized and ran their enterprises. Cultural conflicts associated with nation-building characterized the early years of American consumer society, preventing the free expression and celebration of the multiculturalism that has now become such a familiar part of our own consumer marketplace and sense of national identity.[11]

FOOD, INDUSTRY, AND THE AMERICAN "GENIUS" FOR BUSINESS

In the century after 1840, the United States changed from a nation of rural and small-town dwellers growing and processing much of their own food and drink to a nation of city-dwelling wageworkers and consumers. Urbanites increasingly paid cash to eat products delivered over long distances from fields and processing plants via new systems of transportation. Production for a national market made possible the development of large agribusinesses (later characterized aptly as factories in the fields) as well as large-scale processing and preserving industries. By the early twentieth century, 8 percent of the country's workforce (not including agricultural wage earners) produced and processed food and drink on an industrial scale.

Foreigners and their children were not limited to humble roles as workers or consumers during the industrialization of the United States. Table 1 summarizes the representation of foreigners in varying "occupations and realms of renown" in *American National Biography* (ANB). Overall, a surprising 18 percent of over 17,000 entries in the ANB were persons born outside the United States, exceeding foreigners' representation (12 to 15 percent) in the American population in the nineteenth and early twentieth centuries.[12] Business and industry, ANB reveals, were dominated by leaders of native birth but were also far more open to newer arrivals from Europe than to native-born African Americans or women. Becoming a political leader appears to have been considerably more difficult than building a successful business. Finally, Anglo-Canadian, Irish, English, Welsh, and Scottish immigrants enjoyed linguistic advantages over other foreigners in becoming leaders in industry and politics.[13]

America's food industries were something of an anomaly in both respects. Foreigners generally and immigrants from central and southern Europe (in sharp contrast to the largest native-born minority group, African Americans) enjoyed special prominence as builders of important business enterprises in American food industries. Twenty-one percent of the 78 men and women listed in ANB as leaders of food industries were foreign-born. Of these sixteen, half were from southern and central

Table 1. Nativity and Achievement in *American National Biography*

Number		Born Abroad	British Isles	2nd Generation
17,500	All Entries	18%	43%	N/A
1,087	Non–Food Business*	13%	51%	7%
78	Food Business**	21%	25%	11%
666	Political Figures	9%	95%	N/A

*Includes the following index categories: Advertising Industry Leaders, Automobile Industry Leaders, Barbed Wire Manufacturers, Building Materials Industry, Capitalists and Financiers, Chemical Industry Leaders, Clothing Industry Leaders, Construction Industry Leaders, Department Store Owners, Electrical Industry Leaders, Entrepreneurs, Financial Industry Leaders, Firearms Manufacturers, Household Appliance and Housewares Manufacturers, Industrialists, Insurance Industry Leaders, Iron and Steel Industry Leaders, Machinery Manufacturers, Paper Industry Leaders, Petroleum Industry Leaders, Railroad Industry Leaders, Rubber Industry Leaders, Smelting and Refining Industry Leaders, Telegraph Industry Leaders, Telephone Industry Leaders, Textile Industry Leaders, Tobacco Industry Leaders, Tool Manufacturers.

**Bakers, Brewers, Chewing Gum Industry Leaders, Confectioners, Distillers, Flour Milling Industry Leaders, Fast Foods, Food Business Leaders, Grocery Store Owners, Meatpackers, Soft Drink Industry Leaders, Sugar Refining Industry, Winegrowers and Vintners.

Europe and four were from Germany; only two were from Ireland, and another two from England and Canada.[14] The ANB suggests that Americanization resulted at least temporarily in lower levels of entrepreneurship and leadership: only 11 percent of the food industry leaders were of the second generation.

American food industries were in reality not as plural as Table 1 suggests, for foreigners and natives developed different food industries (see Table 2). Natives from Pennsylvania and northern New England (James S. Bell and his son James F., William Dunwoody, John and Charles Pillsbury, Cadwallader and William Washburn) made the upper Midwest a new center of flour milling in the middle years of the century.[15] During the same years, foreigners from England (Matthew Vassar) and Germany (Virgil Brand, Adolphus Busch, Jacob Ruppert) developed the brewing industry.[16] Foreigners (Julio Gallo, Agoston Haraszthy, Rosa Mondavi, Angelo and Louis Petri, Andrea Sbarboro) dominated wine making and distilling.[17] In sharp contrast, cereal manufacturers and heads of large fruit-and-vegetable canning operations and dairy processing enterprises were largely native Anglo-Americans. Here, among brand names established in the nineteenth century and still familiar today (Dole, Kellogg's, Ralston-Purina, Birds Eye, Campbell's, Post, Carnation, and Knox) the only foreigner was the Canadian James Kraft (cheese processing). H. J. Heinz (canning and preserving) was the lone businessman of European (German) parentage. Founders of large soft-drink, chewing-gum, and fast-food companies in the twentieth century were also Anglo-Americans, with at least three generations in the United States.[18] Meatpacking, along with

Table 2. Nativity of Food Industry Leaders

	N	Born Abroad	Second Generation	Native-Born
ALCOHOLIC BEVERAGES				
Brewing	5	2	2	1
Distilling	5	3	2	
Winemaking	5	4	1	
Subtotal	15	9	5	1
STAPLE FOODS				
Flour	7			7
Cereals	7			7
Baking	4	1		3
Meat	14	2	3	9
Sugar	2	1		1
Dairy	7		1	6
Fruits/Vegetables	4	1		3
Grocery	7	1	1	5
Subtotal	52	5	6	41
SNACK AND FAST FOODS				
Chewing Gum	2			2
Confectioners	4	1		3
Fast Foods	3			3
Soft drinks	2			2
Subtotal	11	1	–	10
Total	78	15	11	52

sugar refining in the nineteenth and retail groceries and confectionery in the twentieth century, was exceptional in having wealthy foreigners, second-generation Irish and German-Americans, and Anglo-Americans all in positions of leadership.

Whether developed by foreigners or by Americans, the food industries represented in ANB were routinized industries, specializing in bulk and mass production.[19] As such, they sometimes struck visitors as the cutting edge of modern American capitalism. Yet neither technical nor marketing innovations nor the acquisition of a national market were products of any peculiarly American national genius for big business. In fact, at first glance there seem to have been few differences in the business practices of foreign- and native-born businessmen in the nineteenth century.

Many of the technical innovations that made mass production possible in American food industries came from Europe in the nineteenth century, giving bilingual foreigners some advantages in locating and introducing technologies developed abroad. The German sugar refiner Claus Spreckels returned to Europe personally to study and then to introduce new techniques of beet-sugar refining.[20] The brewer Adolphus Busch's frequent trips to Germany made him an important conduit for the transfer of technological innovation—notably the diesel engine—to the United States. Busch generally insisted to consumers that he duplicated traditional brewing techniques, but in fact he experimented constantly, substituting rice for barley and pasteurizing beer for long-distance shipping.[21] Although it proved no great impediment to their business successes, Anglo-Americans more often had to hire expertise to introduce technologies from abroad. The adventurous Charles Pillsbury ventured off to France and Hungary while in his thirties, but the considerably older miller Cadwallader Washburn instead hired a French immigrant to engineer the bleaching of the reddish spring wheat processed by Washburn, Crosby and Company in the 1870s. Thirty years later, the native Elbridge Stuart hired Swiss immigrants to install and operate the equipment that processed Carnation's "milk from contented cows."

Foreign-born and native-born entrepreneurs alike sought national markets for their products. In fact, ANB excludes businessmen who achieved success or leadership only within an ethnic or "niche" market of foreign-born consumers.[22] That pasteurized beer brewed from a mix of grains on a large scale in St. Louis tasted little like the beers of Germany was no problem for Adolphus Busch because most who bought his beer were not Germans. On the contrary, consumption of lager beer had become a nationwide fad among young, urban men of all backgrounds in the years during and after the Civil War.[23] Busch's market expanded in the 1870s and 1880s as he leased refrigerated railway cars to ship beer to Southern and Southwestern markets far from German-dominated St. Louis. His use of railroads differed little from the native flour millers of Minneapolis, notably Washburn (an important investor in the railroad industry), or the German, Irish, and American meatpackers of Chicago.[24]

Foreigners in American food industries showed the same creativity in packaging, branding, and marketing exhibited by the natives who made cold cereals a popular new American breakfast nationwide. In fact, the second-generation canner H. J. Heinz's most significant contribution to American business may have been his troops of salesmen and his innovative marketing campaigns. Heinz's slogan, "57 varieties," the pickle charms he distributed at the Columbian Exposition, the colorful wagons of his salesmen, and his "57 culture pier" at the Jersey shore created many of the basic elements of American advertising.[25] In the twentieth century, the Sicilian Giuseppe Di Giorgio transformed fruit marketing throughout the United States by creating auction houses in Baltimore, Chicago, and most other large Midwestern and East Coast cities. Based on European models, auction houses—financed in part by railroads looking for goods to fill empty cars that had delivered meat, canned goods, or beer to rural areas— replaced the older commission houses and their salesmen by selling directly to grocers and restaurant owners.[26]

Searching for the broadest possible markets, foreign-born business-men rarely called attention to their national origins even when nativity might—arguably—have distinguished their products from others. Adolphus Busch could have touted German culture and expertise in adver-tising his Budweiser beer. Instead, German references in Anheuser-Busch trade materials disappeared after 1890 (although they briefly reappeared again during Prohibition). Busch's most popular advertising symbol was instead a much-reproduced painting he purchased of Custer's Last Stand.[27] Similarly, the German-American H. J. Heinz could have emphasized his roots in a country with a rich tradition of pickle making and eating, but instead chose culturally neutral symbols in his innovative campaigns. The business strategies of the earliest big businessmen in American food industries were thus precursors of what business historians later termed "Coca Cola" or "Model T" marketing strategies. They rightly assumed that standardized products appealed to the largest group of consumers.[28] This was the foundation on which products could "become American" as they found a national market.

By far the most striking difference between foreign-born and native-born was not the foreign-born genius for technical innovation, marketing, or mass production but the concentration of the foreign-born in a distinc-tive alcohol niche in the American economy. This alcohol niche alone explains foreigners' relatively high representation in American food indus-tries. Remove foreign-born wine makers, distillers, and brewers from ANB lists, and foreigners' representation in food industries falls to 9 percent, below the average for leadership in business and industry generally, and for political leadership too. Outside the alcohol niche, southern and east-ern Europeans almost completely disappear as industry leaders.[29]

Although brief, ANB biographies suggest that something other than cultural capital or ethnic self-segregation produced the alcohol niche. German immigrants possessed wine-making traditions, and Irish and English immigrants had significant brewing and distilling traditions, yet they did not become prominent business leaders in those industries. In addition, immigrants from countries with rich baking traditions (Germany, Austria, Italy) failed to achieve dominance in that industry.

It seems more likely that foreign entrepreneurs moved into alcohol production because natives and immigrants of British and even Irish origin were abandoning it. Historians have long known that a cultural revulsion against alcohol developed among many middle-class and working-class Anglo-Americans with the second Great Awakening of evangelical Protestantism in the 1830s.[30] Conflicts over alcohol production and consumption soon became a major dimension of the food fights of the country's early consumer society, and historians of temperance and prohibition movements have always acknowledged the xenophobic elements of these reform initiatives.[31] Although mass-produced and marketed nationwide, alcoholic beverages clearly did not become American as a result. Nor were the consequences of this division between foreign and American limited to the shaping of American consumer identities or the prohibition movement. By labeling only some mass-produced foods as clearly "American," the food fights of early consumer society held the potential for shaping American business practices into the twentieth century.

BUSINESS, NATION, AND ALCOHOL NICHE

A strong and growing market for alcoholic beverages, coupled with a politically powerful movement to purge the American nation of the problems associated with alcohol abuse, created a paradoxical business climate in the United States in the nineteenth century. Only foreigners seemed willing to assume the risks of investment under these conditions, but the association of alcohol with foreignness became so pronounced that it affected business practices even in less controversial food industries. A comparison of foreign businessmen in and outside the alcohol industry provides suggestive clues to how business and industry became sites of nation-building during this period.

The life of Agoston Haraszthy (1812–1869) illustrates the problems immigrant entrepreneurs faced in industrializing the production of alcohol. An American market for wine—fueled by wealthy plantation owners and urban merchants alike—had already existed before the American Revolution, as steady imports of wines and spirits revealed. Efforts to produce wine from native grapes repeatedly failed, while distilling alcohol from corn and other native grains expanded rapidly.[32] Industrialization in the next century produced a steadily growing market for wine among Americans eager to emulate the consumption habits of Europe's aristocracies, among immigrants with more plebeian traditions of wine drinking, and among bohemians rejecting Victorian Anglo-American respectability.[33]

Haraszthy, a Hungarian immigrant from an old and wealthy family of large landowners, fled his homeland as a political exile in 1840. After a succession of failures as construction entrepreneur and town builder in Wisconsin and southern California, and assayer in a government mint in San Francisco, he began raising grapes and making wine at his Buena Vista vineyard in Sonoma County in the 1850s. Haraszthy attempted traditional wine-making techniques on a large scale but also experimented with new growing and processing technologies, with an all-Chinese workforce, and with the construction of huge underground vats for processing and aging wines.[34]

Haraszthy's repeated business failures, including the collapse of his Buena Vista venture, can be traced to repeated political blunders. Haraszthy seemed to grasp a necessary connection of business and politics in the United States yet remained curiously blind to American moral values as expressed through politics. His closest political ties in the late 1850s were to proslavery Democrats who despised his enthusiasm for his Chinese workforce and may have had doubts about the morality of alcohol as well. Disastrously, Haraszthy misinterpreted California politicians' economic boosterism for a commitment to state-sponsored economic development (a common-enough pattern in Europe). In 1861, as a member of a commission appointed by California's governor to investigate wine-making possibilities in the state, Haraszthy traveled widely throughout Europe and the Mediterranean and returned with over 100,000 vine cuttings purchased on credit for $12,000. He failed to obtain reimbursement from the government as he had expected, in part because the Democrats he supported had lost power to Republicans with the start of the Civil War. Selling off his vines piecemeal to cut his losses, Haraszthy's wine-making venture soon collapsed. His creditors forced him to incorporate in 1863, and an angry board of directors then swiftly ousted him. He died in 1869 in Nicaragua, where he was exploring possibilities with one of his sons for growing sugar for export to California.

A comparison of two German-origin food industry leaders of the period of intensive industrialization—the immigrant Adolphus Busch (1839–1913) and the second-generation H. J. Heinz (1844–1919)—illustrates both the burdens of business in the alcohol niche and the caution required of businessmen of foreign origin outside that niche. Although both men lived transnational lives and exhibited considerable pride in their German origins, the canner Heinz attracted a favorable press throughout his life, while the brewer Busch became the focus of nativist ire for his arrogance and immorality.

Born in 1839 to a wealthy landowner and vintner with twenty children in Germany's Rhineland, Busch followed a brother to St. Louis. There he first became involved in the malt trade, and then, through his marriage to a daughter of Eberhard Anheuser, became owner and then manager of a faltering brewery which he subsequently transformed into the largest beer factory in the world. H. J. Heinz was born soon after Busch to humbler Bavarian parents who had arrived separately in Pittsburgh a year earlier. After an earlier canning business of his failed during the depression of the 1870s, Heinz expanded from horseradish and pickles into "reciped products" (prepared foods) such as baked beans and pork, pepper sauces, ketchup, chili sauce, fruit butters, minced meat, piccalilli, and macaroni with cheese. Heinz's Pittsburgh canneries also became the largest in the United States. The uncanny similarities of the huge, brick, turreted factory blocks built by Heinz and Busch in Pittsburgh and St. Louis might surprise observers who expect architectural form to follow the differing functions pursued within. Both seemed clear statements of the new power of American capitalism, yet they would elicit very different responses from American consumers and consumer activists.

The lives of the two men also shared some common outlines. Both built lavish homes, collected art, traveled widely, and enjoyed transatlantic lives. Busch was an extravagant philanthropist who gave money to earthquake victims in San Francisco and Messina (Sicily) alike; he generously funded cultural institutions, often in the interests of encouraging the study of German culture. Traveling yearly to Germany with his entire family, he owned an estate there, where he died in 1913 during a hunting trip. Beginning in the 1880s, Heinz, his wife, and children took German lessons and Heinz, too, then revived his (already deceased) father's tradition of returning regularly to Germany to visit family and friends. His younger sister married a man from his father's hometown, and Heinz himself sent several sons to Germany to study. Like other wealthy American businessmen of the era (and much like the Busch family too), Heinz and his family enjoyed European spas and visited the usual shrines of European culture.

Perhaps unsurprisingly, Busch became one of the robber barons America's early consumers most loved to hate. Unlike the Scottish immigrant philanthropist Andrew Carnegie in the steel industry, Busch and his family endured almost universally negative press that became harsher in its criticisms of them as the strength of the prohibition movement and political conflicts over the saloon and brewing industries peaked after 1900. Busch died just before war broke out in Europe, but within months his family members (who were in Germany at their home there at the time) found themselves accused of German sympathies. Anheuser-Busch fell under the control of the federal government during the war. Thereafter, during prohibition, Busch's sons scrambled unsuccessfully to create new products; the company survived prohibition but in a chastened condition.[35]

With his business fortunes firmly in the alcohol niche, Busch could scarcely escape opprobrium as a foreigner. But even the American-born Heinz seemed to recognize the risks of xenophobia while working outside the niche. Heinz gave every appearance of being fully American in his moral sensibilities. A German Lutheran during childhood, he married a native Anglo-American, and then ecumenically attended Methodist, Presbyterian, and Baptist churches, becoming a Sunday school teacher and an outspoken supporter of temperance. Like Anglo-American businessmen in the canning, preserving, flour, and cereal industries, Heinz emphasized the sanitary and healthful qualities of his products. He initially packed all his foods in glass bottles so customers could see what they were buying and only after his business boomed did he switch reluctantly to tin cans. Women in his cannery wore uniforms with white caps that evoked nurses' garb. In 1906 his son and brother-in-law became full-time lobbyists in Washington, making the H. J. Heinz company one of the industry's most vocal supporters of the Pure Food and Drug Act. A vigorous paternalist who emphasized his humble origins, thus appealing to the emerging Horatio Alger myth, Heinz decorated his corporate headquarters with uplifting homilies and instituted an extensive program of welfare programs for his largely female and foreign-born workforce. He attracted positive attention as a benevolent employer and business role model even from the generally critical authors of the *Pittsburgh Survey*.[36]

Within the alcohol niche, businessmen of foreign origin obviously faced special business risks. It seems quite likely that they responded by keeping leadership and ownership of their businesses strictly within their families, sometimes over several generations. In his early years as town builder and assayer, Haraszthy repeatedly formed partnerships and small corporations with native Anglo-Americans. When he began his Buena Vista winery, however, his widowed father (who followed him to the United States and married an Anglo-American in Wisconsin) and three sons became his only business associates until failure forced him into incorporation. Strategically (and as a Catholic), he encouraged two of his sons to marry daughters of the native California rancher, wine maker, and political figure, Mariano Guadelupe Vallejo, and sent one to France to train as a champagne maker. Both sons remained wine industry activists, but Haraszthy's business failure prevented them from pursuing the most common business strategy of foreigners in the alcohol niche—taking over a family business from their father.

In the following decade, Adolphus Busch began his business life in partnership with his father-in-law before incorporating in 1879 as Anheuser-Busch. Both management and stock of the Anheuser-Busch corporation remained in family hands for four generations. (After 1890, the Italian immigrants who succeeded in finding a national market for California wine before and after prohibition would also keep their businesses in family hands.) Even in the 1950s, the Busch and Anheuser families held almost all stock in the company, and grandson August ("Gussie") Busch had become its chief manager; August III later succeeded Gussie.

To a surprising degree, foreign businessmen outside the alcohol niche did the same. After the failure of an early partnership in the 1870s with Anglo-American businessmen (and with capital borrowed from a local bank), H. J. Heinz emerged morally stricken and in debt. In 1876, he formed a new partnership with his brother and cousin. He rejected bids by East Coast financiers to purchase the business, and he incorporated only in 1905. Even then, the original six partners (four family members and two longtime family friends and business associates) were the sole stockholders and officers. The company offered shares for public sale only in 1946. Management, too, remained within the family. Heinz's son Howard assumed leadership of the firm after H. J's death in 1919, and Howard's son, the third-generation H. J. Heinz II, remained president of the corporate board into the 1970s. The uncontroversial Heinz company was just as much a family dynasty as the controversial Anheuser-Busch or Gallo businesses.

Giuseppe Di Giorgio, the produce marketer, lived well after the worst of the food fights of the early twentieth century and purchased vineyards in California only in the waning days of prohibition. Yet his business, too, developed through family ties. Di Giorgio had first arrived in Baltimore (where relatives of his mother's fisherman father already lived) from Sicily in 1889, accompanying a shipment of his father's lemons. After working briefly in the New York commission (food wholesale) house of his father's former importer, Di Giorgio returned to Baltimore to open his own import business. He then paid for the college education of several brothers who followed him into the business. Di Giorgio gained access to necessary capital for his fruit auctions through a number of partnerships with native-born businessmen, while simultaneously building a transnational family enterprise. (A brother with a French wife oversaw the banana import business from a Cuban office but sent his sons to be educated in the United States. Another brother managed the Baltimore auction house; a third oversaw Di Giorgio's subsequent expansion into produce growing in Florida and California.) Although married, Di Giorgio had no children and acknowledged his dependence on his brothers and sisters "to build the family." Family members maintained a controlling 51 percent interest in the company even after the first public offerings of company stock in the 1930s. After a heart attack in 1939, Di Giorgio created a trust for his six nephews, who took over management of the company after his death in 1951. One nephew somewhat wistfully told an interviewer in 1983 that he expected "the day will come where there won't be a Di Giorgio running this company." In fact, as he spoke, the CEO was already an outsider named Peter Scott.

Family-owned and managed businesses were of course common in the United States in the nineteenth century. In ANB listings, native-born and foreign-born businessmen formed partnerships with their brothers and cousins in equal proportions, suggesting that family savings—not banks or ethnic community associations—long remained the main source of capital for food industry entrepreneurs regardless of origin. Beginning in the late nineteenth century, however, raising capital through incorporation and public ownership, bureaucratic management by paid corporate experts, and consolidation into ever-larger trusts and conglomerates began to redefine the national and supposedly American genius for big business.[37] While it took many decades before these newer business practices became the norm, foreigners and natives cited in the ANB already made different choices in the nineteenth century, raising questions about the impact of xenophobia and food fights on business strategy more generally during this transition.

Certainly three- and even four-generation family dynasties resembling those founded by Busch, Heinz, and Di Giorgio were common in food businesses founded by foreigners. Even after incorporating, twelve of the sixteen foreign-born businessmen (75 percent) included in ANB saw their children replace them as presidents and managers of their businesses. In sharp contrast, only a quarter of the much larger group of American leaders of food industries turned over management of their companies to their children. Different managerial cultures apparently marked native- and foreign-origin food businesses well into the twentieth century. Corporate and bureaucratically managed enterprises, along with their products, increasingly defined what seemed modern and "American" in American business. By contrast, familist and foreign strategies of business characterized both smaller mom-and-pop enterprises and the much larger enterprises associated with the alcohol niche and foreignness in the food fights of America's emerging consumer society.

CULINARY NATION-BUILDING AND ITS CONSEQUENCES

Even a rather brief summary of biographies in the ANB raises questions about the evolution of this country's food industries, sharply divided as they were between foreign- and native-born economic niches. Controversies over the nature and definition of American foods and the American nation have also cast a long shadow over the history and biography of the people most involved in organizing and regulating this country's food industries.

This account of foreigners in American food industries suggests that the relative decline of food processing as important mass-production industries might be traced to the food fights of early consumer society. In 1860, measured by value created, the milling of flour and meal was already a nationally significant industry—the fourth largest in the United States. By 1880, two food industries were among the country's ten largest industries; the native-dominated milling industry had dropped to seventh place and the foreign-dominated malt liquor industry (mainly beer brewing) had become the country's tenth-largest industry. By 1900, malt liquor was sixth in rank, while meatpacking, a culturally diverse industry, had replaced it in tenth place.[38] In terms of value added, however, most food industries already fell below the national average by the early twentieth century; other industries were becoming more innovative or efficient.[39] Measured by numbers of employees, too, food industries declined relative to the expanding workforces of foundry, iron and steel, lumber, printing, textiles, and garment industries.[40] After 1900, food industries disappear from America's list of top ten industries. The peculiar risks of business and the significant numbers of entrepreneurs reluctant to seek capital outside family enterprises may hold at least some clues to changes like these.

The rather belated consolidation of food industry businesses into conglomerates might also fruitfully be interpreted with an eye to risks and controversies peculiar to nation-building in the food marketplace. Unfortunately the speed with which the native- and foreign-born industry leaders incorporated could not be compared systematically in ANB biographies. But it is clear that food conglomerates emerged only in the late 1920s, more than thirty years after consolidation of steel, oil, and railroad trusts. Movements toward consolidation had begun in meatpacking, the country's second most important food industry, in the 1890s. Significantly, perhaps, the majority of foreign-born and second-generation meatpackers (notably Michael Cudahy and George and Jay Hormel) refused to join the movement and chose instead to remain independents during the formation of the National Packing company, a combination of the four largest meatpackers. Trust-busting and regulation of the meatpacking industry followed the intense consumer scrutiny that accompanied publication of Upton Sinclair's *The Jungle* and passage of the 1906 Pure Food and Drug Act.[41] In the country's largest food industry—brewing—consolidation through trust-building was simply too risky, and prohibition threatened to destroy the industry completely. The result was that neither of the country's largest food industries in 1900 could become foundations for corporate consolidation, as occurred in other industries. It scarcely seems coincidental that business enterprises founded by native-born Americans in milling, cereal, and canning later became the foundations of the earliest food conglomerates (General Mills and General Foods in 1928 and 1929; Campbell's Soup soon thereafter).

Although evidence is weaker on this point, it also might be worth considering the possibility that foreign-born businessmen responded to risk and xenophobia in the United States by seeking markets abroad with particular vigor. At least as summarized in ANB, foreign- and native-born leaders of the food industries enjoyed varying degrees of success in foreign markets. Already during the Civil War, the German butcher and cattle dealer Nelson Morris (who would spearhead consolidation efforts of meatpackers in the 1890s) successfully parlayed his Union Army contracts into foreign sales of dressed beef to French, British, and German governments. A decade later, however, the native miller William Dunwoody found that consumers in England rejected his Gold Medal flour as too white. (Cereal manufacturers would later find European consumers equally skeptical about their American product or the notions of healthful eating associated with breakfast cereals.) As brewing came under increasing attack in the United States, Adolphus Busch oversaw the expansion of Anheuser-Busch into new markets in South America, Africa, Australia, Asia, and Europe; these may have allowed the company to survive prohibition.

The canner H. J. Heinz probably established the most successful overseas market of any food industrialist of the nineteenth century. Heinz personally made his first sales in London and Germany in 1886, and by 1901 the 57 varieties were in Toronto and Montreal, Nicaragua, Buenos Aires, Bermuda, the West Indies, and South Africa. Heinz and his salesmen pushed on into Asia, Japan, Australia, and the Philippines in the early twentieth century, dreaming of Asian consumers but more often finding buyers among English-speakers scattered throughout the extensive British empire.[42] After H. J. Heinz's death, his son Howard Heinz gave his own son, H. J. II, responsibility for Heinz operations abroad, and H. J. II subsequently completed a second round of internationalization of Heinz operations in the 1950s and 1960s, shoring up company balance sheets when domestic markets for pickles and ketchup slumped.

Attention to business and industry as places where concepts of the American nation are constructed and continue to evolve has an additional advantage. It might help historians move beyond the moralizing tone characteristic of histories of food industry businessmen and of American food generally. Recent popular biographies of foreign businessmen in the alcohol niche can be dismissed as fundamentally unbalanced when not downright scurrilous, and their persistent characterization of these businesses as dynastic and imperial remains striking. Agoston Haraszthy's detractors continued to rage at his dishonesty and supposedly criminal record into the twentieth century.[43] In the eyes of recent biographers, Adolphus Busch's seemingly reasonable business goal, to "win the American over to our side, to make them all lovers of beer," becomes a plot "to weave beer drinking into the fabric of American life."[44] Perhaps biographers continue to believe that the mass production of alcohol is sufficient explanation for the moral failings—suicides, drug abuse, family feuds, and failed marriages—at the core of most histories of corporate dynasties in the alcohol niche.[45] Even the far more balanced entries of the ANB comment extensively on the family feuds, court battles, murders, and suicides of Italian wine makers, as do full-length books such as the unauthorized biography of the Gallo brothers.[46] Foreign businessmen outside the alcohol niche sometimes suffer the same treatment. The temporary feud that erupted between the nineteenth-century German sugar refiner Claus Spreckels and some of his sons gets full treatment, while ANB entries on the Kellogg brothers dismiss their years of court battles in less than a sentence. In this regard the second-generation H. J. Heinz (who ejected an alcohol-abusing brother with a "morally irregular" personal life from the family business) seems to qualify as fully American, for his ANB entry remains silent on the predictable conflicts of family businesses.

Biographies like these reveal the considerable tenacity of the moral discourses of the food fights of the early twentieth century. To this day, businessmen too often become either barons or heroes in our national narrative; consumers become dupes or brave transgressors; mass-produced American foods become drugs, junk, or democracy-on-a-bun. This recurring linkage of morality and food is also clearly a dimension of American nation-building. Older interpretations of prohibition as a movement dividing Protestant, rural "dries" with deep American roots from recently arrived, Catholic and Jewish, urban "wets" may have been simplistic but focused attention squarely on nation-building.[47] Historians of consumer movements might usefully do the same.[48] What were the ties linking purity and prohibition campaigns? Why did consumer ire in the early twentieth century focus on meatpacking, candy, baking, and brewing, but not flour milling, cereal manufacturing, or canning? By asking new questions, historians of American consumer society might avoid offering updated versions of culturally overdetermined and deeply American tales of good and evil in the marketplace.

NOTES

1. For the European perspective, see Claude Fischler, "The 'McDonaldization' of Culture," in Jean-Louis Flandrin and Massimo Montanari, eds., *Food: A Culinary History* (New York: Columbia University Press, 1999), pp. 530–547.
2. Compare the defenders of regional foods, John L. Hess and Karen Hess, *The Taste of America* (Columbia: The University of Carolina Press, 1989), ch. 1, to the clearest defender of mass-produced American foods, Daniel J. Boorstin, *The Americans: The Democratic Experience* (New York: Random House, 1973), pp. 309–322.
3. A rich and rapidly growing literature already examines the ethnicity of food shoppers, the influence of culture on consumer choices, and immigrants' acculturation to the habits of American consumerism. Tracy Poe, "Food, Culture, and Entrepreneurship among African Americans, Italians and Swedes in Chicago," Unpublished Diss., Harvard University, 1999; Andrew Heinze, *Adapting to Abundance: Jewish Immigrants, Mass Consumption, and the Search for American Identity* (New York: Columbia University Press, 1980); Lizabeth Cohen, *Making a New Deal: Industrial Workers in Chicago, 1919–1939* (Cambridge: Cambridge University Press, 1990), pp. 101–120.
4. But see Faith Davis Ruffins, "Reflecting on Ethnic Imagery in the Landscape of Commerce, 1945–1975," in Susan Strasser, Charles McGovern, and Matthias Judt, eds., *Getting and Spending: European and American Consumer Societies in the Twentieth Century* (Cambridge and Washington: Cambridge University Press and German Historical Institute, 1998), pp. 379–405.
5. Dorothee Schneider, *Trade Unions and Community: The German Working Class in New York City, 1870–1900* (Urbana: University of Illinois Press, 1994); James R. Barrett, *Work and Community in the Jungle: Chicago's Packinghouse Workers, 1894–1922* (Urbana: University of Illinois Press, 1987); Rick Halpern, *Down on the Killing Floor: Black and White Workers in Chicago's Packinghouses, 1904–54* (Urbana: University of Illinois Press, 1997); Roger Horowitz, *Negro and White, Unite and Fight!: A Social History of Industrial Unionism in Meatpacking, 1930–90* (Urbana: University of Illinois Press, 1997); Vicki Ruiz, *Cannery Women, Cannery Lives: Mexican Women, Unionization, and the California Food Processing Industry, 1930–1950* (Albuquerque: University of New Mexico Press, 1987).
6. See Marilyn Halter, *New Migrants in the Marketplace: Boston's Ethnic Entrepreneurs* (Amherst: University of Massachusetts Press, 1995); Ivan Light, *Race, Ethnicity, and Entrepreneurship in Urban America* (New York: Aldine de Gruyter, 1995).
7. On significant national differences in the practice of corporate capitalism, see the comparison of "competitive managerial capitalism" in the United States to Great Britain's "personal capitalism" and Germany's "cooperative managerial capitalism" in Alfred D. Chandler, Jr., *Scale and Scope: The Dynamics of Industrial Capitalism* (Cambridge, MA: The Belknap Press of Harvard University Press, 1990). On the special status of businessmen and corporations in American society, see Thomas C. Cochran, *The American Business*

System (Cambridge, MA: President and Fellows of Harvard College, 1957), p. 2, and chap. 1 more generally. For a critique of Americans' simplistic conflation of mass production with capitalist innovation, see Philip Scranton, *Endless Novelty: Specialty Production and American Industrialization, 1865–1925* (Princeton: Princeton University Press, 1997), pp. 4–7.

8. *American National Biography*, ed. John A. Garraty and Mark C. Carnes (New York: Oxford University Press, 1999). Of the four, only H. J. Heinz left extensive archival materials. Di Giorgio is the only businessman treated here who is not included in ANB.

9. I have chosen to call attention to possible biases and problems of representation in ANB only in the footnotes.

10. Donna R. Gabaccia, *We Are What We Eat: Ethnic Food and the Making of Americans* (Cambridge, MA: Harvard University Press, 1998), chap. 5.

11. Marilyn Halter, *Shopping for Identity: The Marketing of Ethnicity* (New York: Schocken Books, 2000).

12. The editors of ANB note their use of an inclusive definition of achievement and significance but deny they used racial or ethnic criteria to identify and select individuals for inclusion in the compendium. ANB includes significant numbers of biographies from the colonial era and this—rather than any editorial effort at "political correctness"—best explains the high representation of Europeans of foreign birth among the notable Americans included.

13. Similar conclusions can be drawn from the 173 foreigners (15 percent of all listings) in John N. Ingham, ed., *Biographical Dictionary of American Business Leaders*, 4 vols. (Westport, CT: Greenwood Press, 1983). In this work, too, over half of business leaders included were English-speaking Canadian or Irish, Scottish, Welsh, or English. See also Walter Licht, *Industrializing America: The Nineteenth Century* (Baltimore: The Johns Hopkins University Press, 1995), p. 150.

14. I do not attribute the relative paucity of English-speaking foreigners among food businessmen in ANB to the marginal place of food or the pleasures of the table in British culture, for the native-born Anglo-Americans who generally shared that culture successfully developed the majority of American food industries.

15. See James Gray, *Business Without Boundary: The Story of General Mills* (Minneapolis: University of Minnesota Press, 1954); William J. Powell, *Pillsbury's Best: A Company History from 1869* (Minneapolis: Pillsbury Company, 1985); Dan Morgan, *Merchants of Grain* (London: Weidenfeld and Nicolson, 1979); John Storck and Walter D. Teague, *Flour for Man's Bread: A History of Milling* (Minneapolis: University of Minnesota Press, 1952).

16. Stanley Baron, *Brewed in America: A History of Beer and Ale in the United States* (Boston: Little Brown, 1962); Thomas C. Cochran, *The Pabst Brewing Company: The History of an American Business* (New York: New York University Press, 1948).

17. Unfortunately, distilling of hard spirits is both confusingly handled by ANB and sloppily indexed. Most businessmen included were either not particularly important distillers or made their "renown" in other arenas, e.g., Charles Fleischmann.

18. I am hesitant to accept ANB listings as definitive for these industries, however. African American and foreign-born street vendors developed a surprising number of "junk" street snacks into big business; Gabaccia, *We Are What We Eat*, pp. 105–106.

19. Scranton, *Endless Novelty*, table 4.

20. Unless noted otherwise by a footnote, my sources in the section that follows are the individual biographies included in ANB.

21. In addition to entries on Adolphus Busch and his grandson (third-generation) August in ANB, see the flamboyantly written exposé of the Busch family in Peter Hernon and Terry Ganey, *Under the Influence: The Unauthorized Story of the Anheuser-Busch Dynasty* (New York: Simon and Schuster, 1991). A more scholarly, if limited, study is Ronald J. Plavchan, "A History of Anheuser-Busch, 1852–1933," Ph.D. dissertation, St. Louis University, 1969. The documentary history published by the corporation, *Making Friends Is Our Business: 100 Years of Anheuser-Busch* (1953), is of some use.

22. For this phenomenon—exemplified by the kosher food industry—see Gabaccia, *We Are What We Eat*, chap. 3.

23. Ibid., pp. 97–99.

24. The railroad industry, it is worth noting, was almost completely dominated by native-born Americans, along with a very small group of immigrants from the British Isles.

25. Heinz has received the most extensive and balanced study of any food industry leader of foreign origin. Robert C. Alberts, *The Good Provider: H. J. Heinz and His 57 Varieties* (London: Barker, 1973) is a useful summary. See also Stephen Potter, *The Magic Number: the Story of '57'* (London: M. Reinhardt, 1959); Edward C. Hampe, Jr., and Merle Wittenberg, *The Lifeline of America: Development of the Food Industry* (New York: McGraw-

Hill, 1964); Eleanor Dienstag, *In Good Company: 125 Years at the Heinz Table, 1864–1994* (New York: Warner Books, 1994), esp. the chapter focusing on the international business activities of Henry J. Heinz.

26. The absence of Di Giorgio from the ANB (which includes Vito Genovese, the mafia "capo," among its listings of Italian-origin entrepreneurs) is hard to explain. It may reflect the ANB's general omission of food wholesalers and its spotty coverage of food retailers or Di Giorgio's successful efforts to avoid public scrutiny. Di Giorgio and his family business have also not yet attracted the attention biographers have devoted to the Italian wine makers. But see Lawrence J. Jelinek, *Harvest Empire: A History of California Agriculture* (San Francisco: Boyd and Fraser, 1979), pp. 64–68; Donna R. Gabaccia, "Ethnicity in the Business World: Italians in American Food Industries," *The Italian American Review* 6, 2 (Autumn/Winter, 1997/1998): 1–19. Unpublished sources include the oral histories (Robert Di Giorgio and Joseph A. Di Giorgio, "The Di Giorgios, From Fruit Merchants to Corporate Innovators," 1983, and Horace O. Lanza and Harry Baciagalupi, "California Grape Products and Other Wine Enterprises," 1969–1970) completed by Ruth Teicher for the Bancroft Library Oral History Research Center, University of California at Berkeley.

27. See advertising materials in *Making Friends Is Our Business*.

28. Richard C. Tedlow, *New and Improved: The Story of Mass Marketing in America* (New York: Basic Books, 1990).

29. Thomas Carvel, the Greek son of a wine chemist, is the sole example of a food industry leader of southern or eastern European origins who made his mark outside the alcohol niche—as developer of soft ice cream in the confectionery industry.

30. Robert Abzug, *Cosmos Crumbling: American Reform and the Religious Imagination* (New York: Oxford University Press, 1994). On the early temperance movement, see Ian Tyrrell, *Sobering Up: From Temperance to Prohibition in Antebellum America, 1800–1860* (Westport, CT: Greenwood Press, 1979).

31. Richard Hofstadter, *The Age of Reform: From Bryan to F.D.R.* (New York: Vintage Books, 1955); Joseph R. Gusfield, *Symbolic Crusade: Status Politics and the American Temperance Movement* (Urbana: University of Illinois Press, 1966), pp. 50–57, 101–102.

32. Herbert B. Leggett, *Early History of Wine Production in California* (San Francisco: Wine Institute, 1940); Vincent P. Carosso, *The California Wine Industry* (Berkeley: University of California Press, 1951).

33. Gabaccia, *We Are What Eat*, pp. 99–102.

34. The best published sources are Brian McGinty, *Strong Wine: The Life and Legend of Agoston Haraszthy* (Stanford: Stanford University Press, 1998); Theodore Schoenman, *Father of California Wine, Agoston Haraszthy: Including Grape Culture, Wines & Wine-Making* (Santa Barbara, CA: Capra Press, 1979). My account draws mainly on McGinty, but offers a somewhat different interpretation of Haraszthy's life.

35. Again, I offer a rather different interpretation from my main source, Hernon and Ganey, *Under the Influence*.

36. Russell Sage Foundation, *The Pittsburgh Survey*, 6 vols., ed. Paul U. Kellogg (New York: Charities Publication Committee, 1909).

37. Alfred D. Chandler, Jr. *The Visible Hand: The Managerial Revolution in American Business* (Cambridge, MA: The Belknap Press of Harvard University Press, 1977), pp. 8–9.

38. Jeremy Atack and Peter Passell, *A New Economic View of American History from Colonial Times to 1940* (New York: W.W. Norton & Co., 1994), tables 17.2 and 17.4.

39. Scranton, *Endless Novelty*, table 4.

40. Department of Commerce, Bureau of the Census, *Thirteenth Census of the United States*, vol. 8 *Manufactures—1909* (Washington, DC: Government Printing Office, 1913), pp. 40–43.

41. Upton Sinclair, *The Jungle* (New York: Doubleday, Page and Co., 1906).

42. Elizabeth Watkins, "Heinz's 57 Varieties: Traveling Salesmen and the Americanization of Eating," Paper presented at the Ninety-Third Annual Meeting of the Organization of American Historians, St. Louis, MI, April 1, 2000.

43. A distant descendant of Haraszthy, McGinty, devotes his book, *Strong Wine*, to carefully weighing, and ultimately rejecting, one hundred years of attacks on Haraszthy's character.

44. Hernon and Ganey, *Under the Influence*, pp. 12–13.

45. See the very similar treatment of the Coors brewing company and its familial dysfunction in Dan Baum, *Citizen Coors; An American Dynasty* (New York: Morrow, 2000).

46. Ellen Hawkes, *Blood and Wine : The Unauthorized Story of the Gallo Wine Empire* (New York: Simon & Schuster, 1993).

47. For changing interpretations since Hofstadter and Gusfield, see John J. Rumbarger,

Profits, Power and Prohibition: Alcohol Reform and the Industrializing of America, 1800–1930 (Albany: State University of New York Press, 1989); and Thomas R. Pegram, *Battling Demon Rum: The Struggle for a Dry America, 1800–1933* (Chicago: Ivan R. Dee, 1998).

48. Existing studies focus on institutional and political dimensions of pure food and drug movements and the influence of women and big businessmen or the research chemist Harvey Washington Wiley on their development. See James Harvey Young, *Pure Food: Securing the Federal Food and Drugs Act of 1906* (Princeton: Princeton University Press, 1989); Mitchell Okun, *Fair Play in the Marketplace: The First Battle for Pure Food and Drugs* (Dekalb: Northern Illinois University Press, 1986); Lorine Swainston Goodwin, *The Pure Food, Drink, and Drug Crusaders, 1879–1914* (Jefferson, NC: McFarland & Co., 1999).

Chapter 11

COMIDA SIN PAR. CONSUMPTION OF MEXICAN FOOD IN LOS ANGELES: "FOODSCAPES" IN A TRANSNATIONAL CONSUMER SOCIETY

SYLVIA FERRERO

INTRODUCTION

*A*nthropological literature has looked in various ways at ethnic food in multicultural, transnational contexts, largely emphasizing discourses of cultural symbolism and self-identification.[1] In this literature, ethnic food is often regarded as a system of communication[2] that discloses the daily practices and the habits that people enact when they purchase, cook, and eat their ethnic food. In transnational contexts, ethnic food is also seen as a vehicle for understanding the practices of "home cooking,"[3] where food practices represent a symbolic and cultural connection with the homeland. In this respect, ethnic food is considered as a "symbolic marker of identity,"[4] where the boundaries of ethnicity and regionalism are often transcended in new forms of sociality.

The anthropological and sociological literature on consumption of ethnic food at restaurants in transnational contexts also reveals the same tendency to deal with ethnic food in abstract terms, in other words, in ways that extol exotic experiences and solicit pleasure and desire. Ethnic restaurants are regarded as "traveling spaces"[5] where diners take in foreign cultures and, contradictorily, are faced with forms of "staged authenticity."[6] Ethnic restaurants are also seen as "arenas"[7] for the transcendence of ethnic differences and the exploration of the culinary "other." At the same time, the process of consumption of ethnic food in itself is conceived as a device to reconstitute identity and enact strategies[8] where subordinated people engage in critical thinking and change the conditions of their own existence.[9]

However, if one looks closer into the culinary practices of people in transnational consumer societies, one realizes that some paradoxical tensions emerge. Mintz,[10] for instance, draws attention to the relations of political and economic power in which food and eating are often enmeshed. He claims that we often deal with food in terms of pleasure, disregarding or forgetting about the conditions of starvation and embargo under which entire populations are constrained by international political decisions. Such political decisions, Mintz argues, show how food at an international level has become an important source of political power. In the same vein, Donna Gabaccia[11] highlights the tensions emerging in transnational and multiethnic contexts related to ethnic food practices. She claims that food fights occur particularly in times of increasing immigration, food conservatism, and harsh competition between corporate food business and enclave entrepreneurs, in other words, between mass production and anti-corporative behaviors of people who claim authenticity of their food.

In this chapter I argue that there is more to be considered about ethnic food consumption than the aspects that semiotic and symbolic anthropological approaches highlight. For among the strategies enacted by ethnic groups through food consumption, there are cultural and social dynamics that are difficult to grasp in their intricacy and with the full complexity of their widespread global movements, particularly in contexts of transnational consumerism. Yet, we must not forget that in transnational consumer societies, the interactions between individuals and consumer objects become increasingly fleeting, intense, and diverse. In this respect, any form of consumption in transnational consumer societies gives way to new forms of negotiation and new cultural contexts where both the cultural traits of individuals and the intrinsic peculiarity of the objects become "disembedded"[12] from their home categories. In other words, in transnational consumer societies consumerism plays an important role in creating new forms of power relations that are established upon and submit to the influence of consumerism itself. Indeed, the tensions between increasing forms of cultural homogenization and new emerging forms of cultural heterogenization, enacted through consumption, bring about different processes of appropriation, resistance, and commodification.[13] In such societies, the process of globalization blurs the center-periphery distinction upon which previous models of global interaction have been based. Its categories of power blur and create new spaces of action where the relations between the dominant and the subordinated, the self and the other, must be reconfigured.

Yet we must take into account also that in transnational consumer societies the market becomes the mirror of what consumers are, what they want to be, and what they can become. The market becomes the arena where individuals build up new social spaces for themselves. In transnational consumer societies ethnic minorities can insinuate themselves into the rules of the dominant system and make up their own rules of action, their own tactics of action.[14] Marketable objects become, in this respect, the devices to change and perform such new tactics. In this way, objects considered to be ethnic, usually regarded in the anthropological tradition as forms of self-identification and as a means of understanding people's intimate worlds, turn out to be useful and powerful enough to change people's social conditions. By gaining economic and social relevance, ethnic objects enable those who are involved in the economic transactions of these objects to state a position in a dominant social and economic environment.

Ethnic food is invested with such power. I argue, in fact, that it can be used to twist relations of power and knowledge in food markets. Indeed, the strategies and the transactions enacted through ethnic food consumption are enmeshed with daily cultural and social dynamics that cannot be separated one from the other. The daily lives of thousands of immigrants, who are spread all over the world, intermingle and intertwine with the transnational consumer and productive practices of their ethnic communities, their neighbors, their relatives, and their family members. How is it then possible to point out the nature and the consequences of such dynamics in daily practices and at the level of everyday and ordinary life? It is in this respect, and to work out a methodological tool of analysis, that I have extended Appadurai's notion of "scapes"[15] to include one of "foodscapes."

The notion of "foodscapes" will allow an analysis that deals with transnational food practices and their dynamics that usually characterize, and potentially subvert, consumer societies. Appadurai defined the overall dynamics characterizing global cultural movements and transnational consumer societies with five different dimensions. They are: *ethnoscapes*— the changing landscape of tourists, immigrants, refugees, exiles, guest workers, and so on; *technoscapes*—the movements of technologies across any kinds of boundaries, for example, mechanical and information technologies; *mediascapes*—the diffusion of electronic technologies that communicate images, news, and information of any kind; *ideoscapes*—the widespread electronic distribution of images and information throughout the world that are often linked to the ideologies of a state, a political movement, or a movement of opposition; finally *finanscapes*—in other words, the endless and quick movements of money and financial transactions across nations, financial corporations, currency markets, national stock exchanges, and commodity speculation. Any of these "scapes" is able to mobilize cultural paradigms, political movements, market economies, and financial systems and provide an analytical framework for characterizing the complex interrelations between the different forces. The dimension of "scapes" challenges the notion of cultural center and subordinate periphery. It offers the building blocks for individuals and groups who create their "imagined multiple worlds" spread all over the globe. Thus, these five dimensions are powerful enough to subvert a dominant order dependent upon the notion of the nation-state.

In the case of ethnic food, a notion of *foodscapes* highlights the trajectories of specific ethnic food items across the globe. Hence it discloses the different configurations that ethnic food entails and builds up with the other "scapes" around the world. For instance, a notion of foodscape shows how movements of ethnic food are deeply interrelated with ethnoscapes and how the economies developed around ethnic food, for example in the case of multinational corporations, are also linked to configurations of finanscapes. A notion of foodscape traces the emergence of enclave economies and ethnic niches in marketing, agriculture, and labor recruitment. It detects movements of ethnic groups and the immigration flow of such ethnic groups. Hence, it discloses the establishment of new ethnic communities that increase and broaden their social networks and their links between the homeland and the hosting nations.

When we go to a Chinese restaurant in Chinatown in New York, Montreal, or London, we enjoy the flavor and taste of Chinese food but do not think of the intricate social connections that are behind Chinese restaurants in any Chinatown around the world. For instance, we do not think that the renown of Chinese food in transnational contexts can be reason enough for Chinese of diverse origins in Hong Kong, Taiwan, mainland China, and South East Asia to try to settle down with a Chinese restaurant business overseas. We do not imagine also that the variety of Vietnamese, Japanese, and Thai restaurants is often the tip of an iceberg that is the widespread business world of Chinese people in transnational contexts. As Watson argues, it is very difficult to gain a clear picture of immigration processes in transnational contexts if we do not take into account both ends of the migration process.[16] Ethnic food is a very important element of such a process. Chinese food, Watson maintains, has enabled Chinese people to settle down and establish a solid food industry in many parts of the world. Issues of authenticity of Chinese food in the Chinese communities abroad have educated non-Chinese diners to request specialties and, at the same time, have enabled the expansion and empowerment of Chinese immigrants into the takeout trade and the business of Chinese restaurants.[17] Thus, in some communities, the Chinese food industry has consolidated Chinese ethnic enclaves and enabled Chinese people not to assimilate and to perpetuate their forms of sociality and traditional life both at home and in a foreign context.[18]

The same counts for the variety of restaurants and food markets that we happen to come across in Indian, Palestinian, Lebanese, Arab, Iranian, Turkish, Greek, Senegalese, Ethiopian, and many other ethnic areas of many towns and cities all over the world. In those areas we enjoy the colorful sights of outdoor food markets and the aroma of ethnic food coming from nearby ethnic restaurants. However, we do not think of the political and economic links and the financial connections that support that niche of ethnic restaurants and markets. When we go shopping, we are amazed by the variety of new ethnic foods that we find on the shelves of our super-markets. However, we do not think that new ethnic groups might have set-tled down and flourished enough to influence the marketing policy of our supermarkets. To live in London, for instance, with its myriad outdoor food markets and small shops, it becomes even easier to understand how the metropolis is divided and inhabited by the different ethnic groups and enclaves. All sorts of vegetables, spices of any kind, in different colors and with different aromas are daily displayed on the stalls of landed immi-grants, political refugees, and first and second generations of ethnic groups who inhabit the city. Thus ethnic food can be a survival strategy where old forms of antagonism and ethnic hatred are forgotten or silenced in a com-mon need for integration. For example, food is a survival strategy for the Mediterranean community in North London. Turkish, Kurdish, Greeks, and Cypriots live together and share their food business in their common attempt to settle down. Their restaurants and food markets are the busi-ness enterprise of people who came to London with the intention of start-ing a new life, having a family, or helping with remittances to their relatives left in the home country.

In this article I focus on consumption of Mexican food in the transna-tional society of Los Angeles. I look at consumption of Mexican food in Mexican restaurants and Mexican food markets in the areas of East and downtown Los Angeles. I argue that an analysis of these different spaces and food practices, so closely intertwined with one another, allows a com-prehensive understanding of the various facets involved in the concept of foodscape. I also conduct a brief analysis of Mexican cookbooks and claim that cookbooks must also be taken into consideration if we want to under-stand better the tensions crossing over the ethnic world of a foodscape.

First, a closer analysis of consumption of Mexican food and some culi-nary practices in the Mexican restaurants of different areas of Los Angeles presents us with a remarkable arena in which to observe how human beings invest eating, food exchange, and their culinary practices with social meanings, issues of power and class discrimination. It also helps us understand how discourses on ethnicity and authenticity of ethnic food can participate in or challenge the dominant system and its discourses of class and ethnic discrimination. Second, a consideration of Mexican food markets and mass food production in Los Angeles shows that Mexican food, as a foodscape, can become a forceful device to twist power relations in the ethnic food industry and corporate business. It shows how Mexican business people claim authority and cultural capital over the authenticity of Mexican food items and culinary practices. It also reveals how Mexican food becomes a means to break into the American economic and cultural system, a way of legitimizing social networks and establishing new ethnic roots. Thus the steady presence of Mexican food in American food markets in Los Angeles allows the ethnic "I" to build up social networks and new social spaces, and to improve his or her position within a dominant system. Finally, a brief introduction to Mexican cookbooks suggests that they turn out to be the semiotic vehicle of communication of a foodscape. For they describe, support, and challenge the social and cultural practices linked to the consumption of Mexican food at Mexican restaurants in a dominant American system. It is by taking into consideration these three aspects and their various facets that I highlight the importance of a full and holistic analysis of Mexican food in terms of foodscape.

EXPLORING MEXICAN RESTAURANTS IN LOS ANGELES

To give an ethnographic account of consumption of Mexican food at Mexican restaurants in Los Angeles,[19] and to understand Mexican food as a foodscape, one has to identify different "spaces" of the city, namely different areas where different food practices prevail. One has also to take into consideration that each area exhibits different social alliances and perceptions of identity and class.[20] Thus an analysis of the consumption of Mexican food at Mexican restaurants located in the different areas of Los Angeles unveils the discursive practices of power and knowledge linked to Mexican food. These practices are found at Mexican restaurants according to the social spaces in which Mexican food is served and in respect of the expectations of different diners concerning the experience of eating Mexican food.

For instance, in the case of Los Angeles, downtown and East Los Angeles are the areas mostly characterized as Mexican-American and Mexican environments.[21] Here restaurants are reminders of social and communal solidarities within the community of Mexican immigrants. They represent forms of culinary pride that express their *Mexicanness* or *Hispanidad* versus the main ruling system. For Anglos, eating and purchasing Mexican food in downtown and certain areas of East Los Angeles often means having to overcome negative conceptions of class and ethnic discrimination. On the contrary, in more affluent areas of Los Angeles, Mexican food can become a device to express forms of culinary resistance versus the Anglo-American society and non-Mexican diners. It is in the location of the different areas and in the distinction between the different culinary practices enacted at different Mexican restaurants that Mexican food discloses a new dimension. Mexican food becomes a device to voice issues of power, class, and ethnicity. Mexican food reveals a sort of "dual life," dependent upon the different areas of Los Angeles where it was found, and distinguished by class and ethnicity.

The "dual life" of Mexican food can be seen in the distinction between the food for non-Mexican diners, adapted according to their expectations and their experience of eating ethnic food, on the one hand, and Mexican food for Mexican diners, on the other. In the first case, Mexican restaurateurs adjust their culinary practices and the image of themselves according to the expectations of non-Mexican diners. They adopt different attitudes toward their Mexicanness, play with the images imposed by the American society on their culture, and perform specific cultural traits to satisfy their customers' expectations. Following Rodriguez,[22] Mexican restaurateurs in these areas enact a process of "commodification of the self" through which they convey the dominant system's consent. So while the outsider expects to encounter certain behavioral attitudes, the persons who are the objects of such expectation display a "pseudoethnicity" that enables them to mask and at the same time adapt their cultural and ethnic identity.

Mexican restaurants participate in the construction of the mythology of Spanish missions, the Mexican revolution, or the rural ancestry of Mexican culture and invent a tradition that becomes a symbol of cultural voyeurism. Photos of Spanish senoritas, of dome-shaped ovens next to *mestiza* and Indian maids, of Spanish soldiers or Californian cowboys, or of the Mexican hero Emiliano Zapata are elements that enhance such imagined tradition and the associated sense of exotic appropriation. Some restaurants have big *sombrero* hats and Mexican flags hanging from the ceiling, and pictures of relatives and family ancestors stating their family status and extolling a specific class or cultural heritage. Some other restaurants offer plays, music, and different kinds of performance drawn from the Mexican folklorist tradition. In many affluent restaurants one might find in a corner or in the middle of the restaurant a group of Mexican musicians. They all wear the typical *mariachi* suits and play romantic and melancholic Mexican music for non-Mexican diners who are willing to experience the romanticism of imagined Mexican beaches. Other affluent restaurants adopt a different strategy. They entrust their reputation and credibility to their cookbooks, written by their cooks or the owners of the restaurant and wisely displayed for sale at the entrance to the restaurant. In this case, one can understand the "positionality" of the restaurateurs, both with regard to the social environment and in relation to the dominant American system, from their marketing strategy that targets and also constructs potential customers as connoisseurs and from a middle- or upper-middle-class background. In other words, restaurateurs play to a sort of flattering image that customers might like to have of themselves as liberal connoisseurs open to ethnic diversity and culinary adventure people. So Mexican cookbooks give customers the chance to appropriate (for money) that imagined pseudoethnicity of the Other by taking home the detailed proof and testimony of that culinary encounter.

There are, however, many other kinds of Mexican restaurants in Los Angeles. Those who target younger diners will stage humorous entertainment and will even dare to interrupt their customers' peaceful dinner. For instance, in some restaurants one might be taken by surprise by waiters who seem to be wearing a pair of ammunition belts crossed over their chests and with two holsters hanging on their hips. There is nothing to be worried about since it is only an illusion; only when these waiters come closer to one's table will one realize that instead of bullets they have in their ammunition belts only small tequila glasses, and instead of guns they keep in their two holsters two bottles of tequila. What a surprise when these waiters perform a gunslinging routine like those in the Hollywood movies of the Far West. When their customers agree to have some *Tequila Boom Boom,* they will gently put some tequila glasses over the customers' table and move their legs wide apart to balance their body like a real Wild West gun shooter in action. Then they will slowly blow on their hands and bend their arms over each holster. They will ask "Are you ready?" And when one replies "yes" they will shout something incomprehensible and literally shoot some tequila into the small glasses. Everything will occur in the span of a couple of seconds. The sudden and abrupt noise of the glasses filled with tequila being banged against the table will conclude their performance.

Another recent trend has developed especially at Mexican restaurants that want to come to terms with "modern" times. Some Mexican restaurants display in the middle of the restaurant, in sight of their diners, a huge electric machine that makes *tortillas.* The menu, brought by gentle waiters dressed in Mexican farmers' costumes, offers an immense variety of Mexican foods that have to be rolled in freshly made *tortillas.* The message is clear: "In our modern times we must be realistic and keep up with technological development in spite of the glorious tradition of our Mexican ancestors." Freshly made *tortillas* seem to be what really matters for the success of a Mexican restaurant.

Indeed, the concern for healthy and fresh food is something that worries many Americans. In the land that bore the first drive-ins,[23] Mexican food, together with many other ethnic foods, impinges on the daily concern of millions of Americans about slimness, healthy eating, and levels of chemicals and preservatives in their processed foods. There is, in fact, an emphasis on the importance of dieting for health that bears the motto "eat what is good for your health not what you like." Paradoxically, however, an overwhelming number of Mexican fast-food chains and restaurants contradict Americans' concern for dieting and health. In Los Angeles, for instance, the presence of numerous Mexican fast-food chains such as Taco Bell, El Pollo Loco, Baja Fresh, El Gallo Grito, El Torrito, La Salsa—to mention but a few—is evidence of the popularity of particular Mexican food. However, the leaflets distributed to their customers by Mexican fast-food chains and restaurants show that there is an awareness of health issues that makes an explicit response, as well as being a marketing device, to these voiced public concerns. For instance, one Mexican fast-food chain started in 1990 with a brand-new image promoting its cover leaflets by a long list of no's: "No freezers," "No lard," "No can openers," "No styrofoam," "No MSG," "No microwaves."[24]

However, in spite of the main concerns for healthy and low-fat food, in the affluent areas of Los Angeles, cooks at Mexican restaurants are expected to fulfill the expectations of non-Mexican diners eager to have exotic experiences and explore the culinary Other.[25] In these areas, Mexican restaurants become as if they were the "front stages"[26] of exotic tourist sites that hosts prepare for their tourists' curiosity. Hence the presentation of colorful Mexican recipes and food items participates, together with the performances of Mexican waiters and restaurateurs, in the construction of the Mexican imagery. Cooks at these restaurants are expected to prepare Mexican food which their customers will find palatable. Thus their menus open up different worlds. Followed by rather un-Spanish-sounding lists of dishes where a French and German flavor is often added, the repetition of entrees such as *enchiladas, chile con carne, tamales, fajita nachos, quesadillas,* and so forth, signals the appearance of a standardized cuisine. Yet in some circumstances, the issue of good, fresh, and healthy food is left aside. I remember a few times taking my Mexican friend Elia, who migrated to Los Angeles with her family when she was ten, to one of these restaurants. I wanted to understand from her personal experience how she perceived those Mexican restaurants. I wanted to know how she judged the food that we were served. By the time we had visited a few restaurants, Elia became eager to ask the cook or the waiters for "more original Mexican food" and quite often she also managed to upset the personnel. Of course she was aware that those restaurants were not for "real Mexican people" and that the food was either "Americanized," as she kept saying, or "standardized" and "with always the same ingredients, something that non-Mexican diners could not understand."[27] My friend's opinion was further confirmed by other Mexican women whom I met in downtown Los Angeles:

> The food that you generally find at Mexican restaurants in many areas of Los Angeles, as a matter of fact, is not the food that we usually eat at home. That one is too rich and fat and we usually eat it only during our festivities. If we ate all that kind of food everyday we would be absolutely fat by now![28]

Thus the menus of many Mexican restaurants in different areas of Los Angeles demonstrate that their customers are considered as tourist diners who lack the knowledge to demand authenticity of Mexican food. In such circumstances, Mexican food becomes a device to transform Anglos' experiences of going to Mexican restaurants into a "foreign" experience.[29] These Mexican restaurants become "communities" where non-Mexican diners are regarded as tourists who go through the same sense of estrangement that in general any tourists experience when they are in a foreign land. Hence it is through a reverse process that Mexican food inverts the social relation between the "ruled" and the "ruler," though still following to the expectations of the ruled ones. In other words, the knowledge of Mexican food that cooks and owners of the restaurants are expected to have empowers them to take in their non-Mexican diners and guide them into the pretended "traditional" culinary practices. In this case, Anglos and non-Mexican diners in general, being treated as tourists, have to fulfill their role and accept being guided by their host Mexican knowledge-givers. Yet the game becomes evident when the acclaimed authenticity of the Mexican food that is served at these restaurants is questioned by diners who, unexpectedly, know the culinary practices of a particular Mexican cuisine.

Interestingly, however, the search for authenticity leads non-Mexican diners to challenge the stereotypical discrimination based on class and ethnicity that stigmatize Mexican-Americans. Donna Gabaccia maintains that "the pursuit of pleasure with minimal obligation encourages Americans to cross cultural boundaries. . . . But it also exposes us regularly to the fears that cultural differences generate."[30] I argue that the search for authenticity of Mexican food also leads to a reconsideration of issues of class and ethnic discrimination. In a society where class and ethnicity are still high on the list of discriminatory parameters, it is to taste real, authentic, Mexican food that non-Mexicans dare to enter the Mexican communities in East and downtown Los Angeles. For instance, one can go to a Mexican restaurant downtown that is well known by middle-class Mexican-Americans, Anglos, and non-Mexicans as a luxury restaurant with real, authentic, Mexican food and be amazed by the sight of Mercedes, BMWs, and Cherokees parked in the backyard, contrasting sharply with the shabby houses of the shanty area of downtown. In such cases, the search for authenticity and a taste of real Mexican food is powerful enough to overcome the stigma associated with Mexicans and Mexican food. It is through food consumption at these kinds of Mexican restaurants that class distinction is reconfigured. Another aspect of the Mexican foodscape is revealed. Non-Mexican diners enter the social space of Mexicans in order to have a "real" experience of Mexican food. Yet it fosters their awareness that Mexican restaurants in affluent, safe areas are mainly "staged" places where non-Mexican diners are obviously treated as "foreigners." In this respect, Mexican food becomes the catalyst of a behavior that challenges stereotypical concepts about the ethnic Other and class and social status. Thus, seen as a foodscape, Mexican food questions also the cultural assumption of a society that still highly discriminates against Mexican immigrants and Mexican culture.

In East Los Angeles and certain areas of downtown, Mexican-Americans and Mexican immigrants generally run Mexican restaurants for customers who are mainly Mexicans and Latinos. It is in these areas that a new sense of Mexicanness and new forms of social solidarities emerge. It is in these ethnic niches that ethnic food as a foodscape demonstrates its consolidating power. Anglos enjoy Mexican food in these areas only when their workplace is nearby. Such is the case, for instance, of a Mexican restaurant on North Broadway of Los Angeles. The restaurant is located near a police station, and Anglos queue almost every day to have good Mexican food, in spite of the presence of a large number of Mexican fast-food chains and other restaurants in the nearby areas. Indeed, in downtown and East Los Angeles, ethnic and regional restaurants flourish. In these areas Mexican-Americans and Mexicans name their restaurants by the name of the region they come from. Thus names such as Zacatecas, Michoacan, Vera Cruz, Puebla, Oaxaca, Colima, and Chihuaha are reminders of a more-or-less recent process of cultural and social displacement.

In these restaurants getting together to eat or to talk about food can be a confusing but laughter-filled event. Although some standardization and processes of pan-ethnicity are occurring among Mexican and Latino food items, there is a variety of food and so many different ways to name it that often the same item can have various names.[31] Discussing food names can be also a great icebreaker, especially when all discover that there is no "right" word and find out one was talking about the same thing all along. However, the terminology, the use of particular words, and the question of nontranslatability of certain Spanish and Mexican words also entails another issue. It is, in fact, another device to claim a certain authenticity for Mexican food items and to a certain extent, it represents a form of resistance against the Anglos' claim to knowledge of, and appropriation or assimilation of, the cultural practices of other ethnic groups. Yet to talk about names of food items and the history of recipes can also become also an occasion for resentful historical remembrance, since it is through words and the names of Mexican food that the Latino cultural ancestry is openly revealed and proudly declared.[32]

During my research I discovered that some Spanish words are also used to describe the colonial past of Mexico and to trace in the memories of Mexican immigrants the routes and histories of migration. These words become strong devices to preserve tradition, to mark historical transitions, or to symbolize cultural events. For example, many Mexican restaurateurs argue about the origin of the word "*chile*." Some are convinced that it is a Spanish word, coming therefore from Spanish conquerors. Others claim that the word "*chili*," on the contrary, is used as a symbol of *mestizaje*,[33] or as a way of explaining the link to a past of colonial submission.[34] The same happens with regard to the recipe used to prepare *mole poblano.* Some Mexican restaurateurs claim that *mole poblano* was invented by the sisters of the convent of Santa Rosa in Puebla, who wanted to prepare something special to celebrate the arrival of an important Spanish bishop. However, many others argue that all the important ingredients for this recipe— turkey, chiles, *tortillas*, chocolate, and squash seeds—were being used by the Aztecs long before the Spanish arrived.

In East Los Angeles and downtown, Mexican restaurants become ethnic communities and social environments where new forms of sociality and new alliances between Mexican immigrants of different backgrounds are consolidated. In these restaurants, Mexican immigrants foster a *mestizo* way of being in the world, and yet they voice their concerns and complaints against the dominant American system. Distant from standardizing food corporations, Mexican food becomes in these restaurants the purveyor of the culture of *mestizaje*. In other words, it is a culture that stands as a sort of transgression. It insists upon violating culinary boundaries and becoming—not ideologically but pragmatically and culturally—a survival strategy whereby, however contradictorily, boundaries are set against the "ruling" society. In many of these restaurants Mexican people claim authenticity for their food and culinary practices and warn against the Mexican restaurants in other areas of Los Angeles. Some restaurateurs vehemently argue that "to taste the real flavor of Mexican food one must buy Mexican ingredients, pans, and crockery at Mexican markets in downtown and East Los Angeles":

> Anglos will never know the real taste of Mexican food because they do not dare to come here downtown and buy our food. Yet the food of Mexican restaurants in fancy areas is not real Mexican food and it is not even a fresh one!"[35]

Other restaurateurs display astonishment at the idea that some Mexican restaurants serve "freshly made" *tortillas* by means of big electric machines and state proudly their faithfulness to their old *molcajetes*, the ancient tools made out of a porous dark gray stone used to pound corn for their *tortillas*.

However, the contradictions and the conflicts of self-perception within the Mexican community also emerge strikingly when issues of class and ethnicity are brought up. A diet based on beans and *tortillas* can be referred to as cheap food or as food for Mexican farmers, while the middle-class Mexican people can afford to eat meat and eggs. In the same vein, to call a restaurant *tortillieria* and to call someone a *tortillera* is to accuse the restaurant of occupying the bottom social rungs, and the person of passivity, Indian backwardness, and poverty. A conversation on Mexican food and restaurants in East and downtown Los Angeles can also turn out to reveal intraethnic antagonisms within the Mexican and Latino society. For example, the term *mestizo* entails ambiguous implications that are very situational and changing, especially in response to the American environment. The word *mestizo* is associated with class and status, hence with ethnic connotations. For example, to refer to maids as mostly *mestiza* is common amongst those who want to distinguish their social status. However, in response to the discriminating attitude of the dominant society, Indian and *mestizo* can become devices to express an underlying cultural resistance and voice a political position.

Nevertheless, and in spite of resentments voiced within the Mexican community, Mexican restaurants in East Los Angeles and downtown represent amazing arenas of socialization where the boundaries between private and public spaces are blurred. These restaurants serve as living rooms for the homesick. They are great archives of culinary memories. They constitute cozy places for Mexican and Latino businesspeople to arrange their affairs. It is in such areas that Mexican foods manage to survive the melting pot. Nowhere else but in East Los Angeles can one find, in a hot Californian summer, a refreshing Mexican drink based on water and flowers of hibiscus with no preservatives and the guarantee that it is a safe drink. That is a real Mexican summer drink that one can find only at stalls spread throughout the backstreets of Mexican neighborhoods in East Los Angeles. At these stalls, one encounters only customers who are Mexican immigrants.

In conclusion, with a notion of foodscapes in mind, an analysis of consumption of Mexican food at Mexican restaurants in different areas of Los Angeles highlights the tensions arising between the dominant system and the Mexican community as related to issues of class and ethnic discrimination. Mexican restaurants disclose discursive practices of power and knowledge relating to food items and culinary practices as well as to issues of identity and ethnicity. At the same time, Mexican restaurants have a major economic and demographic significance. It has to be taken into account that Mexican restaurants are a powerful source of employment for Mexican immigrants and first- and second-generation Mexican-Americans. Here the economy of the Mexican foodscape gives Mexican people a legitimate way to break into the American economic system and establish social networks. In the next section I argue that the steady presence of Mexican food in American food markets in Los Angeles allows Mexican people to build up social networks and improve their social position in American society.

FOODSCAPES IN A PROCESSED-FOOD WORLD

Donna Gabaccia[36] claims that America is not a "multi-ethnic nation, but a nation of multi-ethnics." In the nation of "multi-ethnics," she argues, multiethnic eating stands as a constant reminder of how widespread and enjoyable ethnic interactions have sometimes been in the United States. I argue that ethnic food, particularly in transnational consumer societies, often turns out to be a social and political symbol that is disputed in forms of negotiation and cultural appropriation between different parties such as business corporations and ethnic groups. Yet, as much as with history, ethnicity, and cultural traits, Mexican food has been one among the several aspects of a culture that in times of conquest have been overshadowed, disguised, and misconceived by the dominant society.[37] Today it is still common to hear non-Mexicans lamenting the greasy, nutritionally poor, and farmerlike quality of Mexican cuisine. In spite of such negative conceptions, American food markets are full of Mexican culinary products.

To offer an ethnographic account of Mexican food markets in Los Angeles, one has to recognize certain characteristics of American food markets more generally. For instance, to compare different food practices in American society one has to take into consideration processes of industrial production and food processing. Yet the lack of ingredients, the use of alternative ingredients with more or less the same flavor, the change of technologies, and the process of coexistence within ethnic American society have determined a process of adaptation[38] of Mexican food practices and products that nevertheless has not diluted the cohesiveness of its ethnic communities. I argue that, particularly with regard to food consumption in food markets, Mexican food is not only a device to express identity and a sense of community but also an occasion to enact strategies that shelter and empower the Mexican community.

In Los Angeles there are two main strains of production: mass-produced Cal-Tex-Mex fast foods and epicurean specialties that, like many other Mexican foods, resist mass marketing and are unknown to the non-Mexican diners. It is the demand for the former, not the latter, that continues to dominate consumption in American food markets. As a snack, Mexican food is perhaps detached from the aspects of Mexican culture that are regarded by the dominant system as inferior. Thus the notion that Mexican food has bad connotations of low status and low class distinctions may demote it to the rank of snack. But we must not forget that Americans continue to increase the frequency with which they eat at fast-food restaurants, and their tendency to snack remains highly important in their eating habits.[39]

There is, in fact, a far more economic reason for such an overwhelming presence of Mexican snacks in American food markets. Mexican snacks seem to be successful because they lend themselves to experimentation in the American food industry, where spicy ethnic food can be combined with processed food to fit well the structures of fast food and snack markets.[40] However, there is also another explanation that goes back to the social realities of ethnic food markets. American food corporations are constantly faced with the reality of food markets where immigration flows are endless, and repeatedly introduce new sources of culinary diversity, new tastes, new expectations of authenticity, and new attitudes related to nostalgia for the homeland. American food corporations, in other words, cannot compete with a food market that is always flexible in its demand for food items and where consumers are also always rigorously in search of authenticity in relation to their ethnic foods. Indeed, big American corporations recognize the existence of enclave markets, as demonstrated by their franchising and marketing to specific ethnic groups with precise consumer tastes. However, although they try to penetrate these markets of ethnic food, they are nevertheless faced with enclave businesspeople who have the cultural capital to compete, knowing their consumers better and being able, in spite of their strong anticorporative behavior, to create quasi-monopoly markets.

Indeed, the Mexican food industry and markets have become a center of activity for many Mexican-American and Mexican manufacturers and marketers in Los Angeles. Growing small-business enterprises of Mexican food, outdoor markets, Mexican food stores, and chains of Mexican restaurants bear witness to the potential of the economic value of Mexican food in the food industry.[41] Market analyses now estimate that Mexican food markets are worth billions of dollars,[42] and corporate analysts see Mexican food as increasing its market share with the increasing immigration of Hispanics. As purveyors of their own foods, Mexican-Americans and Mexicans demonstrate entrepreneurial skills. They take advantage of their cultural capital and knowledge of their home regions to supply specific commodities required by new immigrants, Mexicans, and first-generation Mexican-Americans.

All this has to be considered in light of the demographic statistics that relate to the near future of California and which suggest a continuing increase in the Latin American population. Latinos are projected to constitute 35.5 percent of the Californian population by the year 2030,[43] while the growth level for African American and Asians will remain more or less unchanged. Another significant point is the striking disparity in age bands of Latin Americans and Anglo-Americans. In the not-too-distant future, Hayes Bautista argues, California will be inhabited by old Anglo-Americans and young Latin Americans. It is expected that by the year 2030, 60 percent of senior citizens will be Anglo-Americans while 50 percent of the young population will be Latin American. Of this, 45 percent will be under the age of 15, and 38 percent will be between 16 and 64 years of age.[44] This age group is considered by Anglo-American workers to be the most "intrusive" since it will consist mainly of the working classes. The expectations of a demographic explosion will mean also that the Anglo-American society will soon no longer be the majority in the Southwestern states. Hence, in terms of business and market forecasts, in the year 2030, 48.2 percent of American total consumer growth will be in the Hispanic population. In the same year, only 9.1 percent of American consumer growth will be attributable to the non-Hispanic white consumers.[45]

In times of ethnic tensions and increasing migration, powerful American corporations are suddenly realizing that the Hispanic community, on a national scale, represents more than $100 billion in spendable income but that their market share is still very low.[46] To capitalize on these expanding market opportunities, American corporations have been compelled to invest in costly research into the history and culture of Mexican food. The *Hispanic Market Handbook: The Definite Source for Reaching This Lucrative Segment of American Consumers*[47] gives an idea of how market research on Latino markets can become an anthropological and sociological treatise on Mexican-Americans and Latinos in general! Hence, to be effective, marketing campaigns that target Mexican consumers must be in tune with Mexican culture at all levels: symbolic, explicit, visual, and subliminal. However, despite these great efforts, Latino and Mexican food markets are very complex, still underrepresented, and very much an enigma to the vast majority of Anglo marketing professionals.[48]

The contrasts between the homogeneity of American, processed, mass-produced, food markets and the extraordinary diversity of Mexican food markets are, in fact, striking. Colorful *mercados* and *mercaditos* are found throughout downtown and East Los Angeles. They are overcrowded at any time of the day with Latinos, Mexican-Americans, and Mexicans. Only a few Anglos dare to adventure into those areas since they are the domains of ethnic gangs and have high levels of street and juvenile criminality.[49] From the smallest to the largest—including chains such as Tianguis and Viva that are found throughout Southern California—it is common to find in these markets indigenous vegetables and fruits that have been consumed since pre-Columbian times. Following the traditional custom of *tanguis* (the name given to the markets at the time of the Aztecs), most large Mexican markets in downtown and East Los Angeles have a special section in which ready-to-eat traditional Mexican dishes, from *tamales* to less common dishes, are available. One can also find in these *mercados* and *mercaditos* small Mexican restaurants and stalls where tacos are served hot and ready-made with a wide variety of fillings. The preservation of traditional food patterns is made all the easier by the geographical closeness to Mexico that allows many Mexican-Americans and Mexicans to visit their relatives and maintain close contacts with their cultural heritage.

Indeed, the search for a real Mexican food and the claims for authenticity by immigrants transform Mexican food into a device that shifts power relations in the American ethnic food industry. By being involved in economic transactions of Mexican food, Mexican-Americans and Mexicans are also able to play a position game since they are strongly advantaged by their closeness to immigrant consumers. It is in this ability to affect economic business relations that Mexican food shows its dimension as a foodscape. It is in the claim for authenticity by immigrants—whether based on food habits, nostalgia for the homeland, or pride in one's dietary tradition—that Mexican food shows its potential as a foodscape. It is due to the attachment of Mexican food to Mexican culture and to its pervasiveness in the American food markets that Mexican food is effective as a foodscape. Thus Mexican food not only acquires an economic relevance in the American food industry but it also allows the social and cultural empowerment of new immigrants, Mexicans, and first- and second-generation Mexican-Americans. Mexican food fosters traditional social links with the homeland. It opens up economic routes for immigrants and favors the establishment of social and ethnic networks. It becomes also a means of social "deterritorialization" since it opens economic routes for immigrant Mexican labor to come and consolidate in American society. Enhancing flows of immigrants as labor force, Mexican food provides food entrepreneurs privileged access to sources of low-wage labor and new consumer markets. Thus it allows entrepreneurial activity to flourish and thrive. In the next section, I point out that Mexican cookbooks reveal other narratives that play within a foodscape. As nonofficial channels of communication, Mexican cookbooks turn out to be an important bridgehead between the different pratices developed around Mexican food consumption in the different areas of Los Angeles.

MEXICAN COOKBOOKS AS A MEANINGFUL PRACTICE

Anthropologists have widely considered cookbooks as the expression of a particular cultural environment, the potentially surest sign of the emergence of a national cuisine,[50] the representations of structures of production and distribution,[51] or the growing body of a food-based characterization of the ethnic Other.[52] I conceive Mexican cookbooks as a sort of ethnography that discloses, in conjunction with an analysis of Mexican restaurants and food markets, the contradictions between groups and subcultures and the ethnic tensions within the Mexican community and the dominant system. Carefully exposed on the shelves of fancy restaurants in Los Angeles, sold at the stalls of small Mexican food markets, or neatly displayed in the Spanish/Mexican cuisine sections of bookstores, Mexican cookbooks reveal the social reality that pertains to the daily life of Mexican-Americans and Mexicans in American society.

Mexican cookbooks are atypical books in which each section of the book is intertwined with chapters on personal and family histories, historical accounts, political statements, and cultural reclamation or resentment of the injustice of the American society. In American society, Mexican cookbooks represent alternative channels of communication where Mexican immigrants and Mexican-Americans voice their concerns, wishes, and political standpoints in accordance with their social situation. Mexican cookbooks sold at expensive restaurants will try to persuade the reader that the recipes are the outcome of long-term, elaborate research, the heritage of family traditions, and the careful devotion of the author to Mexican tradition and authenticity. By contrast, Mexican cookbooks sold at the stalls of downtown *mercados* and *mercaditos* will express resentment against American society, disclose personal histories, challenge the American history of colonization, and claim a social role within society. Hence Mexican cookbooks have also to be seen in their diversity and in relation to the particular social practices of their immediate contexts. In this section, I highlight only a few aspects of the social and political engagements that emerge vividly from the variety of issues intermingled with recipes, descriptions of food items, and hints on how to perform certain culinary practices.

As we have seen earlier in relation to restaurants, the issues of class and social status are often contradictorily intermingled with ethnicity. Terms such as *mestizo* and *mestizaje* are ambiguously used either to refer to pride in Mexican ethnicity or to distinguish oneself and one's Spanish heritage from the other Mexicans and the low connotation of their Mexicanness. One can understand such tensions when in Mexican cookbooks writers express their negative considerations toward the word *mestizo* either as an "indeterminate and ambiguous" aspect of Mexican culture[53] or as an assumed hybrid characteristic of Mexican people. In this respect, it is interesting to notice also how the ambiguities of *mestizaje* are juxtaposed and elaborated upon through claims of authenticity of Mexican food and stand in contrast with the negative connotation of *mestizo* relating to class, as illustrated in the earlier section on Mexican restaurants:

> By now I arrived at a cuisine representing, I felt, not just the *mestizo* character of Mexican food generally but my own personal process of *mestizaje*, synthesis. I was making dishes true to their origins . . . but I was also experimenting by juxtaposing different elements.[54]

In such cases, the pride in *mestizaje* represents an instance of "reversed normality"[55] and Mexican cookbooks become a tool of political significance. In other words, the concept of *mestizaje* is used by Mexican writers as a response to the imposition of a stigmatic identity by the dominant society. Hence, in this way, those who are stigmatized assert certain characteristics that reinforce their identity rather than mask them. Through the concept of *mestizaje* Mexican writers invite the readers to get rid of conceptions of purity or wholeness. In this sense, they attempt to forge a new conception, in terms not only of race but also of culture, speech, and lifestyle:

> . . . most *norteamericanos* are, or will become, *mestizos* and border crossers. The real question is whether we will acknowledge our literal and imaginary border crossing. *Mestizo* cultures and cuisines remind us that all cultures drift beyond the boundaries of the familiar. Some are just more honest about it. But the fears provoked by *mestizo* ways of becoming are understandable. Almost always, the hybridizing style, because it transcends or ignores the boundaries of the "official" or "traditional" national culture, threatens sacred categories of gender, language, social class, or race. Here in the Southwest, the culture of *mestizaje* expresses a refusal to prefer one language, or one culture, at the *expense* of the other."[56]

Furthermore, writers express their pride in *mestizaje* to show their pride in the syncretism that enriches and, at the same time, obscures Mexican culture to others. In this respect, we find that *mestizaje* becomes also an underlying form of cultural resistance toward the dominant society:

When the native peoples had been crushed and the present mingling of cultures had taken shape, one legacy was a society of polite self-disguise. Even everyday language in Mexico is filled with ceremonious formulas to cushion the impact of all dealings with others, from buying a newspaper to declining an invitation. People know how to act, they know what each situation calls for so that their true selves will remain somewhat hidden. Escape from the rules and roles takes different forms. . . .[57]

Yet it is to respond to a sense of cultural and social exploitation by the dominant system that Mexican cookbooks become a device to discard stereotypes, to clarify what has not yet been clarified and show resistance to political and cultural biases.

The question of authenticity is the second aspect of Mexican cookbooks that I would like to discuss. Mexican writers use authenticity, paradoxically, as much as the concept of *mestizaje,* both as a form of cultural resistance and as an invitation to explore the Mexican culture. So, for instance, in response to forms of cultural appropriation by Anglos and to misconceptions of their Mexican food, writers insist on the authenticity of flavor of Mexican food. The calls for and claims of authenticity become devices to create a social space that Anglos have to enter as a prerequisite for a real, authentic experience of Mexican food; the real flavor of Mexican food derives from the authenticity of ingredients, pans, and crockery found in downtown and East Los Angeles,[58] as well as from the closeness to culinary practices. In this respect, the claim of authenticity plays a crucial role as a result of transnational immigration in non-Mexican contexts:

A *molcajete's* slightly porous surface texture is required [for] both fresh and cooked sauces. A marble mortar and wooden pestle . . . will do well in a pinch. The same isn't always true of electric blenders and food processors.[59]

Don't make the dish if you can't get the right ingredient.[60]

Thus the impossibility of experiencing the real taste by Anglos turns out to be an underlying subject of culinary and cultural resistance. The impossibility of enjoying the real flavor of Mexican food depends on the fact that Mexican ingredients found in the United States do not correspond, on the whole, to the real Mexican ones, as this writer clearly claims:

Though people in the United States boast of their corn, I find that ours has a more distinctive identity. In the United States "corn" usually makes people think of corn on the cob bred for sugar content and tenderness. To me this sweet corn often seems watery and insipid.[61]

Hence the fact that Anglos cannot know the real taste of Mexican food unless they go to Latin American markets is a way for Mexican writers to declare that Anglos have to know what they want to eat and they have to use real ingredients and proper Mexican equipment. To such an extent,

Mexican food is invested with a register that is accessible to the nonnative only when the writer offers himself as a "cultural translator." It is in this respect that the question of authenticity is linked with the nonaccessibility and exclusion of Anglos from Mexican culture: "In my cooking I was ready to take on the role of an interpreter between different worlds."[62]

In this way the claim for authenticity reveals the cultural resistance of some Mexican writers, especially when they combine the question of real Mexican food and taste with aspects of Mexican language. Some cookbooks emphasize the impossibility of a complete translation,[63] whereby a complete "grasping" and knowledge by Anglos of Mexican recipes is almost impossible. Appending a glossary of Spanish terms to cookbooks allows some writers to remind their readership that reproducing recipes does not necessarily lead to cultural ownership. Yet many Mexican cookbooks have a section on vocabulary and pronunciation, as much as on ingredients, cooking methods, and equipment, to guide their non-Mexican readers.[64] The question of language and pronunciation becomes, therefore, another aspect of the claim to authenticity. For example, it is usual to come across caustic remarks noting the "inability" of non-Mexicans to pronounce and to use Spanish names: "*Chile* to people of the Southwest is so much different from the '*chili con carne*,' mispronounced, and sold widely at restaurants in mid-western college towns!"[65]

The resistance expressed in Mexican cookbooks through the question of authenticity, however, stands in tension with the willingness of some Mexican writers to guide non-Mexican readers in their journey to Mexican culture. Mexican writers recognize the distinction between Mexican food practices and those followed by Anglos, and Anglos' lack of knowledge of Mexican culinary practices. Hence they are aware of the gap existing between Mexican food practices *in* themselves (cooking at home and in Mexican closed social communities) and Mexican food practices *for* themselves (cooking at Mexican restaurants in affluent areas of Los Angeles where Anglos expect to find "real Mexican food"). Such a gap can be filled only with the help of a "bridgehead." Mexican cookbooks, as a means of understanding, become the educational device to inform non-Mexican readers about such differences in a process of "acculturation." In this vein, Mexican cookbooks come to enhance the authenticity of Mexican food practices and invite non-Mexican readers into "the home" experience of Mexicans. Some Mexican writers, therefore, welcome non-Mexican readers into their intimate world:

> There are many home-style dishes served by Mexican-American families which one cannot find in restaurants. . . . In Mexican-American culture . . . the original objective of many home-style dishes was to provide nourishment at minimum cost. Because of this recipes for such dishes often rely on what today would be considered an inordinate amount of lard or oil. Consequently, with today's health

consciousness in mind, for this book I selected typical home-style dishes whose fat content could be reduced to a more acceptable level without seriously undermining their integrity.[66]

To conclude, an analysis of Mexican cookbooks proves useful for a full understanding of the aspects that characterize Mexican food in terms of a foodscape. Mexican food as described in Mexican cookbooks is, in this respect, the means that enables writers to extol a historical heritage, to elaborate class distinctions and ethnicity, to hinder forms of cultural resistance toward the dominant society, or to denounce prejudices against or within the Mexican community. Mexican food items, along with the success of Mexican cuisine in American society, become, therefore, the means to affirm a range of social and cultural positions in the dominant system. Yet Mexican cookbooks function also as a "bridgehead" to link the dominant society with the authenticity of Mexican culinary practices and Mexican culture. In such a process, however, the claim for authenticity of Mexican food and the question of authority granted to Mexican purveyors stand in great contradiction to the ambiguity expressed in relation to questions of class, ethnic origins, and historical heritage. It is in Mexican cookbooks, in fact, that the tensions characterizing the relations between the dominant system and the Mexican community are strikingly revealed. At the same time tensions also emerge within the Mexican community itself. To limit an analysis of consumption of Mexican food to Mexican markets and Mexican restaurants in Los Angeles would therefore miss important insights into the dynamic nature of Mexican food practices seen in terms of a foodscape.

CONCLUSION

Ethnic food is widely regarded in anthropology as an arena whereby ethnicity, conviviality, and community relationships are widely expressed. Anthropological literature regards food activities and food practices in particular as devices to understand how people communicate, interact, and behave. Hence attention is drawn to ethnic food as an expression of social and cultural identity without, however, taking into consideration the possibility that ethnic food may also become an agent of social change. Little attention is given to ethnic food as a means of empowerment of the ethnic "I." Indeed, as an object of consumption and as a tool of social and cultural identification, ethnic food entails forms of power that disclose themselves according to circumstances and contexts. For instance, ethnic food can act as a vehicle to enhance economic and social power within an ethnic community. It enables dislocated, contingent identities to establish social alliances and links of solidarity. It opens paths for immigrant labor and becomes an opportunity for the ethnic "I" to acquire status and social position within a dominant, hostile environment.

Hence ethnic food must be regarded under a different light. It must be considered as a means of empowerment. It must be seen also as a device to establish close ties within a community: ties that blur ethnic and social boundaries and conceptions of space. Ethnic food, to this extent, must be regarded as a foodscape. A notion of foodscape reveals how movements of ethnic food are intertwined with the different movements of ethnic groups, financial capital, and business, hence with different configurations of power. In this respect, the implications entailed in the use of a notion of foodscape are many. For instance, it enables one to focus on ethnic food at an ethnographic level. Furthermore, in transnational consumer societies it allows an understanding of the different relations of power involved in ethnicity, gender, and economic forces. It also shows how different "scapes" are intertwined with one another in everyday life. In a metropolitan city such as Los Angeles, a notion of foodscape helps disclose a variety of interactions, tensions, and alliances in the dominant American society and within the Mexican community.

Hence in this article I have focused on practices of consumption of Mexican food in Mexican markets and restaurants in Los Angeles and conducted an analysis of Mexican cookbooks to demonstrate the validity and usefulness of a notion of foodscape. I have argued that Mexican food empowers the Mexican community to enact different forms of resistance and break into the dominant economic and cultural system. It enables Mexican-Americans and Mexicans to claim a social position within the dominant American society, to challenge discrimination and stereotypes, and finally to voice historical, political, and personal issues by means of alternative channels of communication such as Mexican cookbooks. Thank to its success as a great source of income and to its great potential to strengthen Mexican communities, Mexican food, seen in terms of foodscape, displays its multiple dimensions as an economic source, a social collector, and a tool of cohesion. Mexican food is powerful enough to present Mexicans, Mexican-Americans, and new immigrants with a social opportunity that becomes the bedrock upon which they improve their social position. For instance, it lays the ground for new immigrant arrivals and new workforces. It is thanks to Mexican food and Mexican food markets that Mexican-Americans and Mexicans have the opportunity to consolidate Mexican communities and to gain better positions within the dominant system. Mexican food becomes an agent of change that reconstitutes the possibility for the ethnic "I" of gaining a social position within American society.

Yet to carry out an ethnographic account of consumption of Mexican food in Los Angeles and to understand the impact of Mexican food as a foodscape on American society, one has to take into consideration the aspects that concern American food practices, such as the industrial production, food processing, and homogenization that mostly characterize the

American food industry. One has to identify different "spaces" within the different areas of Los Angeles in which different food practices are enacted. Each area implies different social alliances and different perceptions of identity and class. For instance, in downtown and East Los Angeles, Mexican markets and restaurants represent arenas of social solidarity as much as Mexican restaurants in more affluent areas of Los Angeles, by contrast, foster forms of culinary resistance against American society.

I have therefore shown how the consumption of Mexican food in Mexican restaurants unveils a "dual life" of Mexican food: standardized food for Anglos, and specialties for Mexican-Americans and Mexicans. In this respect, I pointed out a disparity between food practices *in* themselves and food practices *for* themselves enacted by Mexicans and Mexican-Americans. The former are enacted for Mexicans and Mexican-Americans in homely environments and ethnic communities, and the latter are performed for Anglos in restaurants located in affluent areas of Los Angeles. Within such a "dual life," Mexican food becomes a means to enhance forms of solidarity and culinary and cultural resistance toward the dominant system. At the same time, it becomes a positive *mestizo* way of being in the world, since it enables Mexicans and Mexican-Americans to foster discourses of pan-ethnicity and to challenge the forms of discrimination by American society.

Mexican cookbooks prove to be one important semiotic vehicle of communication of such a foodscape. They describe and challenge the social and cultural practices linked to the consumption of Mexican food in a dominant American system. They become educational devices to allow American readers into the homely, "authentic" practices of Mexican cuisine. In this respect, they become a "bridgehead" between Mexican culinary practices, otherwise unknown, and Anglos' stereotypical concepts of Mexican food. However, Mexican cookbooks reveal other narratives hidden behind Mexican food items, culinary practices, and recipes. They disclose the ambiguity with which issues of ethnicity, class, and gender are dealt within the Mexican community and the contradictions in which the Mexican community is enmeshed. In this respect, I highlighted the ways in which issues of class and ethnicity are contradictorily linked with concepts of *mestizaje* either to express a belonging to a social status and class or to claim a pride in the multicultural dimension of Mexican culture, challenging American discriminatory stereotypes. In the same vein, questions of authenticity of Mexican food items may become a means to voice forms of cultural resistance toward the dominant system or to declare a willingness to "acculturate" non-Mexican readers and enable them better to know Mexican culture. To conclude, I argued that the real stakes of Mexican cookbooks lie behind what has been explicitly stated and said, between the lines of recipes and culinary descriptions. In other words, they voice social and cultural discrimination and the ambiguous positionalities of the ethnic "I" with regard to gender, class, and ethnicity within both the dominant system and the Mexican community itself.

NOTES

I am grateful to all those at the Food and Drink in Consumer Society conference held at the Hagley Museum in November 1999 who made interesting and informative comments on an early version of this article. I would like to thank editor Warren Belasco for his support and close reading of the first draft of the paper, and I am also indebted to Kevin Latham for invaluable comments on all drafts of this article. All errors and shortcomings that remain are, of course, my own responsibility.

1. Mary Douglas, "Deciphering a Meal," in *Myth, Symbol, and Culture,* ed. Clifford Geertz (New York: Norton and Company Inc., 1971).
2. Roland Barthes, "Toward a Psychology of Contemporary Food Consumption," in *European Diet from Pre-industrial to Modern Times,* eds. E. and R. Forster (New York: Harper and Row, 1975), p. 50.
3. Pierre Van Den Berghe, "Ethnic Cuisine: Culture in Nature," *Ethnic and Racial Studies* 7 (1984): 393.
4. Theodore Humphrey and Lin Humphrey, *"We Gather Together." Food Festival in American Life* (Logan: Utah State University Press, 1991), p. 2.
5. Pierre Bourdieu, *Distinction: A Social Critique of the Judgement of Taste* (London: Routledge, 1984). Van Den Berghe, ibid., p. 394.
6. Dean MacCannell, *The Tourist: A New Theory of Leisure Class* (New York: Schocken, 1976); John Urry, *The Tourist Gaze: Leisure and Travel in Contemporary Societies* (London: Sage, 1990).
7. Arjun Appadurai, "How to Make a National Cuisine: Cookbooks in Contemporary India," *Comparative Studies in Society and History* 30 (1988): 3–24.
8. Mike Featherstone, *Global Culture: Nationalism, Globalization and Modernity* (London: Sage, 1990).
9. Michel De Certeau, *The Practice of Everyday Life* (Berkeley: University of California Press, 1984).
10. Sidney Mintz, *Tasting Food, Tasting Freedom. Excursion into Eating, Culture, and the Past* (Boston MA: Beacon Press, 1996).
11. Donna Gabaccia, *We Are What We Eat: Ethnic Food and the Making of Americans* (Cambridge, MA: Harvard University Press, 1998).
12. Anthony Giddens, *The Consequences of Modernity* (Cambridge: Polity Press, 1990).
13. Arjun Appadurai, "Disjuncture and Difference in the Global Cultural Economy," in *Global Culture: Nationalism, Globalization and Modernity,* ed. M. Featherstone (London: Sage, 1990).
14. De Certeau, p. 87.
15. Appadurai, "Disjuncture," p. 124.
16. J. L. Watson, "The Chinese: Hong Kong Villagers in the British Catering Trade," in *Between Two Cultures: Migrants and Minorities in Britain,* ed. J. L. Watson (Oxford: Basil Blackwell, 1977), p. 181.
17. Ibid.,p. 191.
18. Ibid., pp. 193–210.
19. I carried out fieldwork in Los Angeles repeatedly in 1990, 1992, and 1996.
20. See for instance M. Blanchard, "Lost in America," *Cultural Anthropology* 7 (1992): 496–507.
21. One of the problems in introducing an article on Mexican-Americans and Mexicans in the United States is that of overgeneralizing the characteristics of one subgroup to the others. In particular, there is the problem of deciding what overarching term to use to refer to all persons who are of partial or whole Hispanic descent [e.g., Amado Padilla and Susan Keefe, *Chicano Ethnicity* (Albuquerque: University of New Mexico Press, 1987); L. Estrada, *The Changing Profile of Mexican-Americans* (Claremont: Tomas Rivera Center, 1985)]. There is, besides, the subtle risk that the terminology which might be adopted to define a group can often be embedded with, and interpreted in, ethnic, racist, and elitist terms. Yet in the case of American society, it is class distinction that becomes a function of ethnicity and race. These multiple class distinctions are made according to an ideology that states that social classes are "open," meaning that the movement between classes is a consequence of personal merit. As a consequence of the relationship between class

and "Hispanic" ethnicity, many Mexican-Americans and Mexicans refuse to recognize their Mexican identity and heritage. Chicano literature is suffused with issues of exploitation by the Anglo society as well as by issues of intraethnic antagonisms based on generational and class differences. See Ernesto Galarza, *Barrio Boy* (Notre Dame: Univ. of Notre Dame Press, 1971); Richard Rodriguez, *Days of Obligation: An Argument with My Mexican Father* (New York: Viking Press, 1992); Rudolfo Anaya, *Bless Me Ultima* (Berkeley: TQS Publications, 1972). In the present article I have adopted the terms "Mexican-American" and "Mexican." With regard to American society in general, I have preferred to refer to it as "Anglo," since in the interviews held during my fieldwork, "Anglos" and "Anglo-Americans" were the terms most commonly used. To refer to the American society as Anglo and to social interactions as only occurring between Mexican-Americans/Mexicans and Anglos does not imply a disregard for the importance and the role of other ethnic social groups. Indeed, the definition itself of "Anglo" is wrong since it does not indicate the diverse mix of peoples that it encompasses.

22. S. Rodriguez,"The Tourist Gaze, Gentrification and the Commodification of Subjectivity in Taos," in *The Changing Images of the Southwest*, ed. Richard Francaviglia (College Station: Texas A & M University Press, 1994).

23. Harvey Levenstein, *Paradox of Plenty: A Social History of Eating in Modern America* (New York: Oxford University Press, 1993).

24. During my fieldwork in Los Angeles I was struck by the conscientious/condescending marketing campaigns that many Mexican fast food chains and restaurants launched before their opening.

25. Appadurai, "How to Make a National Cuisine."

26. A nice definition given by MacCannel and Urry, as opposed to "backstage" where performers show their real identity and attitude.

27. Personal communication with my friend Elia during our visits to four different Mexican restaurants in the areas of Santa Monica, Palo Alto, and San Pedro.

28. Personal communication with Olga, Dolores, and my friend Elia interviewed at the Gate Street Children's Center in East Los Angeles during my research in 1996.

29. Van Den Berghe, id.

30. Gabaccia, id.,pp. 230–231.

31. Forms of regionalism and pan-ethnicity linked to food consumption as a phenomenon among Mexican-Americans, Mexicans, and Latinos need to be further investigated.

32. This was confirmed by analysis of Mexican cookbooks, which voiced the same distinctions and concerns over historical and semantic origins of certain food items. See Zarela Martinez, *Food from My Heart: Cuisine of Mexico Remembered and Re-Imagined* (New York: MacMillan, 1992).

33. The concept of *mestizaje* must not be confused with the concept of *creolization.* See Abner Cohen, *The Politics of Elite Culture* (Berkeley: University of California Press, 1981). *Mestizaje*, literally intermarriage or the melding of different heritages since the Spanish invasion in the sixteenth century, is the fusion of Spanish, Indian, and African racial and cultural elements. It is a process that tends to nurture the expression of cultures and ethnic features that intermingle unmarked by any conception of class layers and status differences. According to the Chicano Manifesto *El Plan de Aztlan*, see J. Wasconcelos, *La Raza Cosmica* (La Plata: Agenzia Mundial de Libreria, 1925), by contrast, *creolization* is a cultural, social, and ethnic process that is more bound to status and the concept of class stratification. In such a process there is the tendency to merge certain features and characteristics in order to maintain a high status without a social context. Interestingly, *criollo* is a term used to refer to Spaniards' American born descendants and it has a peculiar connotation as a colonial caste hierarchy.

34. In his Mexican cookbook, Gallagher explains in detail this controversy; T. Gallagher, *The Green Chile Bible* (Santa Fe: Clear Light Publishers, 1994).

35. Personal communication with a Mexican restaurateur of a small Mexican restaurant in East Los Angeles.

36. Gabaccia, id.

37. Rodolfo Acuna, *Occupied America. A History of Chicanos* (New York: Harper and Row, 1981); Manuel Gamio, *Mexican Immigration to the United States* (Chicago: Chicago University Press, 1930); Carey McWilliams, *North from Mexico: The Spanish Speaking People of the United States* (Westport, CT: Greenwood Press, 1972).

38. That happened especially until the late 1970s as documented in many Mexican cookbooks; see e.g., Fabiola Cabeza de Baca, *The Good Life: New Mexico Traditions and Food* (Santa Fe: The Museum of New Mexico Press, 1982); C. Coy, "On the Trial of the Perfect Tamale," *Hispanic* 8/6 (1989): 45–46; G. Duncann, "Some Like It Hotter," *Nuestro* 9/9 (1985): 50–57; E. Fergusson, *Mexican Cookbooks* (Albuquerque: University of New Mexico

Press, 1973); Martinez, id.; Victor Valle and M. L. Valle, *Recipe of Memory: Five Generations of Mexican Cuisine* (New York: The New Press, 1995).

39. Mintz, id., pp. 117–121.
40. Humphrey and Humphrey, id.
41. Alvarez, id.
42. R. A. Molino, "The Mexican Food Industry," *Caminos,* 4/6 (1983): 7–8.
43. David E. Hayes Bautista, et al., *No Longer a Minority: Latinos and Social Policy in California* (Los Angeles: UCLA Chicano Studies Research Center, 1992).
44. D. E. Hayes Bautista, et al., *The Burden of Support. Young Latinos in an Aging Society* (Stanford, CA: Stanford University Press, 1990), pp. 23–31.
45. Valdés and Seoane, *Hispanic Market Handbook* (New York: Gale Research, 1995), p. 87.
46. Molino, id.
47. Valdés and Seoane, id., p. 198.
48. Ibid., p. 210.
49. I have been able to visit some "secluded" areas of downtown and East Los Angeles thanks to the presence of my friend Elia (Monterey Park).
50. Appadurai, "Disjuncture," p. 109.
51. Jack Goody, *Cooking, Cuisine and Class: A Study in Comparative Sociology* (Cambridge: Cambridge University Press, 1982).
52. Van Den Berghe, id., p. 398.
53. Valle and Valle, id., pp. 34–35.
54. Martinez, id., pp. 297–298.
55. Max Gluckman, "Rituals of Rebellion in South East Africa," in *Order and Rebellion in Tribal Africa,* ed. Max Gluckman (London: Cohen and West, 1963).
56. Valle and Valle, id., pp. 175–176.
57. Martinez, id., p. 199.
58. It is common to find in Mexican cookbooks a section on market places and specialty shops where Mexican ingredients and crockery can be bought.
59. Valle and Valle, id., p. 55.
60. Martinez, id., p. 276.
61. Ibid., p. 193.
62. Ibid., p. 157.
63. Cabeza de Baca, id., p. 45.
64. D. Kennedy, *Mexican Regional Cooking* (New York: Harper Perennial, 1990); Cheryl Jamison and Bill Jamison, *The Border Cookbook: Authentic Home Cooking of the American Southwest and Northern Mexico* (Boston: The Harvard Common Press, 1994).
65. Helen C. Duran, *Mexican Recipe Shortcuts or, the Casserolization of the Classics: A Quick and Easy Mexican Cookbook for Those Who Care . . . but Have Absolutely No Time to Spare* (Palmer Lake: The Filter Press, 1983), p. iv.
66. James W. Peyton, *La cocina de la frontera. Mexican-American Cooking from the Southwest* (Santa Fe: Red Crane Books, 1994), p. 16.

Part Five

FOOD AND NATIONAL POLITICS

Chapter 12

INDUSTRIAL *TORTILLAS* AND FOLKLORIC PEPSI: THE NUTRITIONAL CONSEQUENCES OF HYBRID CUISINES IN MEXICO

JEFFREY M. PILCHER

*I*n January 1999, neoliberal President Ernesto Zedillo eliminated the long-standing subsidy on Mexico's daily staple, corn *tortillas*. It was intended as an efficiency measure to improve competitiveness in the global economy, but many saw the decree as an end to the welfare state that had assured political domination for the ruling party for most of the twentieth century. Nevertheless, as neighborhood *tortilla* factories throughout Mexico City began to close—unable to compete, without the subsidy, against the industrial conglomerate Maseca, a producer of dehydrated *tortilla* flour—Mexicans feared the end of another era: more than two thousand years of eating *tortillas* made from freshly ground corn.[1] This essay will examine the twentieth-century transformation of Mexican cuisine, both the mechanization of Native American *tortilla* making and the introduction of Western-style industrial processed foods. The modernization of food production has been instrumental in drawing *campesinos* into the market economy, but it has done so in a halting and incomplete fashion, creating culinary versions of what Nestor García Canclini termed "hybrid cultures." While this half-baked globalization allowed people to retain elements of rural, often-indigenous identities by "entering and leaving modernity," many paid a high nutritional price, suspended between traditional and modern diets, eating the worst of both worlds.[2]

The modernization of *tortilla* production held enormous promise at the dawn of the twentieth century, because Mexico's subsistence diet involved tremendous work for both male farmers and female cooks. Women labored for hours each morning over the pre-Hispanic *metate* (saddle quern) to feed their families *tortillas*. Despite this backbreaking daily chore, when mechanical mills capable of grinding the moist corn dough began arriving in rural communities in the 1920s and 1930s, women patronized the establishments only with great hesitancy. Their skepticism about the new technology reflected not a reflexive peasant conservatism but justified concerns about the expense of using the mills and about their own identity within the family. The so-called Green Revolution of agricultural modernization was greeted with similar concern by *campesinos* following World War II because of the high cost of hybrid seeds and chemical fertilizers and pesticides, as well as the government's failure to supply adequate irrigation, silos, and transportation. Productivity surged in the 1960s, allowing the government to supply cheap food to urban consumers, thereby helping to hold down the pressure for higher industrial wages. As a result, already low rural incomes plummeted further, driving millions of people to the cities in search of work and adding to the pool of surplus labor. Food policy in Mexico, as in so many postcolonial nations, has therefore sacrificed the countryside in search of industrial development.[3]

The great challenge for Mexico and other emerging countries has been to realize the possibilities of nationalism and industrialization in a democratic manner that preserves the distinctiveness of local cultures. Few areas can claim greater urgency in this regard than food policy. The history of postcolonial Africa and India clearly demonstrates the need for democratic governance of food distribution. Despite a rapidly growing population, India has been spared from famine, not because of the agricultural gains of the so-called Green Revolution but rather through political mechanisms for assuring that the hungriest people get food. Starvation in Africa has meanwhile resulted largely from the actions of armed bands that confiscate and sell food aid shipments and locally grown crops, leaving people to die.[4]

Assuring the nutritional health of the poor is equally difficult without respect for local cooking traditions. Peasant cultures throughout the world have developed nutritionally balanced diets of complementary vegetable proteins, for example, rice and soybeans in Asia, or maize and beans in the Americas, to replace expensive animal proteins. Industrial processed foods such as powdered milk can supplement these diets in important ways, but the devaluation of traditional cooking through transnational advertising and misplaced ideals of modernity has primarily increased the consumption of junk foods based on fats and sugars. The gravest risks lie in the transition between traditional and industrial diets, as poor Mexicans substitute *alimentos pacotilla* (snack foods) for vegetable proteins, but cannot afford the meats that supply protein to the diets of the rich.[5]

The rising domination of the Maseca corporation over Mexican corn production illustrates an equally important point for cultural studies: the homogenizing effects of national food processing companies may pose as great a threat to local cultures as the more visible cultural imperialism represented by Ronald McDonald. With government assistance, Maseca executives are well on the way to achieving their dream of processing all of the maize in Mexico, removing the "imperfections" that many people believe give *tortillas* their character. Global corporations have meanwhile learned that to compete successfully in national markets they need to modify their products to suit native consumers. A Big Mac with fries may taste exactly the same in Mexico City, Beijing, or Oak Brook, but even McDonald's has adapted to local markets, either by serving salsa with the fries or by posing the eponymous clown as Buddha. No doubt the world will continue to grow more like the United States, as the Cassandras of cultural imperialism have warned, but the converse is equally true, as ever more people in the United States eat Maseca *tortillas*. The rise of a uniquely Mexican *tortilla* industry therefore merits careful analysis.

FROM THE *METATE* TO MASECA

The modernization of food production in Mexico has been one of the primary tools for incorporating subsistence peasants into the market economy. The first step in this process came at the beginning of the twentieth century with the development of corn mills to replace laborious hand grinding of corn dough on the *metate*. By midcentury, a cottage industry of *tortilla* factories had automated the skills of patting out and cooking *tortillas*. Fifty years later, corn processing had been centralized in the hands of industrial conglomerates producing dehydrated *tortilla* flour. Each change entailed a loss of taste and texture, to the point that the modern *tortilla* would be virtually unrecognizable to peasant women of a century before. Moreover, agricultural modernization and government policies favoring urban industry depressed rural incomes, ultimately forcing the peasants of Chiapas into rebellion under the name of the agrarian martyr Emiliano Zapata.

Native Americans often referred to themselves as the people of corn, and the basically vegetarian diet eaten by all but a small nobility in pre-Hispanic Mesoamerica clearly justified such identification. Even though maize provided as much as 80 percent of the daily intake, when combined with beans, chiles, and squash, it formed the basis for a nutritionally balanced diet. The complementarity between corn and beans, each of which supplied amino acids missing in the other, assured a regular supply of high-quality proteins in the absence of European domesticated animals such as cattle, pigs, or chickens. The Aztec empire, with a population that has been estimated at as high as 25 million people, comprised diverse regional cuisines comparable with those of China and India. For example, a wide variety of chile peppers imparted subtle flavors to the *moles* (chile pepper stews) of the Mixtecs and Zapotecs in what is now the southern state of Oaxaca, while along the Gulf Coast in the Huasteca (the land of plenty), Totonac Indians specialized in creating *tamales*, dumplings wrapped in cornhusks.[6]

The labor-intensive cooking techniques developed by pre-Hispanic *campesinas* continued to dominate Mexican kitchens at the start of the twentieth century. The basic utensil was the *metate*, a tablet of black volcanic rock, sloping forward on three stubby legs, used to grind corn for *tortillas* and *tamales*, chiles and seeds for sauces, and fruits and chocolate to drink. Women spent up to five hours each day preparing *tortillas* to feed their families. Work began the night before, when the woman simmered the corn in a solution of mineral lime to make *nixtamal*. She arose before dawn to grind the corn into a moist dough called *masa*, and immediately before each meal, she deftly patted the dough into flat, round *tortillas* and cooked them briefly over the *comal*, an earthenware griddle. Elite stereotypes of Native Americans as long-suffering wretches owed much to the image of women kneeling at the *metate*. *Tortillas* could not be saved for the following day, or even the next meal, because they became hard and inedible in a few hours. The dough likewise would not keep more than a day before it began to ferment.[7]

Hard labor at the *metate* at least gave women status and identity within the family and the community. Historian Wendy Waters has examined these social implications using the field notes of anthropological studies conducted from the 1920s to the 1940s in Tepoztlán, Morelos. *Tortilla* making was so essential to domestic life that no woman in the village became eligible for marriage until she had demonstrated this skill. Men complemented women by praising their *tortillas*, and some even claimed to be able to identify the unique taste and texture of corn ground on their wives' *metate*. Women expressed affection through their role of feeding the family, offering favorite children extra helpings of beans or reserving for them the best *tortillas*. As a result, children were sensitive to the size of their portions and to the order in which they were fed. Food served to communicate anger as well as love; a wife could burn her husband's *tortillas* if she suspected him of infidelity.[8] The symbolic connections between cook and food, already present in the daily preparation of *tortillas*, beans, and chile peppers, grew exponentially during festive meals, when women spent whole days and nights bent over their *metates* preparing *moles* and *tamales*. They undertook such arduous work to help assure the stability of the entire community—indeed, memories of *mole* continue to draw modern migrant workers home each year to participate—and women gained respect and authority as a result.[9]

Thus, although water-powered grain mills had come into use in Europe before the birth of Christ, most *campesinas* still prepared corn by hand in the early twentieth century, leading one Mexican politician to exclaim that "we still live in the Stone Age!"[10] Technologically, the need to precook the corn with mineral lime and grind the dough while still wet made stone mills impractical for producing *nixtamal*. The late-nineteenth-century development of portable steel mills powered by electricity made it possible to grind *masa* sufficiently fine to make an acceptable *tortilla*, although it was still coarser and less tasty than corn prepared on a *metate*. By 1900, more than fifty of these mills operated in Mexico City alone, and they gained rapid acceptance among urban women. Women still cooked their own corn each evening, then carried it to the neighborhood mill in the morning to be ground for a few centavos. The adoption of machinery also made it culturally acceptable for men to take over the management of *tortillerías*, once an exclusively female occupation.[11]

Commercial *nixtamal* mills took decades to spread through the countryside because of both the relatively high monetary cost in a largely subsistence economy and the challenge they posed to women's established domestic roles. Technical flaws in the early mills allowed women to demonstrate their superiority over machines and assert their place within the family. Because villages lacked electricity, early models operated on gas engines, which caused the *tortillas* to come out tasting of high-octane fuel. Even when gas generators were separated from electric motors, the corn acquired a metallic taste and rough texture. Women could avoid these unpleasant side effects by briefly regrinding the *masa* on the *metate*, yet many refused to patronize the mills, indicating deeper social concerns about grinding corn. Gossip in the village of Tepoztlán questioned the femininity of anyone who carried her corn to a commercial mill. Many women feared that neglecting the *metate* would lead to a dangerous swelling of the joints called "laziness of the knees."[12]

While the arrival of a *nixtamal* mill often worried village women, it absolutely infuriated men. Many forbade their wives and daughters from patronizing the new establishments, fearing a direct challenge to their patriarchal authority. Without the discipline of the *metate*, some believed women would become lazy and promiscuous. As one old-timer from the Yucatán explained, the mill "starts early and so women go out before dawn to grind their own corn the way they used to at home. They meet boys in the dark and that's why illegitimacy is caused by the *nixtamal*." To prevent such danger, the men of one agricultural cooperative that received a mill locked it away from their wives. In another case, a group of women who attempted to organize for their right to a mill were physically assaulted by disgruntled men.[13]

Some of the first rural women to patronize the new mills were those who had fled the countryside during the decade of revolutionary fighting (1910–1920) and discovered the convenience of machine-ground corn in cities or towns. Financial considerations also helped determine who took their corn to the mill. Relatively poor women whose families held little land, contrary perhaps to expectations, often had the greatest incentive to pay for machine-ground corn. Although this service required a few centavos, it freed women from several hours of daily work. They could use that time to engage in artisanal crafts or to become petty merchants, traveling to nearby towns to buy cheaper products, and thus earn enough money to offset the cost of milling. The acceptance of the mill as a natural tool therefore helped draw subsistence farmers into the money economy. Wealthier families who could easily afford the added expense of milling were often the last ones to give up the *metate*. Some considered home-ground corn a status marker, a way of asserting that they lived better than their neighbors because they ate better *tortillas*. Of course, they could also pay poorer women to do the actual grinding.[14]

Political as well as economic issues influenced the reception of mechanical mills in rural Mexico. Established *caciques* (political bosses) often enriched themselves by asserting monopolistic control over *nixtamal* mills, while aspiring populist leaders used them as a form of patronage to organize supporters. President Lázaro Cárdenas (1934–1940) used grants of *nixtamal* mills to encourage membership in the official party and to discourage rival church organizations. Women learned to phrase their requests for cooperative mills within the dominant developmentalist discourse; for example, the women of Rancho Las Canoas, on the shores of Lake Pátzcuaro, Michoacán, formed a Women's Anticlerical and Anti-Alcohol League to petition the president for a corn mill and in this way to liberate them from the "bitter, black stone with three feet called the *metate*."[15]

Tortilla production was mechanized further in the postwar era with the development of an integrated factory comprising a *nixtamal* mill that ground the corn, a rotating press to form it into the proper shape, and an "endless *comal*" conveyer belt to cook it. Mexican inventors had first attempted to duplicate the subtle skills of the *tortillera* in the late nineteenth century, but it was not until the 1950s that they resolved all the technical problems to mass-produce an adequate *tortilla*. By the 1970s, these small-scale factories, capable of producing a few thousand *tortillas* per hour, operated conveniently in urban barrios and rural communities throughout the republic. *Tortilla* aficionados clearly recognized the difference between hand-patted and factory-pressed *tortillas*. Relatively wealthy peasant women, who could afford to devote themselves exclusively to domestic work, rejected machine-made *tortillas* as "raw" because they stuck together. While ordinary *campesinas* began to purchase tortillas for everyday consumption and used the time saved to earn outside income, the *metate* and *comal* came out for festive occasions, when only a philistine would eat *tortillas* that "tasted like electricity" because they had not been cooked over a wood-burning fire.[16]

The arrival of *nixtamal* mills in the countryside transformed the lives of Mexican women, freeing them from hard labor at the *metate* while drawing them into the money economy and often into political organization as well. The male activity of growing maize underwent equally dramatic changes as the government shifted its goals from an agrarian revolution to the Green Revolution, emphasizing large-scale commercial agriculture to support urban industrialization. Land reform had culminated under President Cárdenas, who distributed nearly fifty million acres to *campesinos* in the form of communally owned *ejidos*. Nevertheless, the very magnitude of the reforms, together with financial crises and a fierce conservative reaction, prevented Cárdenas from providing the infrastructure of machinery, irrigation, and credit necessary to make even the most favorable of *ejido* grants into viable commercial operations, and this neglect only grew worse under subsequent administrations. In 1943, a team of agronomists sponsored by the Rockefeller Foundation arrived to supplement Mexican programs aimed at increasing farm productivity, which had been ongoing since the 1920s. Within two decades, the use of hybrid seeds, fertilizers, and pesticides had doubled the production of Mexican corn and quadrupled that of wheat, but the profits accrued primarily to affluent commercial farmers who had the resources to benefit from the technological improvements.[17]

Historian Enrique Ochoa has shown how the Mexican State Food Agency, founded in 1937 by Cárdenas to help small farmers compete in the marketplace, was diverted to support the goal of industrialization. Political crises, particularly urban inflation and food shortages, invariably disrupted rural development plans, as bureaucrats purchased staple crops from a few commercial growers in the Pacific Northwest and imports from the United States rather than from large numbers of small *ejidos* in central and southern Mexico. The construction of grain storage facilities around urban centers and in ports on the Gulf of Mexico perpetuated this bias in the 1950s. The agency provided cheap food to the cities in order to win populist political support while at the same time containing union demands for higher wages, thereby indirectly subsidizing private industry. For example, the agency supplied low-cost corn to the politically powerful *nixtamal* millers in Mexico City, who then sold *tortillas* to the public at fixed prices, gaining substantial profits for themselves in the process. By the 1960s, decades of official neglect led impoverished farmers to begin taking up arms and demanding a return to agrarian reform. The government responded by repressing the rebels and then extending the welfare programs to supply industrial processed food to the countryside as well. This expansion into food processing to provision the new rural stores prompted cries of socialist intervention by business leaders, who nevertheless continued to profit from agency supplies of subsidized raw materials for their own factories.[18]

The creation of a dehydrated *tortilla* flour industry illustrates this mutually beneficial relationship between state-owned and private enterprises. In 1949, the federal government established the first *masa harina* or *nixtamal* flour mill, called Maíz Industrializado, S.A. (Minsa) in

Tlalnepantla, Mexico, the site of giant corn silos for the Mexico City market. That same year, Roberto González opened a rival facility in Cerralvo, Nuevo León, under the trade name Molinos Azteca, S.A. (Maseca). The two firms collaborated on research and development for more than a decade before arriving at a suitable formulation that could be turned into *tortilla masa* with just the addition of water. By the mid-1970s, *tortilla* flour production surpassed 500,000 tons, 5 percent of all the corn consumed in Mexico, with the majority of the market going to the private firm, Maseca, in part because the powerful corn millers used political channels to slow the growth of the state corporation, Minsa.[19]

Government officials justified support for the industry by pointing to economies of scale, since cornmeal could be produced, transported, and stored more cheaply than whole corn. Centralized production also limited the risk of irregularities within neighborhood *tortilla* factories in addition to offering nutritional benefits. For the nominal cost of $10 a ton, Maseca could enrich its *masa harina* with enough protein and vitamins to satisfy minimum daily requirements, but the company has nevertheless resisted implementing the strategy. Although vitamin and protein enrichment would make little difference in taste beyond the already significant change from freshly ground to dehydrated corn, the politically powerful company feared that any additives would undermine its market share.[20]

By the end of the millennium, the dismantling of the State Food Agency by neoliberal governments left the *masa harina* industry poised to dominate Mexican corn markets. President Carlos Salinas de Gortari (1988–1994) first cut the subsidy to corn millers in an attempt to target welfare assistance. In its place he established a program giving poor people *tortilla* vouchers called *tortivales*, which were quickly dubbed *tortivotos* by political opponents who accused the government of using food to buy votes. The president also privatized the state firm, Minsa, selling it to a rival consortium of Maseca. Finally, in January 1999, his successor, Ernesto Zedillo (1994–2000), eliminated the *tortilla* subsidy completely along with price controls. The nutritional consequences of this policy remain to be seen, although standards of living for poor Mexicans have already slipped dramatically in the past two decades.[21] Nevertheless, the demise of family-owned *tortilla* factories has already become clear. Alma Guillermoprieto graphically explained that "when the privatization program of Mexico's notorious former President Carlos Salinas delivered the future of the *tortilla* into their hands . . . [the *tortilla* magnates] served up to the Mexican people the rounds of grilled cardboard that at present constitute the nation's basic foodstuff."[22] Many would apply that same description to the processed foods offered by multinational corporations, and while the reception of those foods has followed a unique trajectory, the effects on Mexican nutrition have been equally grim.

THE OTHER PEPSI GENERATION

The Tzotzil Indians of San Juan Chamula may never appear on television commercials in the United States, but they nevertheless form part of the Pepsi Generation. While Mexicans usually celebrate religious festivals with beer or tequila, in this highland Chiapas community toasts are invariably made with Pepsi Cola. The Tzotzil devotion to soft drinks illustrates the ubiquitous presence of industrial processed food in even the most remote indigenous regions—and the fact that the *cacique* controls the Pepsi distributorship. The arrival of Pepsi and other junk foods has brought tremendous changes in food consumption, with serious nutritional consequences for the lower classes, yet cultural imperialism has not overwhelmed traditional Mexican cooking. At worst, a form of hybridization has taken place as Mexicans have incorporated foreign foods into established eating patterns. Balanced against this have been the efforts of middle-class cooks to create a unified cuisine as part of a self-conscious nationalist program.

The vision of a billion Chinese just waiting to buy Big Macs, Coca-Cola, and other consumer goods formed a crucial element of Western propaganda during the Cold War. This image was as simplistic as it was ethnocentric, and yet it provides a useful corrective to the likewise oversimplified view of neocolonial agribusiness producing luxury goods in the former colonies for sale in the affluent markets of the old colonial powers.[23] The capitalist dream that the fall of Communism would make all the world into a giant McDonaldland overlooked the global ecosystem's inability to sustain the livestock needed to serve billions of hamburgers daily. Moreover, rural incomes in China, as elsewhere in the developing world, were insufficient to purchase even fries and a shake. Nevertheless, multinational food corporations developed long-range plans to transform those rural masses into loyal customers as incomes gradually rose. Businesses built their rural marketing infrastructure from the ground up, starting with low-cost, easily transportable items such as bulk vegetable oils and dehydrated baby formula, in order to reach the eventual goal of a McDonald's drive-through window.

Meanwhile, the urban middle classes in these developing countries provided an immediate market for the whole range of industrial foods, from breakfast cereals to fast-food chains. One of the images used most frequently to prove the West had won the Cold War was the opening of McDonald's restaurants in Moscow and Beijing. It seemed irrelevant that Chinese customers did not particularly like the hamburgers and were more interested in the restaurants as a medium for experiencing life in the United States.[24] Fast foods and soft drinks likewise became fashionable among India's urban elite as economic "liberalization" in the 1990s led the country to abandon its gastronomic nonalignment.[25] Food-processing businesses producing refrigerated meats, canned vegetables, and bottled drinks emerged in Mexico during the industrial boom of the 1890s, yet their expansion was also limited to small urban markets. By the 1940s, the first Mexican supermarket chains, SUMESA and Aurrera, had opened in upper-middle-class neighborhoods, selling Aunt Jemima pancake mix and the Mexican version of Wonder Bread, known by the brand name Bimbo. Housewives not only began replacing crusty *bolillos* (rolls) fresh from neighborhood bakeries with chewy, plastic-wrapped *pan de caja* (bread from a box), they also conducted bizarre experiments using mass-produced ingredients to create such hybrid dishes as shrimp and cornflakes, calf brains with crackers, macaroni and milk soup, and pork loin in Pepsi Cola.[26]

These examples may well illustrate a dark side of mass production, but they do not portend the annihilation of Mexican gastronomy. Cultural differences make it risky to generalize between the Mexican middle classes and their counterparts in the United States. Simple household appliances demonstrate subtle but important distinctions. For example, Mexicans used their newly purchased refrigerators to store soft drinks and beer instead of a week's worth of groceries. And while the most valuable appliances north of the border may have been electric toasters and cake mixers, Mexicans preferred the electric blender, the juice press, and the pressure cooker. The blender's facility in grinding chile sauces relegated the *metate* to the status of a kitchen curiosity, and the juicer turned Mexico's ubiquitous oranges into daily glasses of fresh juice. The pressure cooker solved the age-old problem of boiling water at high altitudes in central Mexico. Beans can now be prepared in less than an hour, saving on fuel costs as well as time, and the toughest beef can be made edible in minutes.

Perhaps the limitations of culinary technology could be used to demonstrate the relative "underdevelopment" of Mexican kitchens: housewives continued to shop for groceries every day and spurned such conveniences as canned beans and frozen orange juice concentrate. Yet the Mexican woman's skepticism of the doctrine that time is money may reflect a more realistic view of the limitations of household technology. Ruth Schwartz Cowan observed that mechanizing housework in the United States had the ironic effect of creating "more work for mother." Time saved by laundry machines, for example, was spent in the automobile working as the family chauffeur. Mexican women at least had the satisfaction of feeding their families fresh food.[27]

Moreover, many foreign manufacturers won customers in the 1940s and 1950s by demonstrating the utility of their products for making national dishes. Glasbake Cookware ran a series of newspaper advertisements featuring recipes for Mexican regional dishes such as *mole michoacano*. Appliance makers depicted giant *cazuelas* simmering on top of their modern stoves, and an advertisement for pressure cookers made the justifiable claim that "Mexican cooking enters a new epoch with the *Olla presto.*" Even Coca-Cola appealed to Mexican customers with nostalgic scenes of picnics at Chapultepec Park.[28]

Mexicans also appropriated elements of foreign culture to their own purposes. Domestic soft-drink manufacturers such as Mundet competed with Coke and Pepsi by introducing lines of soda flavors adapted to Mexican tastes for orange, mango, and apple cider. Local chip makers such as Sabritas and Bali contracted with the North American food technologists who had manufactured MSG in the 1950s to transform wheat pellets into artificial *chicharrones* (fried pork skins).[29] The habit of eating eggs for breakfast, when transferred from the United States to Mexico, stimulated creative experimentation rather than slavish imitation. In searching for national counterparts to eggs benedict, Mexican chefs served *huevos rancheros* (ranch-style eggs) fried with tomato-and-chile sauce, *huevos albañiles* (bricklayers' eggs) scrambled with a similar sauce, and *huevos motuleños* (from Motul, Yucatán) fried with beans, ham, and peas. Soon, no hotel with pretensions to luxury could neglect having its own "traditional" egg dish on the breakfast menu.

The modern desire to preserve traditional Mexican cooking, or to create new traditions when appropriate ones could not be found, also inspired a flurry of folkloric studies in the countryside. Josefina Velázquez de León brought together the country's diverse regional cuisines for the first time in a single work, *Platillos regionales de la República mexicana* (*Regional Dishes of the Mexican Republic,* Mexico City: Ediciones J. Veláquez de León, 1946; Mexico City: Editorial Promama, 1965). Virginia Rodríguez Rivera published another classic volume, *La cocina en el México antiguo y moderno* (*Cooking in Ancient and Modern Mexico,* Mexico City: Editorial Aomamma, 1965), featuring nineteenth-century dishes with recipes drawn from oral history interviews. Mexican women thus displayed a mania for preserving their culinary past even as it began to slip away. When electric blenders finally began to replace the grinding stone, a society columnist warned women to save their *metates,* "because this Mexican cooking utensil has still not been supplanted by any modern appliance."[30]

Nevertheless, they had mixed success in preserving traditional cooking. Attempts to construct a national cuisine reduced complex regional cooking styles to a few stereotyped dishes, which often misrepresented the foods eaten in those areas. Even an author as sensitive as Josefina Velázquez de León adapted traditional village recipes to the needs of urban cooks. For the *zacahuil,* the giant Huastecan pit-barbecued corn cake, wrapped in banana leaves and capable of feeding an entire community, she instructed readers to use a scanty three kilograms of maize and to bake it in the oven. Arjun Appadurai has described a similar process of imagining culinary communities in postcolonial India, as middle-class cookbook authors presented their regional foods to readers across the subcontinent, but he noted also that "one of the results of the exchange of culinary images is the elimination of the most exotic, peculiar, distinctive, or domestic nuances in a particular specialized cuisine."[31]

Just as middle-class cooks struggled to adapt traditional Mexican foods to new urban lifestyles, multinational corporations attempted to transform eating habits in the countryside. Creating an infrastructure of rural marketing networks for processed foods required significant investments. Pre-Hispanic merchants had carried on an extensive trade in nonperishable, relatively high-value goods such as cacao and dried chiles, supplemented in the colonial period by coffee, sugar, and spices, but it was more difficult to transport Pepsi by mule. Fortunately for businessmen, revolutionary governments of the 1920s and 1930s placed a high priority on road-building to unify the country and its markets. Soft-drink and beer distributors were among the first entrepreneurs to take advantage of these highways to send glass bottles from regional plants to consumers and then to return the empties safely for refilling—an essential step to keep prices affordable. Both Coke and beer arrived in the village of Tepoztlán within six years after the opening of a road from the state capital in 1936. The appearance of Pepsi in the 1940s and the growth of national breweries helped foster competition in local markets.[32]

Food distributorships therefore developed in a hybrid fashion, combining modern and traditional marketing methods. Even today, supermarket chains remain concentrated in upper-middle-class neighborhoods, while manufactured foods reach the rest of the population through small-scale grocers, often in municipal markets, and ambulant vendors. These merchants depended on corporate distributors for credit as well as business supplies such as display cases and refrigerators.[33] One shopkeeper considered the Coke deliveryman so important to his livelihood that he invited the driver to his daughter's fifteenth birthday party. The costs of establishing and maintaining these delivery routes encouraged the centralization of Mexican food processing within large industrial groups. The largest Coke franchise in the world, for example, Fomento Económico Mexicano SA, also included Cervecería Cuauhtémoc within the Monterrey-based Garza Sada conglomerate. Pepsico, meanwhile, diversified into the complementary snack-food industry, merging with Frito-Lay in the United States, then acquiring Mexican chip makers Sabritas and Bali.[34] As in the case of *tortilla* flour, the government encouraged the growth of these companies through ostensibly competitive state food corporations. Rural stores established in the 1960s and 1970s by the State Food Agency stocked products such as animal crackers and soft drinks, either produced by state factories or purchased from private groups, thereby helping to incorporate rural consumers into larger national markets.[35]

Mexican politicians have meanwhile foregone many potential health benefits that their economic ventures might have achieved. They conceded to food manufacturers the educational power of the mass media, allowing massive advertising campaigns for soft drinks and snack candies, with "small print" advice to eat fresh fruits and vegetables included as the only concession to public health.[36] Programs to supplement processed foods, including *tortilla* flour, have been initiated periodically but never carried through. Perhaps the most nutritionally irresponsible example of state assistance to private enterprise lay in the subsidies on flour and sugar given to snack-food producers, which made this business, in the words of one health official, a *"negociazo"* (scam).[37]

Even with government assistance, transnational advertising campaigns had a difficult time instilling North American and western European values in the Mexican countryside. The example of Pepsi in San Juan Chamula illustrates the ways that modernizing societies adapt consumer products to fit their cultures. Rather than drinking Pepsi as a daily snack in imitation of the middle classes in either Mexico or the United States, the Chamulans incorporated the soft drink into the community's ritual life, for example, giving cases of Pepsi as dowries for brides. Religious leaders celebrated church services with Pepsi instead of wine, telling parishioners that carbonation drives off evil spirits and cleanses the soul. The natives even hung Pepsi posters in their homes beside the family crucifix, for as one person explained to an anthropologist: "When men burp, their hearts open."[38]

The resilience of local customs has not offset the nutritional damage of the transition from traditional to industrial diets. Studies by the National Nutrition Institute and by numerous anthropologists from the 1960s to the 1990s have documented a fundamental trend toward the replacement of corn and beans by sugar and fats. Well-to-do Yucatecan peasants and working-class Mexico City residents both derive an average of 20 percent of their calories from processed foods, including soft drinks, beer, chips, and candy. The rural poor, unable to afford such snacks except on special occasions, dump heaped spoonfuls of sugar into weak coffee. So pervasive has sucrose become that one study recommended vitamin-enriched sugar as the most efficient means of improving rural nutrition.[39] The convenience of processed foods often came at the expense of nutrition, as when cooks used dried consommé instead of tomatoes and onions, in effect replacing vegetables with salt. Poverty further distorted the diets of *campesinos* subsisting on the fringes of the market economy. The rising price of beans forced many poor families to buy cheaper wheat pasta, with grave dietary consequences. While corn and beans together provide high-quality protein, corn and spaghetti do not.[40]

The food processing industry has waged a century-long campaign to remove consumers from the source of their nourishment, to make packaged foods seem natural and living plants and animals unwholesome. For example, transnational executives hoping to establish modern chicken packing plants in Mexico expressed the long-term goal of persuading consumers that poultry tastes best when purchased from a plastic bag in the refrigerated section.[41] The combination of manufactured foods and traditional cooking styles has had mixed results, introducing valuable new sources of protein to poor consumers, but also destabilizing their nutritional intake. It remains to be seen how successful the chicken packers will be in convincing Mexicans that "parts are parts."

CONCLUSION

This essay has attempted to untangle the complex negotiations of identity and markets among traditional peasant cooks, progressive urban gourmets, food-processing corporations, and an unfortunately far from impartial state. Connections between food consumption and elite identity can be seen in the current fad for the so-called *nueva cocina mexicana*. Chefs have turned to Native American plants and animals in order to claim an equal standing with the great cuisines of Europe and Asia, while preparing these ingredients with the difficult techniques of European *haute cuisine* to maintain their cultural distinction from the popular masses. Thus Arnulfo Luengas, chef of the Banco Nacional de México's executive dining room, created avocado mousse with shrimp, Beef Wellington with chiles, and chicken supremes with *cuitlacoche*.[42] Some might question the *mexicanidad* of such dishes, but the prominent cookbook author Alicia Gironella De'Angeli insisted that this was "the same food we serve at home. It is one of two tendencies in Mexican cooking. The other is the popular Mexican food, the kind with the grease and cheese and everything fried. It is the traditional food that we are reinterpreting." She asserted that the new dishes actually are derived from pre-Hispanic origins. "We did not have the lard and the grease that most people think of as Mexican in our roots. The Spaniards brought the pigs."[43] In this way, she appropriated Aztec authenticity for elite cuisine and associated lower-class foods with the villainous conquistadors.

The popular sectors would not allow her to have such international sophistication and eat it too with a nationalist flourish. They formulated their own diverse ideas of what constituted authentic Mexican food. Maize of course constituted the quintessential cuisine of rural Mexico. During a drought in the Huasteca, when corn shipments arrived from the United States to relieve local shortages, *campesinos* claimed that even the pigs turned up their snouts at the imported grain.[44] Meanwhile, authenticity meant something entirely different to cooks patting out *tortillas* by hand in restaurants on scenic Janitzio Island, Lake Pátzcuaro, where they started with Maseca brand *masa harina* then reground it on the *metate* for the tourists' benefit.

The government has likewise had its say in defining Mexican cuisine through an often-contradictory set of food policies. The National Nutrition Institute developed programs to improve the health of rural and urban poor through educational campaigns about the best ways to use both traditional staples and vitamin and protein supplements. The state food agencies also provided infrastructure to assist small farmers in selling corn to lucrative urban markets, thus preserving their livelihoods. Far more of the government's resources went to promoting domestic manufacturers, even to the point of subsidizing the junk-food industry. These businesses have in turn adopted the mantle of authenticity, even when they represented foreign owners. Advertising billboards informed Mexicans that "*tortillas* taste good, and better with Maseca." Transnational corporations meanwhile adapted their products to Mexican tastes in order to face off local competitors. Bags of Sabritas *chicharrones* (pork rinds) shared counter space with Fritos potato chips, while Mundet *cidral* (carbonated apple cider) sat in the refrigerator with Pepsi-Cola. This goes to show that Macario, the Tzotzil Faust, does not need a North American Mephistopheles to sell his soul.

The nutritional consequences of this partial transition from peasant to industrial diets were profound regardless of their source. Adolfo Chávez, director of the Community Nutrition Division of the National Nutrition Institute, has described an epidemiological trap in which Mexicans have fallen victim to the dietary diseases of the rich world without escaping the nutritional deficiencies of the poor world. Serum cholesterol levels among residents of the wealthy, meat-consuming areas of northern Mexico average higher than those in the United States. Heart disease has become a serious problem throughout Mexico, and ranks as the leading cause of death even among indigenous peasants in Yucatán and other southern states. Excessive sugar consumption has meanwhile created an epidemic of diabetes, the fourth leading cause of death nationwide. Hypoglycemia, hypertension, arteriosclerosis, and various forms of cancer have likewise grown more common. These diseases seemed all the more tragic given the continuing prevalence of serious malnutrition in Mexico. Adults often suffered from both obesity and anemia at the same time, and the nutritional consequences for infants were even worse. The economic downturn of the 1980s led to a rise in mortality from nutritional deficiencies from 1 percent to 5.2 percent among infants and from 1.5 percent to 9.1 percent among preschool-age children.[45]

The hunger of Mexico's poor also portends an ominous future for the national cuisine, which has always derived inspiration from *campesino* kitchens, regardless of the pretensions of European-trained chefs. The heart of this cuisine, *tortillas* made of freshly ground corn, has become particularly vulnerable to industrialization. Economist Felipe Torres Torres explained that "the business of the *tortilla* has expanded under the articulation of an economic model, and not of the historic preferences of consumers, who deep down maintain a vigilant rejection of the new product, although . . . [neoliberal political economy has] not permitted them any alternative; in such a case, it is possible that future generations will defin-itively abandon the consumption of maize before the low quality of a food that is especially sensitive to the criteria of modernity."[46] Of course, gour-met boutiques will always exist, recreating a folkloric past through the per-formances of women, perhaps with indigenous features or costumes, making *tortillas* of organically grown and freshly ground corn for affluent consumers. Indeed, one of the modern world's great ironies is that only the wealthy can afford to eat like peasants.

NOTES

1. Enrique Ochoa, *Feeding Mexico: The Political Uses of Food Since 1910* (Wilmington, DE: SR Books, 2000), p. 219; Alma Guillermoprieto, "In Search of the Real Tortilla," *The New Yorker* (November 29, 1999): pp. 46–48.
2. Nestor García Canclini, *Hybrid Cultures: Strategies for Entering and Leaving Modernity* (Minneapolis: University of Minnesota Press, 1996).
3. Cynthia Hewitt de Alcántara, *Modernizing Mexican Agriculture: Socioeconomic Implications of Technological Change, 1940–1970* (Geneva: United Nations Research Institute for Social Development, 1976); Ochoa, *Feeding Mexico*, pp. 7–9, 225–232.
4. Jean Drèze and Amartya Sen, *Hunger and Public Action* (Oxford: Clarendon Press, 1989), pp. 9–10, 68, 91, 122.
5. Alberto Ysunza Ogazón, et al., *Dietas de transición y riesgo nutricional en población migratoria* (Mexico City: Instituto Nacional de Nutrición, 1985); Lucia Batrouni, et al., *Situación de bar-rios marginados de Teziutlán* (Mexico City: Instituto Nacional de Nutrición, 1983); Adolfo Chávez, et al., *La nutrición en México y la transición epidemiologica* (Mexico City: Instituto Nacional de Nutrición, 1993).
6. On the nutritional value of the pre-Hispanic maize complex, see William T. Sanders, Jeffrey R. Parsons, and Robert S. Santley, *The Basin of Mexico: Ecological Processes in the Evolution of a Civilization* (New York: Academic Press, 1979), p. 376; Hector Arraya, Marina Flores, and Guillermo Arroyave, "Nutritive Value of Basic Foods and Common Dishes of the Guatemalan Rural Populations: A Theoretical Approach," *Ecology of Food and Nutrition* 11 (1981): 171–176. The population estimate comes from Woodrow Borah and Sherburne F. Cook, *The Aboriginal Population of Central Mexico on the Eve of the Spanish Conquest* (Berkeley: University of California Press, 1963).
7. Margaret Park Redfield, "Notes on the Cookery of Tepoztlan, Morelos," *American Journal of Folklore* 42, no. 164 (April-June 1929): 167–196; Nathanial Whetten, *Rural Mexico* (Chicago: University of Chicago Press, 1948), p. 305; Oscar Lewis, *Life in a Mexican Village: Tepoztlán Revisited* (Urbana: University of Illinois Press, 1951), p. 72.
8. "Roads, the Carnivalesque, and the Mexican Revolution: Transforming Modernity in Tepoztlán, 1928–1943," M.A. thesis, Texas Christian University, 1994, pp. 165–170.
9. Lynn Stephen, *Zapotec Women* (Austin: University of Texas Press, 1991), 186.
10. *El Universal* (November 11, 1933).
11. Dawn Keremitsis, "Del metate al molino: La mujer mexicana de 1910 a 1940," *Historia Mexicana* 33 (October-December 1983): 297; John Mraz, "'En calidad de esclavas': obreras en los molinos de nixtamal, México, diciembre, 1919," *Historia obrera* 6:24 (March 1982): 2–14.
12. Quote in Redfield, "Notes on Cookery of Tepoztlan," 182; *El maíz, fundamento de la cultura popular mexicana* (Mexico: Museo Nacional de Culturas Populares, 1982), p. 82.
13. Archivo General de la Nación, Mexico City (hereafter cited as AGN), Ramo Presidentes, Lázaro Cárdenas, 604.11/21, 149, 155; quote from Arnold J. Bauer, "Millers and Grinders: Technology and Household Economy in Meso-America," *Agricultural History* 64, no. 1 (Winter 1990): 16.
14. Waters, "Roads and the Mexican Revolution," 167, 173.
15. AGN, Cárdenas, exp. 604.11/67, 91, 92, 121; Keremitsis, "Del metate al molino," 297.
16. Robert V. Kemper, *Migration and Adaptation: Tzintzuntzan Peasants in Mexico City* (Beverly Hills: Sage Publications, 1977), pp. 29, 152; Maria da Glória Marroni de Velázquez, "Changes in Rural Society and Domestic Labor in Atlixco, Puebla, 1940–1990," in *Creating Spaces, Shaping Transitions: Women of the Mexican Countryside, 1850–1990*, ed. Heather Fowler-Salamini and Mary Kay Vaughan (Tucson: University of Arizona Press, 1994), p. 223; Jaime Aboites A., *Breve historia de un invento olvidado: Las máquinas tortilladoras en México* (Mexico City: Universidad Autónoma Metropolitana, 1989), pp. 39, 47; *El maíz*, p. 82.

17. Joseph Cotter, "The Origins of the Green Revolution in Mexico: Continuity or Change?" in *Latin America in the 1940s: War and Postwar Transitions*, ed. David Rock (Berkeley: University of California Press, 1993); Deborah Fitzgerald, "Exporting American Agriculture: The Rockefeller Foundation in Mexico, 1943–1953," in *Missionaries of Science: The Rockefeller Foundation in Latin America*, ed. Marcos Cueto (Bloomington: Indiana University Press, 1994); Hewitt de Alcántara, *Modernizing Mexican Agriculture*, pp. 118–120, 173–180.

18. Ochoa, *Feeding Mexico*, chaps. 3, 5, 8.

19. Nacional Financiera, *La industria de la harina de maíz* (Mexico City: NAFINSA, 1982), pp. 13–14; *La industria de maíz* (Mexico City: Primsa Editorial, 1989), pp. 108–114; Adrian Cópil, "La guerra de las tortillas," *Contenido* (July 1992): 42–47; Ochoa, *Feeding Mexico*, p. 121; Aboites, *Breve historia de un invento*, pp. 50–51.

20. Nacional Financiero, *La industria de la harina de maíz* (Mexico City: NAFINSA, 1982), p. 51; Ana Naranjo B., *Informe de programas y proyectos de doce años, 1976–1987* (Mexico City: Instituto Nacional de Nutrición, 1987), pp. 225–226.

21. Ochoa, *Feeding Mexico*, pp. 210–212, 219.

22. Guillermoprieto, "In Search of the Real Tortilla," p. 46.

23. See, for example, Richard W. Franke, "The Effects of Colonialism and Neocolonialism on the Gastronomic Patterns of the Third World," in *Food and Evolution*, ed. Marvin Harris and Eric B. Ross (Philadelphia: Temple University Press, 1987), p. 455.

24. See the fascinating studies in James L. Watson, ed., *Golden Arches East: McDonald's in East Asia* (Stanford: Stanford University Press, 1998).

25. Uma Narayan, "Eating Cultures: Incorporation, Identity and Indian Food," *Social Identities* 1:1 (1995): 69.

26. Jeffrey M. Pilcher, *¡Que vivan los tamales! Food and the Making of Mexican Identity* (Albuquerque: University of New Mexico Press, 1998), p. 127.

27. Ruth Schwartz Cowan, *More Work for Mother: The Ironies of Household Technology from the Open Hearth to the Microwave* (New York: Basic Books, 1983).

28. *Excelsior*, April 15, July 14, September 1, December 16, 1945; June 2, 1947.

29. Robert Sietsema, "My Father the Formulator," *Gourmet* (February 2000), p. 91.

30. *Excelsior*, August 13, 1947. See, for comparison, Eric Hobsbawm and Terence Ranger, eds., *The Invention of Tradition* (Cambridge: Cambridge University Press, 1983).

31. Arjun Appadurai, "How to Make a National Cuisine: Cookbooks in Contemporary India," *Comparative Studies in Society and History* 30, no. 1 (January 1988): 17.

32. Waters, "Roads and the Mexican Revolution," p. 78; J. C. Louis and Harvey Z. Yazijian, *The Cola Wars* (New York: Everest House, 1980), pp. 46, 60.

33. Fernando Rello and Demetrio Sodi, *Abasto y distribución de alimentos en las grandes metropolis* (Mexico City: Nueva Imagen, 1989), pp. 68–80.

34. José Antonio Roldán Amaro, *Hambre y riqueza en la historia contemporanea de México*, anexo 1 of *Historia del hambre en México*, ed. Pablo González Casanova (Mexico City: Instituto Nacional de Nutrición, 1986), p. 40; Carol Meyers de Ortiz, *Pequeño comercio de alimentos en colonias populares de Ciudad Nezahuacóyotl: Análisis de su papel en la estructura socioeconómica urbana* (Guadalajara: Editorial Universidad de Guadalajara, 1990), p. 33; Matt Moffett, "A Mexican War Heats Up for Cola Giants," *Wall Street Journal* (April 26, 1993): B1, 6; Young and Yazijian, *The Cola Wars*, p. 133.

35. Ochoa, *Feeding Mexico*, p. 165.

36. David Márquez Ayala, "Las empresas transnacionales y sus efectos en el consumo alimentario," in *Transnacionales, agricultura, y alimentación*, ed. Rodolfo Echeverría Zuno (Mexico City: Editorial Nueva Imagen, 1982), p. 218; Naranjo, *Informe de programas*, pp. 228–234.

37. Quote from "La entrevista: Dr. Adolfo Chávez Villasana," *Cuadernos de Nutrición* 6, no. 9 (July-September 1983): 12–16.

38. Matt Moffett, "Mexicans Convert as a Matter of Politics," *Wall Street Journal* (June 1, 1988).

39. Gilberto Balam, "La alimentación de los campesinos mayas del estado de Yucatán (Primera parte)," *Cuadernos de Nutrición* 16, no. 6 (November-December 1993): 41; Chávez, *La nutrición en México*, pp. 33, 78; Jesús Ruvalcaba Mercado, *Vida cotidiana y consumo de maíz en la huasteca veracruzana* (Mexico City: Centro de Investigaciones y Estudios Superiores en Antropología Social, 1987), pp. 31, 39. The Mexican case thus confirms the hypotheses put forward by Sydney Mintz, *Sweetness and Power: The Place of Sugar in Modern History* (New York: Viking, 1985).

40. K. M. DeWalt, P. B. Kelly, and G. H. Pelto, "Nutritional Correlates of Economic Microdifferentiation in a Highland Mexican Community," in *Nutritional Anthropology: Contemporary Approaches to Diet and Culture*, ed. Norge W. Jerome, Randy F. Kandel, Gretel H. Pelto (Pleasantville, NY: Redgrave Publishing, 1980), p. 213; Serrano Andrade, "El consumo de alimentos industrializados," p. 29; Chávez, *La nutrición en México*, p. 28; Balam, "Alimentación de los campesinos mayas," p. 43.

41. Personal communication from John Hart, Mexico City, July 16, 1997.
42. *El universo de la cocina mexicana: Recetario* (Mexico City: Fomento Cultural Banamex, 1988), pp. 18, 40, 48.
43. Quoted in Florence Fabricant, "Mexican Chefs Embrace a Lighter Cuisine of Old," *New York Times* (May 3, 1995): B3.
44. Ruvalcaba Mercado, *Maíz en la huasteca*, p. 85.
45. Chávez, et al., *La nutrición en México*, pp. 47–78; Ochoa, *Feeding Mexico*, p. 208.
46. "Antecedentes del debate actual sobre el maíz en México," in *La industria de la masa y la tortilla: Desarrollo y tecnología*, ed. Felipe Torres, et al. (Mexico: UNAM, 1996), p. 26.

Chapter 13

BERLIN IN THE *BELLE ÉPOQUE:* A FAST-FOOD HISTORY

KEITH ALLEN

*N*ot far from Bahnhof Zoo, perhaps the best-known train station in Berlin, the most Berlinese of all restaurants languishes in obscurity. The name Aschinger has been forgotten, the restaurant chain's claim to fame usurped by an unlikely alliance of American burger moguls and entrepreneurial Turkish immigrants.[1]

A little over twenty-five years ago, when McDonald's first began operations in Germany and the first Turkish *Dönerkebap* sandwich was served in the Berlin district of Kreuzberg, the last Aschinger lunch counter still offered hungry citizens their favorite dishes: *Bockwurst* and potato salad, pigs' knuckles with pureed peas, and its famous sandwiches.[2] As West Germany's economic recovery reached full pitch, patrons washed down the heavy meals with a few glasses of beer, and, best of all, as many free white-bread rolls as diners might wish to eat accompanied every dish.[3]

Little remains today of the old Aschinger empire. At a commemorative eatery on the Ku' damm, the city's fanciest shopping street during the Cold War, the old rolls free of charge are gone, and so is the old cuisine. With its rustic booths, the old photographs on the wall, and the generous slabs of grilled meat and sauerkraut, Germany's first successful fast-food chain today presents itself as an undefined "Old German" eatery.

The Aschinger restaurant group has reasons to hide its past. We will explore Aschinger's infamy in due course, but first, let us turn to an examination of the company's phenomenal success at the turn of the twentieth century. In its heyday, Aschinger was Europe's largest restaurant and hotel concern. Its empire encompassed nearly five thousand employees and over a hundred cafés, hotels, bars, restaurants, and bakeries. Aschinger owned such Berlin landmarks as Café Kranzler, the Hotel Kempinski, the amusement center Luna Park, the cafeteria at the UfA film studio in Potsdam, and the most sensational building ever constructed in Berlin, the Haus Vaterland.[4] The largest eatery in the world, Haus Vaterland held three thousand guests and a dozen different speciality restaurants all under one roof. Bedecked in Turkish fezzes, waiters brought tiny cups of steaming-hot mocha to customers. Next door, waitresses in *Dirndls* heaved steins of beer, while a full orchestra performed on a massive balcony. And the decor—surrounded by the landscape of the Rhine, completed by the Lorelei, guests marveled at a thunderstorm staged every hour.

While the Aschinger empire found its ultimate expression in such examples of Gilded Age gigantomania as the Haus Vaterland, the company's beginnings were much more humble. Like Ray Kroc, Harland Sanders, or Dave Thomas, the Aschinger saga begins as a story of bootstrapping and derring-do. A restaurant giant that could have written the Golden Arches playbook more than sixty years before McDonald's first burger was flipped, the Aschinger tale demonstrated what Germany's civil servants never ceased to deny: the viability of the mass kitchen.[5]

In 1892, two brothers, August and Carl Aschinger, opened their first quick luncheon buffet, or *Bierquelle*, on the Rosenthalerstraße. Within eight years, the brothers had opened thirty units throughout the capital, each a close replica of the original outlet.[6] In 1900, the former cook and waiter listed their enterprise as a public company on the city's stock exchange.

The key to Aschinger's success lay in its uncommonly low prices and its adoption of the new, popular "cold" fare. In no small measure, its good fortune stemmed from the liberal use of the city's most popular foodstuff, the humble white-bread breakfast roll, the *Schrippe*. The first restaurants in the chain served exclusively cold sandwiches made from the much-coveted *Schrippe*, such as the popular *Hackepeter*, minced raw meat garnished with onions and served on a soft bun. If you could not afford a *Hackepeter*, the brothers fed you anyway. As long as customers had enough money to order a beer, a basket of free rolls lay at their disposal. After initial successes, the brothers added more sandwiches to their menu, as well as a number of equally popular warm dishes. For thirty pfennig, customers relished such regional favorites as pea soup with bacon fat, roasted goose with apple sauce, and *Bockwurst* and potato salad. As the Aschingers expanded their menu to include warm entrées, some of them at prices near a mark (roughly a dime today), they kept old favorites on the menu. Other sandwich-and-beer combinations sold for less than half a mark.

From the beginning, Aschinger sought to unite the spirits of Bacchus and Gambrinus. To wash down the many rolls and warm entrées, the brothers offered customers their preferred beverage, beer, at lower prices and in greater quantity than their commercial competitors. Besides the city's famous *Weissbier* (a light, fizzy beer made using top-fermentation

yeast, typically abetted with a shot of syrup—raspberry, woodruff, and car-
away remain the most popular), customers could also imbibe Dortmund,
Munich, and Kulmbach beers.[7] All beers at Aschinger's were priced at ten
pfennig.

At these prices, one is tempted to conclude, like the *Mainzer Tageblatt*
of 1911, that Aschinger was equally popular among rich and poor.[8]
Arguably Aschinger held a better claim to the title, "restauranteur of the
people,"[9] than many of its pub-on-the-corner competitors. At Aschinger's,
customers came early and left late. A day in the life of an Aschinger quick
luncheon buffet mirrored a day in the life of a modern city. Early morn-
ings witnessed the descent of the customers on the run: skilled laborers,
artisans, and porters. At the noon hour, clerks, minor civil servants, and
office staff from nearby buildings sat down to lunch; when the shops
closed, the department store clerk, the soldier, and the laborer sauntered
up to the counter, while late-night hours brought a different customer altogether, as tourists, students, and thrill-seekers filled the restaurant's booths
and bars.[10] Hard-luck cases could order at the counter and take their food
to their table themselves, and thus skip the obligation to tip.[11]

Around 1900, the confluence of four factors—the rise of the wage
economy, growing distance between residence and workplace, shorter
lunch breaks, and, most important of all, the expansion of women's paid
labor outside the home—created the need for the mass provision of meals
in large industrial cities. Particularly around the turn of the century, the
urban metropolis, in Europe as well as North America, witnessed a variety
of novel public and private responses to the dilemma of midday feeding:
Aschinger, I would like to emphasize, was only one among many.[12] As city
officials, philanthropists, and working women changed their attitudes
toward the hitherto family affair of the midday meal, they redefined
boundaries between households and markets, workplaces and sites of
leisure.

As Berliners of different social origins gathered to consume time-honored favorites, the dining room at Aschinger's witnessed a partial subli-
mation of class. Like other staples of mass consumer culture, such as the
movies, variety shows, and tabloids, the quick-service restaurant blurred
conventional bourgeois class and gender distinctions.[13] Transitional
moments of transgression, when shopgirls rubbed elbows with the stock-
brokers and students, were possible within the disorderly spectacle of the
modern fast-food restaurant, as they were throughout the modern industrial city. In the wake of public neglect, Aschinger's created, albeit unwittingly, a distinctly modern midday habitus: a public space where real class
differences receded behind the reality of tasty food at reasonable prices
and a veneer of equal opportunity.

More than any other restaurant, Aschinger's exploited the advantages
of mass production. The engine of high-revenue, mainstream success was

predictability, the chain its vehicle. To this end, the Aschinger brothers moved quickly to integrate their business vertically, much like other Gilded Age manufacturers. Massive factory installations allowed the brothers to produce all of the components for their prefabricated meals, and ingredient-by-ingredient specifications described in painstaking detail the kitchen items, sauces, and garnishes. Now that the science of production had superseded the whims of individual chefs, nearly complete standardization of fare had become possible. The Aschinger brothers' bread factory alone, their first such acquisition, produced one million rolls a day. Soon thereafter, the firm's own slaughterhouse and *Wurst* factory ensured strict uniformity in food production.

At Aschinger's, each customer's *Bockwurst* emerged from a can fresh off the firm's assembly line, rather than out of a street vendor's hot-water container. Unlike their mom-and-pop competitors, the brothers could be sure that their sandwiches and dishes were always of the same quality. The dictates of uniformity, portion regulation, and the tightest operating controls in the business provided customers with the serene confidence that the dishes placed before them tasted, looked, and cost the same as all of those they had eaten before in the chain's many outlets. The fare at Aschinger's represented the perfect symbol of the machine age, the standardized response to the demands of limited time and fixed incomes. Aschinger's millions upon millions of sandwiches, cheese straws, and bowls of pea soup with bacon fat dwarfed the output of many other manufactured consumer products. At Aschinger's, a growing number of Berliners gladly traded the serendipity of an independent restaurant for predictability.[14]

Vertical integration enabled the brothers Aschinger to secure their hold on the customers' heart, while other innovations allowed the pair to remain in the public eye. They first placed their restaurants in the center city, then quickly expanded into the working-class neighborhoods of the north and east. Before World War I, rail passengers were denied the means to satisfy their hunger on long journeys (*Mitropa* dining cars were first joined to German trains in 1916), so the brothers saw to it that when passengers arrived in the capital, an Aschinger outlet greeted them. A quick bite-on-the-run was available at all hours of the day and night at the city's central train stations.

Visibility was an important element in the Aschinger firm's success. Aschinger's fiercest competitors, the neighborhood eateries then patronized by working Berliners, were located below ground. In an era before refrigeration, the cellar location helped restauranteurs keep their beer cool and meats and vegetables from spoiling. The Aschinger brothers, by way of contrast, placed their restaurants aboveground, always in the first story of a larger building. Unlike the basement cafés found on many city corners, where customers might find a comb, or worse, in the butter dish,

Aschinger's dishes were placed in long glass windows for all to observe.[15] From the sidewalk, the passer-by could watch the barman pour beer before customers' eyes, not, as was frequently the practice in those days, in a dark corner or behind a wall. Here customers could always see what they were getting.

As one of the Aschinger firm's detractors noted: "the little patron is mistrustful. Before he takes the bait, he loves to inspect his merchandise, to subject the wares to his thorough, drawn-out surveillance. This was, of course, all part of the reason these Aschinger characters were able to secure their mass following." Placed behind large glass windows for all to see, "the splendid yellow-red of smoked salmon, the silver luster of sardines, and the golden cheese straws" made a lasting impression even on skeptics.[16] Transparency helped to ensure that Aschinger's fare met with diners' approval, and visual guides for the presentation of customer favorites (like oysters on the half shell) whetted appetites. The quick luncheon buffet was subjected to the discriminating eye of all customers, just like "some sort of fashion boutique, a tie shop, or a book store."[17] All patrons enjoyed the service normally reserved for the propertied classes. "Indeed, one has never seen anything like this," the same skeptic concluded, "where the most prosaic wurst emerges from a glass-fronted cupboard, the architecture of which, in its ornate complexity, recalls a small Buddhist temple."[18]

At Aschinger's, both the fare and the decor celebrated modern life. The storefronts, often compared to pharmacies, with their large, single-pane glass windows, symbolized the triumph of industry.[19] Above the entrance, customers found the words, "Serve Yourself," an invocation not only to self-sufficiency but to quick dining as well. The firm equipped each restaurant kitchen with the latest implements, including gas stoves, electric appliances, a beer cellar, and a walk-in freezer. Aschinger's venues were among the first in the city to boast modern ventilation and to advertise in neon light.[20]

Like so many staple features of mass culture, the Aschinger lunch hall enshrined an intriguing amalgam of needs and desires. Modernity, technology, and rugged individualism, the cornerstones of Aschinger's corporate ethos, dominated, nonetheless tempered by careful homage to tradition. True, the brothers Aschinger stopped short of hanging farm implements on the walls, as a few of their competitors did. Still, much like the Massachusetts businessman, Howard Johnson, who decorated restaurants in New England in colonial style with "white clapboard exteriors, homey lamps glowing in fake dormer windows, and roofs topped by prim cupolas and weathervanes,"[21] the Aschingers felt compelled to invent traditions of their own, based, appropriately enough, on the brothers' attachment to their fictional birthplace, Bavaria. Tempered rusticity began with the unmistakable emblem of Germany's proudest province, fields of baby blue diamonds set in snow-white. Storefronts, delivery trucks, tablecloths, even employees' uniforms sported the colors. Bavaria, then as now, connoted purity, tradition, and a sense of comfort. To metropolitans, the province's rolling hills and idyllic villages appeared far enough away to be exotic, close enough to be visited one day. Adding to the sense of ambiance, reportedly every time an Aschinger bartender appeared in *Lederhosen*, or an Aschinger waitress in *Dirndl*, the gathered assemblage shouted "Cheers!"[22]

The best evidence of Aschinger's adherence to tradition came, oddly enough, from Quisiana, an American competitor and Berlin's most prominent purveyor of automated restaurants. "The mechanical furnishings are arguably the most complete one could imagine," boasted a Quisiana brochure; and rightly so: certainly no outfit kept sandwiches as fresh as Quisiana did, in refrigerated, letter-sized chambers.[23] Beer, too, came made to order, always the same temperature, always the same taste, and in cups always filled to the brim. At the drop of a coin, patrons enjoyed food and drink in simple, comfortable, and, in stark contrast to Aschinger's, quiet surroundings. At Quisiana's outlet in the center of the city's entertainment district, no patron suffered the nuisance of a feckless server or a nosy barkeeper, to say nothing of the indignity of ringing cowbells and waitresses in *Dirndls*.

Yet for all of its novelty, the Quisiana outlet never posed a serious threat to the Aschinger empire. Unlike New York, where, by the 1930s, one chain of coin-gobbling Automats attracted a quarter of a million customers a day, Berlin never took to the self-service cafeteria.[24] At Aschinger's quick lunch buffet, the waiter might ignore you, or your beer might have more of a head on it than your neighbor's; still, Berlin diners seemed to prefer it that way. Like the fast-food giants that now dominate America's culinary landscape or the successful London penny eateries of the day, such as Lyons, A.B.C., and other "corner houses," Aschinger's stopped well short of the machine-age monotony offered by Quisiana's self-service vending machines.[25] Guaranteed excitement and conviviality, within comfortable limits, provided Aschinger's diverse range of customers with a place of refuge from the city's daily rigors.

A distinct breed of patron, referred to by company officials as the "shamed," captured one newspaperman's imagination. Rubbing elbows with the lower orders was fine with some, but for other Berliners, the associations were too powerful, and obvious, to admit to friends, neighbors, or family members. Near the end of the month, before paychecks had come, many a salaried employee would "clandestinely take refuge at a Blue and White, a course of action they contemptuously deny."[26] On the day in question, the "shamed" blended in among the crowds: "They don't show themselves in these parts (so they claim!), and they cannot, for heaven's sake, be discovered by acquaintances. But they are so incredibly hungry, they agree to part with their last mark and toss down a *Brat*. Oh how good it tastes, oh how the will to live once again begins to course through the veins. Cheers to Aschinger!"[27] While customers from the polite classes denied their pleasure in the fare of commoners, the owners joined in the game of masks. In order to hide their small-town roots, the brothers pretended to be Bavarians (their southern German accents demanded some sort of explanation), originally from Nuremberg. In fact, the pair hailed from the Swabian village of Derdingen in Württemberg.

Contemporaries knew of the brothers' humble origins, if not their place of birth, a state of affairs the brothers sought, with considerable success, to turn to their advantage. August, the younger brother, was known to the public as a "modest, rather patient personality," whose passion for deer hunting met with approval among virtually all German men.[28] His brother Carl was a bit more colorful, perhaps even truer to the pair's roots. According to one report, the elder sibling spent most evenings in the company's restaurant on the Leipziger Street, where he could invariably be found at the table reserved for regulars. When his coachman appeared before the entrance to take him home for the evening, Carl ordered the waiter to present his driver with a mug of "the good stuff."[29]

Aschinger's ethos reflected the ambition and energy of Europe's young metropolis. On their frequent lunchtime inspection tours, the brothers often stopped to chat with customers or at least to shake men's hands. In August's view, his customer was too busy to spend much time at the lunch counter; "a quick bite is enough," he allowed, for Berlin's workmen. As long as they "remained seated for ten minutes," the restaurateur was pleased. As the bottled-beer merchant (and later foreign minister) Gustav Stresemann observed of Aschinger: "the constant hurrying and scurrying, coming and going, barely leaves anyone time to sit—one downs a beer standing up and, with a glance at the watch, rushes on."[30] With pride, the brothers referred to their rushed customers, in English, as "makers" and "self-made men."[31] The Aschingers' "self-made man" credo was the mantra for a class that refused to see itself as a class. For these men, the experience of eating out at Aschinger's was not a class-specific phenomenon; on the contrary, the restaurant chain succeeded precisely because it placed the individual at the pinnacle of society.[32]

Low margins, low prices, high stock returns, and high volume provided the brothers with operating capital, and in 1908, with nearly fifty luncheon buffets citywide, the brothers decided to move into the upscale restaurant business. Perhaps they were seeking to diversify their enterprise or to establish their credentials as serious gastronomes. Whatever the reason, their investments did not meet with great success. Their first acquisition, the wine tavern and Hotel Rheingold, cost the brothers over five million marks. The Rheingold's architect, Bruno Schmitz, had designed such other symbols of Gilded Age gigantomania as the Völkerschlachtdenkmal in Leipzig and the Deutsches Eck in Coblenz.[33]

The Rheingold's enormous dining hall sat five thousand, large enough, as one critic surmised, to host a production of *Oedipus Rex*.[34] Whereas the Aschinger lunch counters were unpretentious, the new restaurants, the one at the Rheingold, as well as the Fürstenhof, were palatial and pompous. Neither love nor money, nor the crawfish specials (at ninety pfennig a dozen), brought either colossus out of the red.

In a decision the firm would repeat in the 1920s, the brothers sought to compensate for their losses in the upscale restaurant business through the creation of new markets for old products. In particular, the steady stream of dinner buns rolling off the company's bread factory assembly line demanded the exercise of creative salesmanship. In a few short years, the brothers opened 23 special bakery outlets, most of them small booths that peddled pretzels, breakfast rolls, and cheese sticks. The Aschingers also reached agreements to sell their breadstuffs in cake shops, cafés, and quick luncheon buffets. Yet here, too, though, the Aschingers seemed to have missed the mark: a huge advertisement campaign could not bring bread sales anywhere near projections.

Notwithstanding the company's unfortunate investments, Aschinger's continued to post record sales: in the immediate prewar years, profits near a half-million dollars annually permitted the company to offer stockholders a handsome annual rate of return between 8 percent and 12 percent. Part of the reason for Aschinger's success was low labor costs. Crowds, mass production, and mind-numbing repetitive labor had created the need for meals outside the home at noon. Meanwhile, new innovations, particularly the telephone, the electric light, the cash register, and the escalator, increased the efficiency, safety, and ease of producing, as well as consuming, meals outside of the home. In Aschinger's, the restaurant trade offered its correlative to the innovations that had spurred the emergence of consumer society.

In the company's boom years, Aschinger's had become not only the largest restauranteur in Berlin, but also one of its largest landlords. Before opening a new quick luncheon buffet, the brothers acquired the entire building and refurbished the upper floors as housing for workers. The company's policy held a special allure for recent arrivals to the city, particularly women. With the southern German atmosphere came "service from a tender hand." Waitresses were at the time something of a novelty in northern Germany.[35] Aschinger offered newly arrived women work, half-price meals, and, most important, a place to live, all in one fell swoop. By 1914, about half of the company's employees were female.

Each woman employee of Aschinger received a room of her own; in return, she agreed to dormitory cleaning duty, a ten o'clock curfew, and the oversight of an in-house landlady.[36] A decision to quit one's job meant both a loss of livelihood and the roof over one's head. Those who approached managers with the wish to seek new accommodations were told they could seek employment elsewhere as well.[37] Aschinger's remarkably low labor turnover helped to keep prices down for its customers and profits high for stockholders.

Aschinger's labor record, at least before World War I, was not as abysmal as this saga might suggest. Though closed to female employees (German women were not legally permitted to join national political organizations before 1908), the main German unions were represented at Aschinger's. The socialist-affiliated "free" trade unions, the Central Association of Restaurant Employees, as well as the main national metal, woodworkers, food, and transportation unions, had members in the company's restaurants and factories. Through the foundation of a company union for the waiters, the Waiters' White and Blue Association, the owners nonetheless maintained their own strikebreaking force.

Strikes, at least before World War I, were rare at Aschinger's, in part because of the industry structure, due in part, as even Social Democrats acknowledged, to the company's relatively humane labor record. "In the first years, working conditions and the treatment of employees were widely praised," reported the sober socialist daily, *Vorwärts*.

> Working hours were, although quite long, at least somewhat regulated. Wages were generally good. As long as August Aschinger maintained dominant influence [within the company], employees were never referred to a professional mediator, for disputes were mediated directly by one of his managing directors. The favorable influence of the firm's founders has, in recent years, been increasingly on the wane. Particularly in the recently established, larger restaurants, above all in the wine tavern, "Rheingold," working conditions have, often enough, provoked a public outcry.[38]

Many employees in the larger enterprises, the socialist opinion maker reported, were not paid at all but instead required to live from tips.

Cheap labor, low turnover, and massive economies of scale helped Aschinger's to turn the social need for the provision of meals into a business success. Even after August's death in 1911 (Carl had passed away two years earlier), the Aschinger firm continued to post profits of over a half million marks a year. Led by August's eighteen-year old son, Fritz, and the founders' close personal friend, the Bavarian businessman Hans Lohnert, the company weathered the upheavals of war, revolution, and hyperinflation.

The new directors' accomplishment was no mean feat, for the call to arms sharply reduced restaurant revenues, as loyal customers left for the front. Workers lost their jobs and families saved on food. Military authorities made life especially difficult for restaurateurs, forbidding officers and soldiers to consume alcohol, forcing the city's pubs to shut early, and closing the dance halls. Beer was, in any case, in remarkably short supply, for most barley had come from the Russian Empire.

From 1914 to 1923, shortage was the hallmark of the day. Coal, wood, and electricity, to say nothing of foodstuffs, were always in short supply. Aschinger's wartime menu reflected the changes. Potato and fish dishes replaced the time-honored meat favorites. Yet a *Schnitzel* was a lot easier to prepare than a vegetable dish. Chronic shortages of red meat, fresh game, chicken, coffee, tea, chocolate, and sugar made substitution nearly impossible. Even cleaning became a taxing chore. Linen, sponges, mops, and other cleaning items could only be obtained with great effort and in limited quantities.[39] Periodic confiscations of appliances made of nickel, aluminum, copper, and brass frustrated the best of plans. Even the table linens were not immune from confiscation by military procurement officers. Employee fealty, a cornerstone of Aschinger's success, was anything but assured. Cooks, waiters, and bartenders were called to arms, and women, especially sought after to chop, wash, and peel vegetables, increasingly left the company for more lucrative work in the armaments industry.[40]

Aschinger's insisted upon special treatment from the city's much-harassed rationing authorities. In a 1916 letter to the city's chief rationing authority, Georg Simonsohn, the company's director, pronounced that: "through our efforts to secure the allegiance of our regular customers—the core of Berlin's gainfully employed—we believe to have, on the one hand, fulfilled our duty to the Fatherland, and, on the other, served the future of our business." Through their efforts to meet customers' demands in extraordinary times, the directors believed they were "entitled to special consideration and assistance from state and local authorities for the duration of the war and during the transition to normal economic conditions."[41]

As the city prepared its own venture in the meal business, and Berlin's philanthropists offered the first serious challenge to the company's position in a generation, Aschinger's rested its claim for special treatment on its role as the chief provider of a much-needed, if little appreciated, social service. While Hermann Abraham, the city's leading philanthropic restaurateur, was firmly, if politely, shown the ration office's door, Simonsohn granted Aschinger's request for "special consideration and assistance." On the commodity most important to the firm's success as well as to the city's own rationing scheme—bread—municipal authorities agreed to break their own rules. While citizens waited hours for loaves of adulterated bread, the city granted Aschinger's an exemption from its onerous ration card system. In an unprecedented offer, the city allowed the firm to bake as much bread as it could sell. Not surprisingly, the "exceedingly palatable baked goods" enjoyed what the company's directors described as a "flourishing demand."[42]

The nod and the wink of rationing authorities allowed Aschinger to emerge from the war in solid shape. The hyperinflation, in turn, proved to be a blessing in disguise, because it wiped out the debts incurred with the construction of the Fürstenhof and Haus Vaterland and, much to the delight of Aschinger's new directors, a number of smaller competitors as well. Tough times shrank the restaurant industry—the number of restaurants and pubs in Prussia declined from 223,881 in 1913 to 167,338 in 1922.[43] Like so many other branches of the economy under the Weimar Republic, much of Berlin's restaurant trade fell into the hands of a small number of large companies.

Already before the war, the Aschinger brothers had treated the lunch counters less like a golden calf than a cash cow. Not content with the enterprise's fame as the preferred bistro of the common folk, in the 1920s the new directors set their sights on the city's grand hotels. Among the firm's acquisitions were the Hotel Kaiserhof at Wilhelm Square, the Hotel Baltic, the Esplanade on the Bellevue Street, the Zentralhotel, the Hotel Bristol, the Grandhotel am Knie, and the Palasthotel. In addition, Aschinger's bought two Berlin landmarks—the Wintergarten, a first-class variety theater near Potsdamer Platz, as well as the Kranzler enterprise, including its famous café on the Ku' damm.[44] The company even built new headquarters, a massive structure on the Saarbrückener Street, near Alexanderplatz in the district of Prenzlauer Berg. By the end of the decade, Aschinger's owned virtually every major hotel in the city, with the significant exception of the Kempinski.

Aschinger's move into the hospitality business proved to be ill timed and the accumulation of high-priced property disastrous to the restaurant group's ever-shakier bottom line. High taxes, the federal government's foreign exchange and tariff policies, and fierce competition among the remaining oligarchs and from a new breed of low-priced guest houses kept Aschinger from realizing a return on its heavily mortgaged investments.[45] The city's reserve of under- and unemployed permitted Aschinger's to squeeze its labor force further; between 1910 and 1913, wages had constituted 15 percent to 17 percent of total sales, in 1924, 14 percent, thereafter, around 10 percent.[46] Soon labor troubles joined the company's ever lengthening list of woes. Forced overtime, refusals to pay for extra hours, illegitimate deductions, and arbitrary dismissals led to a growing number of disputes.[47]

Dominance of the city's hotel business proved beyond Aschinger's expertise and probably beyond the company's means. An eight-million-mark loan in 1926 averted financial disaster, though two years later the firm again faced ruin. As the golden twenties screeched to a halt, the city's highly leveraged high-class eateries and hotels were among the first to lose business. In 1931, the popular Palais de Dance closed its doors, citing "financial difficulties"; a year later, the well-liked Café Josty, with its large terrace onto Potsdamer Platz, declared bankruptcy. Many restaurants changed hands, others died off altogether. Even Aschinger's quick luncheon buffets were affected. As times grew difficult for the firm, the directors raised prices for warm dishes and sandwiches. The soups got thinner, and, in a disastrous move, the famous free basket of rolls disappeared from tables. Once all units had been company-owned, but hard times encouraged the firm's management to license generous, standard-price franchise deals to cafeterias, snack bars, and department stores. The Aschinger chain's attempts to use other penny businesses as an anchor nearly sank the ship. Between 1929 and 1933, sales dropped by nearly 50 percent.

Even before times really got tough, Aschinger's, like so many other big businesses of the day, turned to the state for assistance. While Weimar's democrats had turned a deaf ear to Aschinger's concerns, a new party, the National Socialists, seemed to favor the enterprise from its very beginning. Even before his seizure of power, Adolf Hitler and other prominent party officials had arranged quarters in Aschinger's Hotel Kaiserhof, a hundred yards from the Reich Chancellery. On the night of the Nazis' seizure of power, the hotel served oysters, champagne, and caviar to the nation's new elite, while the movement's thugs enjoyed free pork knuckles, sauerkraut, and beerwurst at the company's franchise on the Schönhauser Allee.[48]

For all of his commercial failings, Fritz Aschinger understood how to change with the times. In 1933, Fritz offered Nazi Party members leading company positions: the directorships of personnel, the bakery and cake operations, technical support, kitchen management, as well as employee training and instruction. Fritz's decision paid big dividends, as Aschinger's was chosen as the party's and the government's chief supplier of foodstuffs. The company received the contract to provide food and drinks for the capital's May Day celebrations; the next day, the Nazis eliminated the nation's independent labor organizations. Aschinger received concession contracts for a number of well-publicized state and party functions, including the commemoration for the new air force ministry at the old Sports Palace, the party's annual conferences in Nuremberg, and, most spectacular of all, the 1936 Olympics.[49] When Nazi propaganda chief Joseph Goebbels entertained foreign dignitaries on the exotic Pfaueninsel, when athletes enjoyed a meal at the Olympic village in Charlottenburg, or when foreign visitors grabbed a snack at the Brandenburg Gate, each contributed to the rising fortunes of Berlin's oldest fast-food establishment.

Most important to the Aschingers company's improved fortunes was the Nazi liquidation of businesses owned by German Jews.[50] After the achievement of full employment in 1936 and with the publicity success of the Olympic Games safely behind them, Nazi leaders endorsed a second wave of Aryanization aimed at the nation's larger Jewish-owned enterprises. The Aschinger concern, under Fritz's active leadership, led negotiations to acquire a major competitor, the Kempinski chain. Kempinski, a firm of more than a thousand employees with complementary strengths in the hotel and restaurant industries, became the feather in Aschinger's cap. Within a few short years, Aschinger's was once again in the black.[51]

After the acquisition of the Kempinski concern, Aschinger's complicity in the crimes of the regime became a matter of course. When the Germans invaded Poland, Aschinger delivery vehicles brought men and munitions to the front. When the National Socialists occupied the Netherlands, Aschinger's acquired Kempinski's assets there, as well as a canned food factory. By 1944, 721 citizens from 23 occupied nations, mostly from France, Italy, and the Ukraine, were transported to Berlin and forced to work in the company's hotels, cafés, cafeterias, and quick luncheon buffets.[52]

As during World War I, the rush on Aschinger's quick luncheon buffets, particularly at noon, had increased. Citizens were unhappy with rationed foodstuffs, and many worked too far from their homes to warrant an extra trip during the lunch hour. Increasingly, air raids forced many women and children to abandon Germany's northern cities for safer zones in the south of the country, leaving men without a warm lunch to return to. In August 1944, the respected Swiss daily, the *Neue Züricher Zeitung*, estimated that over ten million Germans consumed at least one meal each day at a restaurant.[53] As late as 1944, Aschinger's involvement in the crimes of the state yielded substantial financial rewards. Between 1938 and 1944, sales rose higher every year, except in 1940.[54] In 1943, annual profits topped four million marks, and in 1944, the company paid off its hotel debts from the 1920s (an eight-million-mark loan from 1926) and doubled its capital stock to six million marks.[55]

When the Red Army entered the city of Berlin in May 1945, the Aschinger empire, notwithstanding bomb damage to many quick luncheon buffets and hotels, remained intact. Fourteen luncheon buffets, a string of high-class restaurants and hotels (including the Kempinski acquisitions), seventeen bakery outlets, a dozen cafés, a handful of wine cellars, two delicatessens, and even the firm's food canning facilities still operated.

During the summer of 1945, an Allied-appointed Berlin municipal authority set itself to the task of satisfying the workday dietary needs of the city's remaining two and a half million inhabitants. The lack of gas, coal, and shortage of foodstuffs would, authorities quickly surmised, lead to substantial nutritional hardship in the winter. While the Allies, as in 1920, assumed responsibility for an ambitious child-feeding program, the new municipal authority concentrated its efforts on the nutritional needs of the adult population. In thirty "people's restaurants," or *Volksgaststätten*, spread throughout the city, municipal authorities drafted a plan to prepare warm lunches for a hundred thousand hungry citizens.[56] The new kitchens needed tables, chairs, lamps, and cooking utensils. For that reason alone, the new city councillors concluded, their enterprise required partners.[57] To this end, the city fathers invited Fritz Aschinger to join them at the Rathaus conference hall for a discussion.

The Aschinger enterprise, several members knew, had run two mass kitchens during the war, at Spittelmarkt and at the Friedrichstrasse train station. Aschinger's decision had been born, like so many in those days, of political expediency. As Spethmann, engineer of the Kempinski buyout, had declared during the war: "It goes without saying that we also put ourselves at the disposal of the idea of [the Nazi-sponsored] community restaurants, which were however denied a sweeping success. We attribute [this lack of success] to the public's aversion to commit itself to anyone in particular when it comes to food."[58] Because the state had exempted them from the most onerous aspects of the new rationing system, and because the Nazis had rewarded the Aschingers handsomely for their loyalty to the state, company officials could live with the nuisance of a few token "public restaurants." As long as they were allowed to arrange meal production as they saw fit, officials could direct customers' anger away from the enterprise and toward the state's management of the food supply. The Nazi regime had slapped several fines on Aschinger's for price and quality violations, but, on the whole, the state had allowed the company the same freedom it enjoyed during peacetime. As far as the Nazis were concerned, they had little choice but to let the masses enjoy their free rolls if they wished to avoid dissent on the home front.[59]

As Fritz Aschinger approached his meeting with the new city government, he might have well expected a partner as equally pliable as the former municipal administration. Certainly the new authority controlled the food supply, but Aschinger's, so the word at City Hall went, had unlocked the secrets of customers' taste, a mission town officials believed their own predecessors in 1916 had failed to achieve.[60]

The proposed cooperation never got off the ground. Aschinger demanded absolute control over production, a request the city officials, to their credit, refused to honor. In Aschinger's eyes, the city aimed to take his hard-earned monopoly status away from them. The municipal authority, for its part, insisted upon the temporary nature of its proposed program. Aschinger offered the city a donation of 50,000 marks and declined further participation in the new project.

Aschinger's decision to abandon the enterprise failed to weaken the councillors' resolve. On November 1, 1945, the city government, in conjunction with philanthropic organizations, consumer cooperatives, and labor leaders, opened its first people's restaurant.[61] Fifteen months later, the city was operating more than 3,500 eateries: roughly two thirds of the feeding centers were former canteens, the other third were restaurants proper. By the end of 1946, the city government fed about 10 percent of the city's population at least one meal a day.[62]

Not Aschinger, but the Cold War, cut short the magistrater's ambitious plans to serve, albeit temporarily, as the city's chief restauranteur. In the east of Berlin, the new Socialist Unity Party confiscated Aschinger's properties on May 1, 1947, as city planning splintered among authorities in each of the city's four zones of occupation.[63] Along with the new people's restaurants in the Soviet Zone, East German authorities laid the groundwork for the creation of the *Handelsorganisation*, or trade organization, the main, state-sponsored, consumer service enterprise in the future East Germany.

Fritz Aschinger had decided to begin a new life at Germany's zero hour. Shortly after the war's end, he moved from his apartment in the central offices on the Saarbrückener Street to a luxury apartment on the Ku' damm. Though he claimed never to have been a party man, in 1946 Aschinger joined West Germany's new conservative party, the Christlich Demokratische Union, or CDU, and went back to work. In the city's western sectors, he reopened the Delphipalast, the Rütlibar, and, shortly thereafter, the Gasteiner Hof in Wilmersdorf, a quick luncheon buffet in Wedding, and, on the Ku' damm, the café Schloß Marquart.[64] For all of his efforts, however, business did not return to normal. News of the Soviet seizure of company assets, accusations of membership in the Nazi Party, as well as involvement in war crimes led Fritz Aschinger to take his own life.[65]

Aschinger's mass-produced variety at bargain-basement prices laid the foundation for one of modern Germany's most phenomenal commercial success stories. Through a combination of consumer-oriented capitalism and time-honored tradition, Aschinger's was many things to many people. Its low prices enabled the cabman, the skilled workman, even the seamstress to enjoy the same fare and clubby, dark-wood atmosphere as the minor clerk, the civil servant, and the student. And yet, though the champion of meal provision, the once-famous Aschinger firm proved a poor custodian of the public interest.

NOTES

1. *Hamburger Tageblatt* (January 31, 1911), Landesarchiv Berlin (hereafter cited as LA Berlin), Rep. 225 Aschinger AG, 853 Zeitungsausschnitte zum Tode August Aschingers.
2. Eberhard Seidel-Pielen's book, *Aufgespießt. Wie der Döner über die Deutschen kam* (Hamburg: Rotbuch Verlag, 1996), provides insights into the world around the *Dönerkebap*— its producers, its customers, and the bonds the Turkish sandwich has fostered between Germans and Turks. Throughout Germany, the Döner industry (admittedly a hodgepodge of many very small operations) boasts higher sales than McDonald's; in Berlin, Döner sales of 920 million top McDonald's numbers by nearly two and a half times. Seidel-Pielen, *Aufgespießt*, 13, 14. The *Currywurst*, a favorite among culinary traditionalists, is (popular lore notwithstanding) a distant third.
3. Walter Henry Nelson, *The Berliners: Portrait of a People and a City* (New York: D. McKay, 1969), pp. 282, 283.
4. Karin and Arno Reinfrank, *Berlin. Two Cities Under Seven Flags, A Kaleidoscopic A-Z* (New York: St. Martin's Press, 1987), p. 12. Siegfried Kracauer once described the Haus Vaterland as "not the world as it actually is, but the world as it is portrayed in hit songs. A world which has been gone over by a vacuum cleaner, so that not a single speck of the dust of everyday life remains," Siegfried Kracauer, *Die Angestellten* (Frankfurt: Suhrkamp, 1971), p. 96. This quote is cited in Detlev J.K. Peukert, *The Weimar Republic: The Crisis of Classical Modernity* trans. Richard Deveson (New York: Hill and Wang, 1989), p. 158.
5. On restaurants (soda fountains, lunchrooms, main-street cafés, diners, and automats) in the United States before widespread use of the automobile, see John A. Jakle and Keith Sculle, *Fast Food: Roadside Restaurants in the Automobile Age* (Baltimore: Johns Hopkins University Press, 1999), pp. 20–39.

6. LA Berlin, Siebente Beilage zum *Hamburger Fremdenblatt*, no. 26 (January 31,1911), Rep. 225 Aschinger AG, 853 Zeitungsausschnitte zum Tode August Aschingers.

7. LA Berlin, *Leipziger Neuste Nachrichten* (January 30, 1911), Rep. 225 Aschinger AG, 853 Zeitungsausschnitte zum Tode August Aschingers.

8. LA Berlin, *Mainzer Tageblatt* (January 31, 1911), Rep. 225 Aschinger AG, 853 Zeitungsausschnitte zum Tode August Aschingers.

9. LA Berlin, "Der Gastwirt des Volkes," *Deutsche Nachrichten Berlin* (January 31, 1911), Rep. 225 Aschinger AG, 853 Zeitungsausschnitte zum Tode August Aschingers.

10. LA Berlin, *Kölnische Zeitung* (February 6, 1911); "Onder de Streep. Berlijnsch Allerlei," *Algemeen Handelsblad*, Amsterdam (February 7, 1911), Rep. 225 Aschinger AG, 853 Zeitungsausschnitte zum Tode August Aschingers.

11. LA Berlin, *Barmer Zeitung* (January 30, 1911), Rep. 225 Aschinger AG, 853 Zeitungsausschnitte zum Tode August Aschingers.

12. Restaurants as we know them today were only one among the many new repositories of social meaning organized around the most important daily act of reproduction, eating. I discuss at length the full range of forces which informed the development of restaurants, school meals, philanthropic eateries, wartime rationing, the instruction of young women in cookery, and home meals in Keith Allen, *Hungrige Metropole. Essen und Wohlfahrt in Berlin, 1870–1930* (Hamburg: Ergebnisse, 2001). See also, Harald Dehne, "Das Essen Wird Also Auch Ambulando Eingenommen, in *Brot, Brei Und Was Daztuglehört* (Urich: Chronos, 1992), pp. 105–123; Jakob Tanner, *Fabrik-Mahlzen. Ernährung-Wissenschaft, Industrie-Arbeit und Volks Ernährungl in Der Schweiz 1890–1950* (Zurich: Chronos, 1999).

13. In this sense, my findings support the arguments of Lynn Abrams, *Workers' Culture in Imperial Germany: Leisure and Recreation in the Rhineland and Westphalia* (New York: Routledge, 1992), pp. 169–195, and Peter Fritzsche, *Reading Berlin 1900* (Cambridge: Harvard University Press, 1996), 127–169.

14. Americans, too, increasingly sought reassurance in culinary sameness, as illustrated by the success of the Wichita-based chain, White Castle. As a company brochure distributed to customers read: "When you sit at a White Castle, remember you are being served on the same kind of counter; the coffee you drink made in accordance with a certain formula; the hamburger you eat is prepared exactly the same way over a gas flame of the same intensity; the cups you drink from are identical with thousands of cups that thousands of other people are using at the same moment; the same standard of cleanliness protects your food," Harvey Levenstein, *A Social History of Eating in Modern America* (New York: Oxford University Press, 1993), p. 51.

15. In Germany as in the United States, concerns about food purity led entrepreneurs to create restaurants which placed a premium on cleanliness. The concern with hygiene, however, appears to have been much stronger in the United States than in Germany. See Harvey Levenstein, *Revolution at the Table: The Transformation of the American Diet* (New York: Oxford University Press, 1988), pp. 183–193. Through the elimination of the "saloons," Prohibition in the United States greatly accelerated the growth of chain restaurants. Jakle and Sculle, *Fast Food*, pp. 20–39.

16. LA Berlin, *Tageblatt für Nord-China* (February 18, 1911), Rep. 225 Aschinger AG, 853 Zeitungsausschnitte zum Tode August Aschingers.

17. LA Berlin, Walter Turszinsky, "Das Problem Aschinger," *Berliner Montagszeitung* (February 6, 1911), Rep. 225 Aschinger AG, 853 Zeitungsausschnitte zum Tode August Aschingers.

18. LA Berlin, Walter Turszinsky, "Das Problem Aschinger," *Berliner Montagszeitung* (February 6, 1911), Rep. 225 Aschinger AG, 853 Zeitungsausschnitte zum Tode August Aschingers.

19. LA Berlin, *Frankfurter Zeitung* (January 31, 1911), Rep. 225 Aschinger AG, 853 Zeitungsausschnitte zum Tode August Aschingers.

20. LA Berlin, Nr. 697–T2/33, Rep. 225 Aschinger AG, 697 Kurz-Chronik der A. A-G.

21. Harvey Levenstein, *Paradox of Plenty: A Social History of Eating in Modern America* (New York: Oxford University Press, 1993), p. 48. By 1940 the New England chain had grown to 125 restaurants, two thirds of which were franchised.

22. "Aschinger, Carl, Aschinger, August," *Berliner Biographisches Lexikon*, ed. Bodo Rollka, Volker Spiess, and Bernhard Thieme (Berlin: Haude and Spener, 1993), p. 19.

23. *Quisiana-Automatenfabrik G.m.b.H. Sonderdruck aus: Die Entwicklung Groß-Berlins. Die Führenden und ihr Werk. Abtl. 3, Gewerbe, Handel, Industrie nach 1910*, p. 50.

24. Levenstein, *Paradox of Plenty*, p. 50. Jakle and Sculle claim that automats were perfected in Sweden; according to them, Philadelphia, not New York, boasted the first automats. They also argue that, as in Berlin, vending was too impersonal to enjoy widespread succees. Jakle and Sculle, *Fast Food*, pp. 34–36.

25. On "popular catering" in 1920s England, the best guide is John Burnett, *Plenty and Want: A Social History of Diet in England from 1815 to the Present Day* (London: Nelson, 1966), p. 296.

26. LA Berlin, *Tageblatt für Nord-China* (February 18, 1911), Rep. 225 Aschinger AG, 853 Zeitungsausschnitte zum Tode August Aschingers.
27. LA Berlin, *Deutsche Nachrichten Berlin* (January 31, 1911), Rep. 225 Aschinger AG, 853 Zeitungsausschnitte zum Tode August Aschingers.
28. LA Berlin, *Berliner Lokal Anzeiger* (January 28, 1911), Rep. 225 Aschinger AG, 853 Zeitungsausschnitte zum Tode August Aschingers.
29. LA Berlin, *Leipziger Neuste Nachrichten* (January 30, 1911), Rep. 225 Aschinger AG, 853 Zeitungsausschnitte zum Tode August Aschingers.
30. Gustav Stresemann, "Die Entwickung des Berliner Flaschenbiergeschäfts," Ph.D dissertation, Leipzig, 1900, pp. 22–23, cited in Gottfried Korff, "Mentalität und Kommunikation in der Großstadt: Berliner Notizen zur 'inneren' Urbanisation," in *Großstädt: Aspekte empirischer Kulturforschung*, ed. Theodor Kohlmann and Hermann Bausinger (Berlin: Staatliche Museen Preussischer Kulturbesitz, 1985), p. 352.
31. LA Berlin, "Der Gastwirt des Volkes," *Deutsche Nachrichten Berlin* (January 31, 1911), Rep. 225 Aschinger AG, 853 Zeitungsausschnitte zum Tode August Aschingers. I have not found evidence to suggest that the Aschinger example influenced fast-food marketers in the United States. On the receptivity of American economic model in Germany in the post–World War I period more generally, see Mary Nolan, *Visions of Modernity. American Business and the Modernization of Germany* (New York: Oxford University Press, 1994).
32. In its celebration of the modern—particularly the ostensibly American urge to rationalize (the Aschingers' commercial innovations were, after all, years ahead of American and British developments)—the Aschinger phenomenon challenges the myth of the "special path," or *Sonderweg*, of nineteenth-century German history. David Blackbourn and Geoff Eley, *The Pecuilarities of German History* (New York: Oxford University Press, 1984).
33. *Berlin und seine Bauten. Teil VIII Bauten für Handel und Gewerbe. Band "B" Gastgewerbe*, ed. the Architekten und Ingenieur-Verein zu Berlin (Berlin: Eigentum des Vereins, 1980), pp. 61, 62.
34. LA Berlin, Walter Turszinsky, "Das Problem Aschinger," *Berliner Montagszeitung* (February 6, 1911), Rep. 225 Aschinger AG, 853 Zeitungsausschnitte zum Tode August Aschingers.
35. Alexander Meyer, *Aus guter alter Zeit. Berliner Bilder und Erinnerungen* (Stuttgart: Deutsche Verlags-Anstalt, 1909), pp. 110–119.
36. LA Berlin, Rep. 751/1 VEB "Aktivist," 80 Betriebschronik des VEB Aktivist 1945–49, "Wie lebten nun Arbeiterinnen und Arbeiter bei Aschinger?" p. 4.
37. See "Die Aschinger Kaserne," *Rote Fahne* (March 23, 1930). Room and board was also provided to women working in prewar France's largest department store. See Michael Miller, *The Bon Marché. Bourgeois Culture and the Department Store, 1869–1920* (Princeton: Princeton University Press, 1981), pp. 105–108, 220–221, 223.
38. LA Berlin, *Vorwärts* (February 1, 1911), Rep. 225 Aschinger AG, 853 Zeitungsausschnitte zum Tode August Aschingers.
39. LA Berlin, Rep. 225 Aschinger AG, 191 Geschäftsbericht und Bilanzrechnung.
40. *Kriegswuchervorschriften. Heft 3: Kriegsverordnungen für Gastwirtschaften und Lebensmittelhandlungen*, ed. Herbert Conrad (Berlin, 1918).
41. LA Berlin, Rep. 225 Aschinger AG, 191 Geschäftsbericht und Bilanzrechnung.
42. LA Berlin, *Bericht des Vorstandes der Aschinger's Aktien-Gesellschaft für das Geschäftsjahr 1916*, Rep. 225 Aschinger AG 192 Geschäftsbericht u. Bilanzrechnung.
43. Schubert, "Die wirtschaftliche Lage des Schankgewerbes in Preußen," 13.
44. See *Handelzeitung des Berliner Tageblatts* (September 22, 1926); *Berliner Tageblatt* (August 26, 1926).
45. Pracht, *M. Kempinski & Co.*, p. 65.
46. LA Berlin, Nr. 697–T2/33, Rep. 225 Aschinger AG, 697 Kurz-Chronik der A. A-G.
47. *Bericht der Hauptverwaltung 1921–1923. Zentralverband der Hotel-, Restaurant- und Café-Angestellten* (Berlin, 1924), pp. 3–7.
48. LA Berlin, Rep. 751/1 VEB "Aktivist," 80 Betriebschronik des VEB Aktivist 1945–49, "Nach 1933 nahm der Betrieb einen beträchtlichen Aufschwung," 12.
49. LA Berlin, Vertag zwischen der Gaudienststelle Berlin der NS-Gemeinschaft "Kraft durch Freude" vertreten durch den Gauwart, Pg. Günther Adam, und den Gau-Kassenwart, Pg. Günther Walde, in folgendem Verpächter genannt und der Aschinger, Berlin, den 15 Juli 1936, Aschinger's Aktien Gesellschaft, Rep. 225 Aschinger AG, 268 Olympiade 1936.
50. LA Berlin, Rep. 225 Aschinger AG, 548 Preiseinhaltung in Restaurants.
51. See Pracht, *M. Kempinski & Co.*, p. 65; Walter Kiaulehn, *Berlin, Schicksal einer Weltstadt* (Munich: Brederstein, 1958), p. 225; "Berthold Kempinski," *Berliner Biographisches Lexikon*, p. 216.
52. LA Berlin, Nr. 697–T2/33, Rep. 225 Aschinger AG, 697 Kurz-Chronik der A. A-G.

53. LA Berlin, *Neue Züricher Zeitung* (August 9, 1944), Rep. 225 Aschinger AG, 486 Zeitungsausschnitte über Aschinger 1901–1944.
54. LA Berlin, Nr. 697–T2/33, Rep. 225 Aschinger AG, 697 Kurz-Chronik der A. A-G.
55. LA Berlin, Rep. 751/1 VEB "Aktivist," 80 Betriebschronik des VEB Aktivist 1945–49, "In dem besetzten Holland," 14, 15.
56. During the winter of 1947, schoolchildren in all sectors of the city were provided with a midday meal of 300 calories from British army stocks. Adults, too, profited from the charitable efforts administered by the occupied armies. The new people's restaurants served as feeding centers for an American relief program for the aged. See The United States National Archives II, CRALOG Meeting 24 Oct 1947, RG 260 Records of the United States Occupation Headquarters, World War II. Box No. 212 Office of Military Government for Germany (U.S. Zone) (OMGUS) Records of the Berlin Sector, Records of the Public Welfare Branch: Records Concerning CRALOG Activities, 1946–1949.
57. LA Berlin, Voraussichtlicher Bedarf an Ausstattungsgegenständen für Großgaststätten, Mummert, 4. September 1945, Rep. 10 B Sen. für Wirtschaft und Kredit. Geschäftsbereich Ernährung, Acc. 1877, 467 Gemeinschaftsverpflegung (1945–48).
58. LA Berlin, Nr. 697–T2/33, Rep. 225 Aschinger AG, 697 Kurz-Chronik der A. A-G.
59. Examples of minimal state oversight can be found in LA Berlin, Rep. 225 Aschinger AG, 548 Preiseinhaltung in Restaurants.
60. LA Berlin, Mummert, Aktennotiz zur Frage der Volksspeisung und Großgaststätten, 1. September 1945, Rep. 10 B Sen. für Wirtschaft und Kredit. Geschäftsbereich Ernährung, Acc. 1877, 467 Gemeinschaftsverpflegung (1945–48).
61. LA Berlin, Vortag zur Vollversammlung am 26. September 1947—16 Uhr im Alten Ballhaus, Berlin C., Joachimstr., p. 3, Rep. 10 B Sen. für Wirtschaft und Kredit. Geschäftsbereich Ernährung, Acc. 1877, 554 Gemeinschaftsverpflegung—Verpflegung in Volksgaststätten, Großküchen, Gastwirtschaften (1945–47).
62. LA Berlin, Abschrift. Gemeinsame Resolution der 20 Bezirksdelegierten aller Volksgaststätten und Werkkantinen und des Volksgaststätten-Beirats, p. 1, Rep. 10 B Sen. für Wirtschaft und Kredit. Geschäftsbereich Ernährung, Acc. 1888, 554 Gemeinschaftsverpflegung—Verpflegung in Volksgaststätten, Großküchen, Gastwirtschaften (1945–47).
63. See "Aschinger beschlagnahmt," *Telegraf* (May 3, 1947); "Fritz Aschinger als Gestapo-Agent. Warum die Aschinger-Betriebe beschlagnahmt wurden,"*Berliner Zeitung* (May 7, 1947); "Was will Herr Aschinger noch?" *Neues Deutschland* (May 8, 1947). Authorities in the Eastern Zone believed that Aschinger had been a member of the Nazi Party since 1937; Aschinger, for his part, denied these allegations. Aschinger admitted that he applied for membership in that year, but at the same time knew he would be denied membership on the basis of his former marriage to a non-Aryan. Their divorce had, however, been final before 1933, so it is hard to imagine there is much to this claim. Aschinger actively supported the Nazi state well before the war and profited handsomely from the Nazis' war of aggression.
64. LA Berlin, Rep. 751/1 VEB "Aktivist," 80 Betriebschronik des VEB Aktivist 1945–49, "Die nächsten Aufgaben der Herstellung der Aktionseinheit der Arbeiterklasse im Kampf zur Entmachung des Monopolkapitals, 44. See also Christine von Oertzen and Gabriele Jäger, *Boulevard Badstrasse: Großstadtgeschichte im Berliner Norden* (Berlin: Bezirksamt Wedding von Berlin, 1993), p. 251; Patrice Poutrus, "Lebensmittelkonsum, Versorlunskrisen und Die Entscheidung Für Den Goldbroiler" Archiv Für Sozialgeschuente 39 (1999): 391–421.
65. Pracht, *M. Kempinski & Co.*, pp. 144, 145.

Chapter 14

FOOD AND THE POLITICS OF SCARCITY IN URBAN SOVIET RUSSIA, 1917–1941

Mauricio Borrero

*S*carcity pervades popular constructions and images of daily life in the history of the Soviet Union. Shortages in Soviet Russia encompassed a wide range of goods and services, including basic personal necessities such as food, housing, and clothing. Their presence is so extensive and deeply rooted that some scholars have posited the existence of a "culture of shortages."[1] Of these various shortages, food shortages were perhaps the most politically charged, a powerful presence in many of the crucial junctures of early Soviet history from 1917 to 1941. Indeed, the major events of these decades, such as the 1917 revolutions, the Civil War of 1917 to 1921, and the Stalin revolution of 1928 to 1932, cannot be fully understood without reference to the presence or the threat of food shortages. But the importance of scarcity in general as a defining characteristic of early Soviet life transcends these well-known turning points. Scarcity was also a main force behind the unique network of breadlines, ration coupons, black markets, and informal barter arrangements that became a central part of the fabric of everyday Soviet life.

In the first decades of Soviet power, a "politics of scarcity" developed in response to the government's claims to control all aspects of food supply (production, transportation, and distribution) and its inability to perform these activities in a consistently reliable manner. A complex food discourse—sometimes complementary, sometimes antagonistic—evolved between the government and the urban and rural populations of Soviet Russia. Building from the rhetoric of 1917, where the promise of bread was one of the three components of the Bolshevik banner of "Peace, Land, and Bread," issues of food distribution figured prominently in the evolving moral economy by which the ruled judged their rulers. Food also occupied a central place in the utopian agendas of communal dining that Bolshevik leaders and activists proposed in part as vehicles for the advancement of women's liberation. In the context of persistent shortages and widespread social upheaval that was sometimes spontaneous (Civil War) and sometimes state-induced (the Stalin revolution), the government's control of food supplies became one of the "sticks" by which it sought to restore order and enforce discipline.

This essay explores the urban side of this politics of scarcity, focusing on two crucial aspects of food distribution—rationing and public dining—which by their very nature brought urban populations into daily contact with governmental agencies. In the early years of Soviet power, we find a tension in rationing between an egalitarian and a hierarchical approach, and in public dining a tension between a "utopian" and a "pragmatic" approach. Indeed, these tensions encapsulate the challenges and realities confronting the Soviet government. Thus, with sharply reduced food stocks at its disposal, government rationing policies alternated between notions of food as a right to be given to all and as a privilege to be awarded by the state to selected groups of people. Likewise, evaluations of the extensive public dining network developed by the Bolsheviks were caught between the idealistic aspirations of those who envisioned a communal substitute for home dining, and the less inspiring reality of dingy, over-crowded, unsanitary establishments where large numbers of people were fed affordable but hardly appetizing meals.

As with Soviet political discourse in general, the egalitarian and utopian features gradually gave way to the hierarchical and pragmatic ones.[2] In the process, a uniquely Stalinist synthesis had developed by the eve of World War II. By then, rationing had been a frequent, although not constant, feature of Soviet urban life and one that arguably facilitated the transition to wartime rationing after the German invasion of 1941.[3] The utopian visions of communal dining had given way to a more prosaic net-work of state-run cafeterias for the common Soviet citizen, and a rather elaborate system of "closed distribution" restricted to the emerging privi-leged classes. The issue of access to food, seemingly a temporary by-prod-uct of the revolutionary crisis of 1917, now became a permanent feature of Soviet life.

THE POLITICS OF SCARCITY, 1917–1941: AN OVERVIEW

From the marches of Petrograd women that sparked the February Revolution of 1917 and the collapse of the Romanov dynasty, food short-ages helped define many of the crucial junctures in Soviet history through the next few decades. Up to the violent imposition of collectivization in 1929, the struggle for control of food supplies in the countryside lay at the root of the tangled relations between the state and the peasantry. Similarly, the struggle for access to scarce food supplies lay at the root of urban politics, from the marches of hungry Petrograd women in February

1917, through the urban protests of early 1921, to the procurement crisis of 1927 that foreshadowed the turn toward collectivized agriculture.

The food shortages that struck with such intensity during the revolutionary year of 1917 dated back to Russia's entry into World War I in 1914. As in other European countries, Russian political leaders both inside and outside government grossly underestimated the severity and duration of a war they had initially endorsed with great enthusiasm. The Great War opened up more fully than before the issue of urban provisioning as a political issue in Russia and other European nations. The war also made state intervention in food supply far more palatable than before, especially in the area of rationing, where leaders and urban populations agreed on the government's responsibility for providing equitable supplies at a time of shortages.

It is important to stress the common European origins of the Russian crisis, because the subsequent Soviet experience with food and scarcity belongs inside and not outside the European continuum, despite its distinctive communist contours. Recent research on European capitals in wartime has posed an interpretive continuum with London at one end, Paris in the middle, and Berlin at the other end. Judged against the experience of the other three capitals, Moscow stands next to Berlin, further down along a spectrum of distress.[4]

Soon after the outbreak of the war, the Russian government began to face enormous problems feeding both its urban population and its swollen army of several million men. The effects of the unexpectedly long war became especially evident in the area of food supply, where the Tsarist government proved unable to maintain a smooth mechanism of food procurement that would prevent rampant speculation while offering agricultural producers a fair return for their grain. Inflation and food shortages soon gripped the large urban centers of Russia, particularly Petrograd and Moscow. Successive governments—Provisional and Soviet—also proved unable to solve this basic conundrum, thus ensuring the periodic recurrence of food shortages in the following decades.

The Bolsheviks rode the wave of urban discontent over food shortages (among other issues) to victory in October 1917, but after October they had to face the realities of ruling over a hungry population with limited resources at their disposal. With the Bolsheviks in power, the question became "Bread for whom?" since there was not enough food to supply everyone. The origins of the Russian and European food crises were indeed similar, but in Soviet Russia, with the victory of the Bolsheviks, rationing came to be seen not as a temporary solution to shortages, but as the foundation for distribution in a new society. In turn, public dining became not just a vehicle for providing cheap meals to the needy, as in other European nations, but a possible substitute for private kitchens and restaurants.

By 1918, inflation, food shortages, rationing, and black markets had become common throughout wartime Europe.[5] Nowhere, however, did they reach such alarming proportions so quickly or become so closely tied to drastic changes in politics and society than in Russia. The events of the Russian revolutions and Civil War (1917–1921) took place against this background of unremitting hunger and growing political restlessness. As war led to revolution and revolution to civil war, hunger became a permanent component of urban life, and the search for food a daily concern for urban residents, public organizations, and government officials. Passengers traveled back and forth on overcrowded trains from city to country, purchasing food in violation of a government monopoly on the purchase of grain. State-sponsored armed squads attempted to enforce the grain monopoly by requisitioning grain from reluctant peasants. In the cities, bread rations ensured a consumption minimum but became smaller during the course of the civil war, dropping from one pound to as little as one eighth of a pound per day, and often were not distributed on a daily basis. Municipal authorities tried to provide alternative venues for inexpensive dining by organizing a network of public cafeterias, but their efforts were hindered by an overall lack of resources. Outdoor private markets, places where anything could be bought for a steep price, thrived during these years, providing an awkward contrast between the promises of a new communist society and the realities of civil war daily life.[6]

The end of the Civil War removed the notion of sacrifice for the revolution as justification for the drastic food policies of the previous years. Faced with widespread protests, ranging from peasant rebellions in the countryside, the uprising at the Kronstadt naval base outside Petrograd, and street demonstrations in Moscow and Petrograd, the Communist Party decided to change course. At the Tenth Party Congress in March 1921, it adopted with some reluctance the package of policies that came to be known as the New Economic Policy (NEP). The central planks of the New Economic Policy were the abolition of food requisitioning quotas, their replacement with a food tax, and the loosening of previous restrictions on private trade, especially petty trade such as the food trade. With regard to food procurement, certainly the changes brought about by the NEP were important, and the abolition of food procurement quotas and the overall confiscatory character of Civil War policies was important, although short-lived, in terms of peasant politics.

The New Economic Policy brought the Soviet government the "breathing space" it had sought since the October Revolution. Likewise, Russian peasants came as close as ever possible to the "golden age" of relative autarchy of which they had long dreamed. But by 1927 a food crisis similar to that of the Civil War, with low state procurement prices and peasants withholding their grain, resurfaced again at a time when criticism of NEP itself was gaining ground within the Communist Party. In this changing political environment, Joseph Stalin was able to gain politically with his well-known trip to Siberia, by advocating a forceful Civil War–type solution to the crisis. The Siberian episode marked the beginning of a series of steps that led to the implementation of the First Five-Year Plan and Collectivization and the abandonment of the more gradualist approach of the New Economic Policy.

With the consolidation of collectivized agriculture in the 1930s, the issue of food procurement changed substantially. This is not to deny that after collectivization the issue of providing a regular supply of food from the countryside to the cities continued to bedevil the Soviet government. But throughout most of the period between World War I and collectiviza-tion, the state's overall weakness had left it and the peasantry almost as equals. With collectivization, relations between state and peasants became more one-sided than ever before. With the peasantry defeated, the issue of food procurement lost the political connotations of struggle between state and peasants that it had during the long decade between World War I and collectivization.

At the other end of the food procurement question lay the issue of pri-vate trade, particularly as it pertained to markets and other forms of food distribution not controlled by the state. For a state engaged in an ongoing ideological battle with private trade, the continued and brazen existence of private markets and trade was a source of great resentment and awkward-ness. During the Civil War, the Bolsheviks abolished private trade as part of their initial attempt to build Communism in Soviet Russia. The editors of *Krasnaia Moskva* (*Red Moscow*), an informative anthology of the achieve-ments of Soviet rule in Moscow that was published in 1920, sought to con-vey the impression that private trade had been successfully replaced by "a system of organized distribution of goods and manufactures . . . where products are issued only by means of ration cards, according to a plan, and in controlled quantities."[7] But the reality was very different, as private trade continued to coexist with state distribution in an uneasy but almost symbiotic relationship.

There was perhaps no stronger symbol of the persistence and scale of private trade in Soviet Russia than the Sukharevka Market that flourished in Moscow, a few miles to the north of Red Square. An old market whose origins dated back to the aftermath of Napoleon's occupation of Moscow in 1812, the Sukharevka became the place to find (albeit at extravagant prices) scarce goods such as flour, cheese, eggs, milk, and tea, all which were officially rationed and had long disappeared from state stores.[8] The Sukharevka grew in direct proportion to the Bolsheviks' attempt to estab-lish control over private trade, and by late 1920 it was the only place to find basic necessities such as soap, wood, boots, and tobacco. The series of decrees and resolutions curbing or abolishing private trade succeeded in dismantling official networks of trade, but did not destroy the spirit of trade, which was now channeled into the black market. The power of the Sukharevka was such that by the end of the Civil War even government institutions were obtaining many of their supplies from the market.[9]

The Sukharevka was closed with great fanfare in December 1920, but with the adoption of the New Economic Policy in March 1921, which permitted small-scale private trade, was soon back in business. Within a few months trade was thriving again, and certainly by the mid-1920s, the Sukharevka was once again the magnet it had long been for pickpockets, prostitutes, and street children seeking a place to sleep or to sell stolen goods.[10] The passage of the New Economic Policy brought back to life the cafés and restaurants that had either disappeared or gone underground during the difficult years of the Civil War. During the peak years of the NEP, the food trade accounted for 40 percent to 50 percent of the total volume of trade. By 1928, however, private trade in food and restaurants had begun to decline, in great part as a response to increasing government restrictions and outright harassment.[11] The Sukharevka itself survived only a few more years. In 1930, the market was shut down, and the Square was renamed Kolkhoz Square.[12]

The existence of private markets in Soviet Russia is generally associated with the Civil War period and the years of the New Economic Policy. It would seem that with the closing of powerful symbols such as the Sukharevka Market, the government had finally won its long struggle against private trade. But the truth was that the relationship between the government and private markets was not only one of conflict but also of mutual dependence. The markets owed their growth to low fixed prices for grain and the general scarcity that resulted from Bolshevik attempts to replace trade with planned distribution. During the Civil War, the government came to rely tacitly on the market to feed those left out from its ration programs. Indeed, the hallmark of private trade in Soviet Russia was not its abolition but its rather dysfunctional existence. Harassed and persecuted, never fully rooted out, and forced to assume odd clandestine forms, private trade survived in Soviet Russia even in the harshest years of Stalinist rule.[13]

With the sudden and arbitrary turn to policies of rapid industrialization and collectivized agriculture, food shortages once again became an almost permanent feature of urban life in the 1930s. Breadlines reappeared in 1929 and the government reinstituted rationing as a way to alleviate shortages while increasing its condemnation of *kulaks* and other saboteurs who were blamed for the shortages. In 1932 and 1933 famine broke out in Ukraine and spread to Russia, Kazakhstan, and the North Caucasus. Severe shortages brought back lines in 1936 and then again in 1939 to 1940, to the increasing frustration of urban residents, who often waited ten to twelve hours for meager amounts of bread. In a reversal of the patterns of the Civil War, when urban residents traveled to the countryside for food supplies, the urban shortages of the 1930s were aggravated by the presence of peasants coming into towns because there was no grain in the villages.[14]

Indignant Soviet citizens, puzzled by the persistence of shortages, wrote in vain to their leaders, including Stalin, complaining of the shortages. These signed letters give us an insight into a Soviet popular mind-set that accepted (or at least utilized) the government's rhetoric of enemies and conspiracies as explanations for the shortages. In also blaming private trade for the renewed shortages, they also show how deeply ingrained was the dichotomy that equated socialist distribution with rationing and private trade with speculation or profiteering. Underlying it all, however, the letters convey an unshakable conviction that it was the government's duty to provide bread (at the very minimum) to its citizens.[15]

RATIONING

European governments first introduced rationing during World War I as way to compensate for the various shortages caused by the war effort. Through their rationing programs, governments acknowledged their responsibility to distribute scarce goods equitably, thus ensuring that the burden of shortages was spread evenly throughout society. Under the impact of the "total wars" of 1914 to 1918 and 1939 to 1945, rationing assisted in the development of modern nationhood by appealing to a citizenry's sense of patriotism and civic duty through the notion of sacrifice for the common good. Rationing itself was ideologically neutral, even though the details of specific rationing systems and the discourse that surrounded them reflected distinctive conceptions of distributive justice. Thus it is not surprising to find it featured with equal prominence in Soviet constructions of distributive fairness as well as in the U.S. government's appeals to American housewives during World War II that "rationing is good democracy."[16]

The Russian experience with rationing grew from this common foundation. But whereas European governments and the Provisional government intended rationing to be a temporary solution, the Bolshevik government soon came to see rationing as the foundation of a distribution system that would eventually replace market relations. In time, rationing and the centralized planned distribution of goods came to be one of the cornerstones of the hierarchical social edifice of Stalinism and an integral part of the planned, bureaucratic economy that took root in the 1930s.[17] In the discourse that accompanied Bolshevik ration programs we also see the outlines of an urban moral economy that, while rooted in the original model elaborated by E. P. Thompson, also contained traits that are peculiar to early Soviet Russia.[18]

European wartime rationing systems were generally based on two basic principles: that all citizens were entitled to the same basic ration, but that workers in physically demanding jobs required a ration supplement.[19]

Thus all citizens received a ration card that entitled them to the same amount of bread, initially set at one *funt* (one pound) a day. In addition, selected groups engaged in physical labor received supplementary rations, essentially a double ration of bread.[20] This was the basic system that the Bolsheviks inherited from their predecessors and, with few substantial modifications, it continued in place until the summer of 1918.

As with other Civil War policies, practical necessities as well as ideological considerations shaped Bolshevik rationing policies. Under the pressure of ever more severe food shortages and the outbreak of the full-fledged Civil War, Bolshevik officials confronted difficult decisions regarding priorities in food distribution. Faced with declining food stocks at its disposal and continuing urban discontent over shortages, the Bolshevik government chose to supply workers first, on the grounds that "bourgeois" groups could always turn to the black market. The pressure of ever-worsening shortages led the Bolsheviks to develop "class-based" rationing programs that divided urban populations into three or four categories and entitled them to receive different amounts of food.[21] But even with this reduced conception of who would and would not be supplied, there was not enough food for the government to distribute. By 1920 when the "labor ration" formally replaced the "class ration," class background or occupation alone did not entitle recipients to larger rations as it had in 1918. Instead rations were to be distributed, almost as a payment, only on the basis of work already performed in the previous weeks.

The change from a "class ration" to a "labor ration" points to an equally important "state-building" dimension to Bolshevik food policies.[22] Faced with labor shortages and declining labor productivity, the government used the promise of larger and guaranteed rations as a mechanism for recruitment and the threat of withholding rations as a way to enforce discipline. Much like the nineteenth-century Caribbean planters discussed by Sidney Mintz in *Sweetness and Power*, the Bolsheviks found themselves resorting to the "discipline of hunger" to control scarce labor.[23] They began to emphasize slogans such as "he who works, eats" and to construct rationing systems based on a hierarchical understanding of the relative importance of one's labor to the revolution or the state. While the formulation of rationing programs reflects the necessities and political preferences of the Bolshevik government, their implementation reveals the same process of mutual adaptation evident in other areas of food supply policy. In the case of rationing, we see a recurring cyclical pattern to each of the programs implemented during the Civil War. Initially, a new rationing program involved the creation of privileged categories that entitled a select group of people to receive more food than others because of the nature and perceived importance of their work. Gradually these privileges were extended to cover broader segments of the population who had petitioned persistently to be included in the higher categories. Finally, in the last stage of the cycle, the privileges were overextended to the point that they were diluted and lost their initial meaning. The government then created a new set of privileged categories, and the cycle started anew.

With the passage of the New Economic Policy, the government phased out rationing by 1923, and with the abolition of the People's Commissariat of Food Supply (Narkomprod) in 1924, the last remnant of Civil War food policies was seemingly removed. While the NEP brought about important changes in the areas of food procurement and private trade, the Bolsheviks still clung to the idea of planned distribution as a viable and desirable alternative to the market. Thus, in the area of food distribution, the NEP years witnessed a mixture of state distribution systems such as "targeted distribution" (*tselevoe snabzhenie*) for favored enterprises and workers, and private markets for the rest.

Rationing was again introduced in Soviet urban centers in 1928 in connection with the accelerated industrialization drive of the First Five-Year Plan.[24] The Civil War experience with hierarchical rationing systems again served as a model, with the difference that the Soviet government of the late 1920s and early 1930s no longer paid lip service to the ideals of egalitarianism. Rationing continued in most urban areas until January 1935. By that time, the Soviet leadership had now begun to reevaluate the meaning of rationing in a system that now sought to present itself as a beacon of material progress and to convince its population that, in the words of Stalin: "Life has become better, life has become merrier." But the relative caution with which the leadership dismantled rationing (in several stages) in 1935 shows its concern with the political implications of this decision, a concern that was not without foundation.[25]

On the surface, it would appear that the Soviet urban population would welcome the end of rationing as a return to "normalcy" in food distribution. Instead, recent scholarship that explores the previously closed topic of popular opinion in the 1930s suggests that the announcement of the impending abolition of rationing in January 1935 was the source of great concern for many of the less-privileged Soviet citizens.[26] An approximation of the 1930s moral economy of the Soviet crowd emerges from letters to Soviet leaders in connection with the end of rationing and from internal Communist Party reports that were often drawn from eavesdropping at breadlines. In their anger and search for villains, some letters denounced the end of rationing as "Molotov's vile deception."[27] More ominously, the December 1934 assassination of Sergei Kirov, second only to Stalin in the Communist Party hierarchy and Leningrad regional and city party boss, was linked in some people's minds to the impending end of rationing, which had been prominently announced in the newspapers only a few weeks before. "Kirov was killed because the Leningrad workers are unhappy about the repeal of the rationing system for bread," went one of the more restrained *vox populi* explanations of his assassination, whereas another put it more bluntly: "They raised prices for bread, so that's what you get."[28]

The political dimension of Soviet rationing expressed itself most forcefully in the unresolved tension between egalitarian and hierarchical rationing. Soviet egalitarianism of the revolutionary period was driven more by leveling tendencies rather than by a true belief in the equality of all citizens. This egalitarian ethos, seen through the prism of food, remained a powerful element in Soviet political discourse well into the 1930s, even as the Communist Party sought to abandon rationing as an emblem of a previous era of scarcity and embarked on a process that hardened the differences between the new elites and the masses.

Early Bolshevik rationing policies built on the same principles that in 1917 allowed for supporters of "Soviet" democracy to define it as one that included all supporters of socialism but excluded "bourgeois" parties, such as the Kadets (Constitutional Democrats). Rationing policies initially drew from the twin beliefs that it was politically permissible to set up hierarchical systems that discriminated against groups outside the working class but not to discriminate within the working class. Viktor Nogin, a prominent Bolshevik involved in economic administration, succinctly articulated the dilemma facing the Bolsheviks as they tried to extend hierarchical rationing to the working class itself. "The issue," he remarked at a meeting held in 1919, "is not how much bread we should assign to the working class, but whether we should differentiate within the working class when distributing bread."[29] Nogin's concerns echoed the widely held reservations among various Bolshevik and working-class sectors in Moscow about the overall direction of the government's rationing policy, particularly its increasing reliance on designating groups of privileged workers entitled to receive more rations than others. By 1921, resentment over preferential treatment for certain groups of workers surfaced loudly at plenary meetings of the Moscow Soviet.[30]

Rationing also allowed the Bolsheviks to play to the sentiments of an urban population open to the idea of revenge on previously privileged classes. This is the context for Grigorii Zinoviev's well-known comment from 1919 that the lowest ration category, providing minimal amounts of food (on the days when there was enough food to distribute to all) was created especially for the bourgeoisie, so that they would not forget the "smell of bread."[31] Fanning the resentment against privileged classes would, however, backfire once the Bolshevik leadership began to be seen as the new recipient of privilege. While some leaders lived modestly, others—including Zinoviev himself—quickly became known and resented for flaunting privileges that in the context of the times were considered "bourgeois."

Ration cards and breadlines, generally symbols of temporary distress, became "institutionalized" during the first decades of Soviet power. The former often served as an alternate currency, the latter a part of a new urban landscape with its own rules and etiquette. Breadlines were also a place for government agents, from Provisional government to Stalinist, to gauge public opinion. Despite radically different political contexts, there is a direct line between rallies like the one held in April 1917 in Moscow's working-class Presnia district, where the crowd shouted "Where is the bread and flour? Down with the police! Down with the Provisional government!" and the grumbling voices heard in Leningrad breadlines after Kirov's murder in December 1934.[32]

Thus in the first decades of Soviet power, rationing became more than a mechanism to alleviate hunger and ensure minimum norms of consumption. Through the Civil War years, rationing became less of a tool to provide equitable access to scarce food supplies and more of a tool for selecting groups that were to receive preferential supply treatment. In the government's view, it evolved from a right shared by all citizens to a privilege granted to groups whose labor and preservation the Bolshevik government considered crucial to the survival of its revolution. Rationing also provided one of the ways for the government to adjust to its changing urban constituency—represented by the growing bureaucratic sector of public employees (*sluzhashchie*)—as shown by the changing social composition of Civil War Moscow. It became a way to reward labor productivity and to punish recalcitrant workers who resisted "Bolshevization" of their trade unions.[33] This punitive dimension of rationing continued to figure prominently through the Stalin years, serving, to paraphrase Elena Osokina, as the carrot and the stick of the Soviet industrialization effort.[34]

PUBLIC DINING

If the discourse over rationing reflects changes in the original egalitarian ethos of the Russian revolution, changes in the theory and practice of public dining reflect important changes in terms of women's policies as well as the overall utopian tenor of the revolution. Rationing and public dining were closely connected in early Bolshevik food distribution programs, as the development of an extensive network of communal kitchens and public cafeterias complemented rationing programs. Both rationing and public dining presented Bolsheviks with ideologically acceptable alternatives that in theory also made better use of scarce resources. Where rationing was part of an attempt to replace markets with a system of planned distribution, public dining was initially part of an attempt to replace private individual kitchens and private restaurants with a network of communal kitchens and restaurants.[35]

The Bolshevik revolutionary agenda included an attack on the restaurants and kitchens of urban Russia as part of an attempt to change the ways in which people ate by replacing, in the words of the economist Evgeny Preobrazhensky, the household pot with "a great public cauldron."[36] The establishment of communal dining facilities provided Bolsheviks with an ideologically acceptable vehicle that would economize scarce resources and liberate women from oppressive housework. A network of public cafeterias would replace the private restaurants and taverns, where food was served at prices far beyond the reach of the average worker, while communal kitchens would free women from the tyranny of the home kitchen, where they spent long hours preparing food for their families.

In their advocacy of communal kitchens and public cafeterias as vehicles that would help expedite the liberation of women from the drudgery of domestic work, the Bolsheviks drew upon long-standing socialist tradition. Owenite utopian communities such as New Harmony featured common dining rooms. In the phalanxes of Charles Fourier's followers, cooking, laundry, and child care were performed on a communal basis. In their writings Karl Marx and Friedrich Engels continued to emphasize the importance of communalizing domestic activities, but transferred regulatory responsibilities to the domain of the state. Beginning with Nikolai Chernyshevsky's influential novel, *What Is to Be Done?* (1863), which features a heroine who finds personal liberation through communal living, the Russian revolutionary movement had also developed an affinity for the theory, if not always the practice, of communal domestic arrangements. In the early months of the revolution, women Bolsheviks such as Inessa Armand and Alexandra Kollontai argued forcefully for the liberating potential of communal kitchens, dining rooms, laundries, and clothes-mending centers. Lenin added the stamp of his authority to these discussions in his pamphlet "*Velikii pochin*" (*A Great Beginning*), where he wrote favorably of public or state-sponsored dining as living examples of small-deeds communism in practice.[37]

Public dining grew rapidly after 1917 in the context of the revolutionary idealism and widespread hunger and deprivation that is familiar to students of this period. To some, public cafeterias had the potential to elevate dining to a new level and to serve as one of the foundations of a new society. To others, their many shortcomings provided ammunition for critics of the regime. Thus one food activist wrote about the ability of "communal dining to truly become a communal event, bringing people together as in a family," while another warned that "ten counterrevolutionary agitators cannot cause as much harm as one director of the cesspools that go by the name of soviet cafeterias."[38]

During the Civil War, public cafeterias and communal kitchens were built on the sites of former hotels, restaurants, student dormitories, and even private homes. The famed Yar restaurant in Moscow, a place where the "rich went to amuse themselves" in prerevolutionary times, became a "kitchen-factory" (*kukhnia-fabrika*) that served close to fifteen thousand daily meals for children.[39] In Petrograd, which led the movement toward public dining, all private restaurants had been closed and replaced by public cafeterias by November 1918, and in Moscow over 90 percent of the city's remaining population was receiving some amount of food from state-sponsored dining by 1921.[40] The shortcomings of these cafeterias were readily visible: most were located in dingy, unsanitary places, and the food they served often bordered on the inedible. Nevertheless, the achievements of the Soviet government were impressive, especially when compared to the Tsarist government, which had yielded all initiative in this area to consumer cooperatives and charitable institutions.[41] Thus it was not surprising to find Bolshevik officials in Petrograd including cafeterias as obligatory stopping points in the tours they gave to foreign visitors, such as the British trade union delegation that visited Soviet Russia in 1920, highlighting the achievements of the new Soviet republic.[42]

The NEP years are often seen as a period of relative calm surrounded by the two stormy bookends of the Civil War and the Second Revolution, launched by the ascendant Stalinist wing of the Communist Party by the end of the 1920s. Certainly in terms of public dining, the New Economic Policy signaled the return of private restaurants and the relative decline of public dining. By the end of the decade, however, ideological militancy and state activism were on the rise, and public dining benefited from this renewed impetus. Women activists who had felt disappointed that the social agenda of the Civil War had been sacrificed to the necessities of political survival in 1921 were now in the forefront of the revival of public cafeterias and communal dining.[43] Once again, as during the Civil War, plans were made for the development of "kitchen-factories," although this time at the grand scale typical of the "gigantomania" that characterized Soviet industrial projects in the 1930s.

Although far more research needs to be done on communal and public dining, and available statistics for this period must be used with caution, a brief statistical excursion through the years between 1924 and 1931 highlights several trends that support the main outline of this story. Between 1924 and 1928, the combined total number of public (state and cooperative) and private eating establishments almost doubled, from 23,902 to 42,491 establishments. Between 1928 and 1931, however, as a result of the drastic change in political course, the total number of eating establishments declined by almost one half, to 24,860. All of these were now either state or cooperative establishments, since private establishments had officially disappeared.[44] Behind these numbers we see some of the broader processes of these years: the growth of private trade, especially small-scale trade under NEP, followed by the onslaught of state-imposed centralization. Together with the virtual disappearance of private food establishments by 1931, the government was implementing a process of centralization that was in character with its overall preference for fewer but larger economic units.

These ideological and utopian components make the Soviet case distinctive, and they stand out in any account of the experience with public dining. But we also need to mention, if only briefly, the broader global context of twentieth-century automatization and "massification" of the production, preparation, and consumption in which it took place. Here, one may be surprised to find that the United States—the other leading mass society of its day, albeit a capitalist one—served as a role model for Soviet large-scale efficiency and cultured consumerism.[45] Thus we find Soviet leaders and theorists, beginning with Lenin, commenting positively on efforts such as Frederick Winslow Taylor's work on labor organization and Henry Ford's revolutionary impact on management and the assembly line. To Soviet eyes, Taylorism and Fordism were the twin pillars of an "American model" that, combined with the Russian revolutionary impulse, would introduce efficiency and economy on a grand scale. Closer to public dining, we find positive endorsements of New York City's "automats," where food was "untouched by human hands." Likewise, Soviet delegations sent by the People's Commissariat of Trade to study commercial techniques wrote back "wildly enthusiastic articles" on American department stores, which, operating on a large scale, were considered superior to small shops.[46]

There was another way in which the two mass societies underwent a similar transformation—a "revolution at the table" (to borrow Harvey Levenstein's phrase), albeit in markedly different political contexts. Levenstein argues that one of the (perhaps unintended) impacts of Prohibition on American eating habits was to "help destroy the higher echelon of the restaurant industry [and] spur a tremendous expansion in the levels below, particularly those catering to the middle and lower-middle classes of both sexes." In Soviet Russia, the municipalization of private restaurants (part of a broader prohibition on private trade) provided the Bolsheviks with the infrastructure on which to build their network of public cafeterias and other eating establishments. And just as Prohibition brought forth speakeasies where liquor was served in violation of the law, Soviet prohibitions on private restaurants brought forth a series of "underground" establishments where access was on the basis of passwords or the correct sequence of knocks on the door.[47]

One final dimension relevant to public dining deserves mention in this discussion. Recent studies of the Stalin years have begun to examine issues of consumption within the context of what Russians have long called kulturnost, ("culturedness"). Going back to prerevolutionary times, the Russian intelligentsia—as the self-appointed vehicle of "culturedness" in Russian society— had adopted the education of peasants and workers as one of its missions. In Soviet times, with a veritable flood of uneducated, peasant migrants as well as the creation of new Soviet elites that aspired to a "cultured" lifestyle, kulturnost, became a watchword of the Stalinist era.[48] One of the areas where this "civilizing mission" was evident was in the world of public dining. As with other areas of Stalinism, the roots of this concern go back to the Civil War years. In the writings of early public dining enthusiasts, we find sustained discussions of how, through the use of art and music, public cafeterias would provide the setting for the cultural and educational advancement of workers.[49]

In hindsight, the history of public dining in early Soviet Russia reveals how the "utopian" elements of the original Bolshevik conceptions of public or communal dining were gradually overshadowed by the practical concerns of feeding large numbers of hungry urban residents. The development of public dining reveals again the tremendous gap between idealistic visions of the future and the harsh realities of daily life that was characteristic of other aspects of Bolshevik social policy and urban life in Civil War Russia. Public dining encountered the same obstacles of other social-engineering programs in the early Soviet period: lack of money, lack of resources, and inadequate infrastructure. Women did not rush to embrace communal cafeterias, visions of the "ideal" cafeteria were far removed from what customers dealt with on a daily basis, food was barely edible, and ultimately public cafeterias did not replace home cooking or outside dining.[50] By the mid-1930s the problems remained similar, even though public dining was now being promoted at a grander scale and with greater resources than in the Civil War. As Halina and Robert Rothstein have noted, "food supplies were limited, food was of low quality and inexpertly prepared, [they were] places where chaos, flies, dirt and terrible service reigned. . . . The workers refused to eat the food and often derisively called the cafeterias 'grub-halls.'[51]

CONCLUSION

On the eve of World War II, food shortages had long been part of the fabric of Soviet daily life. From the revolutionary days of 1917 through the turbulent first two decades of Soviet rule, they had also come to occupy a strategic central place in the unfolding discourse between government and society. In the absence of traditional market mechanisms that allocated food on the basis of one's ability to pay, this contact manifested itself in peoples' attempts to exercise control over food supplies, attempts to gain access more privileged ration categories, and informal barter arrangements between individuals, groups, or enterprises.[52]

It seems that large segments of Russia's urban population, especially the urban poor, came to share many of the Soviet government's assumptions about the sources of food shortages; thus the tendency to explain shortages in conspiratorial terms, the resentment of kulaks and speculators who allegedly profited from the hunger of others, and the need to restrict the market to ensure fairness in distribution. But faced with the time-consuming task of daily existence, Soviet urban residents proved to be—above all—survivors. They tried to obtain as much as they could from the government's ration plans, joined consumer cooperatives when they were still a viable independent source of food up to 1919 (many of them joined more than one cooperative to improve their chances to get food), and resorted to private markets when their budgets allowed.[55]

A complex relationship developed between government and people with regard to food. The government's extensive claims to control over food supply and distribution were challenged obliquely, not directly. There seems to have been a general acceptance that the government had an important role to play in food distribution, but with the government's poor track record in this area, Soviet citizens came to see it as only one of several supply options. To many, the state provided only a safety net that could be generally but not always trusted to deliver minimum amounts of food. It was not always clear, however, which was the true safety net: Did the state protect individuals from the inequalities of the market or did the market protect individuals from the inefficiencies and incompetence of the state distribution system?

NOTES

I am grateful to Warren Belasco, Julie Hessler, Lars Lih, and David Shearer for their comments on earlier drafts of this article. I also wish to thank St. John's University for providing financial assistance that supported the research and early stages of writing.

1. Julie M. Hessler, "Culture of Shortages: A Social History of Soviet Trade, 1917–1953," Ph.D. dissertation, University of Chicago, 1996; Hessler adapts the term from the work of the Hungarian economist Janos Kornai, as developed in works such as *Economics of Shortage* (Amsterdam: North Holland Pub. Co. 1980), 2 vols.

2. For an excellent discussion of this process, see Richard Stites, *Revolutionary Dreams: Utopian Vision and Experimental Life in the Russian Revolution* (New York: Oxford University Press, 1989).

3. See William Moskoff, *The Bread of Affliction: The Food Supply in the USSR During World War II* (Cambridge: Cambridge University Press, 1990).

4. On a series of issues (organization, infrastructure, ability to draw on civic solidarity, and the existence of a black market, for example) London and Paris were better equipped than Berlin to deal with wartime dislocations in food supply. Despite the extensive and overbearing presence of the Soviet state in the food economy of the 1920s and 1930s, enough features of the market survived in these first decades of Soviet rule—even in a distorted manner—to include it at the far end of the continuum of Western consumer societies. See Jay Winter and Jean-Louis Robert, eds., *Capital Cities at War: Paris, London, Berlin, 1914–1919* (Cambridge: Cambridge University Press 1997), passim. On Berlin, see Belinda J. Davis, *Home Fires Burning: Food, Politics, and Everyday Life in World War I Berlin* (Chapel Hill: University of North Carolina Press, 2000). On Moscow, see Mauricio Borrero, *Hungry Moscow: Scarcity and Survival in the Russian Civil War, 1917–1921* (New York: Peter Lang Publishers, 2001).

5. For a comprehensive study of the impact of World War I on the home front, see Thierry Bonzon and Belinda Davis, "Feeding the Cities," in Winter and Robert, eds., *Capital Cities at War*, pp. 305–341.

6. Descriptions of food shortages and hungry, desolate cities are prominent in the accounts of contemporary observers. For examples, see Victor Serge, *Memoirs of a Revolutionary, 1901–1941* (Oxford: Oxford University Press 1963), pp. 70–156; Emma Goldman, *Living My Life* (New York: Knopf, 1934); Iurii. V. Got'e, *Time of Troubles: The Diary of Iurii Vladimirovich Got'e—Moscow—July 8, 1917 to July 23, 1922*, ed. Terence Emmons (Princeton: Princeton University Press, 1988); and Marguerite E. Harrison, *Marooned in Moscow: The Story of an American Woman Imprisoned in Russia* (New York: Doran, 1921).

7. *Krasnaia Moskva* (Red Moscow) (Moscow: 1920), p. 302.

8. On the history of the Sukharevka, see Vladimir Giliarovskii, *Moskva i moskvichi. Ocherki staromoskovskogo byta* (Moscow and Muscovites: Sketches of Old Moscow Life) (Moscow: Sovetskii pisatel', 1935), p. 52; G. M. Shcherbo, *Sukhareva bashnia. Istoricheskii ocherk i problema ego vossozdaniia* (Sukharev Tower: A Historical Sketch and the Problems of Its

Reconstruction) (Moscow: Ianus-K, 1997), pp. 27–28; and Borrero, *Hungry Moscow*, chap. 7.

9. By late 1920, the government felt compelled to issue decrees regulating the purchase of goods on the market by employees of Soviet institutions. See Borrero, *Hungry Moscow*, chap. 7.

10. Alan M. Ball, *And Now My Soul Is Hardened: Abandoned Children in Soviet Russia, 1918–1930* (Berkeley: University of California Press, 1994), pp. 30, 43, 58, 65, 70, 119.

11. Alan M. Ball, *Russia's Last Capitalists: The Nepmen, 1921–1929* (Berkeley: University of California Press, 1987), p. 103.

12. Shcherbo, *Sukhareva bashnia*, pp. 27–28. See also P. V. Sytin, *Iz istorii moskovskikh ulits. Ocherki* (Sketches from the History of Moscow Streets) (Moscow: 1958), pp. 504–508.

13. Julie Hessler, "A Postwar Perestroika? Toward a History of Private Enterprise in the USSR," *Slavic Review* (Fall 1998): 516–541.

14. Sheila Fitzpatrick, *Everyday Stalinism: Ordinary Life in Extraordinary Times: Soviet Russia in the 1930s* (New York: Oxford University Press, 1999), pp. 42–44.

15. E. A. Osokina, "Krizis snabzheniia 1939–1941 gg. v pis'makh sovetskikh liudei" (The Supply Crisis of 1939–1941 in the Letters of Soviet Citizens), *Voprosy Istorii* (Problems of History), 1 (1996): 3–23.

16. See Amy Bentley, *Eating for Victory: Food Rationing and the Politics of Domesticity* (Urbana: University of Illinois Press, 1998), p. 14.

17. E. A. Osokina, *Ierarkhiia potrebleniia. O Zhizni liudei v usloviiakh stalinskogo snabzheniia, 1928–1935 gg.* (Hierarchies of Consumption: On People's Lives under Stalinist Supply, 1928–1932) (Moscow: Izd-vo MGOU, 1993), p. 12 and n. 8.

18. E. P. Thompson, "The Moral Economy of the English Crowd in the Eighteenth Century," and "Moral Economy Reviewed," in *Customs in Common* (New York: New Press, 1991), pp. 185–258 and 259–351.

19. For a recent discussion of rationing practices in wartime Europe, see Bonzon and Davis, "Feeding the Cities," in Winter and Robert, *Capital Cities at War*, pp. 316–322. See also the contemporary discussion by Soviet food officials in *Sbornik statei i instruktsii po rasprede-leniiu i kartochnoi sisteme* (Collected Articles and Instruction on Distribution and Rationing) (Moscow: 1920), pp. 7–10.

20. The Provisional government introduced bread rationing in April 1917. *Sistematicheskii Sbornik po Prodovol'stvennomu Delu* (Systematic Collection on Food Supply Affairs) (Moscow and Nizhnii-Novgorod, 1919–1921), vol. 1, pp. 208–209. For rationing policies before October 1917, see N. Fidelli "Ocherk istorii kartochnoi sistemy, 1915–1917" (A Sketch of the History of Rationing, 1915–1917) in *Prodovol'stvie i revoliutsiia* (Food Supply and Revolution), 1923, no. 7–12, pp. 142–162.

21. This terminology reflected contemporary Soviet usage and political exigencies at a time of great social flux.

22. The classic study of this aspect of food supply is Lars T. Lih, *Bread and Authority in Russia, 1914–1921* (Berkeley: University of California Press, 1990).

23. Sidney J. Mintz, *Sweetness and Power: The Place of Sugar in Modern History* (New York: Viking Press, 1985), p. 70. Mintz uses the term in the context of Caribbean planters trying to maintain their position after the abolition of slavery in the region.

24. The following quantities were issued to workers in the city of Smolensk to the west of Moscow as of 1929: 600 grams of bread a day and an additional 300 grams for each member of his family; 200 grams to 1 liter of vegetable oil a month; 1 kilogram of sugar a month; and 30 to 36 meters of cotton cloth a year. The authors note that these quantities were subsequently reduced. See Mikhail Heller and Aleksandr Nekrich, *Utopia in Power: The History of the Soviet Union from 1917 to the Present* (New York: Summit Books, 1986), pp. 226–227.

25. Osokina, *Ierarkhiia potrebleniia*, passim; Julie Hessler, "Cultured Trade: The Stalinist Turn Toward Consumerism," in Sheila Fitzpatrick, ed. *Stalinism: New Directions* (New York: Routledge, 2000), p. 186.

26. Sarah Davies, "Us against Them": Social Identity in Soviet Russia, 1934–41," *Russian Review*, 56, 1 (January 1997): 70–89; reprinted in Fitzpatrick, ed. *Stalinism*. For a fuller treatment, see Sarah Davies, *Popular Opinion in Stalin's Russia: Terror, Propaganda and Dissent, 1934–1941* (Cambridge: Cambridge University Press, 1997). See also Lesley A. Rimmel, "Another Kind of Fear: The Kirov Murder and the End of Bread Rationing in Leningrad," *Slavic Review* (Fall 1997): 481–499.

27. Davies, "Us and Them," p. 81. See also, Davies, *Popular Opinion in Stalin's Russia*, pp. 27–31.

28. Rimmel, "Another Kind of Fear," pp. 484–486.

29. Gosudarstvennyi Arkhiv Rossiisskoi Federatsii (State Archive of the Russian Federation)

GARF, f. 5451, op. 3, d. 362–b, l. 23. "Soedinennoe zasedanie predstavitelei VSNKh, VTsSPS, i professional'nykh soiuzov (MSPS), 21 maia 1919 g.: O provedenii edinogo klassovogo paika." "Joint meeting of representatives of VSNKh, VTsSPS and trade unions (MSPS), May 21, 1919: On the Introduction of a Single Class Ration."

30. For some evidence of resentment against privileged workers by less favored workers, see *Plenarnoe zasedanie Moskovskogo Soveta R.K. i K. D. sovmestno s plenumami raionnykh Sovetov, M.G.S.P.S., pravleniiami profsoiuzov i predstaviteliami fabrichno-zavodskikh komitetov i kolletivov sovetskikh sluzhashchikh 1 fevrialia 1921 goda* (Plenary Meeting of the Moscow Soviet with Plenums of district Soviets, MGSPS, trade union leaders and representatives of factory committees and collectives of Soviet employees, February 1, 1921) (Moscow: 1921), pp. 1–19.

31. Cited by Mary McAuley, "Bread without the Bourgeoisie," in Diane P. Koenker, William G. Rosenberg, and Ronald Grigor Suny, eds., *Party, State, and Society in the Russian Civil War: Explorations in Social History* (Bloomington: Indiana University Press, 1989), p. 163.

32. "Prodovol'stevennoe polozhenie v Moskve v marte-iiunie 1917 goda" (Moscow's Food Supply Situation, March-June 1917) *Krasnyi arkhiv* (Red Archive) 1937, vol. 2 (81), pp. 128–146; Rimmel, "Another Kind of Fear."

33. Jonathan Aves, *Workers Against Lenin: Labour Protest and the Bolshevik Dictatorship* (London: I. B. Tauris, 1996).

34. The Russian term is *knut i prianik* (the "whip and the cake"). E. A. Osokina, *Za fasadom "Stalinskogo izobiliia." Raspredelenie i rynok v snabzhenii naseleniia v gody industrializatsii, 1927–1941* (Behind the Façade of Stalinist Abundance: Distribution and the Market in the Population's Supply during the Years of Industrialization, 1927–1941) (Moscow: 1998), pp. 89–113. A revised, translated edition of this work was published as Elena Osokina, *Socialist Distribution and the Art of Survival in Stalin's Russia, 1927–1941* (Armonk, NY: M. E. Sharpe, 2001), edited and translated by Kate S. Transchel and Greta Bucher.

35. The Russian term for public dining or public food service is *obshchestvennoe pitanie*. It implies food eaten outside the home in an organized setting, generally organized by the government or a public institution. Communal dining (*kommunal'noe pitanie*) implies eating in a more explicitly communal setting.

36. Cited in Wendy Z. Goldman, *Women, the State and Revolution: Soviet Family Policy and Social Life, 1917–1936* (Cambridge: Cambridge University Press, 1993), pp. 5–6.

37. See Mauricio Borrero, "Communal Dining and State Cafeterias in Moscow and Petrograd, 1917–1921," in Musya Glants and Joyce Toomre, eds., *Food in Russian History and Culture* (Bloomington: Indiana University Press, 1997), pp. 162–176.

38. F. Sh., *Obshchestvennyi stol. Kommunal'noe pitanie* (The Public Table: Communal Dining) (Moscow: 1919), p. 61; Gr. G., "Kommunal'noe pitanie" (Communal Dining) in *Izvestiia Narkomproda* (News of the Food Supply Commissariat) no. 24–25, December 1918, p. 9.

39. Arthur Ransome, *Russia in 1919* (New York: B. W. Huebsch, 1919), pp. 67–68; M. P. Pol'skii, *Leninskaia zabota o trudiashchikhsia. Organizatsiia pitaniia naseleniia sovetskoi strany* (Lenin's Concern for the Workers: The Organization of Feeding for the Soviet Population) (Moscow: Mysl', 1984), p. 96.

40. Mary McAuley, *Bread and Justice: State and Society in Petrograd* (Oxford: Oxford University Press, 1991), p. 285; Pol'skii, *Leninskaia zabota*, p. 102; *Krasnaia Moskva*, p. 125.

41. Goldman, *Women, the State and Revolution*, p. 129; T. M. Kitanina, *Voina, khleb i revoliutsiia. Prodovol'stvennyi vopros v Rossii, 1914–oktiabr' 1917 g.* (War, Bread and Revolution: The Food Supply Question in Russia, 1914–October 1917) (Leningrad: Nauka 1985), pp. 244–247; Pol'skii, *Leninskaia zabota*, p. 27.

42. *Petrokommuna* (The Petrograd Commune) (Petrograd: 1920), p. 55.

43. Goldman, *Women, the State and Revolution*, pp. 130–131.

44. Pol'skii, *Leninskaia zabota*, pp. 153.

45. In the early years of Soviet rule, Bolshevik officials looked to Germany as the model of capitalist efficiency. Although German rationing models were used to validate Bolshevik rationing programs in the Civil War, it is not clear whether the German experience discussed by Keith Allen in another essay in this volume was ever considered by Bolshevik food officials. It is also not entirely clear when the American model comes into vogue for Soviet officials, but certainly by 1933, the German model was no longer a viable one.

46. Stites, *Revolutionary Dreams*, pp. 146–149; Halina Rothstein and Robert A. Rothstein, "The Beginning of Soviet Culinary Arts," in Glants and Toomre, *Food in Russian History and Culture*, p. 183; Hessler, "Cultured Trade," pp. 191–193.

47. Harvey A. Levenstein, *Revolution at the Table: The Transformation of the American Diet* (New York: Oxford University Press, 1988), p. 185; Borrero, "Communal Dining and State Cafeterias," pp. 171–173. I am grateful to Warren Belasco for alerting me to Levenstein's work and to Joyce Toomre for suggesting the comparison to the speakeasies.

48. For a recent overview of this theme, see Fitzpatrick, *Stalinism: New Directions*, pp. 177–180.

49. F. Sh., *Obshchestvennyi stol*, pp. 60–64; Borrero, "Communal Dining," pp. 165–166. For other examples, see McAuley, *Bread and Justice*, p. 285.

50. Barbara Evans Clements, "The Effects of the Civil War on Women and Family Relations," in Koenker, Rosenberg, and Suny, eds., *Party, State, and Society in the Russian Civil War*, p. 112; E. O. Kabo, *Ocherki rabochego byta* (Sketches of Workers' Daily Life) (Moscow: 1928), pp. 149–150.

51. Rothstein and Rothstein, "The Beginning of Soviet Culinary Arts," p. 183.

52. The widespread theft of "socialist property" was another response, which awaits greater study. For a brief discussion of the Civil War years, see Borrero, *Hungry Moscow*, chap. 3.

53. In some cases people belonged to four, five, or even six consumer societies. *Moskovskii kooperator* (Moscow Cooperator), 13 (June 15, 1918): 2.

Notes on the Contributors

Keith Allen is Director of the Wexner Learning Center at the United States Holocaust Memorial Museum. His work, *Hungrige Metropole: Essen und Wohlfart in Berlin, 1870–1930*, was published by Ergebnisse in spring 2001.

Warren Belasco (editor) teaches American studies at the University of Maryland, Baltimore County. He is the author of *Appetite for Change: How the Counterculture Took on the Food Industry* (1993) and numerous articles on the history, politics, and future of the food system. Professor Belasco was awarded the Sophie Coe Prize in Food History by the 2000 Oxford Symposium on Food and Cookery.

Amy Bentley serves New York University as Assistant Professor in the Department of Nutrition and Food Studies. A cultural historian by training, she is the author of *Eating for Victory: Food Rationing and the Politics of Domesticity* (1998), along with several articles on the politics and culture of food.

Mauricio Borrero is Associate Professor of History at St. John's University in New York City. He has authored *Hungry Moscow: Scarcity and Survival in the Russian Civil War*. While continuing research on food and survival in Soviet Russia, he is presently working on a modern history of Lake Baikal.

Martin Bruegel is a historian with the Consumption Research Laboratory of the Institut National de la Recherche Agronomique in France. He is currently working on the effects the industrialization of food production has had on consumers' food baskets.

Jeffrey Charles is Associate Professor of History at California State University, San Marcos. He is the author of *Service Clubs in American Society: Rotary, Kiwanis, and Lions* and is currently writing a book on the relationship between small farmers and the American consumer market.

Tracey Deutsch, a doctoral candidate in the Department of History at the University of Wisconsin, is completing a dissertation on the rise of supermarkets in Chicago between 1920 and 1950. Her work studies the intersection of gender relations, public policy, and retail strategies in modern consumer society.

Sylvia Ferrero teaches about food and culture at McGill University in Montreal, Canada, and has recently been conducting fieldwork in Sardinia on high schools and information and communication technologies.

Donna R. Gabaccia is the Charles H. Stone Professor of American History at the University of North Carolina at Charlotte. She is the author of many books about immigration and the United States, most recently *We Are What We Eat: Ethnic Food and the Making of Americans* (1998).

Kolleen M. Guy is Assistant Professor of History at the University of Texas at San Antonio. Author of numerous articles on wine and consumer culture, she is currently completing her book *When Champagne Became French*, a study of the champagne industry and the shaping of French national culture between 1820 and 1920.

Sidney W. Mintz is the Wm. L. Straus Jr. Professor Emeritus in the Department of Anthropology of Johns Hopkins University. Mintz's books include *Sweetness and Power* (1985) and *Tasting Food, Tasting Freedom* (1996). He is currently carrying out research on the history of soybeans and the soy food industry in the United States.

Jeffrey Pilcher, who teaches at the Citadel, is the author of *!Que vivan los tamales! Food and the Making of Mexican Identity* (1998), which won the Thomas F. McGann prize. His current research examines the clash between public health and private enterprise in Mexico City's meat supply.

Steve Penfold is a graduate student in the Department of History at York

University in Toronto. He is nearing completion of his Ph.D. dissertation, which examines the history of the donut in Canada and hopes that York will one day endow a Chair in Snackfood Studies.

Philip Scranton (editor) is Board of Governors Professor, History of Industry and Technology, at Rutgers University and coeditor of the Hagley Perspectives on Business and Culture series with Roger Horowitz.

Richard R. Wilk chairs the Anthropology Department at Indiana University. He has conducted field research in Belize, West Africa, and the United States on topics as diverse as beauty pageants, tropical agriculture, and family finances. Most of his recent work concerns the global spread of consumer culture and its impacts on human beings and the natural environment. His most recent book is a text called *Economies and Cultures*.

Index

Coit, J. Eliot, 143–44
Cold War, the, 4, 19, 230, 240, 253
College of Agriculture at Davis, 138
Collins, G. N., 133–34, 136, 143
colonialism: American, 210; British, 71–80;
    European, 3; Western, 24
Colored Merchants' Association, 162, 169
Columbian: Exchange, 3; Exposition, 180
comal, 225, 227
commodification, 195; of the self, 200
Commune, the, 119
Communism, 262, 269
community, 62–63; revival, 17
conch ceviche, 77
Condit, Elizabeth, and Jessie A. Long: *How to Cook
    and Why*, 100
consumer: activists, 184; cooperatives, 168, 172n.
    41, 272; goods, 73
consumerism, 27, 190n. 3, 195, 271; transnational,
    195
consumers, 9, 11, 14, 30, 105, 115, 126, 133, 150, 175,
    177, 180, 190, 207–208, 237; Asian, 189; British,
    188; Canadian, 63; European, 188; foreign-born,
    180; French, 14, 118; immigrant, 209; Mexican,
    209, 234; modern, 15; poor, 235; transnational,
    196; U.S., 133, 142–43, 149, 181, 184; urban, 223;
    white, 208; women (*see* women, consumers)
Consumers Union, 149
consumption, 2, 7, 8, 11, 25, 27, 36, 60, 63, 68, 74,
    118, 157, 169, 271; alcohol, 37–39; conspicuous,
    115–17; elite, 73; food (*see* food consumption);
    male, 16; mass, 63, 157; patterns, 37, 93; politi-
    cal nature of, 157; practices, 126–27; production
    and, 25
cookbooks, 80, 115, 142, 198; ethnic, 13; Mexican,
    198–200, 210–14, 216, 218n. 32; Mexican-
    American, 18
cooking, 8, 70, 76, 160; and enslavement associa-
    tions, 8; Belizean, 76, 83; Chinese, 79; ethnic, 81;
    festival, 83; home, 13, 69–70, 194, 259; national,
    81; practices, 76; traditional, 223
Cooperative: Marketing Act, 141; Society of
    America, 168–69
corn, 3, 77, 182, 226, 229, 234, 235–36; grinding,
    226–27, 237; home-ground, 227; low-cost, 228;
    markets, 229; mills, 224–27, 229; silos, 229
corned beef, 124–26
Cornell University, 98–99, 101; Farmers' Wives
    Reading Courses, 101; Study Clubs, 101
corporate: accountability, 10; business, 198, 208
cost of living, 162–63
Country Style Donuts, 54, 55, 59, 61
Cowan, Ruth Schwartz, 231
Cowan, William F., 146
Creoles, 71, 74–75, 80, 83
creolization, 69, 77, 78, 218n. 33
Cronon, William: *Nature's Metropolis*, 9
Cuba, 133, 142
Cudahy, Michael, 188
cuisine bourgeoise, 119
cuisines, 6, 19, 36, 70, vii; American, 6, 13, 175;
    banquet, 69; Belizean, 16, 67–89; California, 150,
    154n. 68; Canadian, 14; convenience-based, 15;
    Creole, 76; ethnic, 76, 79; *haute*, 235; hybrid,
    222–39; imported, 76; Latino, 149; Mestizo, 148,
    211; Mexican, 203, 206, 210, 214, 216, 222,
    230–32, 235; national, 11–12, 13, 16, 18, 67–89,
    175, 232210; regional, 81, 224, 232; Spanish, 210
culinary: identity, 13, 14; nation-building (*see*
    nation-building, culinary); other, 194, 202; prac-
    tices, 71, 198–99, 202–203, 211–13; resistance,

199; tourists, 18, 201–203; traditions, 86, 143
cultural: capital, 181, 198, 208; displacement, 204;
    environments, 210; geography, 57; heterogeniza-
    tion, 195; homogenization, 195; iconography, 49;
    imperialism, 223, 230; practices, 70, 199, 204,
    216; symbolism, 194
culture, 26, 30, 77, 86, vii; American, 52; Anglo-
    American, 7; Belizean, 80, 84, 86; Canadian,
    52–53, 56, 63; Caribbean migrant, 83; consumer,
    10–11, 36, 67, 132, 242; European, 74, 184;
    German, 181, 184; globalization of, 19; hybrid,
    222; indigenous, 13; Latino, 148; mass, 15,
    48–66, 242–43; Mayan, 69, 78; Mestizo, 75, 211;
    Mexican, 75, 200, 207, 209, 211, 213–14, 216;
    Mexican-American, 213; national, 67–89; peas-
    ant, 223; popular, 49, 52, 55, 56
Curlett, John, 108
Curtin, Deane, and Lisa Heldke: *Cooking, Eating,
    Thinking*, 6

dairy products, 96, 99, 179; processing, 178
Dampier, Captain William, 71
DCA (Donut Corporation of America), 53
de Grazia, Victor, 156
de la Blache, Vidal, 42–44
de La Reynière, Alexandre Grimod, 38
Deutsch, Tracey, 17, 18, 19
Deutsches Eck, 246
Di Giorgio, Giuseppe, 176, 180, 186, 187, 192n. 26
Diamond, Jared, 3
diet, 26, 36, 76; African, 69; Creole middle-class,
    78; elite, 73; industrialized, 223, 236; infant's, 92,
    99–106; local, 24; modern, 222; North American,
    143; subsistence, 70, 222; traditional, 222–23; tra-
    ditional Mexican, 222, 236; U.S., 133, 135, 143,
    271; vegetarian, 99, 224
dietary: diseases, 236; guidelines, 15; traditions, 209
dieting, 7, 144, 201
dietitians, 15, 93, 100, 105–107
dining: public, 253, 259, 261, 268–72, 275n. 35;
    quick, 244–45
diseases, 3, 32, 95, 98
distilling, 179, 181, 182, 191n. 17
diversity, 10, 175, 210
Dole, 178
dominant system, 195, 199–200, 205–207, 210–12,
    214, 215, 216
Donut Diner, 53, 65n. 16
donuts, 13, 60–61, 64n. 3; Canadian, 14; capital,
    57–59, 62–63, 65n. 32; folklore of, 14, 54–56, 59,
    61–63, 64nn. 4, 65n. 29; shops, 50–55, 57–61,
    63n.2, 64n. 2, 65n. 32
Driessens, Charles, 119
drinking: excessive, 37–39; patterns, 36–37; social, 37
drinks: alcoholic, 39, 71, 73, 182, 185; bottled, 231;
    femented, 38; luxury imported, 72, 74; mass-pro-
    duced, 176
Dunkin' Donuts, 49, 54
Dunwoody, William, 178, 188

East: India Company, 8; Indians, 76
East, Edward, 9
eating, 76, 198; food and, 24–32, 195; habits, 31;
    multiethnic, 206; studies, 24
Ecole des Mères, 120
ecological sustainability, 10–11, 17
economy(ies): American, 181; domestic, 119;
    enclave, 197; free market, 16; global, 222; mar-
    ket, 196, 222, 224; multinational, 67; subsis-
    tence, 226; wage, 242
Eddie Shack Donut, 51